God's Rule

God's Rule | The Politics of World Religions |

Jacob Neusner, Editor

GEORGETOWN UNIVERSITY PRESS
Washington, D.C.

Georgetown University Press
© 2003 by Georgetown University Press. All rights reserved.
Printed in the United States of America.

10   9   8   7   6   5   4   3   2   1   2003

This book is printed on acid-free recycled paper meeting the requirements
of the American National Standard for Permanence in Paper for Printed Library Materials.

Library of Congress Cataloging-in-Publication Data

God's rule : the politics of world religions / Jacob Neusner, editor.
    p. cm.
Includes bibliographical references and index.
    ISBN 0-87840-910-6 (hardcover : alk. paper)
1. Religion and politics. I. Neusner, Jacob, 1932–
BL65.P7 G635 2003
291.1'77—dc21   2002013810

Contents

Introduction | **Religion and Politics—a Volatile Mix** |

William Scott Green

No issue has marked the turn of the Christian millennium more deeply than the relation of religion to politics. The September 11, 2001, assaults on the World Trade Center and the Pentagon focused attention on a reality that many thought distant, dormant, or at least benign. Dramatically and suddenly, religion has assumed a central place in contemporary global politics. Understanding a religion's political vision is now as essential for managing our immediate world as is using the Internet.

The events of September 11 did not emerge from a vacuum. During the 1990s, the use of religious language and symbolism for political purposes infected the globe like a cultural mad cow disease. The suicide bombers in the Middle East and the ravages of Bosnia are only the most obvious examples. The Taliban destroyed magnificent Buddhist statues in Bamiyan. Hindus demolished centuries-old mosques in India. In a gesture the *New York Times* called "Welcome man of peace. Let's go hate my enemy," the president of Syria, in the presence of the pope, assailed Jews as the "enemies of all religions," the betrayers of Jesus, and the attempted murderers of Muhammad. The American federal government launched a "faith-based" initiative that seems to blend religion with governmental activity. In the *Nation*, Katha Pollitt expanded and illuminated the list:

> Think of all the ongoing conflicts involving religion: India versus Pakistan, Russia versus Chechnya, Protestants versus Catholics in Northern Ireland, Muslim guerrillas in the Philippines, bloody clashes between Christians and Muslims in Indonesia and Nigeria, civil war in Sudan and Uganda and Sri Lanka. It's enough to make one nostalgic for the cold war as if the thin film of twentieth-century political ideology has been stripped away like the ozone layer to reveal a world reverting to seventeenth-century-style religious warfare, fought with twenty-first century weapons.[1]

All these instances give the topic of religion and politics an urgent freshness and significance.

For Americans, thinking anew about the relation between religion and politics is especially important, primarily because so many of us think our society has solved the problem. The ideology of the separation of church and state and some recent interpretations of the First Amendment to the Constitution have conditioned Americans to regard religion and politics as distinct realms of experience. A norm of American life is that religion should not, and generally does not, express itself doctrinally through the activities of government. Most Americans take it as a given that there is a limit to the political expression of religion. The papers gathered in this volume will encourage us not to be naive about that assumption.

Before continuing, some definitions are pertinent here. For the purposes of this volume, "politics" primarily means governance and statecraft—including such components as the powers to tax, to wage war, to produce money, to enforce public order, to compel behavior, to justify obligations, and to make the institutions of society work for your own ends. As for "religion," Melford Spiro's definition is a useful starting point: "an institution consisting of culturally patterned interaction with culturally postulated superhuman beings."[2] Spiro uses the concept of "superhuman being" as the variable that distinguishes religion from not-religion—from politics or philosophy, for instance. To Spiro's conception, we may add a note of historical and phenomenological description. Religions exhibit a tendency to totalize, to extend their reach to all dimensions of experience. The religions discussed in this volume come to expression not only in speech and writing, but also in art, music, and dance, in smell and taste, in ethics and intellect. They have cosmologies (stories of the origin of the world) and eschatologies (stories of the end of the world), theories of nature, birth, morality, sexuality, marriage, suffering, and death. The comprehensiveness of religion allows it to touch all the transition points of life, both collective and individual, and thus to make definitive claims on the total human being.

Religion and Politics: Different but Inseparable

That religion and politics are necessarily connected is not a new idea. As Brian Smith notes in his discussion of Hinduism below (chapter 8), Gandhi observed that "those who believe religion is separable from politics understand neither one." Because religion is comprehensive, it is fundamentally about power; it therefore cannot avoid politics. Religion has the ability to ground the use of force in a cosmic and moral order; therefore, religion constitutes the ultimate legitimation of any political system. Overtly and covertly, religion influences political structures and activity by encouraging and enforcing some attitudes and behaviors and by discouraging and disparaging others. It articulates frameworks of values and truth that ground and inform a society's sense of destiny, leadership, community, and individuality. Max Stackhouse explains that

> authority in all civilizations is incomprehensible without attention to religion. That is, politics cannot be understood without recognizing that the contours of acceptable wisdom, and the definitions of which interests and which forms of rationality are to be given approval and which are to be repressed, are fundamentally shaped by a governing metaphysical-moral vision. The essence of this conviction is the surpassing conviction about what is 'really real,' the compelling sense of what consti-

tutes ultimate and worthy power in a transcendent sense. Wisdom, influence, interests, intelligence, and political force must serve—and must be understood to serve—powers, principles, or purposes beyond themselves. Concern for these, as well as beliefs and behaviors thought to be appropriate to such concerns, are what human beings vaguely call "religion."[3]

Because politics can compel behavior and thus shape immediate collective experience, it has an unusual capacity to validate or undermine a religion's worldview. A religion cannot persist if it cannot explain how the exercise of coercive power in the world of immediate experience conforms to, is encompassed by, or at least does not refute the religion's own theory of how things are or ought to be. Whether or not a religion itself can legitimately deploy force to compel behavior, it must be able to explain how such force is used in its own world. It must show its adherents that it is not mistaken about the world.

The need for a theory of politics is greater for religions that are out of power than for those that are in power. If the ordinary, repeated experience of everyday life disconfirms what a religion teaches, then the religion can lose plausibility, credibility, and membership. Religions that do not govern must explain why, if they are not running the government, the government is not running them. The relationship between religion and politics is both unavoidable and systemically uneasy. Neither can afford to leave the other alone.

With a focus on this inescapable interconnection, the chapters of this volume aim to offer a basic picture of the political visions of the world's great literate religions: Judaism, Christianity, Islam, Hinduism, Confucianism, and Buddhism. The chapter authors have not sought to supply a full history of the political activity of these traditions. Rather, each has sought to answer systemic questions about politics on the basis of one religion's classical sources. Each chapter thus illustrates how a religion expresses a political vision in its foundational texts and fundamental teachings. Beyond these individual examinations of the various traditions, a full-throated, comprehensive comparison of all of them would constitute at least a volume in itself. But a preliminary observation perhaps will give readers a platform from which to view and think about the traditions as a whole.

There are, to be sure, diverse ways in which one might classify the religions discussed here to compare their political visions. One fruitful approach uses the category of transcendence as a guide. In his intelligent and systematic treatment of religion and politics, Stackhouse suggests four variables by which what he calls the "social logic" of a religion—which can ground its vision of politics—can be understood. Does a religion understand transcendence to be "pluralistic or unitary?" Does it view transcendence as "deep within—although hidden by—the realities of existence," or is transcendence beyond, over, or against existence? Is transcendence "personal or impersonal"? And finally, does transcendence involve "constant stability or dynamic change"?

On the basis of these variables, Stackhouse suggests that monotheistic religions apprehend transcendence as unitary, beyond and over existence, personal, and dynamically involved in change. As a consequence, monotheistic religions distinguish between God and the world and reject political orders that are not in accord with God's will. Alternatively, in the "ontocratic" religions of Asia, "true religion is life in accord with natural being and . . . the harmonious state is the supreme earthly embodiment of cosmic totality."[4] Stackhouse's framework suggests how a religion's fundamental metaphysical and theological principles can shape attitudes about the nature of the state.

Piety and Power: A Comparative Grid

A possible alternative comparative grid emerges from the chapters of this book. Instead of comparing the six religions in terms of their core theological doctrines, we might classify them according to their attitudes toward holding actual political power. That is, we might ask if the classical sources of each religion suppose that the religion holds, or must hold, political power to come to full expression. To fulfill its goals, is it necessary for the religion to rule? If we follow this approach, there is an interesting coalescence. Judaism and Christianity begin without the assumption of political power. Islam, Hinduism, and Confucianism, by contrast, appear to take such power for granted. Buddhism stakes out a middle position, in which it knows it can rule but is prepared not to do so. Let us examine this classification in more detail.

Judaism and Christianity, and the Hebrew Scriptures they share, reflect the circumstances and conditions of political subjugation. The foundational documents of Judaism and Christianity emerge from a context of imperialism, in which the religion itself did not and could not constitute a ruling government. In the ancient Mediterranean, Jewish religion took shape and developed almost entirely under foreign political domination. Judaism—in all its forms—was not a religion of free people. The Pentateuch (also called the Torah), which is basic to both religions, was edited into its final literary form under the domination of the Persian state. Judaism later persisted in the ancient Mediterranean in large measure because of Roman indulgence. Julius Caesar granted privileges to the Jewish religion that lasted for three centuries and made Judaism both politically legitimate and politically dependent.

The sources of Judaism deal with the lack of political power by pretending none exists. The Israelites receive their revelation from God in the desert, the opposite of territory. Although they are a community and a nation, because they have no monarch, they do not constitute a kingdom. The Pentateuch barely mentions a king for Israel, and it assumes that the monarch will consult the Torah before acting. In the biblical texts, Israel's king plays no role in Israel's worship or sacrificial cult. More important, the Hebrew Bible as a whole supposes that whereas God can be king, the Israelite king cannot be a god. It thus draws a clear distinction between religion and government. Jesus's famous admonition to render unto Caesar what is Caesar's and unto God what is God's assumes that Caesar is not (and cannot be?) God and thus presupposes this biblical distinction.

The editors of the Pentateuch depict a cult without a kingdom—a pure religion, as it were. The picture is necessarily fictitious, of course, for no centralized cult can operate without the support of attendant political structures that guarantee adequate taxation, public facilities, and social order. By portraying Israel's religion as autonomous from politics, the Pentateuch's narrative disguises Israel's political dependence and creates an image of religion without politics that is basic in Western religious thinking about both.

Jacob Neusner's discussion of Judaism shows how the biblical tradition of a fictive politics continues in the Mishnah, the foundational text of Rabbinic Judaism (chapter 1). He lists four institutions of political sanction: God, the earthly court, the Temple in Jerusalem, and community consensus. None of these acknowledges the reality of Roman imperial control over Judaism and its institutions. Moreover, the Temple had been destroyed for more than a century by the time the rabbis finalized the Mishnah. And Jewish courts, despite the Mishnah's claim, almost certainly did not have authority to impose the death penalty. Neusner suggests that the Mishnah's "politics . . . rehearses the myth of Adam and Eve in Eden," and focuses on the distinction between deliberate and inadvertent transgression. The Mishnah's politics centers on the interior motivations of individual actors, but it supplies no suggestions or models of how to govern. Instead, it offers a utopian vision of a balanced community, an image of a politics without power.

As a renegade species of Judaism, early Christianity had neither hope of governance nor immediate legitimacy in the eyes of Roman authorities. Indeed, until the conversion of Constantine in the fourth century C.E., Christianity existed under Roman domination but largely outside of Rome's political structures. Early Christian writers, like the producers of the Mishnah, had to develop their religion in the absence of political power. What the Pentateuch and the Mishnah accomplish through denial, Early Christian writing achieves through eschatology. Bruce Chilton suggests below that Early Christianity explained its status by simultaneously acknowledging the reality of alien political powers and denying them ultimate religious significance (chapter 2). As an eschatological religion, Early Christianity focused on the divine kingdom to come, not the world as it was. Chilton explains that Christianity's "literally otherworldly perspective results in a paradoxical acceptance of the institutions of this world. That acceptance is qualified, however, by the observation that all forms of human government are provisional." This approach, which allowed Christians to "accept the legitimacy of institutions that are . . . unjust, because they belong to the structure of a world that is passing away," explicitly denies that attaining political power is a sine qua non for Christianity's religious fulfillment.

The heritage of the Hebrew Bible established the concept of a religion without politics and made the distinction between them basic to Western civilization. Because the mandate to govern was essentially excluded from Judaism's and thus Christianity's earliest texts and visions of politics, the relationship between Christianity and politics has always been somewhat labored and uneasy, and the integration of church and state remains problematic in the West. Indeed, the chapters on Roman Catholic, Orthodox, and Reformation Christianity (chapters 3, 4, and 5, respectively) suggest that actually having political power has created as many problems for Christianity as it has solved. The struggles between popes and emperors, Catholics and Protestants, and among Protestant groups that mark European history amply testify to the challenges Christianity faced in assuming political power.

Discrete theologies can yield diverse politics. The chapters on what we might call developed Christianity illustrate the impact of different religious emphases on the form of a political vision. Charles Curran succinctly describes the elaborate reasoning Roman Catholic Christianity used to think the state into its theology (chapter 3). Its focus on the common good, subsidiarity, and socialization reflects the church's distinctive theology of community and allows the state to have a legitimate religious purpose. Curran also explains how the church has developed its teachings in response to contemporary social conditions and pressures, particularly in the area of religious pluralism. In a different mode, Orthodox Christianity, as described by Petros Vassiliades, derives its political theory from the Liturgy and from the theology of the Eucharist (chapter 4). Its singular model of shared power between emperor and patriarch echoes Early Christianity's relationship with the ruling authorities. Finally, Martin Marty's lucid description of Reformation Christianity shows how its emphases on God's control, scriptural authority, the distinction between church and state, and lay vocation established a tendency—not always realized—toward democracy (chapter 5).

The chapters on Judaism and Christianity suggest that in the West religion and politics are necessary interlocutors but not natural allies. Because Judaism and Christianity were both founded apart from government, in principle neither needs—or assumes the need—to rule politically to come to full expression.

The chapters on Islam, Hinduism, and Confucianism (chapters 6, 7, 8, and 9 respectively) present a rather different picture from those of Judaism and Christianity. In each of these religions, there is an explicit assumption that the realm of government is a basic theater of religious expression and manifestation. All three religions exhibit a focus on the religious character of the political leader that is largely absent from the classical sources of Judaism and Christianity.

According to Mark Csikszentmilhalyi, "The Confucian canon played a central role in the [Chinese] educational system and defined the ethos of . . . government" (chapter 9). The emperor conducted rituals and thus formally integrated religion and politics. The classical Confucian sources emphasize the connection between the emperor's moral perfection and his political authority. *Tianming*, the mandate of heaven, could affect and be affected by the character of the ruler. Confucianism acknowledges the reality of political power but claims that its legitimacy depends on conformity to religious values and principles derived from the sacred realm (*tian*).

The same approach is evident in Brian Smith's description of Hinduism, whose sacred texts also suppose an integration of religion and politics (chapter 8). Hinduism has a highly developed concept of sacral kingship, in which the king has divine qualities. As Smith explains, "Hinduism condones and legitimates political power that verges on the dictatorial." But the king must be self-disciplined and "in subordination to the Brahmins and the principles of religion they represent and embody . . . [to] effectively rule." Like Confucian documents, Hindu texts acknowledge the brute reality of political power and ambition—*artha*, the pursuit of economic and political self-interest, is a key concept—but they temper politics with piety. In effect, Hinduism politicizes the warrior and priestly castes and proposes a bond between king and priest.

Of all the religions discussed in the book, Islam is perhaps the most explicit about the necessity of political power for religious expression. As a religion whose founder spent the last decade of his life developing a religious state, this almost seamless integration is not surprising. It flows naturally from the context of origination. As John Esposito and Natana De Long-Bas explain, in Islam, "faith and politics are inseparable" (chapters 6 and 7). More explicitly, they insist that

> throughout history, being a Muslim has been not just a matter of belonging to a community of fellow believers, but also to live in an Islamic community or state governed by Islamic law (in theory if not always in practice). In this utopian vision of the Islamic state, political authority is understood to be the instrument for carrying out the divine message. Sovereignty, therefore, is the embodiment of the Word of God in the Shariah (Islamic law), rather than a power that belongs to the ruler or the clergy. Thus, the ideal Islamic state is a nomocracy (a community governed by God's law), rather than a theocracy or autocracy.

Finally, in contrast to the other five religions, Buddhism appears to stake out a middle position. According to Todd Lewis, the Buddhist political position assumes the reality, but not the necessity of kingship (chapter 10). The core concern of the Buddhist texts is not political control but rather the ability of householders to contribute to the Buddhist monastic communities. Thus, Buddhism in principle is prepared to cooperate with any political system that allows this activity. If there are a Buddhist king and a Buddhist state, Buddhist religious norms must govern. As in Hinduism and Confucianism, a Buddhist ruler acquires legitimacy by practicing Buddhist virtues, such as justice, charity, concern for the common good, generosity, and forgiveness.

This comparative grid helps to display the discrete political visions of these five major religions not only in terms of theological convictions but also in terms of the explicit relationship between political power and religious expression. Judaism and Christianity begin as religions of politically dependent people, and their classical texts promulgate a vision of religion that does not demand to govern in order to save. The texts of Confucianism, Hinduism, and Islam project a different conception, in which overt political power is either assumed to be present or advanced as necessary for religious fulfillment. Buddhism seems prepared to go in either direction.

Concluding American Postscript

In a particular and wonderful way, this book is a profoundly American exercise. By mandating freedom of and freedom from religion, the First Amendment to the U.S. Constitution made religious diversity a defining trait of American life. Because of the First Amendment, Americans as a society have no need to decide which religion is legitimate or which religion should govern. To be sure, there are and have been Americans who would be content to see religion dominate not only the public square but the halls of government as well. But America's pluralist religious heritage—even if it was initially born among Protestant denominations—is likely to keep that from occurring. The American experiment in religious pluralism has allowed diverse traditions to flourish and has made violence between religions almost unthinkable in an American context. The chapters of this book show both the distinction of the American position and the alternatives to it.

In the aftermath of September 11, Robert Stone wrote in the *New York Times*:

> We witnessed . . . the violent assault of one narrative system upon another. . . . The internal narrative of our enemies, their absolute ruthless devotion to an invisible world, makes them strong. . . . The power of narrative is shattering, overwhelming. We are the stories we believe; we are who we believe we are. All the reasoning of the world cannot set us free from our mythic systems. We live and die by them.[5]

Stone's image of "ruthless devotion to an invisible world" is both insightful and arresting. It suggests that, in the end, the murders in New York and Washington, and of those on the airplane that crashed in rural Pennsylvania, and the range of other religious battles that now afflict the globe, are not—or not only—about material property. They are about the real stuff of life—dignity, identity, coherence, and security. They ultimately are not about money; they are about meaning. Our stakes in the stories we believe about ourselves are as high as they can be.

Acknowledgment

The author is grateful to James Johnson, Gerald Gamm, Emil Homerin, and Jonathan Geen for help in formulating aspects of this introduction.

Notes

1. Katha Pollitt, "God Changes Everything," *The Nation*, April 1, 2002, accessed at www.thenation.com/doc.mhtml?=20020401&5=pollitt.

2. Melford E. Spiro, "Religion, Problems of Definition and Explanation," in Benjamin Kilbourne and L. L. Langness, eds., *Culture and Human Nature: Theoretical Papers of Melford E. Spiro* (Chicago: University of Chicago Press, 1987), 187–222.

3. Max L. Stackhouse, "Politics and Religion," *The Encyclopedia of Religion*, ed. M. Eliade (New York: Macmillan, 1987), 408–23.

4. Stackhouse, "Politics and Religion," 413–15.

5. Robert Stone, "The Villain," *New York Times Magazine*, special edition, "Elements of Tragedy." September 23, 2001, 22.

One | **Judaism** |

Jacob Neusner

WHEN THE STATE OF ISRAEL CAME INTO BEING, IN 1948, NO ONE IMAGINED PUTTING into effect, as state law, the Halakhah, or legal system of Scripture as extended and realized in the law books of formative Judaism, Scripture as amplified by the Rabbinic writings of the first six centuries C.E. The new state did not define its political institutions by opening Scripture and appointing a king, for example, or by opening the Mishnah, a second century philosophical system in the form of a law code, and replicating its plan for a tripartite government of king, high priest, and sage. And the founding prime minister of the State of Israel, David Ben Gurion, was not anointed a prophet. So far as the state of Israel aspired to and did and does form a Jewish state (according full rights of citizenship to its Moslem and Christian minorities), Judaism in its classical sources does not guide the formation of public policy.

That is because, as William Scott Green makes clear in his introduction, Judaism, the religious system defined by Scripture and the authoritative writings of the Rabbinic sages, encompasses the issues of politics within its larger mythic framework, but does not contemplate the practicalities of governing the ethnic community, the Jews, as an autonomous sovereign entity: a state, possessing empowered rulers. Rather, what we see in the Judaic politics set forth in the Mishnah's laws is how politics serves as a medium for the concretization of the generative myth that animates the entire religious system. The practicalities of a fully embodied myth permeating a political system and structure in charge of its own fate, able to negotiate as equal with other political entities, do not register. Rather, what we see is how politics forms a medium of expressing that foundation-story of the Israelite social order, as every other component of social culture embodies that same story in other contexts. The mark of a successful theological system and structure lies in its coherence, its capacity to say the same thing about many things. That is what we identify in the story that follows.

Classical Sources of Judaism on Politics

Whereas the world knows as "Judaism" a variety of kindred religious systems, all Judaic systems fall into a single category. That is because, from antiquity to the present, all Judaisms have regarded as authoritative the Hebrew Scriptures of ancient Israel (a.k.a., Christianity's "Old Testament"), which they have called "the

Torah," meaning instruction. Each community of Judaism, furthermore, has regarded itself as a continuation of the "Israel" of which Scripture speaks.

From late antiquity to the present, moreover, most (though not all) communities of Judaism have interpreted Scripture in light of the documents called collectively, "the Oral Torah" (in contrast to Scripture, known as "the Written Torah"). These texts formed the corpus of Rabbinic writings from the Mishnah (ca. 200 C.E.), a philosophical law code, to the Yerushalmi, Talmud of the Land of Israel (ca. 400 C.E.), through the Bavli, the Talmud of Babylonia (ca. 600 C.E.), a commentary to the Mishnah, along with certain compilations of biblical interpretation known as Midrash books of the same period. When we refer to the foundational documents of Judaisms over time, we always begin with Scripture and ordinarily proceed to the documents of the Oral Torah.

There we find a profoundly political conception of religion. The Pentateuch portrays Israel as "a kingdom of priests and a holy people," and further takes for granted that the "kingdom" or "people" forms a political entity, capable of exercising legitimate violence. By "Israel," the social entity brought into being by those that accepted God's rule set forth in the Torah, Instruction, of Sinai, Scripture therefore understands not merely a church or a voluntary community but an empowered society, with a government, laws, and institutions. Scripture's own portrait of the type of government varies. The Pentateuch read whole takes for granted that Israel is governed by God through the prophet, Moses. Moses further appoints an administration to deal with conflict and secure the public order, and that administration exercises authority and inflicts the death penalty for civil and religious infractions. Other writings describe an Israelite monarchy, still others, a government by the priesthood based on the Temple in Jerusalem. The picture of Israel as a family, descended from Abraham and Sarah, conflicts with this account of Israel as an empowered and political entity and plays no role in the articulation of the politics of the holy people.

The Rabbinic canon of antiquity carries forward the premise of Scripture that the holy people form a political entity in the here and now, not merely a supernatural community of the faithful at the end of days such as is the conception of Israel reflected in the library of the Jewish sectarian religious community living in caves located in the mountains overlooking the Dead Sea. The politics expressed through the Mishnah's Judaism speaks of a social entity treated as a political one as well, of the holy people of "Israel" classified as a state. The Judaism of the Mishnah set forth for its social entity (called, as the social entity of every Judaism is called, "Israel") not merely a mythic and theological picture but also a political structure.

When people would speak of "a state of (being) Israel," therefore, they would also address "the State of Israel," the Jewish State, understanding that they spoke of a political entity like other such political entities. Therefore, this Judaism became in mind and imagination a state not only of (autonomous) being but also of (shared and social) doing, not alone of ontology but of society. That is why this Judaism defines a locus for inquiry into more than theological science, into, especially, social science: economics, politics, and philosophy. The key generative problematic of the Mishnah is the interplay of divine will and the human will, and the relationships that require political scrutiny are between God and Israel, not among citizens or between the state and its citizens. Religion and politics are integrated.

At issue in a politics is who does what to whom, so we turn forthwith to the Mishnah's account of the sanctions that accompany the law, and who enforces those sanctions, God or the Temple authorities or the sages of the Torah, its three institutional foci of power. The encompassing framework of rules, institutions, and sanctions is explained and validated by appeal to the myth of God's shared rule. That dominion, exercised by God and His surrogates on earth, is focused partly in the royal palace, partly in the Temple, and partly in the court. The political myth of Judaism thus explains who exercises legitimate violence and under what conditions, and furthermore specifies the source for differentiation. The myth consequently serves a particular purpose—which is to answer that particular question. Indeed, the Judaic political myth comes to expression in its details of differentiation, which permit us to identify, and of course to answer, the generative question of politics.

Analyzing the myth by explaining sanctions draws our attention to the modes of legitimate violence that the system identifies. There we find four types of sanctions, each deriving from a distinct institution of political power, each bearing its own mythic explanation:

1. The first comprises what God and the Heavenly court can do to people.
2. The second comprises what the earthly court can do to people. That type of sanction embodies the legitimate application of the worldly and physical kinds of violence of which political theory ordinarily speaks.
3. The third comprises what the cult can do to people. The cult through its requirements can deprive people of their property as legitimately as can a court.
4. The fourth comprises conformity with consensus—self-imposed sanctions. Here the issue is, Whose consensus? And defined by whom?

Across these four types of sanctions, four types of coercion are in play. They depend on violence of various kinds—psychological and social as much as physical. Clearly, then, the sanctions that are exercised by other than judicial-political agencies prove violent and legitimately coercive, even though the violence and coercion are not the same as those carried out by courts.

Predictably, when we work our way through sanctions to recover the mythic premises thereof, we begin with God's place in the institutionalization and execution of legitimate violence. Of course, the repertoire of sanctions does encompass God's direct intervention, but that is hardly a preferred alternative or a common one. Still, God does commonly intervene when oaths are violated, for oaths are held to involve the person who invokes God's name and God. Further, whereas when faced with an insufficiency of valid evidence under strict rules of testimony, the earthly court cannot penalize serious crime, the Heavenly court can and does impose a penalty.

Clearly, then, God serves to justify the politics and account for its origin. Although God is never asked to join in making specific decisions and effecting policy in the everyday politics of the state, deliberate violation of certain rules provokes God's or the Heavenly court's direct intervention. Thus obedience to the law clearly represents submission to God in Heaven. Further, forms of Heavenly coercion suggest a complex mythic situation, with more subtle nuance than the claim that, overall, God rules, would indicate. A politics of rules and regulations cannot admit God's ad hoc participation, and this system did not do so. God joined in the system in a regular and routine way, and the rules took for granted God's part in the politics of Judaism.

Judaism's Theory of Politics

At stake in the politics of Judaism is God's rule on earth. In simple terms, Judaism presumes the direct involvement of the sacred in the human realm. Practically speaking, this means that the Kingdom of Heaven is realized by the supernatural, holy community of Israel (not to be confused with an ethnic group of the same name, or a nation-state of the same name) as it exercises political power in accordance with every detail of the dictates of the law given by God to Israel. As was discussed above, the written Torah (Scripture), which gave rise to the Oral Torah, governed personal, social, and political life. Politics, articulated through normative law, from the Mishnah forward forms the key to Judaism.

To examine the politics of the Mishnah in its historical context, we must recall that, among prior Judaisms only the scriptural system finally defined with the closure of the Pentateuch had set forth a politics at all. The appeal to politics in setting forth a theory of the social order of their particular "Israel" will have provoked some curiosity among, for one example, the framers of the Judaism portrayed by the library uncovered at Qumran, and, for another, the framers of the Christianity of the Land of Israel in the first century. Both groups, heirs of the ancient Scriptures as much as were the framers of the Mishnah, found in politics no important component of the systemic structure they set forth.

By contrast, the integration, within a systematic account of the social order, of a politics will not have surprised the great figures of Greco-Roman philosophy, such as Plato and Aristotle. That fact takes on consequence when we note that the Pentateuch simply does not prepare us to make sense of the institutions that the politics of Judaism for its part designs. The Pentateuch's politics invokes priest and prophet, Aaron and Moses, but knows nothing of a tripartite government involving king, priest, and sage; nor do the royal narratives concede empowerment to the priest or sage. Yet knowledge of the *Politics* of Aristotle and the *Republic* of Plato to the contrary gives perspective upon the politics of the Mishnah.

The Pentateuch contributes nothing to the Mishnah's scheme of routine government by king and high priest and sages' court. The Pentateuch's prophetic rule and constant appeal to God's immediate participation in the political process, and, in particular, in the administration of sanctions and acts of legitimate violence, by contrast fall into the category of a politics of charisma. The difference is not merely that the Pentateuchal institutions appeal to prophet and priest; it also is a difference in how the structure works as a political system. For the Pentateuchal myth that serves to legitimate coercion—rule by God's prophet, in the model of Moses, governance through explicitly revealed laws that God has dictated for the occasion—plays no active and systemic role whatsoever in the formulation and presentation of the politics of Judaism. Philosophical systems use politics, by contrast, to set forth the rules and unchanging order of legitimate exercise of power, its teleology and its structure. Plato and Aristotle make no place for godly intervention on any particular occasion.

And for their part, among the types of political authority contained within the scriptural repertoire, the one that the Mishnah's philosophers reject is the prophetic and charismatic, and the one that they deem critical is the authority governing and governed by rules in an orderly, rational way. The principal political figures—king, high priest, the disciple of the sage—are carefully nurtured through learning of rules, not through cultivation of gifts of the spirit. The authority of sages in the politics of Judaism in particular does not derive from charisma, for example, revelation by God to the sage who makes a ruling in a given case, or even general access to God for the sage. So the politics of the Pentateuch—structure and system alike—in no way forms the model for the politics of the Mishnah.

The Medium of Expressing Politics in Judaism

That brings us to the nub of the matter: the exercise of legitimate violence in the law of Judaism from the Mishnah forward. How, specifically, do the sanctions that embody Judaism's politics yield an account of the governing political myth? In the Mishnah's picture, some of the same crimes or sins for which the Heavenly court imposes the penalty of extirpation are those that, under appropriate circumstances (e. g., sufficient evidence admissible in court) the earthly court imposes the death penalty. That is, the Heavenly court and the earthly court impose precisely the same sanctions for the same crimes or sins.

The earthly court therefore forms down here the exact replica and counterpart, within a single system of power, of the Heavenly court up there. There are crimes for which the earthly court imposes penalties, but for which the Heavenly court does not, and vice versa. The earthly and Heavenly courts share jurisdiction over sexual crimes and over serious religious crimes against God. The Heavenly court penalizes with its form of the death penalty for religious sins against God, in which instances a person deliberately violates the taboos of sanctification. And that fact calls our attention to a third partner in the distribution and application of power: the Temple, with its system of sanctions that cover precisely the same acts subject to the jurisdiction of the Heavenly and earthly courts. The counterpart on earth is now not the earthly court but the Temple. This is the institution that, in theory, automatically receives the appropriate offering from the person who inadvertently violates these same taboos of sanctification.

But this is an odd choice for the Mishnah, since there was then—at about 200 C.E.—no Temple on earth. That had been destroyed in 70 C.E. The juxtaposition appears then to involve courts and Temple, and the upshot is that both are equally matters of theory. In the theory at hand, then, the earthly court, for its part, penalizes social crimes against the community that the Heavenly court, on the one side, and the Temple rites, on the other, do not take into account at all. These are murder, apostasy, kidnapping, public defiance of the court, and false prophecy. The earthly court further imposes sanctions on matters of particular concern to the Heavenly court, with special reference to taboos of sanctification (e.g., negative commandments). These three institutions, therefore, exercise concrete and material power, utilizing legitimate violence to kill someone, exacting penalties against property, and inflicting pain. The sages' modes of power, by contrast, stand quite apart, apply mainly to their own circle, and work through the intangible though no less effective means of inflicting shame or paying honor.

Power flows through three distinct but intersecting dominions, each with its own concern, all sharing some interests in common. The Heavenly court attends to deliberate defiance of Heaven, the Temple to inadvertent defiance of Heaven. The earthly court attends to matters subject to its jurisdiction by reason of sufficient evidence, proper witnesses, and the like, and these same matters will come under Heavenly jurisdiction when the earthly court finds itself unable to act. Accordingly, we have a tripartite system of sanctions—Heaven cooperating with the Temple in some matters, with the court in others, and, as noted, each bearing its own distinct media of enforcing the law as well. What then can we say concerning the systemic myth of politics? The forms of power and the modes of mediating legitimate violence draw our attention to a single political myth, one that we first confronted, if merely as a generality and commonplace to be sure, at the very outset. The unity of that myth is underlined by the simple fact that the earthly court enters into the process right alongside the Heavenly court and the Temple; as to blasphemy, idolatry, and magic, its jurisdiction prevails. So a single myth must serve all three correlated institutions.

It is the myth of God's authority infusing the institutions of Heaven and earth alike, an authority diffused among three principle foci or circles of power, Heaven's court, the earthly court, and the Temple in between. Each focus of power has its own jurisdiction and responsibility, Heaven above, earth beneath, the Temple in the position of mediation—transmitting as it does from earth to Heaven the penalties handed over as required. And all media of power in the matter of sanctions intersect at some points as well: a tripartite politics, a single myth drawing each component into relationship with a single source and origin of power, God's law set forth in the Torah. The point of differentiation within the political structures, supernatural and natural alike, lies in the attitude and intention of a human being. We differentiate among the application of power by reference to the attitude of the person who comes into relationship with that power. A person who comes into conflict with the system, rejecting the authority claimed by the powers that be, does so deliberately or inadvertently. The myth accounts in the end for the following hierarchization of action and penalty, infraction and sanction:

1. If the deed is deliberate, then one set of institutions exercises jurisdiction and utilizes supernatural power.
2. If the deed is inadvertent, another institution exercises jurisdiction and utilizes the power made available by that same supernatural being.

A sinner or criminal who has deliberately violated the law has by his or her action challenged the politics of Judaism. Consequently, God or God's surrogate imposes sanctions—extirpation (by the court on high), or death or other appropriate penalty (by the court on earth). A sinner or criminal who has inadvertently violated the law is penalized by the imposition of Temple sanctions, losing valued goods. People obey because God wants them to and has told them what to do, and when they do not obey, a differentiated political structure appeals to that single hierarchizing myth.

This myth has two components: first, God's will, expressed in the law of the Torah; second, the human being's will, carried out in obedience to the law of the Torah or in defiance of that law. The political myth of Judaism has to explain the differentiation of sins or crimes, with their associated penalties or punishments, and so sanctions of power. And in Scripture there is a very precise answer to the question of how to differentiate among sins or crimes and why to do so. Given the position of the system of the Mishnah, the point of differentiation must rest with one's attitude or intentionality. We do have a well-known story of how the power of God conflicts with the power of humanity in such wise as to invoke the penalties and sanctions in precisely the differentiated modes we have before us. That story of power differentiated by the will of the human being in communion or conflict with the word of the commanding God comes to us from the Garden of Eden. We cannot too often reread the following astonishing words:

> The Lord God took the man and placed him in the garden of Eden . . . and the Lord God commanded the man, saying, "Of every tree of the garden you are free to eat; but as for the tree of knowledge of good and bad, you must not eat of it; for as soon as you eat of it, you shall die." . . .
>
> When the woman saw that the tree was good for eating and a delight to the eyes, and that the tree was desirable as a source of wisdom, she took of its fruit and ate; she also gave some to her husband, and he ate . . .
>
> The Lord God called out to the man and said to him, "Where are you?"
>
> He replied, "I heard the sound of You in the garden, and I was afraid, because I was naked, so I hid."
>
> Then He asked, "Who told you that you were naked? Did you eat of the tree from which I had forbidden you to eat?" . . .
>
> And the Lord God said to the woman, "What is this you have done!"
>
> So the Lord God banished him from the garden of Eden. (Genesis 2:15–3:23 passim)

Now a reprise of the exchange between God, Adam, and Eve tells us that at stake was responsibility: who has violated the law, but who bears responsibility for deliberately violating the law:

> "The woman You put at my side—she gave me of the tree, and I ate."
>
> "The serpent duped me, and I ate."
>
> Then the Lord God said to the serpent, "because you did this . . ."

The ultimate responsibility lies with the one who acted deliberately, not under constraint or on account of deception or misinformation, as did Adam and Eve. Then the sanction applies most severely to the one who by intention and an act of will has violated God's intention and will.

Adducing this story by itself poses several problems. First, the storyteller does not allege that Adam intended to violate the commandment; he followed his wife. Second, the penalty is not extirpation but banishment. That is why to establish what I conceive to be the generative myth, I turn to a second story of disobedience and its consequences, the tale of Moses's hitting the rock:

> The community was without water, and they joined against Moses and Aaron. . . .
> Moses and Aaron came away from the congregation to the entrance of the Tent of Meeting and fell on their faces. The Presence of the Lord appeared to them, and the Lord spoke to Moses, saying, "You and your brother Aaron take the rod and assemble the community, and before their very eyes order the rock to yield its

water. Thus you shall produce water for them from the rock and provide drink for the congregation and their beasts."

Moses took the rod from before the Lord as He had commanded him. Moses and Aaron assembled the congregation in front of the rock; and he said to them, "Listen, you rebels, shall we get water for you out of this rock?" And Moses raised his hand and struck the rock twice with his rod. Out came copious water, and the community and their beasts drank.

But the Lord said to Moses and Aaron, "Because you did not trust me enough to affirm My sanctity in the sight of the Israelite people, therefore you shall not lead this congregation into the land that I have given them."

Those are the waters of Meribah, meaning that the Israelites quarreled with the Lord—through which He affirmed His sanctity. (Numbers 20:1–13)

Here we have not only intentional disobedience, but also the penalty of extirpation. Both this myth and the myth of the fall make the same point. They direct attention to the generative conception that at stake in power is the will of God over against the will of the human being, and in particular, the Israelite human being.

The political myth of Judaism now emerges in the Mishnah in all of its tedious detail as a reprise—in now-consequential and necessary, stunning detail—of the story of God's commandment, humanity's disobedience, God's sanction for the sin or crime, and humanity's atonement and reconciliation. The Mishnah omits all explicit reference to myths that explain power and sanctions, but invokes in its rich corpus of details the absolute given of the story of the distinction between what is deliberate and what is mitigated by an attitude that is not culpable, a distinction set forth in the tragedy of Adam and Eve, in the failure of Moses and Aaron, and in countless other passages in the Pentateuch, Prophetic Books, and Writings. Then the Mishnah's is a politics of life after Eden and outside of Eden. The upshot of the matter is that the political myth of Judaism sets forth the constraints of freedom, the human will brought to full and unfettered expression, imposed by the constraints of revelation, God's will made known.

Because it is the freedom of humanity to make decisions and frame intentions that forms the point of differentiation among the political media of power, we are required, in my view, to return to the paradigmatic exercise of that same freedom, that is, to Eden, to the moment when Adam and Eve exercise their own will and defy God. Because the operative criterion in the differentiation of sanction— that is, the exercise of legitimate violence by Heaven or by earth or by the Temple—is the human attitude and intention in carrying out a culpable action, we must recognize the politics before us rehearses the myth of Adam and Eve in Eden—it finds its dynamic in the correspondence between God's will and humanity's freedom to act however it chooses, thus freely incurring the risk of penalty or sanction for the wrong exercise of freedom.

At stake is what Adam and Eve, Moses and Aaron, and numerous others intend, propose, plan, for that is the point at which the politics intervenes, making its points of differentiation between and among its sanctions and the authorities that impose those penalties. For that power to explain difference, which is to say, the capacity to represent and account for hierarchy, we are required, in my opinion, to turn to the story of the fall of Adam and Eve from Eden and to counterpart stories. The reason is that the political myth derives from that same myth of origins its points of differentiation and explains by reference to the principal components of that myth—God's and humanity's will and power—the dynamics of the political system at hand. God commands, but humanity does what it then chooses, and in the interplay of those two protean forces, each power in its own right, the sanctions and penalties of the system apply.

Power comes from two conflicting forces, the commanding will of God and the free will of the human being. Power expressed in immediate sanctions is also mediated through these same forces, Heaven above, human beings below, with the Temple mediating between the two. Power works its way in the interplay between what God has set forth in the law of the Torah and what human beings do, whether intentionally, whether inadvertently, whether obediently, whether defiantly. That is why the politics of Judaism is a politics of Eden. And that further explains why sages' systemic statement turned to politics as the necessary medium for its full formulation. Quite how matters were to be phrased as this Judaism crossed the frontier from the realm of theory and theology to practical issues of public policy is not to be predicted on the basis of the systemic statement we have examined, which, we now see, in no way made provision for the complexities of an ordinary, diverse society. But, then, systems never do. And that accounts, also, for the incapacity of the Judaic system to negotiate with—differentiate among—outsiders, as we shall see below.

The Message of Judaism's Politics

A religion that expresses its theology through law, the Judaism set forth in the classical canon delivers its political statement through its legal system. This is called "the Halakhah," meaning, "the norms of correct conduct," as distinct from "the Aggadah," meaning, the rules of correct conviction, exegesis, interpretation. The Halakhah has always served as the medium of theological expression in Judaism, and it contains the message of the politics as well. The statement that is made by the Halakhah may be set forth in two parts, the one describing the problem facing God in the encounter with Humanity, the other the solution put forth at Sinai through the Halakhic account of the regenerate social order Israel is to realize.

First, the problem: God created nature as the setting for his encounter with humanity. Creation was meant as God's Kingdom for humanity's bliss. But with the sin of Humanity committed in rebellion against God's will, the loss of Eden, and the advent of death began the long quest for the regeneration of humanity. In the unfolding of generations, ten from Adam to Noah, ten from Noah to Abraham and thence to Sinai, it was only Israel that presented itself for the encounter. But then Israel too showed itself to be human. For on the other side of Sinai came the celebration of the golden calf.

Second, the Halakhic solution: What to do now? It is to rebuild God's Kingdom among that sector of humankind that undertakes to respond to God's self-manifestation in the Torah and to realize God's dominion and imperatives: the Torah, the Commandments. God provided for Israel, surrogate of humanity, the Commandments as a medium of sanctification for the reconciliation with God and renewal of Eden, the triumph over the grave. Freed of sin through offerings that signified obedience to God's will, by reason of repentance and atonement, signifying humanity's acceptance of God's will over his or her own, which to begin with had brought about the fall from Eden, either might meet God, the two in mutual and reciprocal commitment. Where Israel atoned for sin and presented itself as ready for the meeting, there God and Israel would found their Eden, not a place but an occasion. In overcoming the forces of death and affirming life through purity, Israel brings into being such an occasion. The Halakhah then serves as the medium of sanctification of Israel in the here-and-now, in preparation for the salvation of Israel and its restoration to Eden.

The classics of Rabbinic Judaism., the Mishnah, Midrash, and Talmuds, set forth in the Halakhah a systematic and coherent response to the Torah's account in the Pentateuch, Genesis through Deuteronomy, and in the Prophetic Books, Joshua through Kings and Isaiah, Jeremiah, Ezekiel, and the Twelve. That account portrays the tragic situation of Humanity from Eden onward, the hopeful situation of Israel from Sinai onward. The Halakhah lays out how Israel's entire social order may be constructed to realize the situation represented by Eden now and to restore Eden then. But it would be this time through the willing realization of God's rule, both in the present hour and at the end of days. That actualization takes place within Israel. How will it happen? Tutored by the Torah to want by nature what God wants but will not coerce them to want—"the Commandments were given only to purify the heart of man"—Israel makes itself able to realize God's will and to form his kingdom within its holy community. Through examining the Halakhah in its native categories or tractates, these propositions are shown to animate the entire Halakhic corpus, which is thus proved to embody a theological system, one that rests firmly upon the foundations of Scripture whole and in detail.

In fact, we have in the Halakhah a reworking of two parallel stories, first the story of the creation and fall of Adam and Eve from Eden, then the story of the regeneration of humanity through the Torah's formation of Israel. The two stories then are linked in the encounter of Israel and the nations, represented by the uncleanness of death that, through the disciplines of purity, Israel is to overcome. The tension between them comes to its resolution in the resurrection of Israel, from death, those who know God being destined for eternal life. The two stories, adumbrated in the heads of the outline that follows, represent the native category-formations of the Aggadah, and, as is clear, the native category-formations of the Halakhah are folded into the Aggadic framework:

The story of humanity and rebellion, sin and atonement, exile and restoration
   » Where and when is Eden?
   » Who owns Eden?

The parallel story: Israel and God, sin and just punishment, repentance and atonement, forgiveness and restoration
   » Israel's Adam and Eve
   » Sin and atonement
   » Intentionality and the civil order

The story of Israel and the nations, specifically, Israel and the Torah, the gentiles lacking the Torah
   » Enemies of Eden, tangible and invisible
   » The contest between death and life
   » Overcoming death
   » The Kingdom of God

Through the sages' philosophical reading of Scripture—its Halakhah and its Aggadah alike—the Torah's account of humanity's story is transformed into the design for Israel's social order: God's Kingdom, Eden realized now, restored at the end. Let us now see things whole. Here are the specific Halakhic tractates that convey the message through the norms of public conduct, and the specific details of that message, viewed whole:

Where and when is Eden?
   » Shebi'it
   » 'Orlah
   » Kilayim
   » Shabbat-Erubin

By Eden, Scripture means that place whole and at rest that God sanctified; "Eden" stands for creation in perfect repose. In the Halakhah, Eden stands for not a particular place but nature in a defined condition, at a particular moment: creation in Sabbath repose, sanctified. Then a place in repose at the climax of creation, at sunset at the start of the seventh day, whole and at rest, embodies, realizes Eden. The Halakhah means to systematize the condition of Eden, to define

Eden in its normative traits, and also to localize Eden within Israel, the people. How so? Eden is the place to the perfection of which God responded in the act of sanctification at the advent of the seventh day. While the Land in the Written Torah's explicit account of matters claims the right to repose on the seventh day and in the seventh year of the septennial cycle, it is the location of Israel wherever that may be at the advent of sunset on the eve of the seventh day of the week of creation that recapitulates Eden:

Who owns Eden?
>> Ma'aserot
>> Terumot
>> Hallah
>> Ma'aser Sheni
>> Bikkurim
>> Pe'ah
>> Dema'i

The story expands, within the motif of Eden, to the matter of ownership and possession as media for the expression of the relationship between humanity and God. God accorded to Adam and Eve possession of nearly everything in Eden, retaining ownership—the right to govern according to His will—for Himself. The key to the entire system of interaction between God and Israel through the Land and its gifts emerges in the Halakhah of Ma'aserot and its companions, which deal—along the lines of Shebi'it and 'Erubin—with the difference between possession and ownership. God owns the world, which he made. But God has accorded to humanity the right of possession of the earth and its produce. This he did twice, once to the primordial human beings—Adam and Eve—in Eden, the second time to Israel in the Land of Israel. And to learn the lesson that humanity did not master, that possession is not ownership but custody and stewardship, Israel has to acknowledge the claims of the creator to the glory of all creation, which is the land. This Israel does by giving back God's share of the produce of the land at the time, and in the manner, that God defines. The enlandized (situated within the land) components of the Halakhah therefore form a single, cogent statement of matters:

Adam and Eve
>> Qiddushin
>> Ketubot
>> Nedarim
>> Nazir
>> Sotah
>> Gittin

» Yebamot
» Sacralization and intentionality

The Halakhah of the family, covering the act of sanctification of a woman by a man (Qiddushin), the marriage agreement (Ketubah), vows and special vows, the disposition of a charge of unfaithfulness against a woman, and the severance of the marital bond of sanctification through a writ of divorce or death, does not ubiquitously invoke the metaphor of Adam and Eve in Eden. Our task, then, is to identify the principal foci of that Halakhah and to investigate the appropriate context in which it is to be interpreted. How here does Eden figure? The connection is made articulate by the (possibly later) liturgical framework in which the Halakhah plays itself out. There, in the liturgy of the marriage canopy, the act of creation of humanity is recapitulated, the bride and groom explicitly compared with Adam and Eve. Not only so, but the theme of the land and Israel intervenes as well—two motifs dominant in the Halakhic theology examined to this point:

Sin and atonement
   » The new moral entity
   » Sheqalim
   » Tamid and Yoma
   » Zebahim amd Menahot
   » Arakhin
   » Bekhorot
   » Meilah
   » Temurah

The Halakhah takes account of the tragedy of Eden and provides for a new moral entity, a reformed transaction accorded that entity, one not available to Adam and Eve. For God at Eden made no provision for atonement for sin, but, in the unfolding of humanity's story, God grasped the full measure of mortals' character and drew the necessary conclusion and acted on it. Endowed with autonomous will, human beings have the power to rebel against God's will. Therefore the Halakhah finds urgent the question, how is humanity, subject to God's rule, to atone for the sin that, by their rebellious nature, men and women are likely to commit? To answer that question, the Torah formulates the rules that govern humanity both (1) when under God's dominion and (2) when in rebellion against God's will. These represent the two aspects of the one story that commences with Eden, leads to the formation of Israel through Abraham, Isaac, and Jacob, God's antidotes to Adam, and climaxes at Sinai. But Israel also is human, so that story accommodates both Adam's fall and Israel's worship of the golden calf, and, as the denouement, Adam and Eve's exile from Eden and Israel's

ultimate exile from the land. How, then, does God propose to repair the world
he has made to take account of humanity's character and Israel's own proclivity?

Intentionality and the civil order
» Legitimate violence: who does what to whom
» Keritot
» Sanhedrin-Makkot
» Baba Qamma-Baba Mesi'a-Baba Batra
» Horayot
» Shebuot

The Halakhah dictates the character of (its) Israel's civil order—its political
institutions and system of criminal justice. It undertakes a labor of differentiation
of power, indicating what agency or person has the power to precipitate the
working of politics as legitimate violence. When we understand the differenti-
ating force that imparts to politics its activity and dynamism, we grasp the theology that animates the structures of the politics and propels the system. The
details of the Halakhah, in particular the sanctions assigned to various infractions,
effect the taxonomy of power, which forms an implicit exegesis of the story of
Eden, translated into reflection on the power of intentionality:

Enemies of Eden, tangible and invisible
» Tangible enemies: Abodah Zarah
» Invisible enemies: death, Ohalot
» Negaim
» Zabim and Niddah

The enemies of Eden take shape around the grand struggle between life and
death, in the here and now meaning Israel and the gentiles, at the end of days
meaning those who will stand in judgment and go onward to the world to come
and eternal life, and those who will perish in the grave. Specifically, the world
beyond the limits of Israel forms an undifferentiated realm of idolatry and
uncleanness. Then how is Israel to negotiate life with the world of gentiles and
their idolatry, corpses and their contamination? Among the sources of uncleanness, tangible and invisible, we begin with the gentiles and proceed to corpse- and
comparable kinds of uncleanness. But the two—gentiles and corpses—form a
single domain. The former bears exactly the same uncleanness as the latter. Gentiles, defined as idolaters, and Israelites, defined as worshippers of the one and
only God, part company at death. For the moment Israelites die—only to rise
from the grave. Gentiles die for eternity. The roads intersect at the grave, each
component of humanity taking its own path beyond. Israelites—meaning, those
possessed of right conviction—will rise from the grave, stand in judgment, but
then enter upon eternal life, to which no one else will enjoy access:

The contest between death and life
- » Uncleanness and sanctification
- » Makhshirin
- » Tohorot
- » Uqsin
- » Kelim

The sources of change and disruption that threaten the cleanness, hence the sanctification, of the Temple are the same sources that threaten the norm of cleanness of the household. If the same uncleanness affects the Temple and the table, then the only difference is one of degree, not of kind, as the Halakhah states explicitly. And the rest follows. The web of relationships between sanctification and uncleanness spins itself out into every corner of the Israelite household, where the system makes a difference. And it is the will of the householder that determines the difference that the distinction between clean and unclean is going to make. Everything is relative to the householder's will; he has it in his power to draw the household table into alignment with the altar in the Temple, that is to say, to place the table and the food set thereon into relationship, onto a continuum, with the altar and the Holy Things of the cult. This he can accomplish through an act of will that motivates an attitude of constant watchfulness in the household for those very sources of contamination that Scripture identifies as danger to the Lord's altar in the Jerusalem Temple:

Overcoming death
- » Parah
- » Miqvaot
- » Tebul Yom
- » Yadayim
- » Home and temple in hierarchical formation: Hagigah
- » Cause and effect: where and why humanity's will matters

From death and its effect upon food and drink, that is, the uncleanness caused by, and analogous to, death, we turn to the media for the restoration of life. Still water unaffected by human agency restores the natural condition disrupted by uncleanness other than that of the corpse and its analogues, while by contrast purification-water systematically subjected to human intervention—constant attention, deliberate action, start to finish—alone removes corpse-uncleanness. We have then to account for the exclusion of humanity from the one process, along with the radical insistence upon humanity's inclusion, in full deliberation, within the other. Uncleanness that comes about by reason of any cause but death and its analogues is removed by the Heaven's own dispensation, not by humanity's intervention: rainfall, sunset suffice. Ordinary purification is done by nature, resulting from natural processes. But as to persons and objects that have contracted uncleanness from death, nature on its own cannot produce the kind of water that bears the power to remove that uncleanness and restore the condition of nature. Only human beings can. And men and women can do this only by the highest level of concentration, the most deliberate and focused action. One person's act of will overcomes the uncleanness of death, just as one person's act of deliberate rebellion brought about death to begin with. Humanity restores what humanity has disrupted. Had the Halakhah wished in its terms and categories to accomplish a reprise of the story of humanity's fall, it could not have made a more eloquent statement than it does in the contrast between the Halakhah of Miqvaot and that of Parah.

The Kingdom of God
   » Accepting the yoke of the Kingdom of Heaven and the Commandments
   » Berakhot
   » Hullin
   » Megillah
   » Rosh Hashanah
   » Pesahim
   » Sukkah
   » Mo'ed Qatan
   » Besah
   » Ta'anit

As much as men and women by their nature rebel against God, these same people tutored by the Commandments willingly accept God's will and therefore his rule. What are the Halakhah's media for the reformation, regeneration, and renewal of humanity? The Halakhah here legislates for not Eden but the kingdom of God. For Sinai's answer to Eden's question transcends the matter of sin and atonement and encompasses the conduct of the ordinary, everyday life lived under God's rule. The normative deals with the normal, so the final solution to God's dilemma with humanity—how to accord men and women free will but to nurture in them freely given love for God—lies in the Torah. That way of life in accord with God's rule means to form the Paideia, the character-building education to transform humanity by making Israelite men and women's freely given obedience to God as natural as was Adam and Eve's obstinate rebellion against God. That is why the Halakhic provision for life in God's kingdom moves from the ordinary day and its duties to the table and its everyday nourishment, then to the meeting with God that is seasonal and temporal, and finally to the climax of the system, confrontation with routine crisis.

This brief precis shows how a few large motifs form of the details of the Halakhah a single coherent system, one that tells a story. Clearly, the Halakhah works from Scripture forward.[1] But, being theologians, systematic thinkers, intent on a philosophical reading of religion in quest of a coherent, proportionate, and rigorously argued statement, they do not randomly rework this detail or that. Rather, the sages' philosophical reading of Scripture—its Halakhah and its Aggadah alike—produces a coherent theology. It leads to the transformation of the Torah's account of humanity's story into the detailed design for Israel's social order. The details all find their place within the structure of the whole, and in its workings, the system that sages have constructed animates the whole, the parts working well together to make a simple statement.

That is easily set forth. In its actualities Israel embodies—or is meant to embody—God's plan for humankind, not on the individual level, but as a social entity: God's Kingdom, Eden both realized in the here and now and restored at the end of time. The Rabbinic Judaism embodied, actualized, and realized in the Halakhah is the religion that publicly, in the sight of all humanity, realizes now and for eternity the imperatives of God, made manifest at Sinai, in the Torah, and that thereby shows the way to eternal life with God.

So we have followed the story about the interior architectonics of Israel's being that the Halakhah tells through concrete action-symbols. The Halakhah brings about the transformation of the here and the now, of the particular occasion (thus: place and time and event, mostly in nature) into the embodiment, the exemplification, of the abstract ground of being. Involved is the relationship of realms of the sacred: the rules of engagement between and among God, land, Israel, time, place, circumstance. Through the fabric of everyday life of the land lived out in the household, village, and the holy metropolis, Jerusalem (the three dimensions of the social order of which the Halakhah takes account), Eden is read not as historical moment but as situation and occasion. That then precipitates thought about the human condition. But Eden does not impose narrow limits on the amplification of that thought. It is not the only condition.

There is also the situation brought about by the second great theme, besides Eden, that is implicit in the Halakhah. It is God's self-manifestation in the Torah: the occasion for the reform and renewal of humanity through Israel, the counterpart and opposite of humankind. The Halakhah therefore will be shown to begin with Eden but to progress to the realization of God's Kingdom within holy Israel's social order, conceiving of Israel both enlandized (defined as being situated within the Land) and utopian (located anywhere), as the category of the Halakhah requires.

A third massive motif involves Eden once more, this time under God's rule, and it too engages with the Torah's account of Israel at Sinai. It concerns the reembodiment of Israel, the restoration that comes about not alone in the end of days when the Messiah comes, but in the here-and-now of the workaday world. It is there that Israelite human beings formed by the discipline of the Torah learn both to atone for, and to overcome, their natural propensity willfully to rebel against God. Within the social order of an enlandized Israel moral humanity constructs a godly society. That reading of the Written Torah and translation of its law into the canons of ordinary life speaks in the acutely present tense to portray for humanity a worthy future well within their own capacities to realize: "The Commandments were given only to purify the heart of Man," and "All-Merciful wants the heart," as the Talmud frames matters. Therein, I identify the political theology of the Halakhah: a massive, closed system that, in dialogue with the Aggadah but in its own category-formations and language, says the same thing about many things, numerous details bearing a single message.

Judaism and Nonbelievers: Politics and People outside the Tradition

At the end we turn to how the Halakhic system sets forth the relationship of holy Israel with everybody else, meaning in the context of the system only one thing: idolaters, severally and jointly. Idolatry represents the tangible enemy of God. When the Halakhah takes up the world beyond Eden, it invokes its own metaphors for death: the gentiles in the tangible world outside the genealogical frontier of Israel, corpse-uncleanness in the invisible, if equally tangible, world beyond the limits of the altar, the Temple, and Jerusalem. The world beyond the bounds of Israel—the people in its household walls, the land within its frontiers—forms an undifferentiated realm of idolatry and uncleanness. Then how is Israel to negotiate life with the world of gentiles and their idolatry, corpses and their contamination? The Halakhah constructs, indeed defines, the interiority of an Israel sustaining God's service in a world of idolatry: life against death in the two concrete and tangible dimensions by which life is sustained: trade and the production of food. No wonder Israel must refrain from engaging with idolatry on days of the festivals for idols that the great fairs embody—then especially.

Among the sources of uncleanness, tangible and invisible, we begin with the gentiles and proceed to corpse-uncleanness and comparable kinds of uncleanness. As pointed out previously, the two—gentiles, corpses—form a single domain. The former bears the same uncleanness as the latter. A picture in cartographic form of the theological anthropology of the Halakhah, indeed, would portray a many-colored and much-differentiated Israel at the center of the circle, with the perimeter comprised by all-white gentiles. For white is the color of death, how the unclean graves are marked off to warn priests and others concerned with cleanness. Gentiles, like their idols, constitute a source of uncleanness of the virulence of corpse-uncleanness. What detail of the Halakhah embodies the principle that Israel stands for life, the gentiles like their idols for death?

An asherah tree, like a corpse, conveys uncleanness to those who pass underneath it, so M. Abodah Zarah 3:8: "And he should not pass underneath it, but if he passed underneath it, he is unclean."

Not only so, but gentiles, always meaning idolaters, and Israelites, defined as worshipers of the one and only God, part company at death. Only for the moment do Israelites die, for they are to rise from the grave. The roads intersect at the grave, each component of humanity taking its own path beyond. Israelites—meaning those possessed of right conviction—will rise from the grave, stand in judgment, but then enter upon eternal life, to which no idolater will enjoy access. So, in substance, humanity viewed whole is divided between those who get a share in the world to come and who will stand when subject to divine judgment and those who will not. And humanity also is divided between Israel, acutely susceptible to a broad variety of sources of uncleanness but also capable of attaining purity, and the gentiles, uniformly unclean always. That is the meaning of the fact that all gentiles—even righteous ones—are sources of the undifferentiated uncleanness of the corpse.

When a gentile abandons idolatry and accepts the dominion of God exercised through His self-manifestation in the Torah, he loses the corpse-uncleanness that afflicted him, is immersed and transformed, and as if newly born in the rite of immersion. Nothing in his past affects his new status as part of Israel (though his status within Israel is subject to those same criteria of hierarchization and differentiation that govern all others within Israel in one way or another). Then the Halakhah distinguishing those who love from those who hate God takes as its religious problem the concretization of that distinction, the demonstration of where and how the distinction in theory makes a huge difference in the practice, the conduct, of everyday affairs. And, as we shall see, invisible, though tangible, sources of uncleanness also form analogues to death.

Idolatry—rebellious arrogance against God—encompasses rejection of the entire Torah. The religious duty to avoid idolatry is primary; if one violates the religious duties, he breaks the yoke of Commandments, and if he violates that single religious duty, he violates the entire Torah. Violating the prohibition against idolatry is equivalent to transgressing all Ten Commandments. Differentiated by genealogy and other indicators, all Israelites are defined by submission to God and acceptance of the Torah as God's will. That conclusion is sustained by a simple inversion of subject and predicate in the Halakhic definition of Israel, which we have already encountered. The Halakhah states, "All Israelites have a share in the world to come. And these are the ones who have no portion in the world to come: He who says, the resurrection of the dead is a teaching that does not derive from the Torah, and the Torah does not come from Heaven; and an Epicurean" (Mishnah Sanhedrin 10:1). Then we may say, those who have a share in the world to come are those who affirm God, self-manifest in the Torah.

What accounts for the identification of idolatry with death? The transaction of Eden lies at the foundation, namely, in the act of rebellion. Idolatry forms a deliberate act of rebellion against God. Gentiles are deniers, their status imposed by their own act of will. That is why, in full deliberation, they are unreconstructed humankind, destined for the grave and classified as corpses even while alive. So the Halakhah maintains that Israel encompasses those who will enjoy eternal life, gentiles are those who perish at the grave. The contrast between life and Israel, death and gentiles, is concrete and practical, for the spit and urine of the gentile are unclean, since gentiles are classified as a Zab (Leviticus 15). That means even a gentile who accepted the seven Commandments that pertain to the children of Noah falls outside of the system of differentiated contamination that pertains to Israel, for example, they are not subject to the uncleanness described at Leviticus 13–14, and Israelite itself before the giving of the Torah was not subject to that uncleanness. If Eden stands for life with God, then beyond the limits lies the realm of death, tangible in gentiles, invisible in corpse-uncleanness and other sources of uncleanness, including the idol. In this world, death is to be held at a distance, uncleanness is to be kept away, from the Temple altar, and, by analogy, from the table of the Israelite household, and, in the world to come, gentiles, idolaters, molder in the grave and death itself will die.

How does the Halakhah respond in practical terms to these convictions? The Halakhah takes as its task the negotiation between Israelites and the pagan world in which they live: how are they to conduct themselves in accord with the Torah so that at no point and in no way do they give support to idolatry and so betray the one and only God. In its basic exposition of the theme of idolatry, the Halakhah rests squarely on the foundations of Scripture, supplying rules and regulations that carry out the fundamental scriptural Commandments about destroying idols and everything that has to do with idolatry. But the Halakhah so formulates matters as to transform the entire topic of idolatry into an essay on Israel's relationships with the gentiles, who, as I said, are idolaters by definition. The Halakhah addresses the condition of individuals, the ordinary life of common folk, rather than concentrating on the situation of all Israel, viewed as a collective entity. The Halakhah therefore tends to find its problem in the condition of the private person and in the interiorities of his life in the Israelite community.

For the Written Torah, the community at large forms the focus of the law, and idolatry is not to be negotiated with by the collectivity of holy Israel. In its land Israel is to wipe out idolatry, even as a memory. Scripture is clear that Israel is to obliterate all mention of idols (Exodus 23:13), not bow down to gentiles' gods or serve them but overthrow them and break them into pieces (Exodus 23:24): "You shall break down their altars and dash in pieces their pillars and hew down their Asherim and burn their graven images with fire" (Dueteronomy 7:5). Israelites are commanded along these same lines:

> You shall surely destroy all the places where the nations whom you shall dispossess served their gods, upon the high mountains and upon the hills and under every green tree; you shall tear down their altars and dash in pieces their pillars and burn their Asherim with fire; you shall hew down the graven images of their gods and destroy their name out of that place. (Dueteronomy 12:2–3)

Accordingly, so far as the Written Torah supplies the foundations for the treatment of the matter by the Oral Torah, the focus of discourse concerning the gentiles is idolatry. Scripture's Halakhah does not contemplate Israel's coexisting, in the land, with gentiles and their idolatry.

But the Halakhah of the Mishnah-Tosefta-Yerushalmi-Bavli speaks to a world that is not so simple. The land belongs to Israel, but gentiles also live there—and run things. The Halakhah of the Oral Torah commences with the premise that gentiles live side by side (whether or not in the Land of Israel) with Israelites. Then Israelites have to sort out the complex problems of coexistence with idolatry. And that coexistence involves not whole communities, corporate Israel, and the peoples, whoever they may be, but individuals, this Israelite living side by side with that gentile. The Halakhah deals first with commercial relationships; second, with matters pertaining to idols; and finally, with the particular prohibition of wine, part of which has served as a libation to an idol. The whole is regularized and ordered. There are relationships with gentiles that are absolutely prohibited, particularly occasions of idol worship; the Halakhah recognizes that these are major commercial events. When it comes to commerce with idolaters, Israelites may not sell or in any way benefit from certain things, may sell but may not utilize certain others, and may sell and utilize yet others. Here, we see immediately, the complex and systematic mode of thought that governs the Oral Torah's treatment of the topic vastly transcends the rather simple conception that animates Scripture's discussion of the same matter. There are these unstated premises within the Halakhah:

1. What a gentile is not likely to use for the worship of an idol is not prohibited.
2. What may serve not as part of an idol but as an appurtenance thereto is prohibited for Israelite use but permitted for Israelite commerce.
3. What serves idolatry is prohibited for use and for benefit.

In reflecting upon relationships with the gentiles, meaning idolaters, the Oral Torah moreover takes for granted a number of facts. These turn out to yield a single generalization: Gentiles are assumed routinely to practice bestiality, murder, and fornication. Further negative stereotypes concerning idolaters occur.

The Halakhah then serves as the means for the translation of theological conviction into social policy. Gentiles are assumed to be ready to murder any Israelite they can get their hands on, rape any Israelite woman, commit bestiality with any

Israelite cow. The Oral Torah cites few cases to indicate that that conviction responds to ordinary, everyday events; the hostility to gentiles flows from a theory of idolatry, not the facts of everyday social intercourse, which, as we have seen, sages recognize is full of neighborly cordiality. Then why take for granted gentiles routinely commit the mortal sins of not merely idolatry but bestiality, fornication, and murder? That is because the Halakhah takes as its task the realization of the theological principle that those who hate Israel hate God, those who hate God hate Israel, and God will ultimately vanquish Israel's enemies as His own—just as God also was redeemed from Egypt. So the theory of idolatry, involving alienation from God, accounts for the wicked conduct imputed to idolaters, without regard to whether, in fact, that is how idolaters conduct themselves. That matter of logic is stated in so many words:

> Sifré to Numbers 84:4:
> ". . . and let them that hate you flee before you:"
> And do those who hate [come before] him who spoke and brought the world into being?
> The purpose of the verse at hand is to say that whoever hates Israel is as if he hates him who spoke and by his word brought the world into being.

The same proposition is reworked. God can have no adversaries, but gentile enemies of Israel act as though they were his enemies:

> Along these same lines: "In the greatness of your majesty you overthrow your adversaries." (Exodus 15:7)
> And are there really adversaries before him who spoke and by his word brought the world into being? But Scripture thus indicates that whoever rose up against Israel is as if he rose up against the Omnipresent.

Israel hates God's enemies, and Israel is hated because of its loyalty to God (a matter to which we shall return below):

> "Do I not hate those who hate you, O Lord? And do I not loathe them that rise up against you? I hate them with perfect hatred, I count them my enemies." (Psalm 139:21–22)
> And so Scripture also says, "For whoever lays hands on you is as if he lays hands on the apple of his eye." (Zechariah 2:12)
> R. Judah says, "What is written is not, 'the apple of an eye' but 'the apple of his eye,' it is as if Scripture speaks of him above, but Scripture has used an euphemism."

Now the consequences of these propositions are drawn:

> And whoever gives help to Israel is as if he gives help to him who spoke and by his word brought the world into being, as it is said, "Curse Meroz, says the angel of the

Lord, curse bitterly its inhabitants, because they came not to the help of the Lord,
to the help of the Lord against the mighty." (Judges 5:23)

The proposition announced at the outset is fully articulated—those who hate
Israel hate God, those who are enemies of Israel are enemies of God, those who
help Israel help God—and then systematically spelled out through examples and
by facts set forth in Scripture.

In line with its focus upon issues of intentionality, the Halakhah insists that,
just as gentiles make choices willfully, so in dealing with idolatry and the gentiles,
Israel too may exercise its own will. Under all conditions, the Halakhah assumes,
Israelites possess freedom of will: they are always human beings, "in our image."
The Halakhah presupposes not gentile hegemony but only gentile power. It further takes for granted that Israelites may make choices, may specifically refrain
from trading in what gentiles value in the service of their gods, and may hold
back from gentiles what gentiles require for that service. Israelites may live in a
world governed by gentiles, but they form intentions and carry them out. They
may decide what to sell and what not to sell, whom to hire for what particular act
of labor and to whom not to sell their own labor. And above all, Israelite traders
may determine to give up opportunities denied them by the circumstance of gentile idolatry.

The Halakhah therefore makes a formidable statement of Israel's freedom to
make choices, its opportunity within the context of everyday life to preserve a
territory free of idolatrous contamination, much as Israel in entering the land
was to create a territory free of the worship of idols and their presence. In the
setting of world order, Israel may find itself subject to the will of others. But in
the house of Israel, Israelites can and should establish a realm for God's rule and
presence, free of idolatry. And if to establish a domain for God, Israelites must
practice self-abnegation, refrain from actions of considerable weight and consequence, well, much of the Torah concerns itself with what people are not supposed to do, and God's rule comes to realization in acts of restraint. So much for
the life of Israel under the Commandments.

The Halakhah, to be sure, recognizes that gentiles also are subject to God's
Commandments. There are seven such religious obligations that apply to the
children of Noah. It is not surprising—indeed, it is predictable—that the definition of the matter should find its place in the Halakhah of Abodah Zarah:

Concerning seven religious requirements were the children of Noah admonished:
setting up courts of justice, idolatry, blasphemy [cursing the Name of God], fornication, bloodshed, and thievery. (Tosefta-tractate Abodah Zarah 8:4–6)

The Halakhah constructs, indeed defines, the interiority of an Israel sustaining God's service in a world of idolatry: life against death in the two concrete and

tangible dimensions by which life is sustained: trade and the production of food, the foci of the Halakhah. No wonder Israel must refrain from engaging with idolatry on days of the festivals for idols that the great fairs embody—then especially. So much for the visible enemies of Eden: animate corpses.

The key to the system presents itself in its account of the outsider. The politics of Judaism is a politics of life against death: forming God's Kingdom in particular, yielding life eternal. The entire politics comes to expression in this language, cited above:

> All Israelites have a share in the world to come, as it is said, "Your people also shall be all righteous, they shall inherit the land forever; the branch of my planting, the work of my hands, that I may be glorified." (Isaiah 60:21; Mishnah-tractate Sanhedrin 10:1)

Conclusion

With the classical political construction fully exposed, we can see the sources for the political confusion that overtakes the religious system and structure of classical Judaism when the practical world of power relationships intervenes. The aspiration on the part of the political parties of the Torah camp to realize the Halakhah, all or in part, in the governance of the State of Israel conflicts with the contents of the canonical Halakhic documents, the Mishnah, Tosefta, two Talmuds, and related writings.

To state the source of the conflict simply: The Halakhah certainly accommodates contemporary practical circumstances and can be extended to serve as a law code for the society of Judaism, but the political theology that explains the Halakhah proves incongruent to the task of politics. That is, the theology that animates the political system of Rabbinic Judaism, beginning in the relationships of Adam and Eve with God and focusing on matters of attitude and intentionality, scarcely intersects with the program of questions of legitimate power that other religious systems of politics address.

Brilliant exegetes of the Halakhah have kept up with the practicalities of the everyday world. The substance of the legal system can be made to work, but the why and wherefore of the political myth that explains the whole and makes the parts cohere, addresses the theological condition of the holy people and not the power relationships that require explanation. Judaism sets forth laws, but no politics.

The classical Judaic system sets forth an account of how the social order should function, but not a transcendent validation of the state as the medium of humanity's regeneration and society's reconciliation with God. In the theology of Judaism, there can be a state encompassing a large ethnically Jewish population. But to witness the formation of a state of Judaism, that is, in Hebrew, *med-*

inat Yisrael, meaning for Judaism a state that embodies Israel the holy people in a political structure in God's service, one must await the coming of the Messiah and the advent of God's realized politics on earth for eternity. The politics of Judaism then is postponed until the end of days, when the royal Messiah will raise the dead, according eternal life to the citizens of Paradise redivivus.

Note

1. See Jacob Neusner, *The Torah and the Halakhah: The Four Relationships* (Lanham, Md.: University Press of America, 2003), for a systematic discussion. The present argument does not address the historical question of how the Halakhic system took shape over time. That is a separate matter; see Neusner, *From Scripture to 70* (Atlanta: Scholars Press, 1999), and Neusner, *The Four Stages of Rabbinic Judaism* (London: Routledge, 2000).

Suggested Readings

Avery-Peck, Alan J., Jacob Neusner, and William Scott Green. *Encyclopaedia of Judaism*. 3 vols. Leiden: E. J. Brill, 1999.

Elazar, Daniel J. *The Jewish Polity: Jewish Political Organization from Biblical times to the Present*. Bloomington: Indiana University Press, 1985.

Finkelstein, Louis, ed. *The Jews: Their History, Culture, and Religion*. 2 vols. Philadelphia: Jewish Publication Society of America, 1966.

Neusner, Jacob. *The Economics of the Mishnah*. Chicago: University of Chicago Press, 1989; Atlanta: Scholars Press, 1998.

———. *Judaism: An Introduction*. London and New York: Penguin, 2002.

———. *Rabbinic Political Theory: Religion and Politics in the Mishnah*. Chicago: University of Chicago Press, 1991.

Roth, Cecil, ed. *Encyclopaedia Judaica*. Jerusalem: Keter Publishing, 1971.

Scholem, Gershom G. *Major Trends in Jewish Mysticism*. New York: Schocken Books, 1995.

Sicker, Martin. *What Judaism Says about Politics: The Political Theology of the Torah*. Northvale, N.J.: Jason Aronson, 1994.

Walzer, Michael, Menachem Lorberbaum, Noam J. Zohar, and Yair Lorberbaum, eds. *The Jewish Political Tradition*. New Haven, Conn.: Yale University Press, 2000.

Two | **Primitive and Early Christianity** |

Bruce D. Chilton

"MY KINGDOM IS NOT OF THIS WORLD" (JOHN 18:36). THE JOHANNINE ATTRIBUTION of this statement to Jesus may fairly be questioned, owing to the abstract nature of the assertion, and to its legendary setting in an extensive interaction between Pontius Pilate and a provincial criminal who (after all) enjoyed no civil rights. But there is no doubt that this principle does represent the conviction of many primitive churches with regard to their loyalty to their heavenly Lord and their earthly masters. This dual loyalty is a persistent dynamic within Christian theology, and the sources of Early Christianity permit us to observe how it emerged, and how the sometimes asymmetrical demands of God and Caesar were sorted out.

Within the present chapter, it is useful to make a distinction between primitive Christianity and early Christianity. The Scriptures of Israel have always been valued within the church, in Hebrew, Aramaic, and Greek. Those were the only Scriptures of the church in its primitive phase, when the New Testament was being composed. In their meetings of prayer and worship, followers of Jesus saw the Scriptures of Israel "fulfilled" by their faith: their conviction was the same Spirit of God which was active in the prophets was, through Christ, available to them.

The New Testament was produced in primitive communities of Christians to prepare people for baptism, to order worship, to resolve disputes, to encourage faith, and like purposes. As a whole, it is a collective document of primitive Christianity compiled during the last decades of the first century C.E. Its purpose is to call out and order true Israel in response to the triumphant news of Jesus's preaching, ministry, death, and resurrection. Early Christianity (between the second and the fourth centuries C.E.) designates the period during which the church founded theology on the basis of the Scriptures of both the "Old Testament" and "New Testament," and it did so without the recourse to the institutions of Judaism that is characteristic of primitive Christianity. From thinkers as different from one another as Bishop Irenaeus in France and Origen, the speculative teacher active first in Egypt and then in Palestine, a commonly Christian philosophy began to emerge. Early Christianity might also be called a "Catholic" phase, in the sense that it was a quest for a "general" or "universal" account of the faith, but that designation may lead to confusion with Roman Catholicism at a later stage.

To trace the political development that is our concern, a chronological approach to the sources is followed here, so that (for example) a consideration of

37

Paul precedes a consideration of the Gospels, because the scholarly consensus is that Paul wrote his letters before the Gospels were written down in their final form. As we engage in this approach, we will consider five central issues. Initially, we will consider

1. How the conviction that believers are called by the Spirit of God influenced their view of earthly authorities,
2. How their consequent acceptance of martyrdom related to distinct kinds of eschatology, and
3. How each of these eschatologies eventuated in characteristic attitudes toward the entire project of human governance.

Once those issues have been traced, we can turn our attention to

4. How Christians were called practically to adjust to the demands of this world and its authorities, and
5. Where they saw the sequence of history as leading them.

Classical Sources of Primitive Christianity on Politics

Christianity conceives of people as having a deep affinity with God, and at the same time it acknowledges that between God and humanity a seemingly unbridgeable chasm sometimes intrudes. As recorded in the New Testament, Paul is the preeminent theologian of the ambivalence of this relationship. He wrote extensively to Christian communities in Rome around 57 C.E. His letter to the Romans is the result, the fullest explanation of Paul's theology, and at the same time the earliest example of political theology in the Christian tradition.

In an opening section, Paul concerns himself with the issue of how God may be conceived of as judging people, when they do not even know Him. Paul's response is that God's power and divinity are ingrained in the very nature of the created universe, and thereby evident to people from the world around them:

> What is known of God is evident to them, because He has manifested it to them. His invisible qualities, His eternal power and divinity, have been demonstrated perceptibly from the creation of the world by the things that have been made. (Romans 1:19–20)

The issue of judgment illuminates how Paul understands God to be known to humanity at large. To Paul, the particular qualities of God, because they are behind the world rather than in it, are invisible. God's being God means that He is transcendent in His divinity, beyond the terms of reference of time and space.

But His power is also evident, as demonstrated by our perception of things made in the world around us. The world is not just an accident of our environment, but that which is created by God. Paul's conviction is consonant with the story of the creation in Genesis 1, and with much else in the Scriptures of Israel.

When, in Galatians 1:15, Paul refers to God separating him from his mother's womb, there is nothing abstract or theoretical about the imagery of creation. The emphasis rather falls on the immediate and personal link between God and Paul's own being. The imagery is not original with Paul; he is picking up the language of the Old Testament. For example, Psalms 22:9 and 71:6 offer praise to God for taking the speaker from the womb and keeping him safe from childhood. The image is also used in the prophetic literature, when the prophet is said to have been taken from the womb for the purpose of giving his prophecy (see Isaiah 49:1 and Jeremiah 1:5). In all these cases, as in Paul's usage, the imagery expresses not only a sense of being in an ordered creation but also of experiencing God's care within that creation. The prophetic usage enhances the emphasis on one's personal sense of purpose by applying the image to a particular mission one is to accomplish. Paul shares that emphasis as well.

The prophetic dimension of Paul's reference to God comes out again in his description of God "calling" him. "Calling" is understood to establish a link between God and the person He calls, so that God's word may be delivered. Who is called? It might be a prophet, or all Israel, or Jesus himself. Matthew 2:15 presents the infant Jesus as being called from Egypt for his vocation in Israel, which echoes the prophetic book of Hosea (11:1). Hosea applies "Out of Egypt I called my Son" to the people Israel, liberated at the time of the Exodus. That wording is then interpreted afresh in Matthew to refer to Jesus. Matthew can apply Hosea's prophecy to Jesus because much of the language of the Old Testament, including reference to God's calling and God's separating a person from the womb, is deliberately developed in the New Testament. The usage of the Old Testament is the point of departure for new applications and unusual developments, designed to convey a sense of intimacy with God.

God initiates the biblical call, but the call must be answered by someone for it to achieve the goal of communicating with people. Indeed, the fact of God's call can be the basis upon which people take it upon themselves to call upon God. "Answer me when I call, O God of my righteousness" (Psalm 4:1) is an appeal that is predicated on the prior response of the psalmist, and the psalmist's community, to God's call.

Paul particularly develops the reciprocity of call and response in his teaching about the Spirit of God. 1 Corinthians 2 shows how, in a letter written a year or two before Romans, Paul sees God's Spirit at work. If one asks how we can know what God has prepared for us, the answer is that Spirit alone is able to communicate divine purposes. The initial terms of Paul's knowledge of God, then, are his awareness of God's power and care, and his access to the Spirit of God (see 1 Corinthians 2:9 above all).

But that is by no means the whole of Paul's conception of knowledge of God. Its distinctive feature is that God was pleased "to reveal his Son in me" (Galatians 1:15): that is how Paul knows in the first place that he has been separated from the womb and called by God. The revelation of God's Son in the midst of one's being is the distinctive basis of Christian knowledge of God. In fact, Paul conceives of the moment of receiving God's Spirit in a highly specific manner, linked inextricably to Jesus (Galatians 4:6): Baptism is the moment at which, by accepting the revelation of the Son, one can accept that Spirit which is truly divine. Only what has come from God can acknowledge and respond to God: that is the revelation of God's Son within.

Paul brings us, then, to the most characteristic aspect of the Christian understanding of the knowledge of God—its emphasis upon Jesus, the Son of God, as the central mediator of that knowledge. One's own acknowledgment of and response to God remain vital, but they are understood to be possible only because God has already been at work within, shaping a spiritual eye to see Him at work and a spiritual ear to hear His call. As Paul conceives of Jesus, he is first of all the Son of God revealed within us. Of course, Paul is aware of the primitive teaching concerning Jesus's deeds and teaching, including a graphic account of his crucifixion (see Galatians 3:1). But his interest in Jesus is not historical. Rather, his attention is taken up by how the revelation of the Son of God might shape our minds and hearts to know God.

The most famous expression of this theme occurs in the letter to the Philippians, which was probably composed after Paul's death, by his follower Timothy (ca. 90 C.E.). It represents a mature Pauline theology, much of it on the basis of what Paul personally had thought. It was composed at a time at which Christians in the Greco-Roman world were largely of the servant class, so that its appeal to the form of Jesus as a servant is especially poignant:

> Let this thought prevail among you, which was also in Jesus Christ: Who, being in God's form, did not consider the presumption of equality with God, but emptied himself, taking a servant's form; existing in men's likeness, and found as a man in shape, he humbled himself, becoming obedient unto death, death on a cross. (Philippians 2:5–8)

The point of Paul and Timothy together (see Philippians 1:1) is that it is possible, on the basis of the revelation of the Son of God within a person, to think as Jesus did, although in one's own circumstances. Here is an example of the imperative to imitate Christ within the New Testament. Its object is not a slavish mimicry of the historical person but an embrace of that humble disposition of Christ that makes the knowledge of God possible, proceeding as it does from God's own loving nature.

Knowledge of God, then, involves the capacity to acknowledge God as the source of one's being, the ability to respond to God's call and to hear Him, and an acceptance within oneself of Christ's own loving disposition—his humility unto death. Christianity's anthropology directly reflects its call to humanity to enter into the vision of God and to be transformed by the divine Spirit.

On a political level, this literally otherworldly perspective results in a paradoxical acceptance of the institutions of this world. That acceptance is qualified, however, by the observation that all forms of human government are provisional. The same Paul who would die in Rome during Nero's persecution of Christians could insist in Romans 13:1–2:

> Let every person be subject to the governing authorities. For there is no authority except from God, and those that exist have been instated by God. Therefore one who resists the authorities resists what God has appointed, and those who resist will incur judgment.

Peter is said to have died in the same persecution (crucified, rather than beheaded, as it is said Paul was),[1] and yet the letter called 1 Peter (composed around 90 C.E., during another period of persecution) attributes the following advice to him (4:19): "Therefore let those who suffer according to God's will do right and entrust their souls to a faithful Creator." Under such adverse conditions, there is every intellectual and practical reason to deny that current experience comes from God. Yet that is exactly what primitive Christianity did not do, and as a result a qualified acceptance of human institutions of governance is articulated.

Early Christianity's Theory of Politics

Out of the spiritual transformation of individual lives, and the communal experience of persecution, Early Christianity developed from its New Testament a theory of politics predicated on God's ultimate control of all creation. Believing that God is both the creator and savior of the world allowed Christians to accept suffering at the hands of civil authorities, and paradoxically to give their allegiance to this same ruling government, because God had vested the ruler with power. There is a particularly poignant passage from what is called "The Acts of the Scillitan Martyrs" in which a Roman judge attempts to reason with some people who have been denounced for their Christianity but are not guilty of any other crime. He explains to them, very patiently, that they can easily walk away from the court, simply by burning some incense before an image of the emperor, and swearing an oath of allegiance to him as God's son. His patience extends to a conscientious recognition that the act does not actually require belief; only conformity to the due form is required.

Many Gnostic Christians would have had no difficulty complying with the judge's request, and no doubt there were other Early Christians, loyal to the Apostles' Creed of Catholic Christianity, who nonetheless went along with such friendly advice. But, to the judge's exasperation, the Scillitan martyrs oblige the judge to condemn them to death, which he eventually does. To his mind (as to that of Marcus Aurelius; *Meditations* 11:3), they were obstinate. Christians were proud of such behavior in their ranks, and they produced an entire literature of martyrdom growing out of stories of such single-minded allegiance to God.

The insistence in 1 Peter 4:19 provides the key to this Christian persistence (or obstinacy, depending upon one's point of view). The fact of God's creation of this world seals it as ultimately good, no matter what our immediate experience of it might make it seem. The beginning of the passage makes its perspective clear:

> Beloved, do not be surprised at the fiery ordeal that is taking place among you to test you, as though something strange were happening to you. But rejoice insofar as you are sharing Christ's sufferings, so that you may also be glad and shout for joy when his glory is revealed. (1 Peter 4:12–13)

God's creation of this world in 1 Peter, in the New Testament as a whole, and in the rule of faith as articulated in the Apostle's Creed, is not to be understood simply as a theoretical expression of where things originally came from. Of course, Christians do and always have understood that God is good and that what he made (and makes) is very good, in the unmistakable assertion of Genesis 1:31. But they do not say on that basis that what seems bad is really good, or that evil is merely illusory or the work of some other power. Instead, they see present experience as in the process of a transformation, sometimes a painful transformation, in which all goodness (including God's) will be vindicated. The here and now, according to the New Testament and Early Christian writings, is not the final bar by which human experience should be judged. Christian faith in creation is more eschatological than anything else; it is concerned with what will happen at the end (the *eschaton* in Greek) of all things.

Because Christianity is committed to eschatology as the single perspective that makes sense of human experience, it has been obliged to spell out for itself what its eschatology means, how the anticipated transformation of the world is to be worked out. Three types of eschatological perspective—temporal, transcendent, and juridical—have characterized Christianity over time, and they are closely related to one another. Christians have advanced all three of them, often at the same time, although given periods usually represent a commitment to one of the three more than the others. Which of the types is emphasized has a profound impact on how a person and a community deal with suffering, and with how they actually perceive pain. For that reason, the distinctions among the three—and their relationship to one another—are quite important to understand.

Temporal Eschatology

By its very nature, eschatology must involve the end of time as we know and conceive of time. But there is no actual necessity that eschatological expectation should develop into what is defined as an apocalyptic expectation. After all, Jesus instructed his disciples to pray, "Your kingdom will come,"[2] without giving a precise indication of when that moment was to come. Apocalyptic thought involves the claim to understand the sequence and timing of the ultimate events in human affairs, up until and including the end.

Jesus does not appear to have taught any single apocalyptic scheme, and it is even said that, after his resurrection, he explicitly told his followers that "It is not yours to know the times and periods which the Father has set by his own authority" (Acts 1:7). But the fact is that, even without Jesus's encouragement, apocalyptic calendars thrived in primitive Christianity, as evidenced in books in the New Testament such as the Revelation of John, 2 Thessalonians, 2 Peter, and Jude, all of which were produced near the end of the first century. There is no single such calendar, so it seems obvious that Jesus did not endorse any single apocalyptic scheme. But then, the variety of the calendars themselves shows how vibrant and diverse apocalyptic expectation was.

Although other forms of eschatology have tended to dominate over temporal eschatology in the subsequent history of the church, there have been notable examples of renewed apocalyptic fervor, especially during times of extreme social change. Examples include some radical Anabaptists during the Reformation in Europe, and groups such as the Shakers in the United States during the nineteenth century.

Transcendent Eschatology

Because thought in the modern (and the so-called postmodern) world is, on the whole, not eschatological, it is easy to dismiss eschatology as a primitive and outdated view of the world. The scientific thought of ancient Greece, which has deeply influenced our own view of science, often conceived of physical reality as static and unchanging, and that has inclined many contemporary philosophers to prefer views of the world that are also static. Now, however, science itself shows us just how conditional human existence is. Physically, not even the universe appears permanent; solid matter seems to be a myth; the very survival of human beings is called into question by the rapid extinction of many other animal and plant species.

Just as our own world has started to seem less stable and unchanging to us, the world of ancient eschatology has proven to be much less simplistic and "primitive" than was once thought to be the case. It was fashionable a century ago to depict eschatology as a strictly temporal teaching, as if time were its only concern. We have just seen that some eschatology is indeed temporal in its emphasis. But to see God as final in human affairs also involves seeing God's Kingdom as working now, transforming the very environment in which we live. As Jesus put it, the Kingdom of God "is like yeast, which a woman takes, hides in three measures of dough, until the whole is yeasted" (Luke 13:21; Matthew 13:33). Because space, as well as time, is a dimension of God's activity, eschatology also involves seeing God at work now in his final revelation, and it involves the possibility of joining God in His Kingdom.

The point of the revelation of the Kingdom within our world is that it points beyond our world. The Kingdom is transcendent: It comes from outside us, transforms us, and directs us outside our selves. No theologian more forcefully or influentially emphasized this aspect of eschatology than the third-century Christian apologist, theologian, and priest Origen. To explain the value of the promises that are ours in Christ, Origen cites John 17:14, where Jesus asserts that neither he nor his disciples are of the world. Origen goes on to explain:

> But there is no doubt that the Savior refers to something more glorious and splendid than this present world, and invites and incites all who believe in him to direct their course towards it. But whether that world, which he wishes us to know of, is one that stands apart and separate from this world in space and quality and glory, or whether, as seems more likely to me, it excels in quality and glory but is nevertheless contained within the limits of this world, is uncertain, and in my opinion an unsuitable subject for the mind and thoughts of human beings. (*On First Principles* 2.3.6)

Origen here expresses a characteristic feature of Christian teaching concerning transcendence. The point is not to speak of something so different that we have no inkling what God would do with us. Rather, God may be perceived to be immanent in the world, and in His immanence to direct our course toward that which He would have us be. ("Immanence" is the usual category used to refer to the divine as existing within the universe as people may perceive it.) Because Christian teaching of divine transcendence is eschatological, it links this world with the world to come in the expectation and the experience of the believer.

Juridical Eschatology

Jesus's well-known parable of a feast to which the host makes surprising, insistent invitations—and equally categorical exclusions—voices another emphatic dimension of his own eschatology (see Matthew 22:1–14; Luke 14:16–24). God is portrayed as celebrating in His kingdom with those who would join Him, and as refusing to include those who have rejected the appointed way of entering His kingdom. Because Jesus was and is rightly known as the supreme teacher of divine love, this aspect of his teaching is frequently (and all too conveniently) ignored. But there is finally no compromise in love; it supersedes what would resist it. As the book of Psalms puts it, God's being king puts an end to everything wicked and those who represent wickedness, whether individuals or nations (see Psalm 10:15–16). In the realm of Early Christianity's politics, this juxtaposition between divine love's all-embracing inclusiveness, and its uncompromising exclusion of those who reject God's love, parallels the paradox between Christians suffering at the hands of the same government they endorse. Disciples of Jesus view their earthly rulers as being subordinate to God, willingly or unwillingly, for they themselves have chosen to subordinate their lives to God by naming Jesus as their sovereign Lord and personal savior.

Without doubt, this acute sense of the judgment which is involved in God's final disclosure is a typical, sometimes even dominant, feature of Christianity. In this, Augustine of Hippo delineates the sort of personal preparation for the judgment which would emerge during the Middle Ages. Speaking during the season of Lent, when the congregation makes ready for the celebration of Easter and Christ's temptation in the wilderness is recalled, Augustine preached as follows:

> Life in this world is certainly the time of our humiliation. These days show—by the recurrence of this holy season—how the sufferings of the Lord Christ, who once suffered for us by death, are renewed each year. For what was done once and for all time so that our life might be renewed is solemnized each year so that the memory may be kept fresh. If, therefore, we ought to be humble of heart with sentiments of most sincere reverence throughout the entire period of our earthly sojourn when we live in the midst of temptations, how much more necessary is humility during these days, when we not only pass the time of our humiliation by living, but call attention to it by special devotion! The humility of Christ has taught us to be humble because he yielded to the wicked in his death; the exaltation of Christ lifts us up because by rising again he cleared the way for his devoted followers. Because, "if we have died with him, we shall also live with him; if we endure, we shall also reign with him" (2 Timothy 2:11–12). One of these conditions we now celebrate with due observance in view of his approaching passion; the other we shall celebrate after Easter when his resurrection is, in like manner, accomplished again. (*Sermon* 206.1)

What Augustine is here signaling to us, in the clearest of terms, is the link between devotion to Christ and eschatology. Devotion to him, the imitation of Christ, is not merely encouraged because of Jesus' goodness, but because his life, death, and resurrection map the path into God's Kingdom. Jesus's example charts the single course for passing through the divine judgment that is necessarily a part of the coming of the Kingdom.

The Medium of Expressing Politics in Primitive and Early Christianity

These three types of eschatology are particularly mentioned here because they correspond to major movements in the formative centuries of Christianity. Temporal eschatology typified the first two centuries (ca. 30–200 C.E.); transcendent eschatology characterized the emergence of Christianity's philosophical dominance between the third and seventh centuries (ca. 200–700 C.E.); juridical eschatology, of which Augustine is an early example, became the hallmark of Christianity from the Middle Ages onward (ca. 700+ C.E.). Although it may seem confusing to think of eschatology in these different ways, they are all a part of conceiving God as truly final. God's finality is such that he will definitively change time, but space and the nature of justice in human relations also will be transformed. Time and space and ethics are not totally different categories; rather, they are essential dimensions of human experience, so that eschatology rightly involves them all.[3]

Eschatology in all of its rich nuances constitutes the fundamental perspective from which Christianity both addresses the problem of suffering and urges a positive engagement with the world. The God who makes the world also redeems the world, and he redeems the world that we know, as it is. That may involve waiting over time (temporal eschatology), transforming the place where we stand (transcendent eschatology), and/or entering into a judgment which will change us (juridical eschatology). But in any and all cases, although from the perspective of this world and its political authorities, suffering is a means of control, for Christians, it is certainly not the last word, but merely a transitional word before glory.

The type of eschatology embraced by Christianity has determined its portrayal of how we encounter our world (and its politics) and how a holy life may be led. That portrayal, in turn, relates to the anticipation of how God in Christ is to transform the world and influence its present structures of authority. The virtue which arises from each eschatology is understood as "power:" *virtus* in the Latin sense of the word.

Once time is perceived as the principal dimension within which God acts definitively, the obvious question becomes: Just when will that be? We have already seen (above) that the book of 1 Peter urges its readers to treat their current persecution as a "fiery ordeal," a test whose end would be glory for those who were proven (1 Peter 4:12–13). But how long was the ordeal to last? Does faith involve the simple assurance that in the end God will triumph, without knowledge of his plan for his people? Or does faith appropriately include a more precise insight into one's own redemption and the redemption of one's sisters and brothers in Christ? It is no coincidence that the letter called 2 Peter addresses just these questions.

The letter called 2 Peter is a second-century work attributed to Peter, who (as we have seen) probably died under Nero in Rome in 64 C.E. It takes up the trait of apocalyptic literature of being attributed to a great visionary from the past.

(That trait is also represented in the Old Testament book of Daniel and in the apocryphal book of 2 Esdras.) Here, 2 Peter beautifully and classically sets out an account of how the pain of eschatological delay is experienced within apocalyptic Christianity, and how it might be addressed:

> This is already, beloved, a second letter I write to you; in them I arouse by reminder your sincere intent, to remember the sayings told in advance by the holy prophets and the commandment of your apostles of the Lord and Savior. First, know this: There will come at the last days scoffers with scoffing, going according to their own desires, and saying,
> Where is the promise of his coming? Because although the patriarchs perished, everything remains the same from the beginning of creation!
> This escapes those who like to think this way: Heavens existed from of old and earth from water and through water subsisted by the word of God. Through them the world then was destroyed, deluged with water. But the present heavens and the earth by the same word are stored for fire, kept for the day of judgment and the destruction of the godless. Do not let this one thing escape you, beloved: one day with the Lord is as a thousand years, and a thousand years as one day (Psalm 90:4). The Lord does not delay His promise, as some people suppose delay, but He is generous to you, not wishing you to be destroyed, but that all might attain to repentance. (2 Peter 3:1–10)

The pain of time, that it remains unfulfilled by the presence of God, is dealt with through the understanding that it provides an interim for the purpose of repentance, through the eschatological lens of faith that pain becomes an opportunity, to the extent that it is used as a preparation. Patient penitence is part of the power that transforms the world.

Just as Origen believed that God through Christ had prepared "something more glorious and splendid than this present world," as we have seen, so he pondered what it means to conceive of God and of divine reward as beyond our ordinary terms of reference. His discussion appears within his use of the imagery of light to understand God:

> Having then refuted, to the best of our ability, every interpretation which suggests that we should attribute to God any material characteristics, we assert that He is in truth incomprehensible and immeasurable. For whatever may be the knowledge which we have been able to obtain about God, whether by perception or reflection, we must of necessity believe that He is far and away better than our thoughts about Him. For if we see a man who can scarcely look at a glimmer of the light of the smallest lamp, and if we wish to teach such a one, whose eyesight is not strong enough to receive more light than we have said, about the brightness and splendor of the sun, shall we not have to tell him that the splendor of the sun is unspeakably and immeasurably better and more glorious than all this light he can see? (On First Principles 1.1.5)[4]

Here the imagery of pain is more than a matter of the discomfort one might feel in the ordinary course of living. The point is rather that our lives at their best do not prepare us to come in contact with God, and the little we know already is itself not something we can sustain. As in the myth of the cave in Plato's *Republic*, a person living in the dark will not readily be accustomed to light.

The difference between Origen and Plato is that, whereas in the myth of the cave, the person can come into the sun's light, for Origen in this life we cannot truly know God *as* God.[5] For that reason, pain is experienced in two directions at once. First, we are not naturally prepared to discover as much of God's light as we do, and that is a painful condition, as in Plato's myth. But second, we are also intrinsically unable to proceed from the intimations of God to the reality they point to, so that we cannot be completely fulfilled even after we have prepared ourselves for the light.

So the pain of this life is both that it offers too much of the reality of God, and too little of it. The dilemma can only be resolved when we are in a different place, when the transcendence of God, which presently impinges on our lives, becomes the whole of life as we know it. And because that can only occur beyond our world, present experience is not merely painful but is itself a kind of pain. That is the reason why Origen emphasizes the irreducible importance for every Christian of the vision of God. Only that vision both enables us to understand and to endure our present predicament, because it anticipates the full reality that is to come—much as the life and teachings of Jesus gave a foretaste of what God is like.

In *Sermon* 205.1, preceding the sermon in which he explains the eschatological link between humility and exaltation, Augustine portrays the Christian life as inherently painful, and yet as inherently hopeful for that reason. What he says at the start of the season of Lent is a classic exposition, which charts a course for the development of spirituality during the Middle Ages:

> Today we commence the observance of Lent, the season now encountering us in the course of the liturgical year. You are owed an appropriately solemn sermon, so that the word of God, brought to you through my ministry, may sustain you in spirit while you fast in body, and so that the inner man, thus refreshed by suitable food, may be able to accomplish and to persevere bravely in the disciplining of the outer man. For to my spirit of devotion it seems right that we, who are going to revere the Passion of our crucified Lord in the very near future, should construct for ourselves a cross of the bodily pleasures in need of restraint, as the Apostle says, "And they who belong to Christ have crucified their flesh with its passions and desires." (Galatians 5:24)

Pain here is actually a gate to the promise of transformation. The fact of our selfish desires, which we experience in our flesh, is what keeps us from appreciating and joining ourselves to the love of God in Augustine's thought (see especially his magisterial work, *The City of God*). So the willing experience of pain actually permits us to know our true selves, to form a cross of what alienates us from God, and so through the death of selfishness to understand who we truly are before God.

Juridical eschatology is the source of Christianity's profound skepticism about the value of human life in the flesh. The problem is not so much the material of which we are made, as what has become of it by means of human selfishness. Flesh is where we try to make gods of ourselves, and in so doing dishonor each other as much as we dishonor God in our abuse of passion. For Augustine, war, crime, exploitation, and the violent results of all three are not happenstances. His is not a sudden realization that life as he knows it (in the flesh) is beset by evil. Rather, it is a recognition that these evils must be overcome by a realization of our truer selves, selves not subservient to that selfishness. That became the most predominant virtue in Christianity from the time of the Middle Ages onward.

The Message of Early Christianity's Politics

Obviously, not all who became Christians in the Church's first three centuries of growth had their faith tested to the same degree. Nor did all believers consciously conceive of their world in terms of a particular brand of eschatology. However, politically speaking, each follower of "The Way"—as Christians were at first known—and each believing member of the community (the local church), had to walk his or her own path on the continuum between the here-and-now and the Kingdom to come. Individually and collectively, they had to figure out what it meant to imitate the life of Christ in their world. This entailed living with the paradoxes of allegiance to God and to Caesar, the human paradox of accepting life as it is while believing passionately in the transformative power of God, and the spiritual paradox of being able to take in only so much of God. By the fourth century C.E., changes in the Roman empire's political landscape dramatically altered how Christians related to the "powers that be," and their balance of the paradoxes inherited from centuries of being the outsiders.

Adapting to the Forms of This World

Gregory of Nyssa inhabited a very different world from Paul's. By his time (the fourth century C.E.), Christianity was in fashion within the Roman Empire. He was the brother of Basil of Caesarea in the Cappodocian region of Asia Minor, and Gregory himself was bishop of Nyssa (between 371 and 394). Together with their friend Gregory, son of the bishop of Nazianzus, they are known as the "Cappodocian Fathers." Champions of the emerging Trinitarian doctrine of their day, Gregory especially represents the interpenetration of the Hellenistic literary tradition with the orientation of Christianity. Deeply influenced by Origen, he also remained married long into his episcopate, and only took monastic vows after his wife's death. More eloquently than any other Christian teacher, he identified the problem of the sincerity of believers, which obviously needed to be questioned as soon as the Christian faith became fashionable. Gregory confronted this issue directly in "On What Is Meant by the Profession 'Christian'":

> Let us, then, consider, first of all, from the term itself what Christianity means. From those who are wiser it is, of course, possible for us to discover a significance more profound and more noble in every way, more in keeping with the dignity of the word. However, what we begin with is this: the word "Christ," exchanged for a clearer and more familiar word, means "the king," and Holy Scripture, in accordance with proper usage, indicates royal dignity with such a word. But since, as Scripture says, the divine is inexpressible, incomprehensible, exceeding all comprehensible thought, the Holy Spirit must inspire prophets and apostles, and they contribute with many words and insights to our understanding of the incorruptible nature, one setting us right about one divine idea and another about another. His dominion over all is suggested by the name of Kingdom, and his purity and freedom from every passion and every evil is indicated by the names of the virtues, each being understood as referring to higher signification. Such expressions are used as "justice itself" and "wisdom and power" and "truth" and "goodness" and "life" and "salvation" and "incorruptibility" and "permanence" and "lack of change" and whatever elevated concept there is, and Christ is and is said to be all of them. If, therefore, the comprehension of every lofty idea is conceived of in the name of Christ (for the other qualities mentioned are included under the higher designation, each of them being implied in the notion of kingdom), perhaps some understanding of the interpretation of Christianity will follow. If we, who are joined to him by faith in him, are called by his name whose incorruptible nature is beyond verbal interpretation, it is altogether necessary for us to become what is contemplated in connection with that incorruptible nature and to achieve an identity which follows along with it. For just as by participating in Christ we are given the title "Christian," so also are we drawn into a share in the lofty ideas which it implies. Just as in a chain, what draws the loop at the top also draws the next loops, in like manner, since the rest of the words interpreting his ineffable and multiform blessedness are joined to the word "Christ," it is necessary for the person drawn along with him to share these qualities with him.

The power of Gregory's analysis is that he identifies precisely the primary engine of Christian ethics: the imitation of Christ. The prosperity of a Christianized Roman Empire put followers of Jesus in the odd position of being prominent and acceptable. In an unexpected way, the non-Christians of Gregory's day were in the position of the second-century C.E. Scillitan Martyrs, having the option to declare their allegiance to the church or not. Since Christianity had become the official religion of the empire, it had become conceivable and practicable to become a Christian out of convenience. Gregory reflects the response of exchanging the inquisition which once came from outside, from Roman magistrates, for a searching inquiry within, to test one's own motivations and sincerity.

Engagement with the world, always a duty within Christianity, brings with it suffering in distinct ways. There is the suffering of time, the suffering of place, the suffering of self. Temporal eschatology longs for a different time, transcendent eschatology for a difference place, juridical eschatology for a different self. What is striking is that these anxieties—of time, place, and self—are precisely the most persistent troubles of modernity, while in Gregory's teaching they are actively embraced as a discipline of life.

Yet just where one might expect that these distinct kinds of suffering would develop into distinct responses, Christianity in fact teaches a single, unambiguous strategy, grounded in the teaching of Jesus, best expressed in the famous advice:

> You have heard that it was said, "An eye for an eye and a tooth for a tooth." But I say to you not to resist the evil one. But to someone who strikes you on the right cheek, turn also the other. And to one who wants to enter judgment with you to take your shirt, give your cloak, too! And with someone who compels a mile's journey from you, travel with him two. Give to the one who asks of you, and do not turn away from one who wants to borrow from you. (Matthew 5:38–42)

Of all the teachings of Jesus, none is more straightforward, and none more challenging. Evil is to be overcome by means of what is usually called nonresistance.

What follows in Matthew states the principle of Jesus's teaching, that we are to love in the way that God does (Matthew 5:43–48; and see Luke 6:36). The fundamental quality of that teaching within Christianity is unquestionable (see Matthew 22:34–40; Mark 12:28–34; Luke 10:25–28; Romans 13:8–10). But in the teaching about turning the other cheek, giving the cloak, going the extra mile, offering the money, everything comes down to particular conditions that prevailed during the Roman occupation of the Near East.

The fact that this formulation only appears in Matthew (written around 80 C.E.) has given rise to the legitimate question whether it should be attributed to Jesus in its present form. The imagery corresponds to the conditions of the Roman occupation in an urban area, where a soldier of the empire might well demand provisions and service and money, and all with the threat of force. But even if we acknowledge (as seems only reasonable) that Matthew's Gospel has pitched Jesus's policy in the idiom of its own experience, the policy itself should be attributed to Jesus.

Why should what is usually called nonresistance to evil be recommended? It needs to be stressed that nonresistance is not the same as acquiescence. The injustice that is done is never accepted as if it were just. The acts of turning the other cheek, giving the cloak, going the additional mile, offering the money, are all are designed to be excessive, so that the fact of the injustice of what is demanded is underlined. Indeed, it is not really accurate to call the behavior "nonresistance," for it is anything but passive. The point is for the person who makes demands that are unjust to realize they are unjust. Precisely that policy served Christians and their faith well during the centuries of persecution under the Roman Empire. It was effective because it brought about an awareness within the empire, even among the enemies of Christianity, that the policy of violent persecution was unjust (and, for that matter, ineffective). Rather than a teaching of nonresistance, this is a version of the advice of how to retaliate. Instead of an eye for an eye, it suggests a cheek after a cheek. This is not nonresistance; it is an exemplary response. That is, it is a form of retaliation: not to harm, but to show another way.

The hope that the other way—God's way—will be seen by means of an exemplary response, and that once it has been seen it will be followed, is basic to Jesus's policy of reflecting God's love. That hope is articulated by the three types of eschatology we have seen, in each of which God's ultimate vindication is what awaits the believer at the end, in the *eschaton*. But in every case, the same basic policy of an exemplary response is urged as the only authentically Christian way to deal with suffering in the present.

A Hope of Justice

Because the principal political forms that Christianity confronted during its formative period were not of its own making, none of them emerges as actually sanctioned with the force of revelation. Instead, what emerges is a pattern of urging justice out of a variety of circumstances—some of them manifestly unjust—by means of the imitation of Christ. Believers' willingness to embrace the pattern of Christ makes them a part of that global transformation that is the sign of the Kingdom of God working itself out in the world.

Although Augustine is chiefly an exponent of juridical eschatology, as explained above, he also provided Christianity with an enduring model of how this world interacts with the will of God. In his *City of God*, Augustine brought his Christian theology of history through its baptism by fire. In 410 C.E., Alaric sacked the city of Rome itself. That event was a stunning blow to the empire generally, but it was a double blow to Latin Christianity. First, the pillage occurred while the empire was Christian; two centuries before, Tertullian had argued that idolatry brought about disaster (see *Apologeticus* 41.1), and now Christianity could be said to have done so. Second, Latin Christianity—especially in North Africa—had been particularly attracted to an apocalyptic, millenarian eschatology. How could one explain that the triumphant end of history, announced by Eusebius and his followers, seemed to be reversed by the Goths?

The explanation of that dilemma occupied Augustine in his *City of God*, a tremendous work of twenty-three books, written between 413 and 426. From the outset, he sounds his theme, that the city of God is an eternal city which exists in the midst of the collective city of men through the ages; those two cities are both mixed and at odds in this world, but they are to be separated by the final judgment (*City of God* 1.1). That essentially simple thesis is sustained through an account of Roman religion and Hellenistic philosophy, including Augustine's critical appreciation of Plato (books 1–10).

In the central section of his work, Augustine sets out his case within a discussion of truly global history, starting from the story of the creation in Genesis. From the fall of the angels, which Augustine associates with the separation of light and darkness in Genesis 1:4, he speaks of the striving between good and evil. But the distinction between those two is involved with the will of certain angels, not with any intrinsic wickedness (*City of God* 11.33). People also are disordered in their desire, rather than in their creation by God (*City of God* 12.8).

The difference between the will God intends for his creatures and the will they actually evince attests to the freedom involved in divine creation. But the effect of perverted will, whether angelic or human, is to establish two antithetical regimes:

> So two loves have constituted two cities—the earthly is formed by love of self even to contempt of God, the heavenly by love of God even to contempt of self. For the one glories in herself, the other in the Lord. The one seeks glory from man; for the other God, the witness of the conscience, is the greatest glory. . . . In the one the lust for power prevails, both in her own rulers and in the nations she subdues; in the other all serve each other in charity, governors by taking thought for all and subjects by obeying. (*City of God* 14.28)

By book 18, Augustine arrives at his own time, and repeats that the two cities "alike enjoy temporal goods or suffer temporal ills, but differ in faith, in hope, in love, until they be separated by the final judgment and each receive its end, of which there is no end" (*City of God* 18.54).

That commits Augustine to speak of eschatological issues, which he does until the end of the work as a whole. It is in his discussion of eschatology that Augustine frames classic and orthodox responses to some of the most persistent questions of the Christian theology of his time. He adheres to the expectation of the resurrection of the flesh, not simply of the body (as had been the manner of Origen). In so doing, he refutes the Manichaean philosophy that he had accepted before his conversion to Christianity. In Manichaeanism, named after a Persian teacher of the third century named Mani, light and darkness are two eternal substances that struggle against one another, and they war over the creation they have both participated in making. As in the case of Gnosticism, on which it was dependent, Manichaeanism counseled a denial of the flesh. By his insistence on the resurrection of the flesh, Augustine revives the strong assertion of the extent of God's embrace of His own creation in the tradition of Irenaeus.

At the same time, Augustine sets a limit on the extent to which one might have recourse to Plato. Augustine had insisted with Plato against the Manichaeans that God was not a material substance but transcendent. Similarly, evil became in his mind the denial of what proceeds from God (see *Confessions* 5.10.20). When it came to the creation of people, however, Augustine insisted against Platonic thought that no division between soul and flesh could be made (so *City of God* 22.12). Humanity in flesh and blood was the only genuine humanity, and God in Christ was engaged to raised those who were of the city of God. Moreover, Augustine specifically refuted the contention of Porphyry (and Origen) that cycles of creation could be included within the entire scheme of salvation. For Augustine, the power of the resurrection within the world was already confirmed by the miracles wrought by Christ and his martyrs. He gives the example of the healings connected with the relics of Saint Stephen, which had been recently transferred to Hippo (*City of God* 22.8).

Even now, in the power of the Catholic Church, God is represented on earth, and the present, Christian epoch (*Christiana tempora*) corresponds to the millennium promised in Revelation 20 (*City of God* 20.9). This age of dawning power, released in flesh by Jesus and conveyed by the church, simply awaits the full transition into the city of God, complete with flesh itself. It is interesting that, where Origen could allude to a saying of Jesus to confirm his view of the resurrection (*On First Principles* 2.10–11; see Matthew 22:30; Mark 12:25; Luke 20:36), Augustine has to qualify the same saying:

> They will be equal to angels in immortality and happiness, not in flesh, nor indeed in resurrection, which the angels had no need of, since they could not die. So the Lord said that there would be no marriage in the resurrection, not that there would be no women. (*City of God* 22.18)

In all of this, Augustine is straining, although he is usually a more straightforward interpreter of Scripture. But he is wedded to what the Latin confession of "the resurrection of the flesh" implies, and therefore he cannot follow Origen's exegesis. There is a double irony here. First, Origen, the sophisticated allegorist, seems much simpler to follow than Augustine, the incomparable preacher. Second, Augustine's discussion of such issues as the fate of fetuses in the resurrection sounds remarkably like the Sadducees' hypothesis that Jesus argues against in the relevant passage from the Synoptic Gospels.

Augustine is well aware, as was Origen before him, that Paul speaks of a "spiritual body," and acknowledges that "I suspect that all utterance published concerning it is rash." And yet he can be quite categorical that flesh must be involved somehow: "The spiritual flesh will be subject to spirit, but it will still be flesh, not spirit; just as the carnal spirit was subject to the flesh, but was still spirit, not flesh" (*City of God* 22.21). Such is Augustine's conviction that flesh has become the medium of salvation now and hereafter. As in the case of Irenaeus, the denial of a thoroughly abstract teaching leads to the assertion of greater literalism than may have been warranted.

In his adherence to a kind of millenarianism and to the resurrection of the flesh in the Latin creed, Augustine is very much a product of North Africa and Italy, where he was active (chiefly as a teacher of rhetoric) before his conversion and his return to North Africa. But his *City of God* creates the greater frame, primordial and eschatological, within which history becomes a theological discipline. Here, he argues, is more than a lesson in how to avoid war and create order. And here there is certainly more than the superficial enthusiasm that comes of histories written by the winners. Rather, history for Augustine—and from Augustine—is the interplay of those two forces, which determine the existence of every society, every person.

Augustine died in Hippo while the city was actually under siege by the Vandals. His passing, and the passing of his church and his city, was a curious witness to his *Christiana tempora*. But his conception that his history and every history reflected the struggle between the two cities prepared him and the global church for that, and for much worse. He had turned back to the Eusebian model of history as apocalypse, and he took it even more seriously than had Eusebius himself. No apocalyptic seer ever promised an easy transition to the consuming reign of Christ, and on to that moment when God would be all in all (so 1 Corinthians 15:28, which Augustine quotes). Smooth, unhampered progress is a model of history that only commends itself to those in the line of Eusebius and historians since the nineteenth century. If history is apocalyptic, because the times of the church are millennial, then human flesh has indeed been blessed, but human history is equally dedicated to struggle.

The struggle, however, is not ultimately between good and evil, but between the love of God and the love of self. That is the key to Augustine's ceaseless, pastoral ministry, as well as to his remarkably broad intellectual horizon. In every time and in every place, there is the possibility that the city of God will be revealed and embraced; now, in the *Christiana tempora*, we at last know its name, and can see the face of that love that would transform us all.

History after Augustine could be painted on canvasses of indeterminate size, because he established the quest to integrate the historical task with philosophical reflection. At the same time, in his *Confessions*, he established the genre of autobiography as an investigation of the dynamics of universal salvation within the life of the individual he knew best, himself. Written large in nations and written small in persons, history attested to the outward-working and inward-working power of God, if only one's eyes could see with the love of God, and be cured of the blindness of self-love.

Early Christianity and Nonbelievers: Politics and People outside the Tradition

Only from the second century C.E. do we find a literature that engages in a spirited, intellectual defense of Christianity across the range of other Greco-Roman religious and philosophical options. That defense was principally conducted in the midst of the religious and philosophical pluralism of the second century. In that environment, in which adherents of various groups were attracted to Christianity, it was imperative to develop an account of the intellectual integrity of faith—an "apology" in the philosophical sense—a justification that made sense to nonbelievers. Such literature developed the paradigmatic attitude of Christianity toward faiths other than Judaism. Christianity's apologists crafted a distinctive view of the divine "Word" (*logos*), which conveys the truth of God to humanity. That *logos* was Jesus Christ, understood as the human teacher who at last fully incarnated what philosophers and prophets had been searching for and had partially seen.

A second-century defender of the Christian faith, Justin Martyr, was the theologian who articulated that doctrine most clearly, on the basis of the Gospel according to John. In 151 C.E., he addressed his *Apology* to the emperor himself, Antonius Pius. Such was his confidence that the "true philosophy" represented by Christ, attested in the Hebrew Scriptures, would triumph among the other options available at the time. Justin himself had been trained within some of those traditions, and by his Samaritan birth he could claim to represent something of the wisdom of the East. Somewhere between 162 and 168, however, Justin was martyred in Rome, a victim of the increasing hostility against Christianity under the reign of Marcus Aurelius.[6]

Justin argued that the light of reason in people is put there by God and is to be equated with the Word of God incarnate in Jesus. The type of Christianity that Justin defended was as much a philosophy as it was a religion. His claim was that the light of reason in humanity, which had already been indirectly available, actually became fully manifest in the case of Jesus Christ. Jesus, therefore, was the perfect sage, and Socrates as much as Isaiah was his prophet. In that sense, Christianity was as old as humanity; it was only its open manifestation that was recent.

To make his case, Justin used arguments that had been employed before by Philo of Alexandria (Jesus's older contemporary), but on behalf of Judaism. Philo had also identified the *logos*, the prophetic word articulated in Scripture, as the reason by which God created the world and animates humanity. Philo even makes out the historical case that Moses influenced the Greek philosophers directly,[7] so that the extent to which Greek philosophy illuminates God's wisdom is derivative. Justin is bolder in his Platonism, in that his argument does not rely on such an historical argument but rather on the contention that in Jesus the primordial archetype of humanity and of the world itself, the *logos*, became accessible and knowable in a way it had not been before.

In his *Dialogue with Trypho, A Jew*, Justin describes his own development from Platonism to Christianity as a result of a conversation with an old man. The sage convinced him that the highest good that Platonism can attain, the human soul, should not be confused with God himself, because the soul depends upon God for life (chapter 6). Knowledge of God depends rather upon the revelation of God's spirit (chapter 7):

> Long ago, he replied, there lived men more ancient than all the so-called philosophers, men righteous and beloved of God, who spoke by the divine spirit and foretold things to come, that even now are taking place. These men were called prophets. They alone both saw the truth and proclaimed it to men, without awe or fear of anyone, moved by no desire for glory, but speaking only those things which they saw and heard when filled with the Holy Spirit. Their writings are still with us, and whoever will may read them and, if he believes them, gain much knowledge of the beginning and end of things, and all else a philosopher ought to know. For they did not employ logic to prove their statements, seeing they were witnesses to the truth. . . .They glorified the creator of all things, as God and Father, and proclaimed the Christ sent by him as his Son. . . . But pray that, before all else, the gates of light may be opened to you. For not everyone can see or understand these things, but only he to whom God and His Christ have granted wisdom.

Here is a self-conscious Christianity, which distinguishes itself from Judaism and proclaims itself the true and only adequate philosophy. Justin's account of the truth of the *logos* depends upon two sources of revelation, resonant with one another: the prophetic Scriptures, which attest to the Spirit; and the wise reader, who has been inspired by the Spirit. Implicitly (and later, with the conversion of Constantine, explicitly), this apologetic theology explained a refusal of Christ in terms of either a rejection of Spirit itself or a lack of insight.

Conclusion

The injustice of human institutions comes as no surprise to Christianity, because the anthropology inherited from Saint Paul has prepared theologians and believers at large for that breach between God and humanity that is called sin. At the same time, each Christian is called to a path of justice, through the transforming power of the Son of God, disclosed within every believer by God's Spirit in baptism.

Paradoxically, therefore, an experience of injustice in this world can be a badge of honor, the seal of one's loyalty to the world to come at the price of one's status in this world. For that reason, one can accept the legitimacy of institutions that are nonetheless unjust, because they belong to the structure of a world that is passing away. The coming of the supernatural world that is to supersede all others, the Kingdom of God in its fullness, extends to the witness of martyrs, who participate in an eschatological transformation over time, through space, and in the revelation of true justice. These distinct kinds of eschatology—temporal, transcendent, and juridical—have resulted in different views of how government should be organized when it reflects the message of the Gospels. Christian theologians over time have portrayed government as an opportunity for individuals to repent, as an educational instrument whose apogee is the vision of God, and as a place to adjudicate humanity's struggle with the flesh.

Because no government can be identified with God's Kingdom, Christian politics has always varied. Yet within that variation, Jesus's teaching of an exemplary response is a constant principle. In specific instances, the believer is called upon to reply to injustice in this world with the justice God provides from the world to come. The conviction that the kingdom that is coming will constantly complement and correct the evils of this world is the foundation of Christian hope in history as a locus of revelation.

Notes

1. See Eusebius, *The History of the Church from Christ to Constantine*, trans. G. A. Williamson (Baltimore: Penguin, 1967), 2.25.

2. For the emphatic wording of the prayer of Jesus, and its Aramaic original, see Bruce Chilton, *Jesus' Prayer and Jesus' Eucharist: His Personal Practice of Spirituality* (Valley Forge, Pa.: Trinity Press International, 1997).

3. In fact, Jesus's own eschatology included two further dimensions. His definition of the Kingdom of God provided for a distinctive view of what made for the purity acceptable to God and for an emphasis on the outward, inclusive range of the Kingdom. See Bruce Chilton, *Pure Kingdom: Jesus' Vision of God*, Studying the Historical Jesus 1 (Grand Rapids: Eerdmans, 1996). Those dimensions are not included here because they did not amount to distinctive types of eschatology within the formative periods of Christianity. Still, emphases upon the purity and upon the outward extension of God's kingdom are characteristic of Christianity in most periods.

4. For the examples and their elucidation, I am indebted to John Dillon, "Looking on the Light: Some Remarks on the Imagery of Light in the First Chapter of the Peri Archon," *The Golden Chain: Studies in the Development of Platonism and Christianity* (Aldershot, U.K.: Variorum, 1990), 215–30 (essay 22).

5. This is Dillon's main point (see "Looking on the Light," 225), and his citation of *On First Principles* 1.1.6 demonstrates it admirably.

6. See Henry Chadwick, *The Early Church* (London: Penguin, 1993), 29, 74–79.

7. For a discussion of this motif (in *Quaestiones et Solutiones in Genesin* iv. 152, for example), see Harry Austryn Wolfson, *Philo: Foundations of Religious Philosophy in Judaism, Christianity, and Islam* (Cambridge, Mass.: Harvard University Press, 1947), 141–43, 160–63.

Suggested Readings

Bettenson, Henry, ed. *Documents of the Christian Church*. Oxford and New York: Oxford University Press, 1999.

Boff, Leonardo. *Holy Trinity, Perfect Community*. Trans. P. Berryman. New York: Orbis, 2000.

Brown, Peter. *Authority and the Sacred: Aspects of the Christianisation of the Roman World*. Cambridge: Cambridge University Press, 1995.

Brown, Raymond E. *An Introduction to the New Testament*. New York: Doubleday, 1997.

Chadwick, Henry. *The Early Church*. New York: Penguin Books, 1993.

Chilton, Bruce. *Pure Kingdom: Jesus' Vision of God*. Grand Rapids: Eerdmans, 1996.

Grant, Robert M. *Augustus to Constantine. The Rise and Triumph of Christianity in the Roman World*. San Francisco: Harper & Row, 1990.

Daniélou, Jean, and Henri Marrou. *The Christian Centuries, 1: The First Six Hundred Years*. Trans. V. Cronin. New York: McGraw-Hill, 1964.

Frei, Hans. *Types of Christian Theology*. Ed. G. Hunsinger and W. C. Placher. New Haven, Conn.: Yale University Press, 1992.

Gunton, Colin E., ed. *The Cambridge Companion to Christian Doctrine*. Cambridge: Cambridge University Press, 1997.

Moltmann, Jürgen. *The Coming of God: Christian Eschatology*. Trans. M. Kohl. London: SCM, 1996.

Niebuhr, Reinhold. *The Nature and Destiny of Man*. New York: Scribner's, 1964.

Norris, Richard A. *God and World in Early Christian Theology: A Study in Justin Martyr, Irenaeus, Tertullian and Origen*. London: A. & C. Black, 1967.

Pelikan, Jaroslav. *The Christian Tradition: A History of the Development of Doctrine*. Chicago: University of Chicago Press, 1971–89.

Torrance, Thomas F. *The Trinitarian Faith: The Evangelical Theology of the Ancient Catholic Church*. Edinburgh: T & T Clark, 1994.

Three | **Roman Catholic Christianity** |

Charles E. Curran

GIVEN THE MULTIPLICITY OF USES FOR THE TERM "CATHOLIC," IT IS IMPORTANT AT THE outset to clarify how it and its permutations are used in this chapter. The very word "catholic" (with a lowercase "c") means universal or all-embracing, from the Greek *katholikos*, used generally in Greek classics to mean "throughout the whole, universal, general." Eventually, Christians appropriated the term to describe the "universal church" (it was originally used by Saint Ignatius, ca. 110 C.E.). As is noted by Petros Vassiliadis in his treatment of Orthodox Christianity in chapter 4 and by Martin Marty in his discussion of Reformation Christianity in chapter 5, this sense of "catholic" is embraced by a large percentage of Christians when referring to the church. In fact, members of more than one Christian denomination routinely reaffirm their identity with the "catholic" church, in an inclusive rather than exclusive way, every time they recite the ancient creeds (e.g., Anglicans, called Episcopalians in the United States; the Greek Orthodox; Lutherans; Presbyterians; and Roman Catholics).

In its capitalized form, the word "Catholic" has, over time and in common usage, come to refer both to the ancient Christian Church before significant schisms, and more specifically to the church whose supreme bishop is the pope in Rome, from which the Protestants broke away in the sixteenth century C.E.—the Roman Catholic Church. In this chapter, unless otherwise defined, "Catholic" and "Catholicism" refer to Roman Catholic Christianity, and "catholic" to the universal church.

While emphasizing the gift and goal of eternal life, Catholicism has consistently had a concern for this world and how life is lived in this world. Catholic faith touches all aspects of human existence. The ultimate basis for such a concern for life in this world comes from the doctrine of creation, according to which God made all that exists and saw that it was very good. Some Christians stress the doctrine of sin as radically affecting the temporal world and making it evil; but the Catholic tradition has insisted that, although sin does affect the goodness of creation, sin clearly does not destroy the basic goodness of humanity and all that God has made.

Contemporary Catholic thought also sees the redemptive love of Jesus and God's grace affecting and transforming the temporal realm, while recognizing that the fullness of justice and peace will never be present in this world. Critics both inside and outside Catholicism have pointed out the danger that Catholicism might be too optimistic about the temporal realm and the political order

61

and not give enough importance to the negative effects of sin. Catholicism today, in continuity with its past, insists that Catholic Christians are called to work together with all people of goodwill for a better or more just temporal order in general and political order in particular.

In this chapter's consideration of the Catholic understanding of the political order, I first discuss the classical sources, texts, method, and audience of Catholic social and political teaching. I then develop the substance of this understanding of the political order and the role of Catholics and others in the political realm.

Classical Sources of Roman Catholicism on Politics

What are the generic sources that Catholicism uses to develop its understanding of the political order? Where does the Catholic approach find wisdom and knowledge for its understanding of how the political order should function?

Sources in General

Catholicism, in keeping with the Judeo-Christian tradition, believes that God reveals God's self to us and that this revelation provides wisdom and knowledge. Revelation includes both Scripture and tradition, but these are not understood today in a dualistic way as two distinctly different realities. The Scriptures, or the Word of God, include the Hebrew Bible (often called the Old Testament) and the New Testament. The Scriptures are the inspired Word of God, although diverse interpretations of inspiration exist. Tradition refers to both the process and the content of what has been handed over in the church from generation to generation. Catholicism believes that the Holy Spirit is given to the church so that down through the centuries the church will be able to understand, live, and appropriate the word and work of Jesus in the light of changing historical circumstances.

The Scriptures themselves are historically and culturally conditioned, so tradition helps us to understand the call of faith in light of the different historical and cultural circumstances in which we now live. Perhaps the best example of tradition in early Catholicism concerns the creeds of the Early Church, which spelled out Catholic Christian belief in such basic areas as the Trinitarian nature of God and the divine and human natures in Jesus. The Trinitarian doctrine of three divine Persons in one God is not found explicitly as such in the Scriptures, but the church proposed this teaching in its early councils and creeds.

Most Christian churches recognize Scripture and tradition as sources of moral wisdom for believers. But Catholicism also acknowledges a distinctive source of moral wisdom and knowledge: The gift of the Holy Spirit has been given to the pope and bishops in the church to assist them in teaching authoritatively about faith and morals for the members of the church. This teaching office, exercised especially by the bishop of Rome or pope, has in recent times proposed authoritative teaching in many moral areas, including the political order. In addition, Catholicism accepts human sources of moral wisdom—reason and experience. Because Catholicism recognizes the goodness of all that God has made, human reason and human experience can be sources of moral wisdom and knowledge. Catholicism relies heavily on human reason for its understanding of the political order. Again, the danger in Catholicism is to forget that limitation and sinfulness also affect but do not totally distort human reason and experience.

Texts

In relation to these sources, various authoritative texts exist in Catholicism. The Bible itself with all its parts is the most significant text, but for the area of politics the Bible does not provide that much guidance and direction. Consequently, Christians often refer to the saying in Matthew to give to God what is God's and to Caesar what is Caesar's (22:15–22). They also recognize the teaching in the letter of Paul to the Romans about the obedience that is due to civil rulers (13:1–7). However, there are also passages in the New Testament that cause problems for many Christians today, such as the apparent acceptance of slavery. Christians have tried to explain in different ways how this came about. The primary purpose of revelation in general and the Bible in particular is not to give details about the political order, although they do provide guidelines and even commandments for life in this world. However, the dramatic difference between political life then and political life today means that any specific biblical teachings might not be applicable to our very different situation.

The Early Church's councils and creeds usually did not address issues of politics, but the writings of the leaders of the Early Church (often called the Patristic Age, embracing the first six or more centuries) frequently did discuss aspects of life in the temporal and political spheres. For example, the question of Christian participation in the army was frequently discussed. Many other issues of daily life, as well as the broader question of what today we call the relationship of church and state, were discussed by these church leaders and thinkers. Augustine of Hippo (d. 430 C.E.), the most famous of these "fathers of the church," wrote on many subjects dealing with life in the temporal and political realms. The writings of this period from these leaders tended to be ad hoc and dealt with particular issues primarily from a pastoral perspective.

A more systematic study came to the fore in the second millennium with the rise of universities under church auspices. Here again, notice the Catholic acceptance of the goodness and power of human reason to arrive at truth. Systematic theology began at this time as an attempt to explain Catholic faith and morals in a systematic way, putting all the parts together into a whole. In the thirteenth century, religious orders such as the Dominicans and the Franciscans came into existence and began to engage in the systematic study of theology.

The most important figure in the thirteenth century was Thomas Aquinas (d. 1274), an Italian Dominican friar whose *Summa theologiae* became the most significant book in Catholic theological tradition. By definition, the *Summa* is a synthesis of all theology. But the second of its three parts deals with the moral life, which Aquinas explains on the basis of the three theological virtues (faith, hope, and charity) and the four cardinal virtues (prudence, justice, fortitude, and temperance)—with justice, dealing with life in the world, receiving the most coverage.[1] Aquinas uses all the five sources mentioned above, but in a distinctive manner he employs Aristotelian thought in trying to explain Christian faith and morals. His discussion of justice relies heavily on Aristotle.

At the same time, the Franciscan School, represented by Alexander of Hales (d. 1245), John Duns Scotus (d. 1308), and Saint Bonaventure (d. 1274), made significant contributions to systematic theology. During the next few centuries, Thomism competed with both Scotism and nominalism, an approach associated with William of Ockham (d. 1347). However, in the sixteenth century a revival of Thomism throughout Europe, beginning in Germany and moving to Italy and especially Spain, made Thomism the primary approach to Catholic theology and understanding. At this time, the *Summa* became the textbook of theology in all universities. Spain became the principal center of the Thomistic renewal, with such leading figures as Francis de Vitoria (d. 1546), who has been called the father of international law, and Dominic Soto (d. 1560), who like many others wrote long commentaries on the *Summa*, especially the section on justice.

In the eighteenth century, however, Thomism lacked vitality and began to wane. In the nineteenth century, Italian Jesuits started a successful campaign to renew Thomism (or Scholasticism, as it was sometimes called). One of their students later became Pope Leo XIII, who in 1879 issued an encyclical (an authoritative letter to the bishops of the world) titled *Aeterni Patris*. This encyclical called for the renewal and teaching of Aquinas in Catholic universities and seminaries "for the defense and beauty of the Catholic faith, for the good of society, and for the advantages of all the sciences" (n. 31).[2]

Later church documents maintained that philosophy and theology in Catholic institutions should be taught according to the method, outline, and approach of Thomas Aquinas. Note here the importance of Aquinas not only for teaching the faith but also for the Catholic understanding of society as a whole. From the nineteenth century onward, Thomism (or neo-scholasticism) reigned as *the* Catholic theology and philosophy, with varying emphases, under the one Thomistic umbrella until the Second Vatican Council (or Vatican II), when Catholicism opened itself to other possible approaches. Many have viewed Pope Leo's imposition of Thomism in the late nineteenth century, which was continued by his successors, as a very forceful way for the church to speak convincingly to the modern world and its problems. But others criticized this as imposing an older approach and showing an unwillingness to open up a dialogue with contemporary thought.

Leo XIII played an even more significant role in developing the Catholic approach to the social and political orders. In 1891, he issued the encyclical *Rerum novarum* (official church documents take their name from the first two or three Latin words of the document), dealing with problems for workers brought about by the Industrial Revolution. The encyclical recognizes the right of workers to a living wage, the need for them to organize into unions, and the proper role of government to intervene to protect the rights of workers and others who are in need. The encyclical inspired other encyclicals and letters by subsequent popes dealing with social, economic, and political questions. Such documents were often issued on anniversaries of *Rerum novarum*, and together they constitute what Pope John Paul II has called the social teaching of the church.

These documents, including those from Vatican II (1962–65), have addressed a broad range of issues pertaining to national and international society in the social, political, and economic realms. In the U.S. context, two pastoral letters by the U.S. bishops on peace (1983) and on the economy (1986) are generally included in the group of documents on Catholic social teaching.[3] Thus, these documents form an authoritative source of official teaching on the social and political order. The documents themselves employ all the sources mentioned above but tend to highlight official church teachings. The documents have spawned many commentaries throughout the world. Before Vatican II, most such commentaries were quite uncritical, but later ones employ more sophisticated hermeneutical principles.

Catholic social teaching, because it authoritatively proposes teaching for all Catholics, tends to be somewhat broad and general, involving principles for reflection, criteria for making judgments, and basic directives for action. On the U.S. scene, the two pastoral letters by the bishops have proposed more specific guidelines (e.g., no first use of counterforce nuclear weapons), but the bishops recognize that on these more specific issues there is room for disagreement among Catholics. The somewhat general nature of the papal documents means that various commentators can and will interpret them differently. The basic thrust of Catholic social teaching, as will be illustrated below, tends to the more progressive side, emphasizing the needs of the poor and workers. However, a group of Catholic neoconservative scholars in the United States have disagreed with the approach taken by the U.S. bishops for being too negative on U.S. policy and capitalism and have interpreted the papal documents from their perspective.[4]

Roman Catholicism's Theory of Politics

On the one hand, Roman Catholicism has a well-articulated theory of politics, in its use of natural law. Fundamentally, this methodology has theological, as well as ethical and social, dimensions. Natural law, from a theological perspective, is the participation of the eternal law in the rational creature. Because Catholic theology believes in mediation—the divine is mediated in and through the human—it posits that God's own reason can be discerned through the world He created and the faculty of reason that He has given us. Within the ethical domain, this theology relates to issues about the degree to which humans can and should be held responsible and accountable for their actions. So also in the social domain, natural law points to issues of social justice and human rights.

On the other hand, because natural law as theory has so often been discussed and debated in the context of its method of expression, the two seem to have become inextricably bound together. Moreover, this methodology touches on such a wide array of issues, and has stimulated so many debates, that it would be counterproductive here to try to separate the theory from the medium of its expression. Therefore, rather than attempting to deal separately below with Catholic political theory and its method of expression, I will take up both together, without attempting to disentangle the discussion of one from the other.

The Medium of Expressing Politics in Roman Catholicism

Thomism, Catholic social ethics (the academic discipline), and Catholic social teaching are obviously interrelated and employ in general a natural law methodology based on that found in Aquinas. Natural law, from a theological perspective, is the participation of the eternal law in the rational creature. As was explained above, from a theological vantage point, natural law is the understanding that divine eternal law exists independent of human opinion or construction, but rational beings participate in it. The eternal law is the plan that God has for the world. How do we discover God's plan? Do we go directly and immediately to God to find out what to do?

The Catholic answer to this question is No. One of the distinctive characteristics of Catholic theology is the idea of mediation, which was explained above. God has created the world and has given us our reason that mediates God's own reason. Human reason, reflecting on the creation that God has made, including of course human beings, can discover how God wants us to act and use what God created. Thus natural law is the participation of the eternal law in the rational creature. Such a natural law approach means that Catholics and all others are called to do the same thing in working for a better or more just temporal and political realm. The later papal encyclicals explicitly address not only Catholics but all people of goodwill.

From an ethical and philosophical perspective, natural law is human reason directing us to our end in accord with our human nature. Of course, there are disputed questions about what is meant by human reason and human nature.

By examining human beings, human reason comes to the conclusion we are not isolated monads but are social by nature and meant to live in many different communities, from the family on up to the broader political community. To fulfill ourselves as human beings, we need to exist in these many different relationships. Another example: Reason discovers that through work human beings earn what is necessary to provide for themselves so that they might have at least a minimally decent human existence. The just wage, therefore, is not simply what the employer and the employee agree on but rather what is necessary to provide the worker with a minimally decent human existence.

Commentators have raised various questions and criticisms about natural law, both from within and from outside the Catholic tradition. More recent documents of Catholic social teaching and commentaries on these have responded to these criticisms and thus modified to some extent the neo-scholastic natural law approach as found in Leo XIII.

A first criticism concerns the fact that the natural law approach does not give enough importance to the central faith aspects of Jesus Christ, revelation, and redeeming grace. Vatican II, which renewed Roman Catholicism, in *Gaudium et spes* (translated as *The Pastoral Constitution on the Church in the Modern World*), lamented that the split between faith and daily life is a major error of our times (n. 41). Neo-scholasticism, perhaps not totally faithful to Aquinas, had seen the temporal as the realm of the natural distinguished from the supernatural aspects of grace, redemption, and Jesus Christ. Subsequent to Vatican II, the documents of Catholic social teaching have tried to understand life in the world also in the light of Catholic faith and all that it entails.

One advantage of the newer Christological or faith approach is the centrality of working for a better human society or, as it is called, the social mission of the church. Previously, the church's mission was seen as twofold—divinization and humanization, with the latter carried out by lay people in their daily life in the temporal, social, and political orders. Divinization occurred on the supernatural level in the life of the church, and humanization occurred on the natural level in the life of the world. *Justitia in mundo* (1971), the document of Catholic social teaching coming from the international Synod of Bishops, maintained: "Action on behalf of justice and participation in the transformation of the world fully appear to us as a constitutive dimension of the preaching of the Gospel, or in other words, of the church's mission for the redemption of the human race and its liberation from every oppressive situation." Working for a better human society in this world was always a consequence of Catholic faith, but before Vatican II it tended to be secondary to the more spiritual and supernatural elements. Now it is a constitutive part of the preaching of the Gospel, which means that without a social mission there is no true preaching of the Gospel or redemptive mission of the church.

A second criticism of natural law concerns its failure to give enough importance to history, change, and development. Natural law is a participation in eternal law, which is understood as absolute, universal, and unchanging. The nature of things is something already given and does not recognize much change and development.

There have been some rejoinders to this criticism within the documents of contemporary Catholic social teaching. First, the teaching itself has developed over time, as this chapter will explain below. For example, Catholic social teaching in the twentieth century came to a greater appreciation of freedom, equality, and participation in public life and even changed its teaching on religious freedom. In other areas (e.g., sexuality and medical ethics), contemporary Catholic teaching has not been that open to change or development.

Second, many more recent documents have employed a more inductive methodology. Thomism, at least as it was interpreted in nineteenth- and early-twentieth-century neo-scholasticism, was deductive in its method. Conclusions were deduced from their premises. Pope Paul VI clearly employed a much more inductive method. Induction by definition begins, as does *Gaudium et spes*, with "the signs of the times," contemporary realities.

Third, Paul VI in *Octogesima adveniens* (1971) explicitly moves away from the backward glance of natural law to eternal law and appeals rather to forward looking utopias as "criticism of existing society [which] often provokes the forward-looking imagination both to perceive in the present the disregarded possibility hidden within it and to direct itself toward a fresh future" (n. 37). John Paul II, the successor of Paul VI, has moved away from the historical consciousness and more inductive approach found in *Octogesima adveniens*.

A third criticism refers to natural law's penchant for insisting on universality, absolute principles, and unity at the expense of particularity, flexibility, and greater diversity. Here again, some effort has been made to meet this criticism, but the documents still propose principles for reflection, criteria for making judgments, and directives for action for the whole world, in all its cultural diversity. At a very minimum, any approach that tries to speak for the whole world must be conscious of its diversity and be self-critical enough to recognize that no perspective is without its limitations and prejudices. In the global reality of the modern world, however, universal ethical concerns touching all human beings seem to be most necessary.

A fourth criticism points to the tension involved in a teaching claiming to be authoritative for Catholics but also claiming to be based on human reason. The criticism has been phrased as seeing the teaching more as law and less as rational. This is obviously a tension within the Catholic community itself in terms of the legitimacy of disagreement within the church about hierarchical church teaching on social and political matters. Within Roman Catholicism, there has been considerably less discussion about disagreement and dissent in the realm of Catholic social teaching than in the areas of hierarchical sexual teaching such as contraception and divorce. Perhaps the very general nature of the social teaching, which by definition allows for different interpretations, makes the issue of dissent or disagreement less likely.

The Message of Roman Catholicism's Politics

In the Catholic understanding, the temporal realm embraces all that occurs in human existence in this world. The temporal realm includes the broad area of the social as well as the cultural and the political. Thus, for our purposes, the political order is narrower than the temporal order and is differentiated from the cultural realm. The political realm refers to the ordered political life of the community.

Anthropology constitutes the grounding for the Catholic understanding of the political order. The Catholic tradition usually addresses the political order in terms of the state. "State" is the word that is usually used to refer to all aspects of government, be it local, state (in the U.S. understanding), or federal. Catholic anthropology insists that the human person (personal language is much more recent; the older term was human being) has an inherent, God-given dignity and sacredness but is also social and political by nature.

Genesis, the first book of the Bible, tells us that God created human beings in God's own image and likeness. The human person has an inherent, God-given sacredness and dignity and is thus different from all other parts of the creation. However, as human beings, we are not isolated monads but are called by the nature God has given us to live together in various structures, such as the natural structure of the family and the natural institution of the state or the political order. This twofold aspect of anthropology grounds the Catholic understanding of the state as natural, necessary, and good but also limited.

The State as Natural, Necessary, and Good

Aquinas, in harmony with the biblical emphasis, accepted the Aristotelian understanding of the human being as social and political by nature. Human beings by their very nature (notice the natural law approach) are made by God and called to live together in political society. Only in and through political society can human beings achieve some of their fulfillment. Again, no human being is an island or an isolated monad.

Such an understanding of the state differs from two other common approaches. Some Christian traditions (especially the Lutheran) see the state as fulfilling the promise made to Noah that God will never again destroy the world. Sin by its very nature leads to death, and sinful human beings cannot live peacefully together. God thus uses the state as an order of preservation, which through the power of coercion tries to keep sinful human beings in check and from killing one another or creating chaos. The state thus has the somewhat minimal and negative function of restraining evil and maintaining order.

In the thirteenth century Aquinas raised what might seem today to be a totally irrelevant question: Would the state or political order exist if Adam and Eve had not sinned (*Summa* I, q. 96, a. 4)? But the question is very relevant. Are the nature and existence of the state due primarily to human sinfulness or to human nature as created by God? Aquinas responded that the state would have existed without sin, because wherever there are a multitude of human beings, they need someone to direct them to the common good. The different orders of angels remind us that even angels need a political authority. In this conception, the state has a very positive role to play in bringing about the common good of society. In the Catholic understanding, the state is primarily directive and not coercive. If citizens feel that their government is primarily coercive, such a government will be very insecure. Note again that the perennial danger in Catholic understanding involves an overly optimistic view of human nature and the state primarily because not enough importance is given to the role of sin.

From a philosophical perspective, the Catholic approach differs from the more individualistic approach that prevails today among many people in the United States. Individualism sees different individuals concerned about themselves wanting to protect their own interests in the light of the existence of other people and their interests. These individuals then come together to work out a contract for a society that can best protect their individual interests, with the realization that some compromises will be necessary to accommodate others. This is often called the contract theory of the state, whereby individuals enter into a contract with each other as the best way of trying to protect their own individual interests. The Catholic approach does not begin with isolated individuals but rather with a person who is social and political by nature and thus destined to live in political community.

The Role of Government

Anthropology also governs the role of the state. An anthropology that recognizes both the inherent dignity or sacredness of the human person and the social and political nature of the person avoids the opposite dangers of individualism and collectivism. Individualism sees only individuals and downplays the role of the community itself. Conversely, collectivism so stresses collective interests that it fails to give enough importance to the individual.

This complex anthropology governs two important roles of the state: its purpose and its relationship with individual persons and other groups in society. In the Catholic tradition, the purpose of the state has been to work for the common good, which differs in theory from both individual goods and the collective good. An individualistic approach acknowledges only individual goods which each one tries to protect and promote as much as possible. The collective good so stresses the collectivity that it denies individual goods and is even willing to sacrifice the individual for the good of the collectivity.

The Catholic tradition insists that the purpose of the state is to work for the common good. In theory, the common good by definition flows back to the good of individuals and does not contradict or limit the proper good of individuals. The state, for example, pursues the good of clean air, which benefits all. The encyclical of Leo XIII, *Rerum novarum* (1891), made explicit, however, that the common good also still requires the good of parts of society. The state can and should intervene to help a particular group such as workers, but this also ulti-mately contributes to the common good and the good of other members of soci-ety (nn. 28–29).

The description of the concrete common good tends to be somewhat gener-al. In *Mater et magistra* (1961), Pope John XXIII describes the common good as "the sum total of these conditions of social living whereby human beings are enabled more fully and readily to achieve their own perfection" (n. 65). The cri-terion of the common good as the purpose of society thus clearly differentiates the Catholic approach from both individualism and collectivism.

In keeping with that same basic anthropology, the state in the Catholic under-standing is natural, necessary, and good—but its role is limited. The proper role of the state is governed by two principles: subsidiarity and socialization. In *Quadragesimo anno* (1931), Pope Pius XI developed the principle of subsidiarity (n. 79), but the basis of this principle is clearly found in Aquinas. The primary limit on the role of the state comes from the dignity and sacredness of the human indi-vidual who is prior to the state. Likewise, the Catholic tradition sees the family as a natural society that is prior to the state.

In addition to the individual person and the family, public society also includes given structures and institutions, such as extended families and neighborhoods. Then there exist voluntary groups or institutions of all types that are necessary for the total good of society—educational, cultural, social, and professional groups. Think of the media, colleges and universities, labor unions, management groups, and also religious groups such as churches, synagogues, mosques, and temples, all of which exist in society and contribute to the good of public society as a whole. Only then do we come to the levels of government, beginning with the local, then the state, and finally the federal (as these are understood in the United States).

Subsidiarity comes from the Latin word *subsidium*, meaning "help." The description of society in the preceding paragraph begins with the most funda-mental level of the human person, moving upward to given institutions and struc-tures, then to voluntary associations, and finally to government with its different levels. According to the principle of subsidiarity, the higher level should do everything possible to help the lower level achieve its own purposes and should only intervene when the lower and more basic level cannot do something on its own.

The way higher education is funded in the United States illustrates well the principle of subsidiarity at work. Individuals and families bear the primary responsibility of providing for higher education. Originally, many colleges and universities were religious in origin; then private institutions also came into existence. However, these alone could not meet the demand, so state governments founded universities—land grant institutions, teachers' colleges, and community colleges. The federal government now helps all types of higher education through grants and low-interest loans. The state government had to start its own institutions to provide higher education for all, but individuals and families must still pay something.

Likewise, state governments do not demand the extinction of private institutions. In fact, many if not most private colleges could not survive if it were not for various forms of government help. Thus the government does not usurp the role of the family or more basic groups but helps them to achieve their purposes while providing for others who otherwise would not have access to higher education. Contemporary political scientists often speak of the need for mediating structures and institutions between the individual and government.

The principle of socialization exists in some tension with the principle of subsidiarity. Pope John XXIII developed this principle in *Mater et magistra* (1961): "One of the principal characteristics of our time is the multiplication of social relationships, that is a daily more complex interdependence of citizens" (n. 59). In this light, to a greater extent than heretofore, public authorities have to intervene in a more organized and extensive way to adapt institutions, tasks, and means to the common good. However, this does not do away with the principle of subsidiarity. Thus the complexity of the modern world—with its many interrelationships, including globalization itself—calls for greater government intervention, because the government alone can direct these complex forces to the common good.

Development in the Values of the Common Good

As has been mentioned above, the common good in Catholic social teaching is described in broad and somewhat vague terms. The values that constitute the common good have changed over time, and the authoritative documents of Catholic social teaching show a very significant development—even though the documents themselves do not explicitly call attention to this change.

One must also see the values that constitute the common good in the light of the Catholic self-understanding of the state as in a middle position between the two extremes of individualism and collectivism. In the eighteenth and nineteenth centuries, the Catholic Church saw the individualism of liberalism as its primary foe. Liberalism extolled the reason and freedom of the individual cut off from any relationship with God and God's law according to the Catholic self-understanding. The Catholic Church was the implacable enemy of all forms of liberalism. (The term is used here as it is used in philosophical thought, not in contemporary political thought.) Religious liberalism, according to a generally understood Catholic approach, started with Luther, who exalted the conscience of the individual believer over the authority of the church. Philosophical liberalism emphasized human reason cut off from God and God's law.

Political liberalism supported democracy and the rights of the majority over the rights of truth. Economic liberalism in the form of capitalism affirmed the freedom of owners and entrepreneurs to make as much money as possible and forgot about the rights of workers and the poor. Leo XIII's *Rerum novarum* (1891) emphasized the role of government to intervene and protect the workers and the poor. In a very triumphalistic way, in *Quadragesimo anno* (1931) Pope Pius XI maintained that "*Rerum novarum* completely overthrew those tattering tenets of liberalism which had long hampered effective intervention by the government" (n. 27).

Pope Leo XIII's authoritative writings clearly illustrate the opposition to liberalism with its emphasis on human freedom. Leo strongly attacked the modern freedoms, including freedom of religion, which violates the "highest duty" of worshiping the one true God in the one true faith; freedom of speech and the press means that truth will not remain sacred. In addition Leo did not see human equality as a value because in his concept of the organic society each individual has a different role to play for the good of the whole. Civil society is based on an analogy with the human body, which has many distinct and unequal parts that have to work together for the good of the whole. If all the parts were the same and equal, there would be no unified human body. Equality erodes the glue that keeps society together. Also, Leo did not advocate the participation of people in government. His favorite word for the leaders of society was rulers (*principes*), and he saw the people as the illiterate multitude that had to be led.

As the twentieth century unfolded, however, the Catholic Church began to see totalitarianism, especially in the form of communism, as the biggest problem. In the 1930s, Pius XI issued encyclical letters condemning totalitarianism on the right (Nazism and Fascism) and especially totalitarianism on the left in the form of communism. Communism trampled on the dignity, freedom, and rights of the individual. In this context, Pius XI was happy and proud to wage the good fight for the liberty of consciences, which he was quick to point out did not mean the absolute independence of conscience from God's law.

In the two encyclicals issued by John XXIII in the early 1960s, one can observe a fascinating development. *Mater et magistra* (1961) develops a vision that the values of truth, justice, and love constitute the good society (nn. 212–65). But *Pacem in terris* (1963) adds a fourth value to this triumvirate: freedom (nn. 86–129). The documents themselves do not call attention to this very significant change, but the growing importance of freedom comes to the fore here.

Vatican II moves even further in its promotion of human freedom in general and freedom in political life, as is illustrated in its changed teaching on religious freedom, which will be analyzed below. In *Octogesima adveniens* (1971), Pope Paul VI develops two aspirations that have come to the fore in the light of recent developments: "the aspiration to equality and the aspiration to participation, two forms of human dignity and freedom" (n. 22). At the end of the nineteenth century, the Catholic Church strongly opposed freedom, equality, and participation. But in the twentieth century, the same Catholic Church became a strong proponent of human dignity and freedom. Pope John Paul II has made human freedom and dignity an essential part of his many teachings on the political order.

The shift to a greater emphasis on freedom, equality, and participation in political society helps to explain the Catholic movement toward acceptance of and support for democratic forms of government. The Catholic Church strongly opposed the French Revolution and even supported the monarchy and the ancien régime. Liberal democracy seemed to involve all the negative aspects of liberalism in general. Catholic teaching did not give that much emphasis to the form of government but simply insisted that, in whatever form it existed, it should strive for the common good of society.

As the twentieth century progressed, however, the developments mentioned above called for an acceptance of democracy. In his 1944 Christmas message, Pope Pius XII stated that a democratic form of government appears to many people as a natural postulate imposed by reason itself. Catholic thinkers such as Jacques Maritain and Catholic Christian Democratic parties in Europe after World War II espoused the cause of democracy. Vatican II firmly accepted the democratic form of government. John Paul II has been a strong advocate of democracy, both in the countries behind the former Iron Curtain and in the developing countries of the world.[5]

Church and State

Historically, Roman Catholicism has been associated with the union of church and state. In fact, it was only at Vatican II that the Catholic Church accepted religious freedom and the so-called separation of church and state.

The Gospel of Matthew recognizes the duality between church and state with the warning to give to God what is God's and to Caesar what is Caesar's (22:21–22). The Catholic tradition has recognized two different orders—the spiritual and the temporal—with different authorities ruling each order. In the course of history, however, the Catholic Church has accepted significantly different relations between church and state.

HISTORICAL DEVELOPMENTS

At the time of the Roman Empire, the conversion of Emperor Constantine brought about a very close relationship between church and state. Constantine and his successors saw themselves as defenders of the faith who could and did intervene directly in the spiritual affairs of the church, as was illustrated by their calling ecumenical councils. The Middle Ages witnessed an attempt by popes in the Catholic Church to establish a Christian commonwealth with all people and princes bound together under obedience to the pope. The confessional state arose after the Reformation in accord with the famous principle—*cuius regio eius religio*—that the religion of the place (and the people) follows the religion of the prince. The Peace of Augsburg (1555) established the confessional state, which was based on the understanding that religious unity was necessary to achieve civic unity. Thus there came into existence Protestant and Catholic states. Note how the founding of the United States in the eighteenth century introduced a new reality: the possibility of political unity in the midst of religious diversity.

Catholic theology in general fought against control of the church by the state, and it developed various theories for understanding the relationship. In the Middle Ages, many Catholic theologians espoused the direct power of the papacy and the church over the state and thus supported the Christian commonwealth of the Middle Ages. This hierocratic theory, however, still recognized the existence of two different powers or societies but maintained that Christ—who was both priest and king—delegated to Peter and his successors, the popes, direct jurisdiction over temporal affairs as well as spiritual ones. According to the metaphor, the pope has the two swords but delegates the temporal sword to the princes. If the prince is delinquent, the pope can take the temporal sword away. Such was the justification of Christendom. During the Reformation, Robert Bellarmine (d. 1621) supported a theory of the indirect power of the pope over the temporal realm. For spiritual reasons, the pope can depose the ruler.

By the nineteenth century, official Catholic teaching still called for the state to publicly support the Catholic religion. Individuals could privately practice different faiths, but the state should prohibit the public expression of all faiths except the Catholic faith. A distinction, however, was made between thesis and hypothesis. The thesis, which should prevail, called for the institution of legal establishment of the Catholic Church and legal intolerance for all others. In certain circumstances in which a greater good could be achieved or a greater evil avoided, however, the hypothesis involving the legal toleration of all religions could be accepted. What happened in practice was that where Catholics were a vast majority, the thesis existed; where Catholics were a minority, as in the United States, the hypothesis could be tolerated. This remained the official teaching until Vatican II.

It is helpful—especially in our own age, which is so different—to give the reasons behind the denial of religious freedom. First, the primacy of the spiritual order called for the temporal to be in service of the spiritual. They were two different realities, but they had to work together.

Second, the most important reality involved was objective truth. The truth—which, according to the Catholic understanding, meant that the Catholic Church was the one "true religion"—is primary. But what about the consciences of people who disagreed? The response was that error has no rights. Just as one is not free to sell poisons that can cause death to our physical life, one cannot permit religious errors that can cause spiritual death. Objective truth is the primary consideration.

Third, the understanding of the state bolstered this denial of religious liberty. The state is a creature of God, and like all creatures of God it also must acknowledge the one true God and the one true religion. The state has an ethical and even religious function of directing the illiterate multitude to their spiritual and ethical good. Such a state is authoritarian or paternalistic at best.

Fourth, the Catholic Church strongly opposed the European arguments in favor of religious freedom as proposed in the name of continental liberalism. According to this theory, there was no dyarchy (no two societies—the temporal and the spiritual) but only a thoroughgoing political and juridical monism—one sovereign, one society, one law, one secular faith. This complete secularism would remove the church entirely from the public realm and leave it existing only in the private sphere. Such a church could have no influence whatsoever on public life.

CHANGE AT VATICAN II

At Vatican II in 1965, however, Roman Catholicism accepted the principle of religious liberty, meaning that no one is to be forced to act against one's conscience in religious matters or prohibited from acting in accord with religious conscience. What brought about this significant change?

The primary reality in this change was the greater appreciation and acceptance of the dignity, rights, and freedom of the human person that had been developed earlier. Its implications for religious liberty are decisive.

First, the emphasis moved from the primacy of the objective reality of truth to the primacy of the subjective reality of the human person and her or his conscience. The freedom of the human person calls for a free response, and no secular authority can take away the basic freedom of the individual person in one's response to God.

Second, the growing emphasis on the freedom and dignity of the human person dramatically changed the understanding of government and its role. For Leo XIII, the state was authoritarian, or at best paternalistic, in directing the illiterate multitude to their own good. Now the freedom of the individual limits the role of the state. The *Declaration on Religious Freedom* of Vatican II insists that "the usages of society are to be the usages of freedom in their full range. These require that the freedom of human beings be respected as far as possible and curtailed only when and insofar as necessary" (n. 7).[6] Here the Catholic Church accepts the principle of the free society and of limited constitutional government.

Third, the contemporary understanding of religious freedom as enshrined in limited constitutional government does not call for the removal of the church from the public realm and its relegation only to the private sphere. The church is free to carry on its own mission in the world, including the mission of working for a more just human society. The church has a right to influence the temporal society in and through the conscience and works of church members, who are both members of the church and citizens of the nation. The government thus recognizes the freedom of the church to carry out its mission, and in this way the primacy of the spiritual is safeguarded. The recognition of religious freedom also means the acceptance of a limited constitutional government and the rejection of the authoritarian, paternalistic, and ethical state that Leo XIII had proposed in the late nineteenth century.

On the basis of the teaching found in the *Declaration on Religious Freedom*, Catholic teaching insists on the important distinction between the broader public society and the narrower concept of the public order where the coercive power of government is employed. The broader public society includes all individuals, natural groups, and voluntary associations that influence and affect public society. The end of public society and all those who participate in it is the common good. The political order or the state with its power of coercion has the limited purpose of protecting and promoting the public order. The basic principle of a free society is as much freedom as possible with government intervening for the sake of public order.

The question then naturally arises: What is public order? According to the *Declaration*, public order involves the three goods of justice, public morality, and public peace (n. 7). Government can and should intervene and promote these three values. In keeping with the anthropology and understanding of the state developed above, I add social justice to the generic concept of justice because of the danger that people often do not give enough importance to social justice in our society.

Public order with its threefold goods or values also puts legitimate limits on religious freedom. In the United States, despite the prevailing rhetoric, we recognize restrictions on religious freedom that are basically governed by the threefold values of public order. If a religion calls for child sacrifice, public authorities can and should stop this because of justice—the need to protect the right to life of all citizens. If your religion calls for you to march through a residential neighborhood at 3 A.M. with a hundred-piece band, the need to keep the peace justifies the government in preventing such a march.

In the nineteenth century (in a disputed move), the Supreme Court ruled that polygamy for Mormons was illegal despite the directives of their religion to practice polygamy. Note that the criterion of public morality by definition differs from private morality, but there exists much discussion about what constitutes public morality.

The *Declaration on Religious Freedom* thus sets forth the contemporary Catholic acceptance of limited constitutional government. But in a surprising move, subsequent papal documents of Catholic social teaching issued by Paul VI and John Paul II fail to mention public order as the end of the state but still regularly invoke the common good. The possible reasons for this somewhat astonishing silence lie beyond the scope of this chapter. Because Catholic social teaching deals primarily with justice issues, however, both the criterion of public order and the criterion of the common good would come to the same conclusions about the role of the state with regard to justice. The following section deals with justice in Catholic social teaching.

Justice

In this section, I discuss material goods, private property and the poor, the different types of justice, human rights, and the economic systems of capitalism and Marxism.

MATERIAL GOODS, PRIVATE PROPERTY, AND POOR PEOPLE

The Catholic tradition based on the Scripture and influenced by Thomistic Aristotelianism has maintained that material goods are not the most important human goods but are always subordinate to more spiritual goods. Human dignity, however, requires a sufficiency of the material goods of this world. In any society or government, the primary issue concerns the just distribution of material goods.

Catholic social teaching emphasizes the universal destiny of the goods of creation to serve the needs of all people. In *Sollicitudo rei socialis* (1987), Pope John Paul II succinctly summarizes the teaching: "It is necessary to state once more the characteristic principle of Christian social doctrine: the goods of this world are *originally meant for all*. The right to private property is *valid and necessary*, but it does not nullify the nature of this principle. Private property, in fact, is under a "social mortgage," which means that it has an intrinsically social function, based upon and justified precisely by the principle of the universal destiny of goods" (n. 42).

Since the beginning of the church, Catholic teaching has recognized both a social and an individual dimension to material goods, in keeping with its basic anthropology, but there has been some development over time about the exact relationship between the two aspects. The social aspect of the goods of creation rests on the intention of the Creator that the goods of creation exist to serve the needs of all people. On this basis, the criterion of distributive justice that will be developed below insists that all human beings have a right to the material goods necessary to live a minimally decent existence.

The social dimension also limits the understanding of private property as something that one owns as one's own. Thomas Aquinas accepts the general teaching of the Early Church that private property is justified not on the basis of natural law but on the basis of human sinfulness. He acknowledges there would be no need for private property if it were not for sin. However, granted the need to possess things as one's own in this imperfect and sinful world, the use of private property insists on its function to serve the needs of all (*Summa* Ia, q. 98, a.1, ad. 3).

In the question of the distribution of material goods, the Catholic tradition has insisted on a special care and concern for poor people. According to the Hebrew Scriptures, God is the special protector of poor people, and God will hear their cry and take care of them. The New Testament also shows this special concern of God and Jesus for poor people, as is illustrated in the so-called last judgment scene in Matthew, where eternal reward is based on what one does for poor people and the least of our brothers and sisters (chap. 25). In the very beginning of *Rerum novarum* (n. 2), Leo XIII insists that "some remedy must be found and quickly found, for the misery and wretchedness which press so heavily at this moment on the large majority of the very poor." John Paul II insists on the preferential option for poor people. The economic pastoral of the U.S. bishops spells out the priorities involved in the preferential option for poor people (nn. 87–95). A preferential option is not an exclusive option. God loves all people but has a special concern for poor people. On the basis of the preferential option for poor people, three priorities emerge. First, the fulfillment of the basic needs of poor people is the highest priority. Second, increasing active participation in economic life by those presently excluded or vulnerable is a high social priority. Third, the investment of wealth, energy, and human talent should be specifically directed to benefit poor people.

THREE TYPES OF JUSTICE

In keeping with an anthropology that stresses both the dignity and social nature of the human person, the Catholic tradition insists on three types of justice: commutative justice (coming from the Latin *commutare*, meaning exchange) governs one-to-one relationships such as contracts; distributive justice governs how society distributes its goods and burdens among its members; and legal, social, or contributive justice governs the obligation of individuals to society and the state. Scholastic theologians, especially Thomas Aquinas and commentators on his work, developed a similar understanding of justice and applied it to the problems of their own day. The economic pastoral of the U.S. bishops (1987) describes these three types of justice and indicates their application to contemporary problems (nn. 68–76).

Commutative justice involves arithmetic equality, is blind, and is no respecter of persons. If I borrow ten dollars from you and ten dollars from the wealthiest person in the world, I owe each of you ten dollars. The characteristics of the individual person do not enter into the consideration. Those who propose a more individualistic anthropology see commutative justice as the primary or only aspect of justice.

Distributive justice governs the relationship between society or the state and the individual. As was pointed out above, society is broader than the state. In the light of space constraints, this subsection discusses how the state should distribute its goods and burdens. A just distribution rests on a recognition that the political community includes members who have an equal human dignity.

Take first the distribution of material goods. What is a fair and just distribution of material goods in society? An individualistic approach asserts the right of individuals to acquire as much as possible for one's self, provided equal opportunity is afforded to all. Often the metaphor of the race is invoked. Extreme collectivism argues for total equality in the distribution of material goods. The Catholic tradition, once again, finds a middle way between these two approaches.

A fundamental criterion for the just distribution of material goods is human need. As was mentioned above, in the Catholic understanding all human beings have a right to a minimally decent existence. Above and beyond this criterion of need, other criteria such as creativity, hard work, risk, and reward all come into play. Not everyone should have the same amount of goods, but all should have that basic minimum necessary for a minimally decent existence. In addition, the equality of members of society is jeopardized if there exists a huge gap between the highest and lowest economic strata in the possession of material goods.

Take now the distribution of burdens. The primary societal burden involves taxation. What is a just tax system, according to the principles of distributive justice? Those who earn or have more money should contribute more. Distributive justice maintains that those who have more should pay not only arithmetically more but also should pay a higher percentage. A progressive tax system is called for.

Legal justice, or what is today sometimes called contributive justice, involves the relationship of the individual person or citizen with society and the state. In an older understanding, the primary obligation was to obey the just laws of the state; hence the name legal. Now, however, the emphasis falls on the responsibility of individuals to participate actively in the total life of the state and their community and on the corresponding obligation of society to recognize and encourage such participation. Especially today, when many people feel they have no say or control over our political and economic institutions, we desperately need institutions that are open to participation by all.

HUMAN RIGHTS

Until comparatively recently, Roman Catholicism has shied away from talk of rights. Aquinas does not treat subjective rights. Rights language in the nineteenth century was associated with liberalism, the Enlightenment, and individualism. However, in keeping with the development in the twentieth century traced above, Catholic social thought began to appreciate more the freedom, dignity, and rights of the human person. Only in *Pacem in terris* in 1963 did Pope John XXIII, for the first time, develop a theoretical understanding of human rights in the context of Catholic social teaching. Today John Paul II has made human rights and solidarity the cornerstone of his social teaching.

Catholic social teaching arrived on the human rights bandwagon somewhat late and out of breath. To its credit, however, Catholic teaching insists on both political and civil rights, as well as economic or social rights. Political rights such as freedom of religion, speech, press, and association are cornerstones of liberalism. Conversely, socialist countries have stressed the social and economic rights of individuals to food, clothing, shelter, and health care. By insisting on both political and economic rights and by insisting on duties as well as rights, Catholic social teaching today tries to avoid the one-sided extremes of individualism and collectivism.

As might be expected, the Catholic social tradition with its basic anthropology has historically criticized both capitalism and communism. Because this chapter deals primarily with the political order and its responsibilities, it does not include a detailed discussion of these two economic systems.

Roman Catholicism and Nonbelievers: Politics and People outside the Tradition

Is the message or teaching of Roman Catholicism about politics intended just for Catholics and Christians or for all humankind as well? The documents coming from the hierarchical teaching office in the Roman Catholic Church insist that the teaching is for all humankind. From a methodological perspective, the teaching has traditionally been based on the natural law approach, which by definition is open to all human beings and has no religious presuppositions with regard to its content. From a content perspective, Catholic social teaching insists on one common good for political societies, to which all members of the society, whether they are believers or not, must contribute. Since the 1960s, the papal documents themselves have explicitly been addressed to all people of goodwill. Nowhere do these official teachings propose something different that Catholics are asked to do in the political order. From a practical perspective, the Catholic approach recognizes that its teaching for a more just social order will be effective only if many people work together to try to put this teaching into practice.

Although, in theory, Catholic social teaching is addressed not only to Roman Catholics but to all people of goodwill, in practice, two problems arise. First, as was mentioned above, ever since Vatican II, official church teaching documents have made more explicit references to Scripture, Jesus Christ, revelation, and grace. But, as was also noted above, these documents still address all people of goodwill. At the very least, this new approach creates some tension because it addresses two different readerships. The U.S. bishops in their pastoral letters have recognized this tension, and they claim that they appeal to unique Catholic and Christian sources in addressing fellow Catholics and appeal to others on the basis of common human reason and experience. However, it is impossible to make this clear differentiation all the time.

Second, recall the tension mentioned above between natural law as based on human reason and experience and natural law as authoritatively proposed by the Roman Catholic Church. With regard to non-Catholics, the fact that the teaching is proposed as being in accord with reason and experience means that all people can enter into the discussion. Such an approach facilitates a civil dialogue among all people in a society. However, because the teaching is also proposed as authoritative church teaching, the Catholic Church and Catholic individuals at times have used their political muscle or power to make these authoritative teachings into law. Thus, at times, the paradigm of culture wars seems more fitting than the paradigm of deliberative rational discourse and civil discussion about what is good for society.

Conclusion

This chapter has discussed the Roman Catholic approach to politics in the light of its sources, its theory of politics, the medium or methodology used, its message and content, and finally its relevance for nonbelievers. The very nature of Catholicism, with its authoritative teaching office, means that the official documents have developed in some depth the Catholic understanding of the political order. More than half of this chapter thus has dealt with the message or content of this teaching as found in the official documents of the Catholic Church. The Catholic approach, however, is also intended for all people of goodwill and thus is truly catholic or universal.

Notes

1. For a Latin and English version of the *Summa*, see *Summa theologiae: Latin Text and English Translation, Introductions, Notes, Appendixes, and Glossaries*, 61 vols., ed. Dominicans from English-Speaking Provinces of the Order (New York: McGraw-Hill, 1964–). The treatise on justice is found in the second part of the second part of the *Summa* and is generally referred to as II-II, q. 57–122.

2. For an English translation of Pope Leo XIII's encyclicals, see *The Papal Encyclicals, 1878–1903*, ed. Claudia Carlen (Wilmington, N.C.: McGrath, 1981). Encyclicals and other church documents take their official title from the first two or three Latin words of the document.

3. There is no official canon or list of these documents. For a readily available collection of these documents in English, see *Catholic Social Thought: The Documentary Heritage*, ed. David J. O'Brien and Thomas A. Shannon (Maryknoll, N.Y.: Orbis, 1992). The text will give the paragraph numbers from the documents cited, which can then be found in this volume or any other source.

4. Michael Novak, "Neoconservatives," in *The New Dictionary of Catholic Social Thought*, ed. Judith A. Dwyer (Collegeville, Minn.: Liturgical Press, 1994), 678–82.

5. Paul E. Sigmund, "Catholicism and Liberal Democracy," in *Catholicism and Liberalism: Contributions to American Public Philosophy*, ed. R. Bruce Douglass and David Hollenbach (Cambridge: Cambridge University Press, 1994), 217–41.

6. For an English translation of the Vatican II documents, see Walter M. Abbott, ed., *The Documents of Vatican II* (New York: Guild, 1966).

Suggested Readings

Bokenkotter, Thomas S. *Church and Revolution: Catholics in the Struggle for Democracy and Social Justice*. New York: Doubleday Image, 1998.

Curran, Charles E. *Catholic Social Teaching 1891–Present: A Historical, Theological, and Ethical Analysis*. Washington, D.C.: Georgetown University Press, 2002.

Curran, Charles E., and Leslie Griffin, eds. *The Catholic Church, Morality, and Politics. Readings in Moral Theology No. 12*. New York: Paulist Press, 2001.

Dorr, Donal. *Option for the Poor: A Hundred Years of Catholic Social Teaching*. Rev. ed. Maryknoll, N.Y.: Orbis, 1992.

Froehle, Bryan T., and Mary L. Gautier. *The Catholic Church Today*. Maryknoll, N.Y.: Orbis, 2000.

Gillis, Chester. *Roman Catholicism in America*. New York: Columbia University Press, 1999.

Hellwig, Monika K. *Understanding Catholicism*. 2d ed. New York: Paulist Press, 2002.

Kohmescher, Matthew F. *Catholicism Today: A Survey of Catholic Belief and Practice*. 3d ed. New York: Paulist Press, 1999.

Krier Mich, Marvin L. *Catholic Social Teaching and Movements*. Mystic, Conn.: Twenty-Third Publications, 1998.

McBrien, Richard P. *Catholicism*. San Francisco: Harper San Francisco, 1994.

McBrien, Richard P. *Responses to 101 Questions on the Church*. New York: Paulist Press, 1996.

McCarthy, Timothy. *The Catholic Tradition: The Church in the Twentieth Century*. Rev. 2d ed. Chicago: Loyola University Press, 1998.

Four | **Orthodox Christianity** |

Petros Vassiliadis

IN THE MIND OF THE GENERAL POPULACE, CHRISTIANITY MAY BROADLY BE UNDERSTOOD as the religious tradition devoted to Jesus Christ, which today is most readily identified with a variety of churches and denominations. Furthermore, followers of Christ would logically be known as Christians. Beyond that, however, it would be difficult for most people to keep track of the distinctions within the Christian tradition, even on the denominational level. Particularly with reference to the Orthodox branch of Christianity, a clear, concise definition is in order.

Defining "Orthodox Christianity" is indeed a very difficult task. At a time when the very attribute ("orthodox") is widely understood as having more or less negative connotations, what can we identify as the defining attributes of the "Orthodox Church"? In Western theological and academic circles, Orthodox Christianity has become known through ecumenical discussions, especially within the World Council of Churches, involving Catholic, Protestant, and Orthodox Christians. Some scholars used to identify Orthodoxy either as a kind of Roman Catholicism without the pope, or as a kind of Protestantism with an episcopacy (hierarchy of governance through bishops). Certainly to most Protestants from the "evangelical" stream of the Christian tradition, but sometimes also those from the "ecumenical" one, the "Orthodox Church" has a negative Old World connotation. For them, Orthodox Christianity has come to signify stagnation in church life, strict dogmatic confessionalism, and an inflexibility and unreadiness to adapt to modern situations or to deal with politics in a comprehensible way. At best, Orthodoxy is an "Eastern phenomenon" vis-à-vis the "modern Western mentality" and perhaps theological and academic process.

Orthodox Christianity is normally defined in confessional or denominational terms, that is, as the Eastern branch of Christianity, which was separated from the West around the beginning of the second millennium C.E. In the *Oxford Dictionary of the Christian Church*, the Orthodox Church is described as "a family of Churches, situated mainly in Eastern Europe: each member Church is independent in its internal administration, but all share the same faith and are in communion with one another, acknowledging the honorary primacy of the Patriarch of Constantinople."

In general, most textbooks of church history with a Western perspective make little or no reference to Eastern Orthodoxy after the Great Schism between the Eastern and Western churches in 1054 C.E.—or at least after the fall of Constantinople in 1453 C.E. With regard to our subject of politics, the general impression

85

of most scholars from all church traditions that underwent modernism is that for a very long period of time what actually characterized Eastern Orthodoxy was an intolerable subservience of the church to the state. Another way of looking at is that the church adapted to the existing world order, resulting in church and society penetrating and permeating each other. At the same time, however, others insist that the Eastern Orthodox Church established itself in the world as an institution focused almost exclusively on otherworldly salvation.

Reinforced by recent developments, both these contradictory assessments of Orthodox Christianity hold some truth. But neither one is completely accurate. The former view was reinforced by the political attitude of almost all the so-called Orthodox nations in the near past (e.g., Greece, Russia), which actually gave the impression of a nationalistic inclination of the Orthodox Church. The latter view, found in the writings of some Orthodox theologians, lays disproportionate stress on the mystical aspect of Orthodoxy. It should be noted that these writers are mostly immigrants from prerevolutionary Russia (before 1917), who came in contact with the West after a long period of separation. In a desperate attempt to preserve their ancient Orthodox identity surrounded by a modern world quite alien to them, they underline the mystical aspect of Orthodox Christianity to Western Christians. However, today both these one-sided presentations of Orthodox Christianity (i.e., nationalistic and mystical) are seriously questioned.

To give an accurate description of Orthodox Christianity, we need to redefine the actual understanding of the term to a radical (in the sense of getting back to the root meaning) degree, because current usage is so misleading. According to most serious interpreters of this ancient tradition, if we examine the derivation of the term Orthodox Christianity it refers to the wholeness of the people of God who share the right conviction (*orthe* + *doxa* = right opinion) concerning the event of God's salvation in Christ and his Church. In addition, this label encompasses the notion of right expression, or right practice (*orthopraxia*) of the Christian faith. *Orthodoxia* leads to the maximum possible application in *orthopraxia* of charismatic life in the freedom of the Holy Spirit, the spirit of God, in all aspects of daily social and cosmic life.

Thus, everybody is invited by Orthodoxy to transcend confessions and inflexible institutions without necessarily denying them. Some Orthodox theologians even insist that Orthodoxy is not to be identified only with those belonging to the canonical Orthodox churches in the historical sense and with all their limitations and shortcomings. After all, initially this term was not given to any historical branch of Christianity, but to the One, Holy, Catholic, and Apostolic Church as a whole over against the heretics who, of their own choice, split from the main body of the church. The term is exclusive for all those who willingly fall away from the historical stream of life of the One Church, but it is inclusive for those who profess their spiritual belonging to that stream.

The term Orthodoxy, therefore, has more or less ecclesial (having to do with the essence of what it means to be a church) rather than confessional connotations. And for this reason, one can argue that the fundamental principles of Christian spirituality, of social and political theory, are the same in the East and in the West.

Nevertheless, that ecclesial charismatic community has had a certain historical manifestation, and it has developed concrete political viewpoints, which need to be extracted from a certain background, from certain texts, and from certain sources. Attempting to accomplish this, however, we encounter some major difficulties.

Classical Sources of Orthodox Christianity on Politics

On what ground and from what sources can one accurately establish an Orthodox viewpoint? Roman Catholics have the decisions produced by the relatively recent council known as Vatican II (1962–65 C.E.) to guide them, but the Orthodox do not have an equivalent collection of authoritative statements. The Lutherans have the Augsburg Confession; the Orthodox do not have a confession, and Orthodox Christianity also lacks the equivalent of a Luther or Calvin, to mention just two leaders of the Protestant Reformation who help give Protestant Christians their theological identity. With regard specifically to politics and social life in general, the Catholic tradition has certain encyclicals and declarations, such as *Rerum novarum* (1891), *Gaudium et spes* (1965), and more recently *Justitia in mundo* (1971).

Similarly, Protestant denominations in the wider sense have their confessions and from time to time certain decisions made by their respective collective ecclesial bodies. This has never been the case with the Orthodox, until a very recent exceptional case with regard to the Russian Orthodox Church, to which we will return below. In contrast, the only authoritative sources that Orthodox Christianity possesses are in fact common to all Christians: the Bible and the Tradition, although they have never been considered by Orthodox Christians as "sources" in the strict sense, at least in the way they are thought of in the West. How can one establish a distinctly Orthodox view on a basis which in fact is common to the non-Orthodox as well?

Some Orthodox insist that defining Orthodox Christianity is not a matter of drawing from special sources but rather of interpreting the sources that Orthodoxy shares with the rest of Christianity and partly with Judaism. In other words, it is a matter of theological presuppositions, which suggests a certain problematic and method not always familiar to the non-Orthodox. Naturally then, all their social, ethical, and theological viewpoints, and politics in particular, come only as the logical consequence of these presuppositions. However, even the essence of Orthodox Christianity, vis-à-vis Western Christianity in its entirety—that is, Catholic and Protestant—is even beyond such theological presuppositions. After all, the main theological difference, which resulted in the eventual split between Eastern and Western Christianity, was a different understanding of truth. Eastern Christianity—especially in later Byzantine antiquity—presupposes a concept of revelation substantially different from that held in the West under the influence of Aristotle.

In particular, under the guidance of the Holy Spirit, Orthodoxy believes that in the church every Christian, and the saint in particular, possesses the privilege and the opportunity of seeing (*theorein*) and experiencing the truth. Because the concept of *theologia* (i.e., theology) in Cappadocian and Antiochean thinking was inseparable from *theoria* (i.e., contemplation), theology could not be—as it was at least in Western high Scholasticism—a rational deduction from "revealed" premises, that is, from Scripture or from the statements of an ecclesiastical magisterium. Instead, it was a vision experienced by the faithful, whose authenticity was of course to be checked against the witness of Scripture and Tradition.

A true theologian as understood in later Byzantine thought was for the most part the one who saw and experienced the content of theology. Theological inquiry and insight were considered to belong not to the intellect alone, though rigorous thinking of course is not excluded from the process, but to the "eyes of the Spirit," which place the whole human being—intellect, emotions, and even senses—in contact with the divine existence. In Orthodox Christianity, "truth" is inseparable from "communion."

Therefore, it would be more accurate to say that Orthodox Christianity is a way of life; hence the importance of its liturgical tradition. It is exactly for this reason that the Liturgy plays such a prominent role in the theology of almost all Orthodox Christians in modern times. It is widely held by the Orthodox that the liturgical dimension is perhaps the only safe criterion for ascertaining what might be considered unique or peculiar to Orthodox theology. Given the centrality of the Liturgy, I would suggest that the Orthodox Church is first of all a worshiping community. Worship comes first, doctrine and discipline second. As an old Latin saying goes, *lex orandi lex credendi*, "The rule of prayer dictates the rule of belief" or "As we pray, so we believe."

The *lex orandi* (the law or rule of prayer) has a privileged priority in the life of the Christian Church. The *lex credendi* (the law or rule of belief) depends on the devotional experience and vision of the church, or more precisely on the authentic (i.e., liturgical) identity of the church. The question, therefore, about the principal sources on which one can draw to describe the Orthodox religious system's views about politics is much more complex than for the rest of Christianity.

The heart of Orthodox liturgy, as in all or almost all Christian traditions, is the Eucharist, which is called by the Orthodox "Divine Liturgy." The Orthodox

Church has consistently accepted the priority of the eucharistic *experience* over all theological *views* and *convictions*, the priority of *communion* over *faith* or *belief*, and as a matter of fact the priority of *ecclesiology* over *theology* in its regular meaning. One of the most distinguishing features of Orthodox Christianity is that, contrary to many Western religious systems that have adapted to modernism, Orthodoxy has attempted to distance itself as much as possible from the dominant post-Enlightenment and post-Reformation paradigm that most theologians tacitly accept.

Theologians who have a modernist bent believe that the essence of Christianity is to be found in the articulation of theological statements, based on Scripture, Tradition, or other authoritative pronouncements, and that these truths are upheld by church institutions and promoted by the authority of clergy and scholars. But for the Orthodox, who by the way have not yet undergone the process of modernization, what constitutes the core of Christian faith cannot be extracted from expressed theological views, from a certain *depositum fidei* (depository of faith), be it the Bible or the Tradition (or both), the writings of the Fathers, or the canons and even the decisions of the Ecumenical Councils.

Whereas the modernist outlook inevitably led the Western church to adopt some kind of magisterium, be it hierarchical or scholarly, Orthodox Christianity took a different tack. It is mainly for this reason that the criterion most widely held among the Orthodox of our time in defining the Orthodox Church's response to all ethical, moral, social, and political issues is undoubtedly the *eucharistic* approach. Only in the Eucharist does the church become God's people, the One Church in its fullest sense.

Even with Orthodoxy's emphasis on the Eucharist, I will start my discussion of politics with Jesus Christ, the anointed Messiah. All social ethical issues, and the understanding of politics in particular, are based on and determined in Orthodox Christianity—as in all Christian traditions—by the teaching, life, and work of Jesus of Nazareth. His teaching, however, and especially his life and work, cannot properly be understood without reference to the eschatological expectations of Judaism.

Without getting sidetracked by the complexities of Jewish eschatology, one can very briefly say that this eschatology was interwoven with the idea of the coming of a messiah, who in the "last days" of history ("the *eschaton*") would establish his kingdom by calling the dispersed and afflicted people of God into one place to become one body united around him. As it was expressed in the prophetic tradition of the Hebrew Bible (e.g., Joel 3:1; Isaiah 2:2, 59:21; Ezekiel 36:24), the start of the eschatological period will be marked by the gathering of all the nations and the descent of God's Spirit to the sons and the daughters of God. One particular statement in the Gospel of John about the messiah's role is extremely important. In chapter 11, the writer interprets the words of the Jewish high priest by affirming that "he prophesied that Jesus should die . . . not for the nation only but to *gather into one* [emphasis added] the children of God who are scattered abroad" (John 11:51–52).

Throughout the Gospels, Jesus Christ identifies himself with this eschatological messiah. We see this in the various messianic titles he chose for himself, at least as witnessed by the most primitive sources of the Christian tradition ("Son of Man," "Son of God," most of which had a collective meaning, whence the Christology of "corporate personality"). We see it as well in the parables of the Kingdom of God (e.g., Matthew 13, Mark 4, and Luke 8), which summarize his teaching, the point of which is to proclaim that his coming initiates the new world of God's rule. In the Lord's Prayer, but also in his conscious overt acts (e.g., the selection of twelve disciples, symbolizing Israel's Twelve Tribes), Jesus introduces the eschatological agenda. In short, Christ identified himself with the messiah of the *eschaton*, who would be the center of the gathering of the dispersed people of God.

It is on this radical eschatological teaching of the historical Jesus about God's rule that the Early Christian community has developed its ecclesiology and determined its "political" theory (in the wider sense). Modern biblical research has shown that Jesus's expectation about the rule of God moves dialectically between the "already" and the "not yet"; in other words, it has already begun in the present but will be completed in its final authentic form in the eschaton.

In the first two decades after the crucifixion of Jesus, the Christian community understood its existence as the perfect and genuine expression of the people of God. With a series of terms taken from the Hebrew Scriptures, the Early Christian community expressed its belief that it was the "Israel of God" (Galatians 6:16), the "saints" (Acts 9:32, 41; 26:10; Romans 1:7; 8:27; 12:13; 15:25), "the elect" (Romans 8:33; Colossians 3:12, etc.), and "the chosen race" and "the royal priesthood" (1 Peter 2:9), namely, the holy people of God (*laos tou theou*), for whom all the promises of the Bible were to be fulfilled at the *eschata*.

During this constructive period, the concept with which the Early Christian community understood its identity was that of a people and not an organization or even a religious system. An examination of both the First (Old) and the Second (New) Testament terminology makes this quite clear. The chosen people of God were an *'am* (in Hebrew, especially in the prophets) or a *laos* (in Greek), whereas the people of the outside world were designated by the Hebrew term *goyim* and the Greek *ethne*, meaning Gentile (cf. Acts 15:14).

The second generation after Pentecost is certainly characterized by the theological contribution of Saint Paul. He takes over the above charismatic notion of the church, but he gives it in addition a universal and ecumenical character. To the church belong all human beings, Jews and Gentiles; for the latter have been joined to the same tree of the people of God (Romans 11:13ff). The church, as the new Israel, is thus no longer constituted according to the external criteria of Judaism (e.g., circumcision, sacrifices), but rather on its faith in Jesus Christ (cf. Romans 9:6). The phrase, however, that characterizes Pauline ecclesiology is *Body of Christ*. With this metaphorical expression, Saint Paul was able to express the charismatic nature of the church by means of the Semitic concept of corporate personality. He emphasized that a variety of gifts exist in the church, exercised by the individual members of the community, and necessary for the building up and the nurturing of this body, Christ alone being its only head and authority.

The understanding of politics, and the church's social responsibility in general, stems exactly from this conception of the church. The people of God is an eschatological, dynamic, radical, and corporate reality that struggled to witness authentically to the Kingdom of God, that is, to manifest God's rule, "on earth as it is in heaven" (Matthew 6:10, parallel). The Apostles, Jesus of Nazareth's disciples, were commissioned to proclaim neither a specific political theory nor a set of given religious convictions, doctrines, or moral commands. Instead, they were to announce the coming Kingdom, the Gospel, that is, the Good News of a new eschatological reality, with the crucified and resurrected Christ as its center. He is the incarnate *Logos* (or Word) of God, who nevertheless through the presence of the Holy Spirit continues to dwell among human beings, guiding them to transform the present—"fallen" and unjust—world order, and pave the way toward the ideal and otherworldly Kingdom of God.

On the basis of this Kingdom reality, therefore, all faithful Christians were called—not so much as isolated individuals, but as a corporate ecclesial entity—to behave in this world "politically."[1] Because they understood themselves to be carrying on the line of Israel, the Early Christians took on the political responsibilities required of the chosen race of the people of God. They were considered a "royal priesthood" by reason of the fact that all of them, without exception, have priestly and spiritual authority to practice in the *diaspora* (or the dispersed community of faith) the work of the priestly class. The fact that not just some special cast, such as the priests or Levites (i.e., people with certain political and religious authority), were responsible for this "eschatological holy nation" at the same time reminded Christians to be worthy of their election through their exemplary life and works. That is why they were called to walk toward unity (*"so that they may become perfectly one"* [John 17:23]), to abandon all deeds of darkness and to do justice to the society at large.

We note that the church was able within a few generations of the first century c.e., largely on the basis of the important contribution of the Greek Fathers of the golden age (second–fourth centuries c.e.), to develop the doctrine of the Holy Trinity, and much later to further develop the important distinction between substance and energies of the three Persons of the Trinity. According to some historians, this was only possible because of the eschatological experience of *koinon-*

ia (fellowship, community) in the Eucharist (both vertical with its head, and horizontal among the people of God, and by extension with all of humanity through the church's mission), an experience that ever since has continued to constitute the only expression of the church's self-consciousness, its Mystery par excellence.

No one, of course, can deny that early enough in the history of the Christian community, even from the time of Saint Paul, there began a "paradigm shift" in the understanding of this act (Eucharist) of self-consciousness of community as a *koinonia* of the *eschata*, i.e., in the understanding of the the Eucharist as a manifestation of the coming Kingdom of God in anticipation of the actual eschatological event. Regardless of the reasons, over the centuries there has been a shift of the theological center of gravity of Christianity from the (eucharistic) experience to the (Christian) message, from eschatology to Christology (and further and consequently to soteriology), from the event (the Kingdom of God), to the words and story about the bearer and center of this event (Christ, and more precisely his sacrifice on the cross).

However, the Eucharist (the *theia koinonia*, or divine fellowship with God and among people) has always remained the sole expression of the church's identity. This *koinonia* dimension of the Eucharist recently has been quite strongly reaffirmed in ecumenical circles with its indications that not only the identity of the church, but all its expressions (e.g., structure, authority, and mission) and actions (e.g., ethics, social and moral, and consequently politics) are in fact *relational*.

To sum up: if one wants to approach, and reflect on, any specific issue, like politics, from a distinctly Orthodox perspective, it is eucharistic theology in its broad sense that should guide his or her effort. Of course, one would expect Orthodox Christianity, like all other religious systems, to offer final solutions to common problems, and inevitably to exercise some kind of legitimate power and not only present affirmations of conscience. But the caution to keep in mind with Orthodoxy is that the entire ethical issue, that is, the problem of overcoming the evil in the world, is basically understood neither as a moral nor as a doctrinal issue; it is primarily (and for some even exclusively) understood as an ecclesial one. The moral and social responsibilities of the church (both as an institution and also as its individual members), as its primary witnessing acts, are the logical consequence of its ecclesial self-consciousness.

Orthodox Christianity's Theory of Politics

Given how differently the Orthodox tradition views the relationship between the religious and the ethical, it would be prudent for us to begin our discussion of its theory of politics with a couple of basic questions. First of all, "Does Orthodox

Christianity have a theory of politics and the social order?" Second, "Is politics a tangential and unimportant subject?"

These questions cannot be answered by a simple "yes" or "no." Orthodox Christianity in dealing with the problem of politics in the past has come to a solution, according to which *religion* and *polity* were never to be divorced or even separated from each other, despite the lack of any visible spectacular victory of the church over the empire, and the detrimental impact of the imperial forces on ecclesiastical affairs (dethronements and exiles of bishops and patriarchs).[2]

Most Orthodox churches nowadays still have this model of "in-and-out-of-politics," the model of *symphonia* or *synallelia*—which was fully developed and elaborated in premodernity—as their ideal, and they try to impose it as far as they can on modern constitutions of modern democratic states.[3] Only in the Orthodox diaspora have there been serious attempts to adapt Orthodox ecclesiology to the modern context.[4]

For an explanation of this close relation between *religion* and *polity* in Orthodox Christianity, one has to go back to ancient Greece, where religion was understood as the cultic life of the polis and never conceivable outside it. Having been ideologically shaped (more than any other branch of Christianity) by Greek culture, the Orthodox religious system not only borrowed the word *ecclesia*, the assembly of citizens, from Greek political life to denominate itself but also developed its identity very much embedded in the whole society. Religion as a separate sphere has never found a solid footing in the theological thinking of the Orthodox Church. It would have been impossible to relegate the church, holistic in conception—and relational rather than confessional in character—to a private sphere in civil society.

This idea of the privatization of the church, together with individualism—which for historical reasons was adopted in the historical Protestant churches—was developed in modernity. There the cardinal idea, which still shapes our modern Western culture, is that religion should be altogether separate from the state, being a matter of individual conscience, in an attempt to provide the basis for social peace and stability. In part, this was a reaction to the religious wars in Europe between Protestants and Catholics in the early seventeenth century C.E. At the same time, however, the eschatological inclination of Orthodoxy gives the impression that politics may be a tangential and unimportant issue.

In recent years, and despite the fact that the eucharistic approach to all aspects of Orthodox Church life has been reaffirmed again and again, the Orthodox have drafted a number of official documents to be presented for final approval to the forthcoming Holy and Great Synod of the Orthodox Church. One of these documents or decisions, titled "The Contribution of the Orthodox Church in Establishment of Peace, Justice, Freedom, Fellowship and Love among the Peoples, and the Lifting of Racial and Other Discriminations," deals indirectly with sociopolitical problems.

This document, which was finally officially approved by the third Pan-Orthodox Pre-Conciliar Consultation by all Orthodox Autocephalous Churches,[5] is a first attempt at a theological response from an Orthodox perspective to social issues pertinent to modern challenges. More precisely focused on our subject is an even more recent document, issued by the Russian Orthodox Church, titled *The Basis of the Social Concept of the Russian Orthodox Church.*[6] This document may not have a Pan-Orthodox canonical status,[7] but it accurately describes the present status of the church–state relations in the Orthodox world:

> Today the Orthodox Church performs her service of God and people in various countries. In some of them she represents the nation-wide confession (Greece, Rumania, Bulgaria), while in others, which are multinational, the religion of the ethnic majority (Russia). In still other countries, those who belong to the Orthodox Church comprise a religious minority surrounded by either heterodox Christians (Finland, Poland, USA) or people of other religions (Japan, Syria, Turkey). In some small countries the Orthodox Church has the status of the state religion (Cyprus, Greece, Finland), while in other countries it is separated from the state. There are also differences in the concrete legal and political contexts in which the Local Orthodox Churches live. They all, however, build both their internal order and relations with the government on the commandments of Christ, teaching of the apostles, holy canons and two-thousand-year-long historical experience and in many situations find an opportunity to pursue their God-commanded goals, thus revealing their other-worldly nature, their heavenly, divine, origin.[8]

Having said all this, it is important to underline that some of the theological differences between the Orthodox East and the Christian West were, and in some cases still are, related to the way the church—as the image of the expected Kingdom of God—was and is directly engaged with temporal and secular matters, that is, with politics. It has been argued time and again that toward the end of the first millennium the church in the West adopted, or was forced to accept, a kind of church–state relationship on a legal basis, namely, as a relationship between two distinct institutions, two distinct and independent "temporal" authorities. Thus, the church moved away from the model of *symphonia*, or *synallelia*, and adopted the theory of the "two swords." In certain critical moments, it even argued that, whereas priestly authority is directly derived from God, secular authority can only be assumed through priestly authority.

Even if such political views are no longer officially supported in Catholic Christianity, one can safely argue that during the second millennium—the millennium of the tragic schism between Western and Eastern Christianity—the emphasis of Western theology was more on the historical dimension of the

Christian ecclesial identity, thus being more sensitive to ethics and constantly reminding the church of its responsibility for the world. At the other end of the political spectrum, the Orthodox Church has developed a clear awareness of the eschatological dimension of Christianity, being in fact the only ecclesiastical institution that always emphasizes the eschatological identity of the church, sometimes even disincarnating its historical manifestation from history.

It is mainly for this reason that many of us[9] are in search of a synthesis between Eastern and Western spirituality, believing that a dynamic encounter will enrich both traditions. After all, the authentic catholicity of the Church (in terms not so much of ecclesiology, but of spirituality, of ethics, and in particular of politics) must include both East and West. Only through such a synthesis can the perennial problem of the tension between history and eschaton in Christianity—and by extension in politics—find a proper and permanent solution. Quite simply, therefore, this is the message of Orthodox Christianity's politics, no matter how strange or vague this may sound!

The Medium of Expressing Politics in Orthodox Christianity

Turning next to the question "through what medium does Orthodox Christianity make its point," the answer is certainly through the eucharistic Liturgy, understood as a glimpse and a foretaste of the eschatological Kingdom of God. In its liturgy, however, the Orthodox Church clearly and in a very stylish and sophisticated way reenacts a story: the *story* of God's creation, of human destiny and condition, of God's abundant love for His creation (and, therefore, His intervention in history), His continuous care for His people, by giving them the Law and by making a covenant with them, and finally by sending them His only-begotten Son, who inaugurated his Kingdom on earth, experienced in history by hosts of saints in his church, but expected in its fullness at the *eschaton*.

In Orthodox Christianity, this story is not told as a past event but as a present reality, as personal narrative with far-reaching consequences for the social order of corporate community. It is for this reason that the political role of its members starts after the Liturgy, in the meta-Liturgy, the Liturgy after the Liturgy, in which the Orthodox are sent forth "in peace" to give witness to this ideal by any means, including politics. Those "means," nevertheless, have never been clearly defined (except in a very vague way; i.e., that they should not deviate from the Gospel, as proclaimed by Jesus of Nazareth, his disciples, and the hosts of saints thereafter). This is partly because almost all the geographical areas where Orthodoxy has historically flourished have never faced the process of modernity. As I will assert more fully below, the relationship between religion and politics became an issue only after the Enlightenment.

The Message of Orthodox Christianity's Politics

We have stated above that, although the principal sources of Orthodox Christianity are the same as those of the rest of Christianity (Bible and Tradition), the special nuance is its liturgical (i.e., eucharistic) dimension. To put it a different way, compared with the West, the Orthodox tradition underlines more sharply the eschatological dimension of the Christian faith. In that respect, Orthodox Christianity claims to have followed the Early Church, which entered history not so much as a "doctrine" but as a new, otherworldly "social order," a new "community." Time and again, early Christians insisted that their true citizenship (*politeuma*) was not of this world:

> Our citizenship is in heaven, and it is from there that we are expecting a Savior. (Philippians 3:20)

> Here we have no lasting city (*polin*), but we are looking for the city that is to come. (Hebrews 13:14)

And not only this; the members of the Early Church were almost always addressed as strangers and traveling through (*paroikoi* and *parepoidemoi* 1 Peter 2:11) this world. Although the main issue in politics is who does what to whom, these tasks were consciously, although in certain cases reluctantly, transmitted to the lay members of the church, and in time to the secular authorities. This migration of political responsibility results from the incompatibility of using even legitimate force with being and reflecting that glorious and ideal Kingdom of God, which the church (and especially its priestly members) strives to do. Only in special situations, such as when the people of an organized nation request the head of their local Orthodox Church to assume for a while leadership in secular matters, does one find an Orthodox ecclesiastical figure engaged in the politics of this world. The guiding principle for these tasks, both for those belonging to the laity (which by the way is considered in Orthodoxy an ecclesiastical priestly order, without which no liturgical service is possible) and for those coming from the ordained priesthood, is Jesus Christ's admonition to his disciples:

> The rulers of the Gentiles exercise lordship over their subjects; and those in authority over them are called benefactors. But not so with you; rather let the greatest among you become as the youngest, and the leader as one who serves. (Luke 22:25–26, parallel)

Recall that the Orthodox Church considers as its main task to make manifest proleptically (or in anticipation of the promised future reality) in the Eucharist this new, ideal order of the coming Kingdom. To this end, the faithful literally are sent at the end of the service to "go forth in peace" to transmit the experience gained in the Liturgy—even as a glimpse and as a foretaste—of that glorious expected moment. In this respect, the Orthodox faith in fact embraces all aspects of human life. The ultimate basis for such a concern for life and for all that has been created in this world comes from the fundamental doctrine of creation, according to which God—ex nihilo—made all that exists and "saw that it was good" (Genesis 1:4, 10, 13, 18).

Because God's creation was corrupted by sin, however, it became necessary for all of creation to be transformed ("that the creation itself will be set free from its bondage to decay and will obtain the freedom of the glory of the children of God"; Romans 8: 21), to be renewed, to become a "new creation" (2 Corinthians 5:17; Galatians 6:15), a process that started with the incarnation of God Himself in Jesus Christ. The Kingdom of God that Jesus proclaimed did not have an eschatological character alone, but also an earthly one. And his people, the church, the "true" Israel (Galatians 6:16), was in fact "a city," a polis, a new and peculiar "polity." It was more than "a church," just as ancient Israel was at once a "church" and a "nation."

It was for that reason that in the early stages of their existence, Christians were suspected of civic indifference, even of "misanthropy," *odium generis humani* (literally, the "hatred of the human race," probably contrasted with the alleged "philanthropy of the Roman empire"). Origen, responding to a similar accusation by Celsus, insisted that Christians "have another system of allegiance" (*allo systema tes patridos*).[10] And Tertullian even went to the extreme of declaring that for Christians "nothing is more alien than public affairs" (*nec ulla magis res aliena quam publica*).[11] We find a more balanced position, however, in an anonymous letter from the early years of the second century C.E. In the famous *Letter to Diognetus*, Christians are presented as living in the world but not being of the world:

> While they dwell in the cities of Greeks and Barbarians, as the lot of each is cast, the structure of their polity is peculiar and paradoxical. . . . Every fatherland is a foreign land. . . . Their conversation is on earth, but their citizenship is in heaven.[12]

All these are a common heritage of both Eastern and Western Christianity. Where Orthodox Christianity seems to differ from both the Roman Catholic and the Protestant points of view with regard to politics is the famous "Byzantine synthesis," a unique experiment in political matters, which most Orthodox churches and Orthodox societies (some even use the awkward term "Orthodox nations") unfortunately dream to revive, even in the age of modernity and postmodernity.

This experiment was the first Orthodox adventure in Christian politics. According to the renowned Orthodox historian and theologian George Florovsky, "It was an unsuccessful and probably an unfortunate experiment. Yet it should be judged on its own terms."[13] It was wrongly labeled as a "Caesaropapism" (alluding to the combination of the two roles of Caesar and pope) on the assumption that in Byzantium the church ceased to exist as an independent "political" institution, because the emperor became with the agreement of the church its actual ruler. The emperors were indeed rulers in Christian society, and also in religious matters, but never rulers over the church.[14] In fact, this solution to the perennial problem of the relationship between church and state, initiated by the overall policy of Constantine the Great,[15] had its origin in Pauline theology and his understanding of the role of all secular ruling authorities. The ruling secular authorities are understood as being instituted by God, and therefore are of divine origin:

> Let every person be subject to the governing authorities; for there is no authority except from God, and those authorities that exist have been instituted by God. Therefore whoever resists authority resists what God has appointed, and those who resist will incur judgment. For rulers are not a terror to good conduct, but to bad. Do you wish to have no fear of the authority? Then do what is good, and you will receive its approval; for it is God's servant for your good. But if you do what is wrong, you should be afraid, for the authority does not bear the sword in vain! It is the servant of God to execute wrath on the wrongdoer. Therefore one must be subject, not only because of wrath but also because of conscience. For the same reason you also pay taxes, for the authorities are God's servants, busy with this very thing. Pay to all what is due them—taxes to whom taxes are due, revenue to whom revenue is due, respect to whom respect is due, honor to whom honor is due. (Romans 13:1–7)

It was exactly for that reason that in the so-called Pastoral Epistles the faithful are urged even to pray for governing authorities:

> I urge that supplications, prayers, intercessions, and thanksgivings be made for everyone, for kings and all who are in high positions, so that we may lead a quiet and peaceable life in all godliness and dignity. (1 Timothy 2:1–2)

This compromised solution to all the problems dealing with power and the authorities of this world is in effect in agreement with Jesus of Nazareth's clever answer to the religious authorities of his day:

> Give to the emperor the things that are the emperor's, and to God the things that are God's. (Mark 12:17, parallel)[16]

The response of Early Christians to this dilemma, i.e., how to accommodate their simultaneously belonging to secular and to eschatological worlds, was not unanimous. Paul's accommodating views in dealing with the secular authorities are seemingly in sharp contrast with the more radical views expressed by the author of the book of Revelation (chap. 13). There, the secular Roman authorities are compared with the beast, in contrast to the eschatological identity of the church as the "New Jerusalem," making any dealing and connection of the people of God with the hostile secular authorities impossible.[17] I have argued in other related studies that the solution to our problem, offered by

Paul—and in fact to all other social issues—might not have been as idealistic or radical as in the rest of the New Testament. It was, nevertheless, a realistic solution of the *social integration* of the charismatic (and eschatological) people of God into society at large.[18]

This solution reached its climax in the sixth century C.E. It is expressed in a more detailed way in the preface to Justinian's famous *Sixth Novel*, which is a summary of the basic principles of the Byzantine political system, and which has greatly influenced the political views of Orthodox Christianity, even to this day:

> There are two major gifts which God has given unto men of His supernal clemency, the priesthood and the imperial authority—*hierosyne* and *basileia*; *sacerdotium* and *imperium*. Of these, the former is concerned with things divine; the latter presides over the human affairs and takes care of them. Proceeding from the same source, both adorn human life. Nothing is of greater concern for the emperors as the dignity of the priesthood, so that priests may in their turn pray to God for them. Now, if one is in every respect blameless and filled with confidence toward God, and the other does rightly and properly maintain in order the commonwealth to it, there will be a certain fair harmony established to it, there will be a certain fair harmony established, which will furnish whatsoever may be needful for mankind. We therefore are highly concerned for the true doctrines inspired by God for the dignity of priests. We are convinced that, if they maintain their dignity, God will bestow great benefits on us, and we shall firmly hold whatever we now possess, and in addition shall acquire those things that we have not yet secured. A happy ending always crowns those things, which were undertaken in a proper manner, acceptable to God. This is the case, when sacred canons are carefully observed, which the glorious Apostles, the venerable eyewitnesses and ministers of the Divine World, have handed down to us, and the holy Fathers have kept and explained.[19]

The *Sixth Novel*, of course, does not speak of church and state, but of two ministries. And in addition, it was a secular (legal) not a religious (Christian) document. There the *imperium* is at once an authority and a service. This model, very often called "symphony," or *synallelia*, was further developed in the famous *Epanagoge*, a constitutional document of the ninth century C.E., most probably prepared by Photius, the famous Patriarch of Constantinople:[20]

> The temporal power and the priesthood relate to each other as body and soul; they are necessary for state order just as body and soul are necessary in a living man. It is in their linkage and harmony that the well-being of a state lies.[21]

In the *Epanagoge*, however, we notice a slight centralization of power. In the place of the *imperium* and *sacerdotium*, we now have the emperor and the patriarch,[22] not as rivals but as allies, both parts of a single organism, both essential for the prosperity of the people. This model has helped the church in the East to resist the temptation to acquire temporal secular authority and to avoid the temptation to be "clericalized." In addition, Orthodox Christianity did not feel the need to develop the theory of the "two swords," which held such appeal in the West. This may be due to a more classical Greek philosophical background in its ontological thinking, in comparison with the more Roman (i.e., legal) heritage of Western Christianity. It is to be noted that the famous programmatic model and vision of *De civitate Dei*, by Augustine of Hippo (d. 430 C.E.), which was so influential in Western Christianity, did not play a decisive role in the development of Orthodox Christianity's political theory.

Conversely, this enmeshment between church and state, very tight indeed, which has caused so many tensions and even clashes (e.g., in the *iconoclastic* controversy and later in the imperial unionist policy), was not without opposition. For instance, the emergence of monasticism helped Eastern Orthodox Christianity—not without problems of course—to keep the balance between the eschatological vision and the historical missionary engagement of the church. This is especially true in monasticism's later development not as an arm of the institutional church (cf. some medieval orders of Roman Catholicism) but rather as a strong reaction to it, as a constant reminder of the eschatological character of the church, and the eschatological dimension of the Christian faith in general.[23]

Orthodox Christianity and Nonbelievers: Politics and People outside the Tradition

History has shown that Orthodox churches have traditionally taken a tolerant attitude toward nonbelievers by and large. One case in point is the Crusaders, who found the Orthodox in Constantinople unexpectedly and unacceptably tolerant toward the Muslims. Similarly, more openness and hospitality have been granted by the Orthodox to non-Christian "religious cousins" (e.g., in the case of the expelled Jews from the Iberian Peninsula in the sixteenth century).

These were not accidental occurrences. Instead, they were the result of Orthodoxy's Trinitarian understanding of mission, which goes beyond the "Christocentric Christian universalism" developed in the past by Western Christianity. Underlying its response to nonbelievers is Orthodox Christianity's twofold fundamental missiological (having to do with evangelism and outreach) assumption about God: (1) the divine self, God's inner life, is a life of communion; and (2) God's involvement in history aims to draw humanity and creation in general into this communion with the very life of the divine being. Perhaps for this reason, Orthodox Christianity has never developed a universal proselytizing mission.[24] Without relegating their mission to an optional task and neglecting the imperative of bringing new converts to Christ, the Orthodox normally direct their efforts toward the transmission of the life of communion that exists in God, and not toward the propagation of certain doctrines or moral and social norms.

If one carries this understanding of mission a little further, one can even argue that the church's involvement in this present fallen and sinful situation, i.e., its worldly politics, does not actually allow the use of power and coercion that inevitably includes legitimate violence. Rather, the Orthodox understand their task to be that of *witnessing* in a tolerant, loving, and reconciling way to the pro-leptic experience of God's rule (i.e., the Kingdom of God), gained in their litur-gical and eucharistic communal life. According to Orthodox theology, the mis-sion of the church does not focus on the conversion of "others" by the spreading of the Gospel of the abundant love of God to the end of the world (which inevitably leads to a "confessional and religious exclusiveness"). Its mission is to serve in this multicultural and pluralistic world as the witness of the church's eschatological (and certainly not institutional) identity (this can be labeled "eccle-sial inclusiveness"). That understanding of mission has by and large prevented Orthodoxy from all kinds of aggressive proselytism.

For the Orthodox Church, the real aim of evangelism has never been so much bringing nations and people of other faiths to its own religious "enclosure"; its real aim has always been to "let" the Spirit of God use both evangelizers and those to whom they bear witness to bring about God's rule. According to this under-standing, everything belongs to God, and to His Kingdom. In simpler terms, everything belongs to the new eschatological reality, inaugurated of course in Jesus's messianic work but expected to reach its final stage at the end of history. The church in its historical manifestation does not administer all reality, as was believed for centuries in the West; it only prepares the way to that reality, being an icon of it.

Conclusion

In recent years, as a result of the effect of postmodernism and of the resurgence of religion worldwide, some Orthodox societies (at least those with a powerful institutional church, like the Greek and the Russian ones) have shown signs of willingness to allow their churches to reassert their influence on both politics and public life. This *deprivatization* of religion means that the ideal of modernity—to keep church and state (or religion and society) separate, relegating the former to the private or personal realm and declaring the public realm secular and free of all religious influence—is losing ground.

This deprivatization is, of course, a universal phenomenon, mainly due to the shortcomings of modernism. The post-Enlightenment modern critical paradigm, which has undoubtedly shaped our democratic political process, has overrationalized everything from social and public life to scholarship, from emotion to imagination, seeking to overcontrol and overlimit the irrational, the aesthetic, and even the sacred. In its search to rationalize and historicize all, modernism has transformed not only what we know and how we know it, but also how we understand ourselves within that known world. Hence the desire in a wide circle of intellectuals (not limited to scholars or even to theologians) for wholeness, for community, for what in German is called *Gemeinschaft*, for an antidote to the fragmentation and sterility of an overly technocratic society, and in the end for postmodernism.

To be honest, religion is far too important for human existence to be excluded from politics; and this is undoubtedly both a threat and a hope. It is a threat if fundamentalists assume uncontrolled power, as was the case on September 11, 2001. However, it is a hope if religion can exercise its tremendous potential and power to bring back moral values and to recreate or originate new images of what it means to be human in a just, peaceful, and sustainable universe.

Nowadays, this last option is being seriously considered by the Orthodox, if not for anything else, at least because the basic ecclesiological principles of their religious system are incompatible with individualism, one of the pillars of modernity. There is a lot of discussion that the old "Byzantine symphony" can again become a model of Orthodox political theory, but this time not as a symphony of the church with the state but instead directly with citizens.

In addition, any such symphony could not be implemented in isolation from the rest of Christianity but rather in cooperation with it, as an example of a "common Christian witness." Even people of other faiths are considered as partners on certain political issues, as has been shown by the most recent initiatives of the *primus inter pares* Orthodox Patriarchal See of Constantinople and also of other autocephalous Orthodox churches. In our small global village, that mysterious universe, the values of God's Kingdom are common to all people of goodwill, religious or not! Only wicked people could object to their political implementation, provided of course that the basic democratic rules are observed.[25]

Notes

1. In classical Greek philosophy and language (which was the overall language adopted by Christianity to elaborate its doctrine), "political" behavior, i.e., care for the *polis* (the city, the society) was contrasted to a selfish, egocentric lifestyle, i.e., the behavior of the "idiot" (Greek *idiotes*), a term that universally acquired negative connotations. Cf. 1 Corinthians 14:24, where the term *idiotes* is equated with that of the unbeliever.

2. G. Florovsky was right that "Byzantium collapsed as a Christian Kingdom, under the burden of (this) tremendous claim." G. Florovsky, "Antinomies of Christian History: Empire and Desert," in *Christianity and Culture*. vol. 2 of *The Collected Works of Georges*

Florovsky (Belmont, Mass.: Nordland Publishing Company, 1974), 67–100; the quotation is found on p. 83).

3. The majority of the Orthodox positions with regard to a system of church–state relationship take this Byzantine model as the only acceptable one in the Orthodox world, despite the above-mentioned remarks of Florovsky.

4. Cf. Saint Harakas, "Church and State in Orthodox Thought," *Greek Orthodox Theological Review* 27 (1982): 5–21; E. Clapsis, *Orthodoxy in Conversation: Orthodox Ecumenical Engagements* (Geneva and Brookline, Mass.: World Council of Churches Publications and Holy Cross Orthodox Press, 2000); Th. Hopko, "Orthodoxy in Post-Modern Pluralistic Societies," *Ecumenical Review* 51 (1999): 364–71.

5. The final documents were originally published in the journal *Episkepsis* (December 15, 1986), and they have since received wide circulation, being translated into many languages. According to a decision of the consultation, they all have a binding canonical status for the Orthodox, even before their final synodical (ecumenical?) approval (p. 9 n).

6. The final document (now available at www.incommunion.org/misc) deals with "those aspects of the life of the state and society, which were and are equally relevant for the whole Church at the end of the 20th century and in the near future." It is a document of a local Autocephalous Orthodox Church, primarily aimed at providing her members "the basic provisions of her teaching on church-state relations and a number of problems socially significant today" (preamble).

7. This may be because some of the positions taken reflect rather conservative views, not shared by all Orthodox. In addition, the wide range of themes tackled (anthropological, ecological, bioethical, educational) may need further theological examination. But mainly because of the principles underlined above in the first section. After all, the Russian Orthodox, being aware of all these, does not claim for the document anything more than that it "reflects the official position of Moscow Patriarchate on relations with the state and secular society" (*Basis of the Social Concept of the Russian Orthodox Church*). Despite all these limitations, the document is a courageous first attempt by an official Orthodox institution to deal with social problems, in the way Western Christians have been responding to modern everyday challenges in the last centuries, and for this reason it must be judged accordingly.

8. *Basis of the Social Concept of the Russian Orthodox Church*, III 4.

9. P. Vassiliadis, "Orthodoxy and Ecumenism," *Eucharist and Witness. Orthodox Perspectives on the Unity and Mission of the Church* (Geneva and Brookline, Mass.: World Council of Churches Publications and Holy Cross Orthodox Press, 1998), pp. 7–27, especially 15.

10. Origen, *Contra Celsum* VIII, 75.

11. Tertullian, *Apologeticum* 38,3. Cf. also his statement in *De Pallio*: "I have withdrawn myself from the society (*secessi de populo*)" (5).

12. *Ad Diognetum* 5,6.

13. Florovsky, "Antinomies," 77.

14. Florovsky, "Antinomies." Dvornik was certainly right that "in most ways the Byzantine emperors followed the example of their 'predecessors' David and Solomon when organizing religious life" (*Early Christian and Byzantine Political Philosophy. Origins and Background*, vol. 1 (Washington, D.C., no publisher given, 1966), p. 301.

15. The importance of Constantine's religious policy rests not so much on the implementation of the religious freedom of his subjects, not even on his conversion to Christianity. It rests, instead, on the fact that he introduced a major shift in politics, by replacing the cosmocentric theories of Greco-Roman antiquity with the theocentric worldview of Christianity, a process which was dramatically ended in post-Enlightenment modernity. In the person of Constantine, the church recognized the possibility of implementing its catholicity, but also the founder of its visible ecumenicity, and for that reason it canonized him with the honorable title of *isapostolos* (equal to the apostles).

16. The other biblical reference, which usually enters in the discussion, i.e., Peter and the rest of the Apostles' statement, "We must obey God rather than any human authority" (Acts 5:29), has more general connotations.

17. Theologically interpreted, the book of Revelation expresses the victory of the oppressed over the impersonal and oppressing secular institutions, the victory of the "politics of theology" over the (pseudo-) "theology of politics."

18. P. Vassiliadis, "The Church and State Relationship in the N.T. (With Special Reference to the Pauline Theology)," *Biblical Hermeneutical Studies* (2000): 435–44 (in Greek); cf. also my "Your Will Be Done. Reflections from St. Paul," in *Eucharist and Witness*, 77–84.

19. R. Schoel and W. Kroll, *Corpus Juris Civilis*, vol. 3 (Berlin, no publisher given, 1928), 35ff.

20. The *Epanagoge* was in fact a draft that has never been officially promulgated. However, substantial portions of it were incorporated in later legislation, but most important, it received wide circulation and appreciation throughout the Orthodox world.

21. J. Zepos and P. Zepos, eds., *Jus Graecoromanum*, vol. 2 (Athens: no publisher given, 1931), 240ff.

22. "The Patriarch is a living and animate image of Christ, characterizing the truth in deeds and words." The role of the patriarch (in rank after the emperor) was threefold: (1) to preserve the faith of the Orthodox believers, (2) to make any possible effort that the heretics be reunited to the church, and (3) "finally to behave in such a brilliant, most glorious, and admirable way so that those outside the faith be attracted and imitate the faith" (*Epanagoge*, in *Jus Graecoromanum*, 242).

23. More in Florovsky, "Antinomies," 83ff.

24. Cf. I. Bria, ed., *Go Forth in Peace. Orthodox Perspectives on Mission* (Geneva: World Council of Churches Press, 1986), 3.

25. More in Vassiliadis, *Postmodernity and the Church* (Athens: Akritas Publications, 2002).

Suggested Readings

"The Basis of the Social Concept of the Russian Orthodox Church." Available at www.incommunion.org/misc.

Clapsis, Emmanuel. *Orthodoxy in Conversation: Orthodox Ecumenical Engagements*. Geneva and Brookline, Mass.: World Council of Churches Publications and HCO Press, 2000.

Dvornik, Fr. *Early Christian and Byzantine Political Philosophy: Origins and Background*, vol. 1. Washington, D.C. (no publisher given), 1966.

Fitzgerald, Thomas. *The Orthodox Church*. Westport, Conn.: Greenwood Press, 1995.

Florovsky, Georges. "Antinomies of Christian History: Empire and Desert." In *Christianity and Culture*, vol. 2 of *The Collected Works of Georges Florovsky*. Belmont, Mass.: Nordland Publishing Company, 1974.

———. *Bible, Church, Tradition: An Eastern Orthodox View*. Belmont, Mass.: Nordland Publishing Co., 1972.

Harakas, Stanley S. *Wholeness of Faith and Life: Orthodox Christian Ethics*. Brookline, Mass.: HCO Press, 1999.

Lossky, Vladimir. *The Mystical Theology of the Eastern Church*. London: Clarke, 1957.

Pelikan, Jaroslav. *The Christian Tradition 2: The Spirit of Eastern Christendom (600–1700)*. Chicago: University of Chicago Press, 1974.

Meyendorff, John. *Byzantine Theology. Historical Trends and Doctrinal Themes*. Crestwood, N.Y.: SVS Press, 1987.

Schmemann, Alexander. *Church, World, Mission*. Crestwood, N.Y.: SVS Press, 1979.

Staniloae, Dumitru. *The Experience of God*. Brookline, Mass.: HCO Press, 1994.

Vassiliadis, Petros. *Eucharist and Witness: Orthodox Perspectives on the Unity and Witness of the Church*. Geneva and Brookline, Mass.: World Council of Churches Publications and HCO Press, 1998.

Ware, Kallistos (Timothy). *The Orthodox Church*. Baltimore: Penguin Books, 1964 (and numerous subsequent editions).

Zepos, J., and P. Zepos, eds. *Jus Graecoromanum*, vol. 2. Athens (no publisher given), 1931.

Zizioulas, John. *Being as Communion. Studies in Personhood and the Church*. Crestwood, N.Y.: SVS Press, 1985.

Five | **Reformation Christianity** |

Martin E. Marty

NEARLY FIVE CENTURIES AGO, WESTERN CHRISTIANITY WENT THROUGH A PERIOD OF dramatic upheaval, which changed not only the religious landscape but also the political landscape of Christendom. As with most periods of dramatic transition, no one knew early on exactly what was emerging or what the outcome would be. However, astute observers of the time would have perceived numerous forces coming together all at once, challenging the relatively homogeneous realm of the Roman Catholic Church to reform itself, or else face the breakup of its domain. "Reformation Christianity" is the broad label we apply to the diverse Christian movements that emerged in Europe and the West during the sixteenth century C.E., and the religious and political dimensions of this variegated movement are the subject of this chapter.

Clarifying Theses

In an effort to make things clear and, I hope, memorable, let me propose some theses, in advance of my discussion of the politics of Reformation Christianity. Reformation Christianity left as its legacy at least seven elements of political theory. First, God the Creator is the agent behind politics. God is sovereign, gracious, and mysterious. Humans are to be responsible, but they cannot rightfully claim to be sure that their acts are congruent with God's will. Negatively stated: The political order is never "merely" a human creation.

Second, discernment of the will of God finds its source or reference in the sacred Scriptures of the faith, though such efforts at discernment will not bring respondents to absolute assurance that they have rightly acted. There is no supreme ecclesial authority, such as the papacy—from which Protestants separated—to determine resolutions. Protestants in the tradition of Reformation Christianity are divided over scriptural interpretation, and also over politics.

Third, this tradition is ordinarily dualistic; the sovereign God acts in one order through divine law and promotes justice. The same God, as a gracious deity, acts in the other order through the Gospel and promotes salvation. The former is essential in the political ordering.

Fourth, believers are called to obedience to God even as they act at the side of nonbelievers. Some in this tradition hold in theory to the belief that they must work to see the development of political orders in which believers have privilege or monopoly. Others see God working equally through believer and nonbeliever.

Fifth, in this tradition, there is a strong accent on the vocation or calling of lay people to civic responsibility. "The priesthood of all believers" is supposed to minimize deference to hierarchical authority, at least within the church. The political agent is, in God's eyes, equal to the religious professional as he or she works out this vocation.

Sixth, such an outlook predisposes Reformation Christianity toward democratic thinking. This does not mean that this tradition immediately worked for democratic politics or could have realized it where it exists without partnerships. But when the opportunity came for its development, those of this heritage came to embrace and further it.

Seventh, Reformation Christianity in theory proclaims what has been called "the Protestant principle of prophetic protest." That means that the judgment of God and critical thinking and activity are to be directed as much to one's own people, believing community, cause, nation, or movement as it is to that of "the other." But this is theory; in practice, this motif (like some of the others) is often neglected or muted.

Defining Reformation Christianity as Religion: Protestantism Plus

Heirs of the tradition here called Reformation Christianity seldom think of their "Reformation" background and realization as a "religion." If they use the word religion, as they must in encyclopedias, textbooks, and curricula, they restrict it to the noun: they are Christian. They see their movement(s) as the working out of the Christian faith, church, and culture through the twenty centuries after Christ. So on the large scale of being an altogether separate religion, neither Reformation Christianity, nor Eastern Orthodoxy, is comparable to Judaism or Islam. Yet the adjective "Reformation" tells much about the distinctions of this branch of "the Christian religion," adhered to by several hundred million people around the world.

To most readers in our time who are at all aware of religious history, "Reformation Christianity" equals "Protestantism." All Protestantism is a descendant of European movements of reform in the sixteenth century.

We shall treat the two terms as rough equivalents, after having introduced several cautions about the limits of such an approach. There are four ways to do that. First, the Reformation Christianity that became Protestantism did not have a patent on reform of the Christian Church in Western Europe. (We are talking only of the West; Eastern or Orthodox Christianity may have experienced "reformations" from time to time, but its leaders rather serenely ignored the tensions that led to the breakup in the sixteenth century of unified Western Christianity, which before that time meant exclusively Roman Catholicism.) That is to say, there were many movements of reform that remained in the Roman Catholic Church. Leaders of some of these may have displayed similarities to the accents and trends that became Protestant, but they did not forsake papal obedience, nor were they excommunicated.

One must take great care to remember and to remind others that there was also a "Roman Catholic Reformation" in the late fifteenth and early sixteenth centuries. So it is that some Roman Catholics could say and would say, if it were not confusing to hearers, "*We* represent Reformation Christianity."

A second reservation to keep in mind when roughly equating Reformation Christianity with Protestantism is this: Many reform movements that inspired the causes that became Protestant were cut short and had no chance to develop into a full-blown movement. Thus in the fourteenth and fifteenth centuries, leaders such as John Wycliffe in England and Jan Hus in Bohemia anticipated many of the accents later developed by those historians regard as the originators of the Protestant Reformation. Most such leaders had to challenge both the papacy and their temporal rulers, be they kings or emperors. And that challenge led to their death. Think of their contributions as being "Pre-Reformation Christianity."

A third reason for being a bit cautious about terms has to do with later Protestant movements that do not like to think of themselves as being heirs of Reformation Christianity. This is the case among American-born church bodies such as the Christian Church (Disciples of Christ) and the various bodies that call themselves the Churches of Christ or the Church of Christ. Nevertheless, in the eyes of sociologists of religion or opinion poll-takers, they do not succeed in disentangling themselves from Reformation Christianity. They clearly are neither Orthodox nor Roman Catholic, and they tend to focus on teachings that others associate with the Protestant Reformation.

However, their leaders saw themselves as not deriving from the Christian agencies associated with names of people in the sixteenth century, names such as Henry VIII in England, John Knox in Scotland, John Calvin in the Netherlands and Switzerland—and Huldreich Zwingli also needs to be mentioned, in that case—and parts of Germany, or Martin Luther in Germany and Scandinavia. These nineteenth-century innovators instead believed that they were reclaiming a primitive, pure, original, innocent, apostolic Christian world that had been obscured in Roman Catholicism as well as in what looked to them like a too-complicated set of Reformation churches. Their leaders, Alexander Campbell and Barton Stone among others, taught them to say something like "Where the Bible speaks, we speak; where the Bible is silent, we are silent." For them, most of what happened between the first and the eighteenth centuries was not only beside the point but seriously obscured the true faith of the Apostles. Despite the respect we must show such "primitive" movements for their efforts at self-definition, it is obvious to those who study them that in politics, our present concern, they match Protestant Reformation Christianity in most respects.

A fourth reason to be a bit wary about the terms we must necessarily use is that to anyone who wants to be patient and accurate, there is no such thing as Reformation Christianity. There are only Reformation Christianities. In the United States and Canada alone, there are more than two hundred bodies listed in the censuslike church yearbooks, bodies that are neither Orthodox nor Roman Catholic and would be considered Protestant. The Orthodox Church claims to be "one," even if it has several jurisdictions, based in part on geography and ethnicity. Roman Catholicism, for all its internal variety, claims to be and is "one" because in the end it yields to the papacy in matters of authority and organization. Not so with Protestantism, which from day one—if, indeed, we can isolate such a day—was divided and produced diverse expressions.

What Reformation-Tradition Christians Hold and Reject

Having set out so many qualifications, the reader may wonder what is left. Here come words of cheer to those who would seek a plot, a way of making sense of the realities around them. Alert to the differences among the Protestant churches and with fingers figuratively crossed, we shall find some common features in most of Reformation Christianity, even if some of them are negative—meaning defined by what they are *not*. With these in mind, we shall be free to deal responsibly with those differences.

To get to the positive point as quickly as possible, we note what Reformation Christians unanimously are *not*. Unlike the vast majority of Christians in the West until soon after 1500 C.E., and unlike all Christians at that time who were officially established and had privileges, they were not under papal obedience. That does not mean that many of them did not and do not consider themselves to be "catholic."

Notice that until the previous sentence, the eight times the word "Catholic" appeared it came with an adjective, "Roman." That was the case because again, as a matter of historical accuracy and in the interests of sensitivity, we cannot restrict the word "Catholic" to Roman Catholicism. Many members of the largest non–Roman Catholic expressions, the Anglican Communion, will correct you every time you even call them Protestant, or at least if you forget to say that they are also Catholic. (Many of them will settle for "catholic" with a lowercase "c," which literally means "universal.") Lutherans, Presbyterians, and many others who get categorized as Protestant also recite the ancient creeds and with them confess "I believe in one holy, *catholic*, and apostolic church."

For non–Roman Catholic Christians, this means that they are in continuity with the universal church that dates back to Jesus Christ and has existed throughout the centuries. But if they are "Catholic," they are emphatically not "Roman" Catholic, for the reason mentioned above: They reject the pope as Christ's uniquely legitimate representative on earth. The pope is, of course, a bishop, one of many bishops, at the Vatican and governing Rome.

That situation does not offend non–Roman Catholic bodies that themselves have bishops, again and especially, Anglicans and Lutherans. The fact that there is one "presiding" bishop for Roman Catholics, in this case at Rome, is also not offensive as such to almost any Protestant body. Most of them elect a president, a moderator, a presiding bishop. They may recognize a wide range of powers in such a person. What offended Protestants—who acquired that name when some of them were involved in a protest in German territories in 1529—was the set of claims that came with the papacy. These, of course, had a bearing on their political resolutions.

Protestants rejected the notion that the pope was Christ's vicar. They vehemently refused to believe with Roman Catholics that outside his church, and thus apart from papal leadership, according to official sixteenth-century Catholic doctrine (less stressed today) there is no salvation. This Roman claim left churches in the Reformation tradition incapable of being the bearers of salvation-work. They rejected the notion reinforced and made official only in the late nineteenth century that the pope is infallible with respect to faith and morals. Because he often governed in earthly affairs, at times in congruence with and sometimes in rivalry with emperors and kings, they challenged the role of the pope and broke ties to him, dismissing his authority over them.

Some years ago, I was assigned the task of writing a book called simply *Protestantism*. Having read the doctrines and observed the practices of the Protestant bodies in search of what they held in common and that no one else, in Catholicism or Orthodoxy, held, I could find nothing beside nonpapacy to be a universal Protestant position. Most Protestants, it is true, liked to say that they were gathered around themes such as "grace" and "Scripture," but Catholics would not let them get away with claiming a monopoly on these. Of course, some Catholic teachings were abhorrent to most Protestants. These included prayer to the saints, the elevation of Mary the mother of Jesus to quasi-divine status, "gaining salvation in part by works," and the like. But one can always find Protestants, at least toward the Anglo-Catholic end of the spectrum, who keep some practices that many other Protestants would regard as Roman Catholic.

Here we have made so much of the rejection of the papacy because observation of that theological position opens the door to the many kinds of adjustments the Western Christians who are identified with the Reformation and Protestantism made in governance, in relation to authority, and thus, following the guiding theme of this book, in politics. If the pope was not to govern, not to mediate the spiritual concerns in the temporal world of politics, who would? If the papacy was not to be the authority, but Scripture was, who would decide how to determine what Scripture has to say? That is an important question, because various scripturally based Reformation movements disagreed with each other significantly while each claimed that it derived its approach from Scripture. This fact became the basis for many taunts directed at Reformation Christianity by Roman Catholic and Eastern Orthodox Christians. Because the Bible is held in such high esteem within Reformation Christianity, we need to investigate what it and the other ancient (authoritative) Christian sources say about politics.

Classical Sources of Reformation Christianity on Politics

"This religion," internally divided Protestantism already in the Reformation era of the sixteenth century, was also divided as to which are the classical sources and which have authority. But that there are classical sources is obvious in every case, and we must discern some of the key ones.

The Hebrew Scriptures

Because all of Reformation Christianity claimed itself to be congruent with and faithful to "original" Christianity, as even the "primitive" bodies that were born in the nineteenth century would also contend, it means that they all inherited some of their political views from the Hebrew Scriptures, their Old Testament, and from the New Testament. To mention this may mean that there will be some overlapping of themes in this survey with what others write about Judaism first and then, more closely, about Early Christianity, Roman Catholicism, and Orthodox Christianity. Of course, each interpreted these classical texts in different ways.

The Old Testament was indeed a dominant classical source for political thinking. No Protestants saw themselves as being simply "the children of Israel," which would have meant their being governed by Yahweh through a priesthood and other authorities, though many saw themselves *complicatedly* so. Reformation Christianity inherited and interpreted the Ten Commandments, and many stretched teachings connected with them into the political order. Thus prominent Reformation leaders like Martin Luther expounded the Decalogue in his *Small Catechism* and took the command to honor parents into other realms of obedience, including government. Elders in home as well as church and state demanded and deserved respect and obedience.

Many Protestant reformers (after this, we will capitalize that word to suggest a definite body of people at a particular time in history) derived more political and governmental thought from the Old Testament than from the New Testament, from the Hebrew Scriptures than from the earliest decisively Christian documents such as the Gospels and Epistles. Whoever has read the writings of the American Puritans who settled New England, and had much influence on later

American politics, will have found them citing "the laws of Moses" and telling stories based on the Hebrew Scriptures when determining what positive laws should say. If, for instance, those laws condemned bestiality, the laws of the land had to forbid it as well and to stipulate penalties for offenders, penalties sometimes also stipulated in the Pentateuch, which to those Puritans was "the five books of Moses" in the beginning of their canon, their Bible.

Only a few wilder-eyed and dreaming sectarians—I am momentarily adopting the view of "establishment" Protestants here by using their stigmatizing terms— ever tried to work out simple equations linking governors in their time and governing leaders as recorded in the Hebrew Scriptures. Thus the governor of Massachusetts Bay or Connecticut was not an exact match for figures like Moses and Aaron or the judges and kings of Israel. Sometimes the Protestant movements did aspire to form theocracies founded directly on the Hebrew Scriptures, as many observers saw John Calvin's Geneva or John Winthrop's Massachusetts Bay to be. But most of them were realistic about the differences between the situation of ancient Israel's chosen people and their own circumstances. Still, wherever they could, they wanted to connect earthly rule with divine sanction, whether that meant the sanction of a monarch, a prince, a ruling assembly, or, much later, democratically elected rulers.

The New Testament Gospels

Because New Testament authors, especially the Apostle Paul in his letters, went out of their way to say that the saving work of Jesus Christ freed believers from the bonds of "the law," only the Decalogue served as a universal religious or scriptural guide to governance. Human-made law, in Reformation Christians' eyes, dared not violate those Ten Commandments. But citizens were free from most of the hundreds of ritual laws that governed Judaism.

One example of this pertains to a central issue in both Judaism and Christianity, namely, observing the Sabbath. Reformation Christianity inherited and kept the Orthodox and Catholic practice of moving the Sabbath from Saturday—as specified in the creation accounts of Genesis and observed in Judaism—to Sunday, which in early times, for most Christians, came to be observed as the festival of the resurrection of Jesus on that day. (In the nineteenth century, and in smaller ways in other times and places, "Seventh-Day" Adventists or Baptists went back to Saturday observance. But when most Protestants, especially the already-mentioned Puritans, wanted to legislate Sabbath observance, they chose Sunday.)

Reformation Christianity prioritized responsible interpretation of the *whole* Bible, *both* "Testaments," though ordinarily Protestants did not include the Deuterocanonical books of the Apocrypha, which were equally authoritative for Catholics. They were specially cautious to avoid the perception that their exposition might in fact be rejecting the authority of the Old Testament, even if they did see the New Testament's witness as a rejection of the legalism that they found in the Old Testament. They were most concerned about eternal salvation, about how one became right with God, or "justified." For that, the law was not of positive use. It applied to the earthly realm, including politics.

So the Protestants were selective about what they carried over from the Old Testament. Most Reformation Christian movements, however, made up as they were of believers in salvation through Jesus Christ, were less ambiguously devoted to the New Testament as a classical source for their politics than to the Hebrew Bible.

Here is where trouble came in, trouble that suggests why Puritans and many before them commented more on Old Testament than on New Testament descriptions and prescriptions of the God-pleasing life with respect to the temporal and the political. There is a clear reason for that. Though they may not all have used the term "eschatological," which means "dealing with the *eschaton*," the end of the world as they knew it, they could read that the writers of the New Testament did picture the world ending soon. Of course, fifteen centuries later, believers had to have laws and to govern and be governed socially in the mean time. They were to "occupy" the lands and the times until Jesus would come again. But the words of Jesus as set forth in the Gospels are seldom encouraging to anyone who wants to establish a political order based on them.

That eschatological vision portrays Jesus as always in a hurry, demanding immediate obedience to the reign of God and freeing disciples from many legal and religious bonds and bounds. In the Sermon on the Mount (Matthew 5–7) he was cited as taking one or another of the Ten Commandments and then raising the bar to humanly impossible levels. The law said, "Do not kill." Jesus claimed this also meant, "Do not hate." The law said, "Do not commit adultery." He made this difficult if not, again, impossible to follow: Any man who had even looked with desire on a woman had already committed adultery in his heart.

Jesus was quoted as being emphatic that his kingdom was not "of this world," a fact that logically rendered it nonpolitical. Gospel stories show Jesus having to instruct disciples and would-be followers that he was *not* an earthly Messiah who would occupy the throne of David, throw off the yoke of the Roman Empire and other oppressors, and rule the day-to-day affairs of Israel, including what his supporters saw themselves to be, a New Israel, a chosen people.

While engaging in such intended corrective work, the Jesus of the Gospels, that central classical Christian source, was even portrayed as disdainful of government, earthly authority, as Reformation Christianity, eager to be faithful to the scriptural word, could not help but see in the Gospels. Herod, on any organizational or political flowchart, had to be the immediate temporal authority to whom Jesus must defer; but Jesus sneered at Rome's political puppet as "that fox." That is hardly the kind of term one uses when bowing low in deference and reverence. Out of such an attitude, one could hardly hope to teach and live with "the divine right of kings," which is what most in Reformation Christianity continued for a time to recognize, even when they chafed under unjust or anti-Protestant kings.

A second illustration has to do with a Gospel scene in which some Jews, eager to trap Jesus, asked whether they should pay taxes to Caesar or not. Any direct answer would get him in trouble, with Jews as pictured in such stories and with Rome, whose Caesar was embossed on the coins used to pay imperial taxes. Jesus's indirect answer was a question or two: Do you have a coin to show me? Someone in the crowd must have reached into the coin bag and offered one to him.

A second question: Whose image is on it? Naturally, the modern non-Jewish reader thinks: Caesar's. Let it go at that. Not at all. In the first century c.e., Jews were not supposed to be carrying around images of gods—which Caesar Augustus and other Roman Emperors claimed to be—because that would challenge the uniqueness and authority of Yahweh. In effect, the second question was: What are you righteous people doing practicing idolatry by the very act of cherishing coins with that idol on them? One can almost hear an "Ugh!" from Jesus: a coin with an image is dirty. Give it back to the figure whose image is on it, Caesar. And meanwhile, render to God the things that are God's, including your ultimate allegiance.

Such a text is often put to use positively in patriotic sermons in republics where church and state are somehow separated but mutually to be recognized. It is used to suggest not only separation but also balance. For Jesus, that could not be further from the point; this theme is a valuing of the divine kingdom and a devaluing of the coin of the realm. It would be hard to pursue a political order in which there is no pattern of financing operations. And here is Jesus having little interest in politics and so much interest in a kingdom above, apart from, and beyond politics, giving no charter for Reformation Christianity in its faithfulness to Scripture as it replaces papal rule with a political order of its own.

The New Testament Epistles

Reformation Christianity's New Testament classical source, however, did not draw only on the gospels, which center on the life and teachings of Jesus of Nazareth. Its leaders deduced some political notions from the Epistles, which also center on Jesus Christ, but more specifically on the meaning of his life and teachings for the life of the early church, as interpreted by Paul the Apostle and by others whose Epistles come attached to names such as "Peter" and "James" and "John." Although the letters of Paul were probably written before the Gospels were produced in the form we can read today, Paul never knew Jesus the rabbi of Nazareth, Jesus "after the flesh." Paul's Jesus Christ was the subject of a revelation, an experience matched by all other believers who believed in Jesus but were not eyewitnesses.

Paul, as revered a "classical source" as anyone in Reformation Christianity, was friendlier than the Jesus of the Gospels to the political order. Again, there were ambiguities. Paul the rabbi and Roman citizen could speak of that political order as the locale for "principalities and powers" that could war and did war against Jesus Christ and his believing people. Paul, also eschatologically minded, contended that the time for such authorities to rule was short. Their powers were limited, as was to be evident as the new order that came with belief in Jesus was emerging. Still, there was an indeterminate "meantime," and in that meantime, Rabbi Paul, who made radical breaches with Jewish law, read his Hebrew Bible with an interest in anchoring everything in nonlegal free grace effected by and embodied in Jesus.

In that mean time, Paul the Roman citizen—in some biblical narratives, glimpsed as a proud man who knew how to use his citizenship to survive and make his way—spoke well of the authority that happened at that time to be Roman. In a famous passage in his letter to the church in Rome (Romans 13), he provided a charter taken over wholesale into political interpretation by Martin Luther and fated to be central to the political theory in force in many mainstream versions of Reformation Christianity. Paul commanded every soul to be subject to the higher authority—he was speaking of the very Roman empire that was harassing Christians!—considering it to be ordained of God. Thus, he insisted, it was worthy, even when it acted unworthily; it merited obedience, and because it was appointed by God was not to be resisted. Expressed radically: To resist the authority was to go against the ordinance of God.

Other epistolary advice told believers to "honor the king" and to be supportive of earthly government, something that many found hard to do in early Christian times. They thought it did not pay to offer allegiance because the world was ending and the rule was harsh—after all, the government was persecuting them. Many in the Reformation era of the sixteenth century also found such obedience hard to offer to their ruling authorities, both civil and religious. That "higher authority" was for most of them then a mix of the papacy, which in their eyes had too much of a hold on temporal affairs, and the holy Roman emperor, whose interests did not match theirs and who tried to stem Reformation impulses.

Of course, the New Testament also in the Epistles was concerned that Christians get their priorities right, to give obeisance first to God and to relativize all political orders to God's directives. Such references inspired the politics of some on what is often called the "left wing of the Reformation," the "radical Reformation." These set themselves not only in opposition to the holy Roman emperor and the papacy but also against Protestant orders as these came to prevail in many territories and emergent nations in northern and northwestern Europe. So there is no such thing as an unambiguous Protestant response to the charter documents in their only determinative classical source, the Bible as interpreted by contending and differing Reformers.

Early Christian Thought, Especially Augustinian

Although most Protestant movements adopted the ancient creeds of the church, the Apostolic, Nicene, and Athanasian, these offer no direct word about politics. Most found the ancient creedal formulas about the divine Trinity and the nature of Christ congenial, but these also did not include anything of a political nature. (Historians will note, however, that the way doctrinal formulas turned out was often influenced by politics.) Thus, emperors in the officially established Christian church in the fourth century C.E. took sides on doctrines, and some statements of church councils were influenced by the fact that an emperor was present at, or absent from, a council where these matters were to be decided.

If these classical sources are generally silent on our subject, it was because they dealt with other than political questions. In turn, some unofficial writings from the fourth century, when Christianity officially became the religion of the West, and from the sixteenth century, when Western unity began to break up, *did* have influence, if not full authority. Most notable among these for the Reformers was the work of Saint Augustine of Hippo (d. 430), who in *Civitas Dei* (*The City of God*) wrote what certainly has to be called a classic Christian exposition of religion and politics in the Roman Empire. This was a book that some called a "Charter for Christendom." That suffix "-dom" suggests dominion or rule, and Christendom really meant that part of the world ruled by Christian authority.

Papal Catholics may have read Augustine in one way, but most Protestant Reformers read him in quite another. His classic *The City of God* differentiated between the concerns of the "earthly" and the "heavenly" city. It thus provided perspective as to what was really important—the heavenly city—and relativized the temporal order. Still, Augustine gave that second regimen considerable weight. Someone has said that you do not write a 1,000-page book explaining why Rome "fell" and take pains not to overassign blame to Christians for that fall, unless you have some kind of regard for the temporal city, in that case Rome.

Augustine, in the eyes of the Reformers, did not give very hearty assent to the grandeur of political authority. At one time, he legitimated it as being necessary for human order, using the rather shady analogy (to political leaders) of thieves. Even bands of thieves, he noted, had to select someone among them to lead them. Those Reformers who wanted to undercut the absolute authority of the rulers that they inherited, and even those who sometimes would limit those governances that they themselves had, often indirectly, helped set up, could use such a passage for perspective.

What Protestants mainly took from Augustine and propelled into later history was a formulation of dualism. It was not an approach that left God out of half the picture, but it described different ways God was active in the world and in the "Kingdom of God," then often identified with the church catholic. (One could put a marker here that says: "Watch this. It will show up in Protestant theory.") Some Protestants, Luther preeminently, liked to talk about "two kingdoms," without letting God out of the picture in either one of them. Caution: Do not equate the two cities with "church" and "state," but realize that the church signifies, it points to, the fuller heavenly city.

The Reformers in general found themselves attacking most of the classical sources of the Roman Catholicism of their day. They worked in tandem with a band of scholars called Humanists, who were developing critical historical tools and using them on inherited documents. Some such as the "Donation of Constantine" they showed to be a pure forgery, though it had been claimed as an instrument that gave authority also to the papacy and the Roman Catholic church to rule on earth. Such exposure of forgeries or such revisionist history concerning the contexts in which inherited documents had appeared served to help make possible the setting up of an alternative authority to that of Rome, though it did not provide classical sources for the positive teaching and practice of Reformation Christianity.

Together with Roman Catholicism and Orthodox Christianity, Reformation Christianity subscribed to the authority of the Bible and the ancient creeds. However, because they viewed themselves as both true bearers of the Christian faith and renewers of the existing church, the Reformers devoted much effort to generating documents reflecting their new understandings of Christianity. The classical sources of Reformation Christianity, then, came to include the documents produced by Reformation movements and Reformers. To them we turn next, along with an explanation of the theory (or theories) of politics advocated by Reformation Christianity.

Reformation Christianity's Theory of Politics

Given the centrality of Scripture to Reformation Christianity, it is no surprise that translating the Bible into modern European languages—the languages of the people—became a major thrust of the Reformers. Equally important was their effort to explain and debate the theology, as well as the political theory, they were proposing. These explanations and debates were aimed at swaying the ecclesial powers that controlled the religious realm, and also the emperors and kings who governed their respective domains. For this reason, Reformation Christianity's theory of politics was not identical throughout Christendom, but took different forms in different geographical locations. Our survey of these Reformation era classical sources corresponds to the places where they were created, the languages in which they were articulated, and the respective Protestant groups for which they became authoritative.

The Church of England and Anglicanism

Almost no Reformation movement came into being for the purpose of stating a theory of politics and the social order. At the same time, in almost no such movement can one describe politics as being tangential—or certainly as unimportant. The nearest one comes to an exception as an agent of a political order, and it is an important exception indeed, is the Church of England, which became the mother church for the worldwide Anglican Communion. This is the body that first severed itself from the papacy during the reign of Henry VIII, who had fallen out with Roman Catholicism thanks largely to its disapproval of his personal marital vagaries. Of course, Henry's experience was not all that the Anglican Reformation was about. Decades before he came to power, John Wycliffe and the Wycliffites, the Lollards, and other movements were restless with Rome. They set out on the dangerous task of providing Bible translations in English, the language of the common people, which was a threat to the monarch regardless of whether he or she was Roman Catholic or Protestant. They advocated much more authority by lay people than Rome was willing to tolerate. Some of them wanted to reform practices connected with the sacraments, to accent grace instead of law in the path of salvation, or to attack the immorality of the clergy. But it was Henry's move that occasioned the original and central political adjustment.

When Henry broke with Rome, he appropriated all of the Roman Catholic church's property (e.g., churches, monasteries, and land) and functionaries (e.g., priests and bishops), which were renamed the Church of England, much like a modern hostile corporate takeover. That move meant that the Church of England claimed that it was the direct and proper successor to the Apostles. Its bishops, no longer obedient to the pope, they contended, were in unbroken succession to the Apostles in the "historic episcopate" and possessed special authority for that reason. In a move consolidating the power of the secular and sacred into one office, the English monarch in 1534 officially became the head of the Church of England and, equally officially, the Defender of the Faith. This meant royal supremacy over the church.

Of course, this change did not go unchallenged. Briefly, after 1553, the ardent Roman Catholic Queen Mary Tudor reverted to Catholic monarchical ways. But still much of Henry's approach remained, and it was restored when non–Roman Catholic monarchs again acceded. And there were challenges from those who favored Presbyterian ways—ruling through "elders"—or separatist and "congregational" modes (these related, for example, to the Puritan tradition). But Henry's basic approach dominated. Throughout the centuries, the Church of England domestically has devoted much of its energy to canon law, to retaining a church established by law, to being the would-be official expression of the faith of the English people, and to issues of authority. All the while, it identified ever more with doctrines, embodied in its "Thirty-Nine Articles," that were expressive of Protestant views of divine grace.

There are, indeed, some classical sources for Anglican politics. But in most cases they manifest theologically something of a hit-and-miss character, an adjustment to circumstances, active as these were in the church's necessary political adjustments and inventions. These were urgent because in almost all cases religious reform was connected to impulses of popular dissent. In all those cases, it was necessary to formulate new ways to rule.

Scandinavian Lutheranism

Sometimes the transition was easy. When Reformation Christianity came to Scandinavia—to Sweden and Denmark and what was to become Norway—the Catholic bishops became Lutheran, and the civil rulers, having determined to follow a Lutheran path and to break with Rome, ruled much as they had previously. Of course, they no longer inhibited the Lutherans who represented Reformation Christianity. Instead, they gave them support, and the once–Roman Catholic establishment now became the Lutheran establishment. Even there, however, one would have to say that the theory of politics and the social order was tangential and did not issue in new classical sources.

No Southern European or Mediterranean jurisdiction became part of Reformation Christianity. One looks in vain in Italy and Spain, for example, to discern Protestant theories. That leaves central Western Europe, what became or already was Germany, Switzerland, the Netherlands, and from time to time France, to probe theories of politics in Reformation Christianity. There one must make a distinction between two general families of Protestantism: what may be called the "magisterial" Reformation, and the radical Reformation.

The Magisterial Reformation

First, though there is no good and agreed-upon name for it—but observers recognize it when they see it—we turn to the more "established" form of Protestantism. Some call it "magisterial," because it became expressive of a type of authority that was coexistent with temporal rule. Today, one might call it "mainstream" Protestantism, which in almost all cases had once been the state faith during some regime or in some territory.

Over against this, there is a dissenting version of Protestantism, which was sometimes, as has been noted, called the "left-wing," the "radical Reformation," the nonestablished version. Except for brief periods in isolated circumstances when a charismatic and theocratic ruler declared divine authority for his leadership of a movement, this wing of the Reformation did not set up political authority. On the contrary: It often was inhibited and persecuted not only by Catholic but also by newly established Protestant leaders. Both camps of Reformation Christianity produced documents that, if they often do lack authority, provide perspective and historical reference points. This is the case even where later developments, such as the rise of democracy, both forced and lured such leaders into situations of drastic change.

What I am leading up to here is a fundamental fact about mainstream Protestant Reformation Christianity, a fact that flies in the face of many popular perceptions of Protestant politics and polity. So heartily did most Protestants embrace the separation of church and state when it came, for example, to the young United States, that their heirs like to think that Reformation Christianity invented such separation, such differentiation of authorities.

Not at all—or at least not entirely. Ironically, in the face of such thought, Reformation Christianity in central Europe at the Peace of Augsburg in 1555 found mainstream Protestant leaders accepting the idea that, in Latin form, contended *cuius regio, eius religio*: Whoever rules a region determines its religion. We have already seen this idea operating in realms such as Sweden. The document sealing the Peace of Augsburg may be read by few later Protestants, but it has to be seen as a classical source, even if it serves as an example of what later Protestants repudiate.

Alongside the "magisterial Reformation," and contributing significantly to its formulation of a politics, were several leading Reformers. If one wishes to speak of "classical Reformers," it is natural to turn to Martin Luther and John Calvin.

Martin Luther and Lutheranism

Most influential was Martin Luther, the German Catholic monk turned Reformer, whom many regarded as the prime embodiment of the Reformation. Historians today are less ready than often before to let any of the early-sixteenth-century figures be seen as heroic initiators. They will observe instead that scores of restless people and movements had begun to question Roman authority and politics. Then, as is so often the case, one figure comes forward as a charismatic, beguilingly attractive (and at the same time, to others alienating) personification. It has been said that this Luther-led (and later, Luther*an*) part of the Reformation started as a revolt of the junior faculty at a new backwater university in Wittenberg.

From the start, Luther's reform was definitely not *about* politics. It had to do centrally with the question of how the sinful person found a gracious God and came to proper terms with God. Luther's familiar formula was that the people were "justified by grace through faith" and not by obedience to the law or good works. But one could not use such a teaching as a direct assault on Roman

Catholicism and the Holy Roman Empire, especially if that teaching successfully attracted many, without coming through with theories about what was wrong with the old order and how to address the new.

The official and thus classical Lutheran source for doctrine and for providing coherence was a set of "confessions," such as the Augsburg Confession of 1530 and the collection that included it, the *Book of Concord*, fifty years later. Anyone who compares these to the official writings of the Church of England will see that there is in them very little of positive political construction or comment. The sources here instead are unofficial, chiefly the writings of Luther himself.

At the heart of Luther's political theory and practice is theocentrism—God rules—a theme that similarly pervaded the politics of John Calvin and other branches of Reformation Christianity. For these Reformers, God was the center of it all. Of course, Roman Catholics also would have agreed to that, but they would have applied the affirmation quite differently. Papal Catholicism set out to keep together, if in some tension, Augustine's "two cities"—what Luther called "two regiments." Such Reformation Christians saw little tension between the two, even when relations were in fact practically tense.

For Luther and Lutherans, God ruled the church, representing the heavenly city, through the Gospel, the good news of God's grace in Christ. That realm should not be ruled by law. God ruled the other regiment, the earthly city (or kingdom, or reality), through the law—both divine and human. It dare not be governed by the Gospel. Such governance would cheapen human affairs and sentimentalize them to the point that chaos would result. Sinners cannot live without the Gospel; they cannot be saved apart from it—just as they cannot be saved by the law. Societies cannot live without government; anarchy meant death. So God initiated both regiments and is served in both.

What this has to do with politics in particular is the following. The civil ruler, who may or may not be a Christian, who as Christian would be governed by the Gospel, and who may not recognize God at all, can still serve God through what Luther called "civil righteousness." In slang terms, you do not get to heaven through civil righteousness, but you serve God through it. Luther was more ready to live under a just and intelligent non-Christian ruler than he would be under a fellow Christian who was unjust and unwise. The other regiment meanwhile lives by "the righteousness that avails before God." This means Christian faith in the good news of what the same God has done in Christ.

In some respects, the Lutheran classic approach gives great space to what we can call the secular realm. In its name one does not have to baptize the secular order through terminology (e.g., by calling it a Christian nation, because the majority of people in it identify as Christians). One moves freely in it, seeking justice along with secular people and those of other religions, believers and unbelievers alike. (John Calvin, we shall see, has a somewhat different take on this.)

The upside of the Lutheran approach for participation in the political order is seen in that people who have a sense of vocation, a calling, serve God. This vocation liberates them for all kinds of "secular," "worldly," and ordinary activity that is ecclesiastically on a par with the calling of clergy and monastics in Catholicism. There is a downside, which is the abdication of responsibility for the secular realm. The Lutheran tradition in Europe turned over much church governance to electors, princes, and temporal rulers, who were to be obeyed (after the manner of Paul in Romans 13) more than resisted. Luther did allow for resistance for the sake of the church, but those circumstances were rare. By the way, he himself resisted, when in 1521 at the Diet of Worms he stood before the secular ruler, the emperor and not the pope, and defied him—an act which helped lead to the breakup of unified Western Christendom.

In that legacy, nations with Lutheran majorities among Protestants, most notably Germany, often saw the development of obedient, acquiescent, supine, uncritical Christians in the face of evil regimes—most notably Nazism. The command to be obedient often even led Lutherans into explicit support of "the powers that be" (Paul's term in Romans 13), evil though they be. The Lutheran form of polity works best when the civil order is ruled benignly, where people in ordinary lives can freely live out their vocation in service to God. It works least well when there should well be religious resistance to evil under authority.

Luther was capable of seeing the church as an instrument of criticism in the state, and he wrote a treatise questioning unlimited submission to "secular authority." But his approach had granted so much to civil authority that it was always hard for Lutherans to rise up in criticism and counteraction. The general tendency was for Lutherans to be acquiescent in and supportive of the policies of governing authorities, often at the expense of the prophetic voice they claimed.

Although Luther, more than anyone else, shook up the power bloc of the Holy Roman Empire, the Roman Catholic Church, and the pope, and though other Protestants learned from him, his polity was very much attuned to the changing times, to his moment. It continued to have influence in Germany and Scandinavia. But very little of it ever was welcomed in England or reached America in large enough measure to have a shaping role. That role belongs much more to the heritage of John Calvin, author of other classical sources for Reformation politics.

John Calvin and the Calvinist-Reformed Tradition

John Calvin was a French lawyer who chose to participate in and then lead reforms in Geneva and, through it, in much of Switzerland. In the mix of European boundaries and influences in his time, Calvin also helped shape what came to be called Reformed Protestantism in the Netherlands and in John Knox's Scotland (e.g., Puritanism, Presbyterianism, and Congregationalism). The Reformed tradition also came to have more influence on the Church of England's theology than did Lutheranism.

As a lawyer, Calvin was better trained and more capable of envisioning the implications of a political order than was his German counterpart Luther, who was a professor of Scripture. Calvin's Geneva became the model for a Reformed polity, just as Massachusetts Bay, under the Calvin-influenced Puritans, was later to become. Formal Calvinism did anything but "separate church and state" or, in James Madison's term, it only drew a thin, blurred, and interrupted "line of distinction between religion and the civil authority." Geneva, Switzerland's urban center, had no room for outsiders or dissenters. Under Calvin's leadership, its laws were to be divine laws. The confessions of the Calvin-influenced churches, documents such as the Westminster Confession, reflected more concern than did the Lutheran confessions for political order.

Halfway through the twentieth century, theologian H. Richard Niebuhr wrote a seminal book called *Christ and Culture*, which offered a useful typology of how Christians related to their social and political environment. Two of the five types matter here. Luther's approach, says Niebuhr, saw Christ and culture "in paradox." Such a theory could negate *and* it could affirm the political order, seeing church and culture always in tension. In contrast, according to Niebuhr, Calvin was devoted to "Christ transforming culture." That is, through responsible citizenship and activities one worked to see the "secular" order transformed into ever more correspondence with what the eternal city, the regiment of God, would effect.

Calvin was as theocentric as Luther. Indeed, some see Luther as being so Christ centered and Gospel centered that he slighted the sovereignty, the majesty, and the governing will of God. Calvin started with that sovereignty, and in a way "fit grace in" as the second theme. Calvin, like Luther, drew distinctions between church and state, between the two regiments that they represented. But in Calvin's view, the state should be Christian, promote Christianity, live by Christian norms, and develop laws congruent with Christian calls to justice as defined in the Bible. In some respects, Calvin's approach was a kind of reversion to what medieval Catholicism had represented.

Calvinism was more ready and able to confront evil in the governmental realm than Lutheranism because for it the church had the mission of purging the political order of evil and even of running that political order where possible. Churchly officials held some forms of state power. The classic source of Calvinism is Calvin's monumental *The Institutes of the Christian Religion*, which was quite explicit about theories of politics and governance. The civil order was to promote religious life. It was not to be neutral. Calvin's also was more of a reworking of Old Testament motifs, because he was less afraid of elders and rulers being active on the lines of Mosaic rule. The language of American Puritans showed that they wanted to be seen as a city set upon a hill, a colony that ruled out outsiders, an authority that legislated on the basis of divine law.

In qualified ways, this approach entered the American mainstream. It is seen most regularly almost half a millennium after Calvin when, even in a pluralist society, there are impulses by some to create a kind of "evangelicaldom." In this case, the "dominion" would be a church-informed government that promotes piety and religiously based morality. John Knox in Scotland, by the way, in the style of Calvinism, resisted monarchs when they, in his terms, "command[ed] impiety." Knox was also more ready than Luther to authorize insurrection against ungodly rulers.

The Radical Reformation

From all these magisterial figures and movements, we turn to the radical Reformation—left-wing, radical, dissenting, outsider forms of Reformation Christianity. Often in their day they were called Anabaptist (literally "rebaptizer"), because most of them did not believe in infant baptism, which they associated with Rome and magic or superstition. Because they strongly advocated that theology be rooted in the Bible, and they concluded that the New Testament called for adult baptism, they insisted on "believers' baptism," involving adults who could make their own profession of faith. So they rebaptized; hence, the name.

Under the umbrella of Anabaptism are subsumed highly diverse movements in which theories of politics and social order, largely negations of the Catholic and magisterial Reformation resolutions, were central. For their radical beliefs and practices these Anabaptists, none of whose leaders had names to match Henry VIII, Luther, or Calvin for recognition, suffered under both Catholic and Protestant regimens. Menno Simons, after whom Mennonites are named; Conrad Grebel; Sebastian Franck; and the truly radical Thomas Muentzer—all led smaller movements against the dominant theological stream.

These often downplayed the sacraments (Baptism and the Lord's Supper), to which they felt mainstream Protestants gave too much stress. Their theme was discipleship, or following after Christ, which demanded high standards of personal appropriation of faith and a willingness to criticize officials of both church and state. They were leaders in promoting what became a major Protestant theme: separation of church and state. Their heirs in late colonial America, some Baptist and some Quaker, teamed up with leaders like Thomas Jefferson, no friend of orthodox Christianity, to help topple establishments in religion.

Many Anabaptists, though they regarded government or magistracy as ordained by God, were not free to hold office. It was too compromising. In H. Richard Niebuhr's terms, they represented "Christ against culture." The mainstream Reformation culture's theocentrism remained but came now with a different twist. In the radicals' argument, government held the sword, and the fact of that possession left it a priori outside the realm of Christ. Good government in that respect was as bad as bad government. Out of this view came some of the pacifist movements. These "peace churches" thought that the discipleship of believers, not citizen-in-government activities, was the instrument by which God would work justice in the world. In the respect that a Christian's relationship with God is viewed as paramount, the Anabaptist stress on discipleship more closely echoes the Orthodox emphasis on the Eucharist than it does the variety of Protestant political theories.

Because Anabaptists did not recognize Anglican ("Henrician," if you will), Lutheran, or Calvinist authority any more than they would a Roman Catholic regimen, they were harassed or persecuted, sometimes even executed by Protestant and Catholic alike. In America, their heirs also often suffered, most notably when Quakers of their lineage kept this pacifist and dissenting heritage alive. Mary Dyer, a Quaker, was the only person hanged for religious reasons by Massachusetts Bay colonists (in 1662). Quakers, Mennonites, and other dissenters living in Pennsylvania during the Revolutionary War after 1776 met stigma and suffered harassment. At the same time, many of them gained admiration for their personal ethics and their voluntary contributions to human good. Thus they present still another model of Reformation Christianity and (anti-)political theory.

The Medium of Expressing Politics in Reformation Christianity

Reformation Christianity, being so internally diverse, issued many forms of relation to the external world. The Church of England and, insofar as they were established by law, other Protestant churches, had to be preoccupied with law, though Lutherans generally took pains to note that the laws were not as such "Christian." They were merely laws—congruent, one hoped, with what one knew of God's commandments and justice. Calvinism, however, was more ready to use the medium of law.

Theology was strong in the Reformations of Knox, Luther, and Calvin. Most of their political thought came in preaching and theological proclamation. Each of them would have described his work and vocation as being wholly centered in theology. Unlike Anglicans, they would have had to say that political theory and action, however urgent and God pleasing, were secondary.

Liturgy played a part in the established Protestantisms, most notably in the Church of England. In lands where the ruler and thus the realm turned Protestant, the leaders took over the great Catholic cathedrals from medieval times. In those surroundings, they enacted coronations, blessed military forces, mourned those killed in battle, and sanctioned the acts of lawmakers. These milieus conjured up a sense of importance, of divine authority standing behind human action. Even in a highly pluralist society like the United States, Catholic and Protestant alike keep something of this sense alive. In September 2001, after terrorist attacks on New York and Washington and thus on the whole nation, it was natural that memorial observances be held in the awesome arched nave of Washington National Cathedral, an Episcopal sanctuary. The solemn event signaled to all the gravity of the occasion, and the blessing and care of God over the civil order, celebrated on religious soil. It was not a direct "sectarian" expression of Episcopalianism, which by now in the United States represents an out-of-power religious minority.

As for institutions, these varied. In some cases, there were efforts to replicate all the supportive institutions inherited from medieval Catholicism. The universities with their law faculties in Germany and Scandinavia turned Lutheran and enhanced the claims of Reformation Christianity. In Geneva, Calvin invented "the academy" to sustain and reinforce the themes of his politics under God. But most institutions were tangential to the understanding of churchly political theory and action.

Narrative played its part in developing political theory and action among Reformation Christianity's founders and heirs. Protestantism is more often a storied faith than a chiefly sacramental one. Lutherans and Calvinists could honor theologians and promote their tomes among specialists. But by telling their stories, they also made it possible for the laity to grasp what was going on. Many of these stories appeared in sermons, which took narratives from the Gospels and applied them to daily contemporary life.

Often these and other stories developed against the background of the narrative of developing freedom apart from the medieval Catholic political order. John Foxe's *Book of Martyrs*, a bestseller in England and the American colonies, was one of the better known of the accounts of what dire things happened as a result of Catholic monopolies and oppression. Over against these, authors told stories of freedom, deliverance, and covenant making among the heirs of the Reformation.

The Message of Reformation Christianity's Politics

Despite all the diversity, the seven theses mentioned at the beginning of the chapter, which have been developed above in detail, are constant and appear across much of the scope of Reformation Christianity. Therefore, in summing up the message of the Reformers' politics, we return to the theses.

First, God is in control. God is at the center of life and all that happens. Politics that is not God-centered may be effective, but Christians have to bring God-centered interpretations to any polity. Thus they might live under "the Turk," the Muslim authority, a constant threat that they would not welcome. But they would not say God had abandoned the world, creation, or the political order simply because the Turk came to rule in the southeastern part of the Western Catholic-turning-Protestant territory.

Second, the Scriptures tend to be normative. Although humans may use their intellect and imagination to set up institutions of church and state, in the end most leaders in Reformation Christianity wanted to make their case by referring to the Bible, however much adapting they must do because they were not ancient Israel and much had happened since the period of Scripture formation.

Third, God works in two different ways through two different cities, realms, or regiments. In one, clearly, the Gospel rules, though there may be church laws to support it. Its purpose is the salvation of sinners and the developing of community among members, before they go out into the world to do good. In the other, the law of God, the effort is to establish and support a sphere in which God is active for the sake of human good, through agencies of justice and protection. For Reformation Christianity, these can be related in a variety of ways. But it is rare to picture any responsible leader or follower who would advocate doing away with the civil sphere, and it would be unthinkable to see him or her let the instrument of salvation slip.

Fourth, Christians are called to obedience in the civil and political realms, but rarely is their response seen as absolute obedience. Most of Reformation Christianity could picture the legitimation of dissent and, when the Gospel is at stake, even of insurrection. Christians are called to live under the Gospel in the churchly realm. There may be many degrees of intermingling between the two cities, realms, or regiments, but Reformation Christians do not picture a complete blurring of the lines or merger of one into the other.

Fifth, Reformation Christianity was a move away from the secluded monastery and convent, from the hierarchical church into a world that celebrated and authorized the vocation of lay people. This was called the "priesthood of all believers" and was easily rendered by analogy from the churchly to the civil realm.

Sixth, democracy thus was being prefigured but never fully realized in early Reformation Christianity. Protestants who claimed that they invented democracy were well advised to send a card of thanks to leaders in the Enlightenment and forces of modernity. But as democratic thinking and republican realization developed, Protestants could find many anticipations of it and authorizations for it.

Seventh, in the twentieth century Paul Tillich discerned better than most what he called "the Protestant protest" in the name of "prophetic Christianity." (One did not have to be a Protestant to exemplify it.) In the political realm, the heirs of Reformation Christianity—responsive to the language of the Hebrew prophets, who criticized Israel and not only its enemies, and to Jesus, who attacked the religious and civil forces on which people around him relied—must criticize their own polis, their city, nation, church, and cause.

Reformation Christianity and Nonbelievers: Politics and People outside the Tradition

How does Reformation Christianity's politics deal with nonbelievers? To this final question, no single answer suffices, partly because the definition of "nonbeliever" varies to such a great extent from age to age. Predominantly, given the nature of the times, the different subgroups of sixteenth-century Reformation Christianity tended to label anyone not of their particular stripe a nonbeliever, regardless of whether they were from a different Christian denomination or simply non-Christian. In the twenty-first century, a greater degree of tolerance prevails.

Inevitably, those forms of Reformation Christianity that are established hand in glove with government will be more ready to demean and inhibit or even exile or execute radical and open dissenters who are members of other faiths. Almost inevitably, clashes developed between the various expressions of Reformation Christianity and Catholicism, even to the point that each saw the other as "nonbeliever," or "anti-Christ." Terrible experience such as the Thirty Years' War (1618–48) showed that the "other" could be demonized and subjected to death.

At the same time, almost from the beginning, there were theologies, theories, and patterns of action that worked for some measure of tolerance. Some on the left wing of the Reformation in England, the Puritan sects, first openly promoted tolerance of the other. With the infusion of Enlightenment thought and the politics of tolerance in England and in northwestern Europe, very gradually more "live-and-let-live" policies developed. Some Reformers, like Luther, voiced a theology that provided great space for the nonbeliever. However, in action it was often obscured, and Luther himself spoke obscenely of exiling Jews and burning synagogues, and of making war against "the Turks." Yet most of the dealing with the "other" occurred between Protestants and Catholics.

Centuries later, most versions of Reformation Christianity promote tolerance, dialogue, and constructive engagement with Muslims, Jews, Catholics, and others, though some in reaction have withdrawn into "fundamentalism" or sought purity through isolationist sectarianism. As they confront other religions and other polities, the heirs of Reformation Christianity are free to develop subthemes from their spiritual heritage, which in a pluralist and interactive world can become major themes.

Conclusion

In the many parts of the world where Protestants are not well represented—places where Muslims, Jews, Hindus, Buddhists, or others dominate—the Protestant role in politics is negligible. At the same time, nations that interact with Western European, North American, and now Sub-Saharan African and other nations where Protestantism has a presence will find good reason to study Protestant approaches to politics. Such study will help explain some of the actions of these nations and their residents.

At the same time, citizens of nations such as the United States have a special reason for tracking Protestant ways in the political order. Well over half the American people identify themselves as members of religious bodies that are classified as Protestant, and the more intense among them try to put some aspects of this Protestant faith to work in the political and governmental orders.

Thus, in the United States—where people speak of "the new Christian right," which is almost wholly Protestant, or of "mainline Protestant activists"—Protestants and non-Protestants alike need to make sense of the deposit of Reformation Christianity and the Protestant presence in society. They will rarely meet someone who exactly replicates or puts to work the politics that such Reformers as Luther, Calvin, or the New England Puritans wanted to establish. But the aftereffects of their movements remain in the new century and show few signs of dissipating.

Suggested Readings

Bouyer, Louis. *The Spirit and Forms of Protestantism*. Cleveland: World, 1964.

Brown, Robert McAfee. *The Spirit of Protestantism*. New York: Oxford University Press, 1961.

Dillenberger, John, and Claude Welch. *Protestant Christianity Interpreted through Its Development*. New York: Scribner's, 1954.

Forell, George. *The Protestant Faith*. Englewood Cliffs, N.J.: Prentice Hall, 1960.

Martin, Martin E. *Protestantism: Its Churches and Cultures, Rituals and Doctrines, Yesterday and Today*. New York: Holt, Rinehart, and Winston, 1972; New York: Doubleday, 1974.

Mehl, Roger. *The Sociology of Protestantism*. London: SCM, 1970.

Pauck, Wilhelm. *The Heritage of the Reformation*. Glencoe, Ill.: Free Press, 1961.

Sanders, Thomas G. *Protestant Concepts of Church and State: Historical Backgrounds and Approaches for the Future*. New York: Holt, Rinehart, and Winston, 1964.

Schmidt, Jean Miller. *Souls or the Social Order: The Two-Party System in American Protestantism*. New York: Carlson, 1991.

Tillich, Paul. *The Protestant Era*. Chicago: University of Chicago Press, 1957.

Tinder, Glenn. *The Political Meaning of Christianity*. Baton Rouge: Louisiana State University Press, 1989.

Wald, Kenneth D. *Religion and Politics in the United States*. New York: Saint Martin's Press, 1987.

William, George H. *The Radical Reformation*. Philadelphia: John Knox, 1962.

Wolf, Donald J., S.J. *Toward Consensus: Catholic–Protestant Interpretations of Church and State*. New York: Doubleday, 1968.

Yoder, John Howard. *The Politics of Jesus*. Grand Rapids: Eerdmans, 1972.

Six | **Classical Islam** |

John L. Esposito with *Natana J. De Long-Bas*

ISLAM IS OFTEN DESCRIBED AS A "TOTAL WAY OF LIFE," ENCOMPASSING BOTH THE PRIVATE and the public spheres. Islam's holistic worldview does not recognize a division between public and private life, asserting instead that one's private beliefs should serve as the guiding force in all decision making. In Islam, faith is not simply a matter of what one believes (orthodoxy) but also includes what one does (orthopraxy). Thus, in the Muslim understanding of the meaning and purpose of faith, religion cannot be separated from social and political life because religion informs every action that a person undertakes.

"Islam" is an Arabic word meaning "submission." A Muslim is one who submits to the will of God, seeking to follow and actualize God's will in history at both the individual and communal levels. Adherence to Islam means membership in the worldwide community of believers, giving the Muslim both an individual and a corporate religious identity and placing upon the Muslim the responsibility not only to obey God's will but also to implement it on earth in both the private and public spheres. The responsibility of the believer to Islam and the Muslim community overrides all other social ties and responsibilities, whether to family, tribe, ethnicity, or nation. Politics is therefore central to the Muslim faith because it represents the means by which Islam is to be carried out in the public sphere.

Classical Sources of Islam on Politics

The principal sources of Islam, to which Muslims look for guidance and inspiration, are the Quran (the Word of God) and the Sunnah (example) of Muhammad. Muslims believe that the Quran is the eternal, literal, uncreated, and final Word of God, revealed to the prophet Muhammad one final time over a period of 22 years (610–32 C.E.) to serve as a guide for humankind (Q 2:185). Rather than being a new revelation, the Quran claims to be the corrective to the one eternal message of God initially revealed to but corrupted by Jews and Christians (Q 5:19). It contains 114 chapters (*surahs*) with a total of 6,000 verses (*ayat*) that are arranged according to length, rather than chronology.

As God's Word, the Quran is essentially a religious document proclaiming God's existence, sovereignty, and will for humankind. It contains examples and lessons of God's intervention and sovereignty in human history (Q 30:2–9) in order to make His will for humankind known. It is neither a law book nor a collection of legal prescriptions per se. Rather, it presents an ethical guide for moral behavior (doing good and avoiding what is wrong) and building a just society according to God's will. These guidelines for behavior necessarily have both private and public dimensions.

Muhammad's role is that of an intermediary who received God's message and communicated it. He is a purely human prophet, rather than a divine figure. Muhammad enjoys special status among Muslims both because of the message he received and because he is believed to have been a perfect living model (sometimes popularly referred to as the living Quran) and interpretation of that message. Thus, the Sunnah of Muhammad in both his words and deeds enjoys authoritative scriptural status among Muslims. The Sunnah are recorded largely in the *hadith* (tradition) literature. The *hadith*, or prophetic traditions, are narrative reports that record the sayings and deeds of Muhammad, demonstrating the living out of the Quran's precepts and teachings. They are used in conjunction with the Quran to determine appropriate behavior and values. Muhammad and the Quran have thus been pivotal to the formulation and development of Islamic law, traditions, rituals, and social practices.

Central to Islam is the doctrine of *tawhid*, or absolute monotheism, in which God is the creator, sustainer, judge, and sovereign of the universe. God's will, as expressed in Islamic law, and rule are therefore comprehensive and applicable to all creatures and aspects of life. Unlike a secular approach, which considers human reason to be the fundamental point of reference, Islam, like many other religions, looks to God as the ultimate source of authority and as the center of the universe. All power and authority come from God and should reflect Quranic values. In cases where human reason and God's Word are in conflict, Muslims believe that God's Word should take precedence.

The Quran's overarching message about God is that God is a God of mercy (36:5, 21:107, and 29:51) and justice (21:47). As judge, God is the source of all rewards and punishments. The purpose of human beings is to serve as God's vicegerents or representatives, caring for all of creation and carrying out His Will. Islamic ethics are derived from Quranic values and the special status and responsibility of human beings.

The social order prescribed by the Quran and Sunnah emphasizes the themes of social justice, the responsibility of all Muslims, particularly the wealthy, to care for the less fortunate and oppressed, and the right and responsibility of the Muslim community to defend itself from aggression. Women and orphans enjoy special protection in the Quran. Redistribution of wealth is prescribed through the requirement that Muslims pay *zakat*, or an alms tax, of 2.5 percent of their total wealth. Usury, or the collection of interest, is forbidden because it serves as a means of exploiting the poor. False contracts are also denounced.

Through all of these declarations, the Quran emphasizes the responsibility of the rich toward the poor and dispossessed. The previous guiding principles of tribal vengeance and retaliation are subordinated to a belief in God's justice and mercy, so that human-made laws, bonds, justice, and customs are replaced by divinely prescribed laws. This new social order further proclaims that the purpose of all actions is the fulfillment of God's will, rather than serving the desires of tribes or self. By asserting the notion that all believers belong to a single universal community (*ummah*), Muhammad sought to break the bonds of tribalism and place Muslims under a single prophetic leader and authority.

The Quranic basis for consideration of the Muslim community as a political entity comes from Quran 49:13, which proclaims that God "made you into nations and tribes." The Quran proclaims that, like Jews and Christians before them, Muslims have been called into a covenant relationship with God, making them a community of believers who are to serve as an example to other nations (Q 2:143) by creating a moral social order. The Quran states, "You are the best community evolved for mankind, enjoining what is right and forbidding what is wrong" (Q 3:110). This prescription has served as the Muslim rationale for political and moral activism throughout the centuries.

Islam's Theory of Politics

The Quranic prescription to enjoin what is right and forbid what is wrong serves as the springboard for an activist approach to politics in Islam. Muslims look to the Quran and Sunnah not only for specific examples of Muhammad's actions as a political head of state but also for values upon which to base the defense of the Muslim community and Islam (*jihad*) and a theory of the Islamic state.

Muhammad and the State

For Muslims, Muhammad was not only the final prophet and the living embodiment of the Quran through his words and deeds but also served as the religio-political leader of the first Muslim community. Muhammad's first ten years of preaching in Mecca were marked more by resistance and oppression than by mass conversions. His claim to prophethood gave him and his message a legitimacy and authority that undermined the wealthy and powerful in Mecca. He called for allegiance to the broader Muslim community, transcending tribal bonds and authority and breaking away from the power structure based upon leadership by the tribe of Quraysh. The threat of Muhammad's message to the wealthy and powerful in Mecca led to persecution of and attacks against Muhammad and his followers.

After ten years of persecution and violence at the hands of the Meccans, Muhammad and the early Muslims migrated to Medina, where Muhammad was invited to serve as an arbiter and judge between Muslims and non-Muslims. Eventually, Muhammad was recognized as the religious and political leader of the entire community, marking a new phase in the Muslim experience. Rather than being rejected by society and being outside of the power structure, Muhammad and the Muslims now found themselves in the position of leadership and power. In Medina, the Muslim community prospered and grew. From its beginning, therefore, Islam has contained a political dimension, with Muhammad serving as the political leader of an autonomous community.

Muslims look to the emigration (*hijra*) from Mecca to Medina in 622 C.E. as both a turning point in Muhammad's life and a major milestone and paradigm in Muslim history. For Muhammad, it marked the beginning of his political and military leadership, in addition to his continuing role as prophet. During the next ten years, Muhammad forged the identity and religious practices of the Muslim community, consolidated its political base, turned it into a strong military force, and established its legal system on the basis of Islamic religious law. 622 C.E. also marks the first year in the Muslim calendar (1 A.H., or "After the Hijra").

This dating method is significant because it focuses attention on the birth of the Muslim community, rather than on the birth of Muhammad (c. 570 C.E.) or the sending of the first revelation (610 C.E.). Rather than emphasizing the central role of its prophet, selection of the first year after the *hijra* emphasizes the central role of the broader Muslim community, reinforcing the public and this-worldly meaning of Islam as the realization of God's will on earth as carried out by the Muslim community. It is a statement of both the message and the mission of Islam.

As political and military leader of the Muslim community in Medina, Muhammad used both force and diplomacy in his engagements with the Meccans and in order to unite the tribes of Arabia under the banner of Islam. These engagements were initially defensive in nature, serving to protect the fledgling Muslim community from aggression. Several pivotal battles occurred between the early Muslims and the Meccans, providing symbols and paradigms for Muslims of every time and place.

The first major battle between the Muslims and the Meccans occurred at Badr in 624 C.E. In this military encounter, Muhammad and his followers were greatly outnumbered by the Meccans. Nevertheless, the Muslims were victorious. Muslims look to this battle as evidence of the righteousness of the Muslim cause and of God's favor upon the Muslims because the forces of God (monotheism) miraculously defeated the forces of unbelief (polytheism). The Quran (8:42 and 3:123) records God's sanction and assistance to the Muslims, providing them with victory. The Battle of Badr has therefore become a sacred symbol for Muslims and has been remembered, commemorated, and referred to throughout history whenever Muslims have been facing seemingly overwhelming odds. For example, Egyptian president Anwar al-Sadat used the code name "Operation Badr" for the 1973 Egyptian–Israeli war, believing that the use of Islamic symbols and slogans would both inspire and motivate his forces.

The Muslims fought additional battles against the powerful Meccans (Uhud in 625 C.E. and the "Battle of the Ditch" or "Battle of the Trench" in 627 C.E.), after which the two parties agreed to a truce. However, by 630 C.E., Muhammad charged the Meccans with breaking the truce. In response, he led an army of ten thousand against them. The Meccans surrendered without a fight. Although he could have demanded vengeance and plunder according to the norms of the day, Muhammad chose instead to grant his former enemies amnesty. As a result, the majority of the Meccans converted to Islam and became part of the Muslim community, recognizing Muhammad as both prophet and political leader. By 630 C.E., the Muslims controlled most of Arabia.

As the number and strength of this initial Muslim community grew, rulers engaged in offensive, as well as defensive, activities. Although defensive activities were legitimated in the name of self-defense and preservation of the *ummah* (community), offensive activities were launched by rulers and legitimated in the name of Islam, although primarily driven by a desire for political expansion and economic gain.

Jihad

Like many other world religions, Islam is a religion that emphasizes peace and nonviolence. Islam and the Arabic word for peace, *salaam*, from which the common Muslim greeting "Peace be upon you" comes, share the same root. Both convey a sense of order and social harmony, rooted in obedience to God's will. It is only through submission to the will of God and participation in the order that God has ordained that one can be at peace not only with God, but also with other human beings. However, like other world religions, Islam recognizes that there are also legitimate uses for violence.

Jihad is mentioned in both the Quran and the *hadith* and is often referred to as the "sixth pillar of Islam," although it has no such official status. Though it is often mistranslated as "holy war," *jihad* actually means to "struggle" or "strive" and refers to the Quranic command to Muslims to exert themselves to realize God's will on earth, to live a virtuous life, to spread the Islamic community throughout the entire earth by preaching and teaching, and to fulfill the universal mission of Islam. Muslims are generally responsible for carrying out *jihad* both individually and communally.

Jihad is often described as having two levels: internal and external. At the internal level, *jihad*—or greater *jihad*—is a personal struggle within oneself to carry out God's will by leading a virtuous life and by spreading Islam through personal example, teaching, or preaching. The external level of *jihad*—or lesser *jihad*—

refers to the struggle to defend Islam and the Muslim community, whether by words or by taking up arms. God promises blessings upon those who strive to achieve His will. Quran 9:20–22 states, "Those who have believed, emigrated and fought in the path of God with their lives are higher in rank in God's sight; and those are the winners. Their Lord announces to them the good news of mercy from Him, good pleasure and gardens wherein they have everlasting bliss; abiding therein forever. With God is a great reward." That is, one should not fear the loss even of one's own life in such striving because God will reward those who struggle in His cause.

As the obligation to strive or struggle to realize God's will, *jihad* has, at times, been interpreted to justify engagement in holy war to struggle against injustice and evil and to spread and defend Islam. It was in this way that *jihad* became part of Islam's doctrine of war and peace. However, *jihad* is not intended to be a military activity designed to spread the faith or win converts. The Quran (2:156) proclaims, "There is no compulsion in religion." Rather, conversions should be carried out through persuasion, emphasizing the importance of preaching and teaching. Violence is permissible only "'if we are aggressed against, if our land is usurped, we must call for hitting the attacker and the aggressor to put an end to the aggression.'"[1]

Jihad has sometimes taken on aggressive forms, as exemplified by early extremist groups like the Kharijites. The Kharijites interpreted the Quran and Sunnah literally and believed that the Quranic injunction to "command the good and prohibit evil" was a religious mandate that was to be implemented absolutely and without compromise at the political level. All human actions were divided into two classifications: good and permissible or bad and forbidden. There was no in-between category. The Kharijite worldview further divided the world into two clear, mutually exclusive spheres: the realm of believers (*dar al-Islam*), that is, Kharijites, and the realm of unbelievers or infidels (*dar al-kufr*), that is, those who did not share Kharijite beliefs, who were necessarily the enemies of God.

This division was particularly striking because it declared anyone who claimed to be a Muslim but did not share extremist Kharijite beliefs to be a non-Muslim and therefore outside of the true Muslim community. Non-Kharijites were considered apostates guilty of treason against the Islamic community, rendering them liable to punishment. Although they were to be called to repentance and acceptance of the Kharijite interpretation of Islam, refusal to become Kharijites rendered them enemies liable to being fought against and killed, even if such people were pious Muslims and regardless of how minor such sins or differences were.

The Kharijites' literal interpretation of the Quran and Sunnah affected their interpretation of two concepts that became the hallmarks of their movement: *hijra* and *jihad*. The first Muslim *hijra* occurred when the Muslims left Mecca for Medina. The Kharijites interpreted this to mean that all Muslims must engage in a *hijra*, or withdrawal, from their society of origin to live in a Kharijite community. *Jihad* was understood as the literal, physical struggle against unbelief, which the Kharijites interpreted to be necessary against any and all non-Kharijites because all non-Kharijites were classified as enemies of God.

The Kharijites characterized themselves as the soldiers of God fighting against the people of evil. Because they believed that they were instruments of God's justice and God's own righteous army fighting against those who had usurped God's rule, they declared all methods of warfare legal, legitimate, and obligatory for themselves, including violence, revolution, and guerrilla warfare. They continued to lead rebellions against both Umayyad and Abbasid rulers. Contemporary ideologues like Egypt's Sayyid Qutb and extremist groups today like the Armed Islamic Group in Algeria and the international al-Qaida organization, share similar beliefs, although this clearly is not the Quranic vision of how *jihad* is to be carried out because the Quran clearly and expressly forbids aggressive violence.

The proscription against aggressive violence in Islam is based upon Quran 17:33: "Do not kill the life/soul that God has made sacred except for just cause. Whoever is killed unjustly, We have given his heir the power [to demand satisfaction]." The Quran also clearly prohibits aggressive actions (Q 2:190): "And fight for the cause of God those who fight you, but do not be aggressive. Surely God does not like the aggressors." However, the Quran grants permission to fight to people who have suffered aggression. Quran 22:39–40 states: "Permission is given to those who fight because they are wronged. Surely God is capable of giving them victory. Those who were driven out of their homes unjustly, merely for their saying: 'Our Lord is God.' Had God not repelled some people by others, surely monasteries, churches, synagogues and mosques, wherein the name of God is mentioned frequently, would have been demolished. Indeed, God will support whoever supports Him. God is surely Strong and Mighty."

The Quran also gives permission to Muslims to fight for justice for the oppressed. Quran 4:74–76 states, "Whoever fights in the way of God and is killed or conquers, We shall accord him a great reward. And why don't you fight for the cause of God and for the down-trodden, men, women and children, who say: 'Lord, bring us out of this city whose inhabitants are unjust and grant us, from You, a protector, and grant us, from You, a supporter.' Those who believe fight for the cause of God, and those who disbelieve fight on behalf of Satan. Fight then the followers of Satan. Surely the guile of Satan is weak."

Thus, the Quran makes it clear that fighting in God's cause means seeking to reassert God's order on earth, particularly with respect to social justice. Fighting for the sake of justice for the oppressed is permissible. Fighting to maintain an unjust order is not. Classical Islamic law provides very strict and highly detailed regulations about the carrying out of *jihad* as a physical struggle or fight. *Jihad* is never to be an arbitrary action or to be used for the acquisition of personal power, wealth, or property or to forcibly convert anyone to Islam. The only "valid" conversions according to both the Quran and Islamic law are those which occur from the heart due to personal conviction.

The Islamic State

Historically, Islam has served as the religious ideology for the foundation of a variety of Muslim states, including great Islamic empires (Umayyad (661–750 C.E.), Abbasid (750–1258 C.E.), Ottoman (1281–1924 C.E.), Safavid (1501–1722 C.E.), and Mughal (1526–1857 C.E.). In each of these empires and other sultanate states, Islam informed the state's legal, political, educational, and social institutions.

The Muslim vision of political and social order is based upon the purpose for which Muslims believe God created human beings. The Quran teaches that God has given the earth as a trust to humankind (Q 2:30, 6:165). Muslims therefore see themselves as God's representatives with a divine mandate to establish God's rule on earth in order to institutionalize an Islamic Order that is expected to result in the creation of a just society. "You are the best community ever brought forth for mankind, enjoining what is good and forbidding evil" (Q 3:110).

Whereas the Christian West has interpreted Jesus' message as supporting the division of the world into secular and sacred spheres, rendering unto Caesar what belongs to Caesar and to God what belongs to God, Muslims believe that all of creation belongs to God as the Creator and Sustainer of the universe. Indeed, the primary act of faith is to seek to implement God's will in both the private and public spheres, calling all to worship God as well as promoting good and prohibiting evil. Therefore, throughout history, being a Muslim has been not just a matter of belonging to a community of fellow believers, but also to live in an Islamic community or state governed by Islamic law (in theory if not always in practice).

In this utopian vision of the Islamic state, political authority is understood to be the instrument for carrying out the divine message. Sovereignty, therefore, is the embodiment of the Word of God in the Shariah (Islamic law), rather than a power that belongs to the ruler or the clergy. Thus, the ideal Islamic state is a nomocracy (a community governed by God's law), rather than a theocracy or autocracy. The purpose of the state is to provide security and order so that Muslims can carry out their religious duties, particularly the doing of good and the prevention of evil. Legislation is not a function of the state because divine law, the Shariah, is not a product of the state but precedes it. According to the literature, the legal process of a truly Islamic state is a matter of detailing rules and judgments from the broader tenets of the Shariah, rather than creating new legislation. A sense of balance should exist among three groups: the caliph, who serves as the guardian of both the faith and the community; the *ulama* (religious scholars), who are responsible for providing religio-legal advice; and the *qadis* (judges), who resolve disputes in accordance with Islamic law. Over time, Muslims came to believe that this ideal blueprint and state had actually existed and must be reinstated. Contemporary militant movements particularly look back to this utopia as an example to be emulated today.

The Quran and *hadith* do not provide any specific format for an "Islamic state" or even prescribe one as necessary. Instead, they contain general indications of the function of the state as well as ethical considerations. Early Islamic empires and sultanates developed systems that combined elements adopted from conquered societies with religious prescriptions and institutions. During this time period, most states, non-Muslim as well as Muslim, used or controlled religion as a source of legitimacy or to mobilize popular support.

Although no specific form of government is exclusively "Islamic" or "Muslim," there are certain functions that the state is to fulfill in Islam. Examples include caring for the poor, orphans, and widows; the provision of justice; and the punishment of crimes. The Islamic concept of the state emphasized three major themes: *jamaa* or *ummah* (the group or community), *adl* or *adalah* (justice or fairness), and *qiyadah* or *imamah* (leadership). Therefore, politics in Islamic thought focuses more on problems of government, methods of statesmanship, and the conduct of the ruler than on types of states.

The Medium of Expressing Politics in Islam

Fewer than thirty years after Muhammad's death, serious divisions arose within the Muslim community. During Muhammad's lifetime, the community was united by Muhammad's prophetic and political leadership. When situations or questions caused divisions among believers, Muhammad and his continued divine revelations provided immediate and authoritative answers. Muhammad's death marked not only the end of direct, personal contact with him, but also the end of direct revelation from God. Disputes over various issues led to crises, dissent, and even civil wars after Muhammad's death.Immediately following Muhammad's death, his senior Companions sought to reassure the community that Islam had not died with its Prophet. Abu Bakr, a close Companion, trusted adviser, and father-in-law of Muhammad, announced to the Muslim community: "Muslims! If any of you has worshipped Muhammad, let me tell you that Muhammad is dead. But if you worship God, then know that God is living and will never die." Abu Bakr was selected by the Companions as caliph, or successor, to Muhammad as political and military leader of the Muslim community. He did not serve in the capacity of a prophet because the Quran declared Muhammad to be the last of the prophets.

Abu Bakr's reign as caliph lasted only two years (632–34 c.e.). Yet it reflected some of the critical issues facing the early Muslim community that remain relevant to contemporary Muslim debates about the nature of both political leadership in Islam and the meaning of membership in the Muslim *ummah*.

Shortly after Abu Bakr was declared caliph, Muslim tradition maintains, several Arab tribes tried to leave the Muslim community, arguing that they had maintained their political independence despite their conversion to Islam as a religion. According to tribal custom, political pacts and alliances between leaders ended upon the death of one of the parties to the pact. Consequently, from their perspective, the death of Muhammad represented the end of their political allegiance to the broader Muslim community. However, Abu Bakr reminded the Arab tribes of the overarching message of Islam—that membership in and loyalty to the Muslim community transcended all tribal bonds, customs, and traditions. He asserted as both political and religious truth that all Muslims belong to a single community whose unity is based upon the interconnection of religion and the state in which faith and politics are inseparable.

The immediate result of this conflict in perception was the Wars of Apostasy, in which Abu Bakr prevailed, crushing the tribal revolt, consolidating Muslim rule over the Arabian Peninsula, and definitively preserving and reasserting the unity and solidarity of the Islamic community-state on the basis of shared religious beliefs. Abu Bakr made it clear that religion was not simply a matter of personal, private belief, but that those beliefs were intended to be lived out publicly and had political consequences. Abu Bakr did not accept the argument of the Arab tribes that religion and politics were two separate and unrelated entities. Rather, in Abu Bakr's view, religion was intended to guide political decisions and to provide legitimacy to a political system.

Abu Bakr's successor, Umar ibn al-Khattab (634–44 C.E.), continued the policy of the indivisibility of religion and politics. He emphasized the combination of religious and political-military leadership during his reign by adding the title "commander of the faithful" (Amir al-Muminin) to that of caliph, demonstrating the religious basis for political unity among Muslims. Extensive expansion and conquest occurred under Umar's capable military leadership.

By the rule of the third caliph, Uthman ibn Affan (644–56 C.E.), the Muslim community was again experiencing serious divisions. Tribal factionalism and rebellion resurfaced as the Umayyad clan, the clan of Uthman, sought preferential status and power within Uthman's administration on the basis of tribal ties. Uthman was assassinated by a group of mutineers from Egypt in 656 in the first of a series of rebellions that thereafter plagued the Islamic community's development and unity.

Ali ibn Abi Talib, Muhammad's cousin, son-in-law, and close Companion, was selected as the fourth caliph following Uthman's assassination. A major civil war followed, resulting in a permanent division between Sunnis and Shiis over the questions of leadership, authority, and responsibility. Divisions over the question of leadership had existed since the appointment of Abu Bakr as leader of the Muslim community following Muhammad's death. The majority of Muslims supported the appointment of Abu Bakr as being consistent with the teachings of the Quran that all Muslims are equal in God's eyes, with no special status accorded to anyone on the basis of wealth or family. That is, the best Muslim is not the wealthiest or the most powerful, but the one who is the most pious and learned in matters of faith. This majority, known as the Sunnis (those who follow the Sunnah [example] of Muhammad), believed that leadership should pass to the most qualified person, not in hereditary succession. Thus, they supported the appointment of Abu Bakr.

However, a minority believed that succession should be hereditary. Since Muhammad had no sons who survived infancy, this minority, known as the Shiis (the "partisans" or "sect"), believed that succession should pass through Muhammad's daughter, Fatima, and her husband, Ali, who, as Muhammad's first cousin, was Muhammad's closest living male relative. The Shiis believed that the first three caliphs recognized by the Sunnis were, in fact, illegitimate.

This political infighting came to a head when Ali finally succeeded to the caliphate. Ali faced two immediate crises upon his accession to the caliphate. First, a group of Muslims led by Aisha, Abu Bakr's daughter and Muhammad's favorite wife, launched a military challenge to Ali's authority. The ensuing "Battle of the Camel" (so named because Aisha directed her troops from her palanquin on the back of a camel) ended in Aisha's defeat. The more important and lasting effect of this battle was its marking the first military engagement between Muslims, resulting in the permanent split between Sunnis and Shiis.

The second major crisis with which Ali had to contend was to find and punish Uthman's murderer. When he failed to do so, he was confronted by two groups. One group was led by Muawiyyah, the governor of Syria and a relative of Uthman. Disgusted with Ali's failure to provide justice, Muawiyyah sent his soldiers against the Muslim army. When it looked as if the army of Muawiyyah would suffer defeat, Muawiyyah's soldiers raised Qurans on the tips of their spears and declared that they would let the Quran decide the outcome of the conflict. The arbitration process that followed was inconclusive, and both armies returned home.

The second group to challenge Ali's leadership, the Kharijites (those who "go out" or secede), then emerged. Claiming that Ali's failure to find and punish Uthman's murderer and to subdue his opponents rendered him no better a leader than Muawiyyah, the Kharijites permanently broke away from the broader Muslim community. The Kharijites proclaimed that both Ali and Muawiyyah had sinned against God, rendering them unbelievers who deserved to be punished by death. The Kharijites brought their extremist proclamation to political reality when one of their number assassinated Ali in 661 C.E. Muawiyyah subsequently seized power and established an absolute monarchy, creating the Umayyad Dynasty (661–750 C.E.).

Following these events, both the Sunni and Shii traditions established a body of literature addressing the nature of political authority and political legitimacy in an Islamic state and detailed the qualifications of the appropriate leader for the Muslim community—the caliph for Sunnis and the imam for Shiis.

The Sunni Caliphate

Sunnis believe that the most qualified person should become the head of the Muslim community. They understand political leadership in Islam to be strictly political in nature because the caliph succeeded Muhammad as political leader, not as prophet. Because Muhammad was the last of the prophets, leadership of the Muslim community following Muhammad's death ceased to be a religio-political position and became strictly political. Sunnis believe that the leader (caliph) of the Muslim community possesses human and worldly, rather than divine, authority.

Sunnis look to the lifetime of Muhammad (610–32 C.E.) and the rule of the Four Rightly Guided Caliphs (632–61 C.E.) as a special normative period in which God's favor was clearly upon the Muslims. During this time, the conquest of Arabia was completed and Islam spread throughout most of the Middle East and North Africa. This physical expansion of Islam was the putting into social and political action of the religious principles preached by Muhammad. The two successive Sunni dynasties, the Umayyad (661–750 C.E.) in Damascus and the Abbasid (749–1258 C.E.) in Baghdad, consolidated Muslim power by expanding the Islamic empire as a world political force covering a geographical space that was greater than that of the ancient Roman Empire and encouraged the flourishing of Islamic civilization. Sunni Muslims considered this expansion and civilizational development to be a sign of God's guidance and favor, as well as validation of Islam as a faith.

The Sunni juridical theory of the state focuses on the institution of the caliphate, beginning with the question of the legitimacy of the institution. The caliphate was legitimated by the first two of the Rightly Guided Caliphs, Abu Bakr and Umar, by tying it to tribal principles of government: *shura* (consultation), *aqd* (the contract between the ruler and the ruled), and *bayah* (oath of allegiance). Although these principles were used in the selection of the third caliph, Uthman, by the time the Umayyad Dynasty was established following the death of the fourth caliph, Ali, these principles had fallen into disuse and were replaced by a hereditary, semiaristocratic monarchy.

The rise of the Abbasid caliphate raised the question of the relationship between the legitimacy of the government and the unity of the community. Ahmad ibn Hanbal (d. 855 C.E.), the founder of the Hanbali school of Islamic law, declared the primacy of the unity of the community over the legitimacy of the government in cases where the two were in conflict. After this, juridical theory emphasized the authority of the caliph as a political symbol, whereas the unity of the community was a human base. In the Sunni political literature, the concept of rights is divided between those of the caliph and those of the community (ummah). Civil individual rights exist only with respect to one's life and personal property. No mention of public or political individual rights is made. Instead, emphasis is placed upon the relationship between the ruler and the ruled. The ruler is responsible for persuading or coercing the population into obeying him. The state is intended to be the expression of a religio-cultural mission that is universalistic in its orientation. No physical or ethnic boundaries are recognized. The state is defined by its moral content and does not recognize any distinction between the public and private spheres.

The Sunni literature addressing the caliphate tends to focus on the person of the caliph, particularly the qualifications and traits he should possess. As the ruler of an Islamic polity, the caliph or sultan as a head of state was seen as the political successor of Muhammad whose responsibility was to protect the faith, lead the faithful, implement Islamic law as the official legal system, and spread Islamic rule. The Sunni practice of at times merging spiritual leadership with political leadership in the institution of the caliphate made it difficult to religiously justify disobedience against an unjust or usurping ruler. Resistance to the government was possible only via open militancy or spiritual disdain.

One of the most contentious questions faced by religious scholars throughout Muslim history has been whether the character of the ruler was a decisive factor in determining whether the state was truly Islamic. That is, if the ruler is known to be immoral, did this necessarily render the state un-Islamic so that its citizens were obligated to overthrow the ruler? The majority of religious scholars (ulama) determined that maintaining social order was more important than the character of the ruler and therefore determined that the decisive factor rendering a state or society "Islamic" is its governance by Islamic law.

However, a minority of ulama, most notably the thirteenth-century Hanbali scholar Taqi al-Din Ibn Taymiyyah, determined that the character of the ruler was, in fact, decisive. In a case where the ruler was perceived to be unjust, immoral, or otherwise a "bad" Muslim, this minority declared that rising up against him and overthrowing him was not only permissible but in fact required. Although this minority opinion never enjoyed broad acceptance or support, it is significant in that it has continued to influence radical extremist movements throughout Muslim history up through today, especially and including Osama bin Laden.

Ibn Taymiyyah asserted that a legitimate Islamic government was one that not only was governed by the Shariah as law but also had to be capable of defending

Muslim lands militarily against invaders. Ibn Taymiyyah's influence is also seen in doctrines such as *"din wa-dawlah,"* which assert the necessary synthesis between religion and the state in Islam, and in his judgment that the use of Islamic discourse does not render a ruler, or anyone else for that matter, a Muslim. In Ibn Taymiyyah's thought, words and actions must be consistent. Someone who claims to be a Muslim but does not act like one cannot be considered a true Muslim. Ibn Taymiyyah also viewed the world in a bipolar manner, in which the only two choices were Muslim and non-Muslim.[2]

Ibn Taymiyyah's influence on contemporary Islamic movements is significant. Particularly relevant with respect to political concerns is the tendency of contemporary extremist movements to look to Ibn Taymiyyah's division of the world into two spheres and proclamation that actions must be consistent with words for a person to truly be a Muslim. Those not in agreement with the movements' interpretation of Islam are labeled as *kafirs*, or unbelievers. This is particularly important in cases where rulers and religious authorities are targeted as unbelievers who must forcibly be removed from power, as was the case, for example, with Anwar al-Sadat of Egypt, who was assassinated by al-Jihad in 1981.

The Shii Imamate

Shiis believe that succession to leadership of the Muslim community should be hereditary and passed down to Muhammad's male descendants, beginning with Ali, his cousin and son-in-law. Ali's caliphate began only after three other caliphs had been appointed by the community and had ruled, and it ended with major power struggles. Ali was assassinated by opponents, and the caliphate was seized by his enemy Muawiyyah. Shiis believe that Muawiyyah was an impostor and that the rightful next caliph was Ali's son Hussein. When Muawiyyah's son Yazid came to power, Hussein was persuaded by some of Ali's followers living in Kufa (in modern Iraq) to lead a rebellion against Yazid in 680 C.E.

The support promised by the Kufans never materialized, however, and Hussein and his army were slaughtered by the Umayyad army at Karbala (also in modern Iraq). The martyrdom of Hussein and his followers, commemorated by Shiis every year during Ashura, shaped the Shii worldview and paradigm of the suffering and oppression of the righteous, the need to protest against injustice, and the requirement that Muslims be willing to sacrifice everything, including their lives, in the struggle to restore God's rule. The struggles between Ali and Muawiyyah and Hussein and Yazid are understood to represent the struggle of God's righteous rule against the overwhelming forces of evil (Satan).

Over the centuries, this paradigm and reading of history has been reinforced by the fact that Shiis have remained in the minority in the global Islamic community (constituting a total of about 15 percent of all Muslims) and that they have experienced discrimination because of their minority status and their theological disagreements with Sunnis, who have constituted the majority at about 85 percent of all Muslims. Politically, Shiis were therefore not concerned with legitimizing the authority of an inherently illegitimate government, but, rather, with legitimizing Shii participation in and obedience to Sunni governments and public life in Sunni majority territories. Their purpose was to cooperate with those in power while refusing to accept responsibility for the existence of an illegitimate government. In other words, Shiis granted de facto recognition of Sunni government and complied with it while avoiding legitimating it.

Historically, Sunnis have almost always ruled over Shiis. Because Shiis existed as an oppressed and disinherited minority among the Sunnis, they understood history to be a test of the righteous community's perseverance in the struggle to restore God's rule on earth. Realization of a just social order led by the imam became the dream of Shiis throughout the centuries. Whereas Sunni history looked to the glorious and victorious history of the Four Rightly Guided Caliphs and then the development of imperial Islam under the Umayyads, Abbasids, and Ottomans, Shii history traced the often tragic history of the descendants of Ali and Fatima.

Thus, whereas Sunnis can claim a golden age when they were a great world power and civilization, which they believe is evidence of God's favor upon them and a historic validation of Muslim beliefs, Shiis see in these same developments the illegitimate usurpation of power by Sunni rulers at the expense of a just society. Shiis view history more as a paradigm of the suffering, disinheritance, and oppression of a righteous minority community that must constantly struggle to restore God's rule on earth under His divinely appointed Imam.

In the twentieth century, this history was reinterpreted as a paradigm providing inspiration and mobilization to actively fight against injustice, rather than passively accept it. This reinterpretation has had the most significant impact among the Shiis of Lebanon, who struggled to achieve greater social, educational, and economic opportunities during the 1970s and 1980s, and among those of Iran, where the Shah was equated with Yazid and Ayatollah Khomeini and his followers with Hussein during the Islamic Revolution of 1978–79 so that the victory of the Islamic Revolution was declared the victory of the righteous against illegitimate usurpers of power.

In contrast to the Sunni caliphate, Shiis believe that leadership of the Muslim community should follow an imamate structure in which the leader, or imam, is a direct descendant of Muhammad and serves in a religious, as well as political-military, capacity. Although the imam is not considered to be a prophet because the Quran states that Muhammad was the last of the prophets (defined as one receiving direct revelation from God), the imam is nevertheless considered to be divinely inspired, infallible, and sinless, and to be the final and authoritative interpreter of God's will as formulated in Islamic law. Shiis therefore consider the sayings, deeds, and writings of the imams to be a source of scripture, in addition to the Quran and Sunnah.

There are three major subdivisions of Shiis which reflect the number of imams they believe succeeded Muhammad: the Zaydis (also called the Fivers), the Ismailis (Seveners), and the Ithna Ashari (Twelvers). The Zaydis split with the other Shiis by recognizing Hussein's grandson, Zayd, as the fifth imam. They believed that any descendant of Ali who was willing to assert his claim to the imamate publicly and fight for it could become Imam. The Zaydis were the first Shii group to achieve independence. They founded a dynasty in Tabaristan on the Caspian Sea in 864 C.E. Another Zaydi imamate state was founded in Yemen in 893 and lasted until 1963.

The split between the Ismailis (Seveners) and Ithna Ashari (Twelvers) occurred in the eighth century over the question of who succeeded the seventh Imam, Jafar al-Sadiq (d. 765 C.E.). The Ismailis (Seveners) recognize seven Imams, ending with Jafar al-Sadiq's son, Ismail, who was designated as the seventh imam but who predeceased his father and left no son. This group formed a political revolutionary movement against the Sunnis and established their own Fatimid Dynasty, which stretched from Egypt and North Africa to the Sind province of India between the tenth and twelfth centuries.

An offshoot of this group, the Nizari Ismailis, was particularly opposed to the Sunni Abbasid rulers and engaged in a policy of striking at them, earning them the epithet of the Assassins. One of their descendants fled to India and established the line of Imams known by the honorific title of Agha Khan, which has ruled over prosperous communities in Canada, East Africa, South Asia, and the United Kingdom. The current Agha Khan functions as a living Imam and oversees the cultural and spiritual lives of his followers, in addition to looking after the educational, social, and commercial institutions of the community.

The third and most populous group of Shiis, the Ithna Ashari (Twelvers), are a majority in Bahrain, Iran, and Iraq. This group recognized twelve legitimate successors to Muhammad. The twelfth, Muhammad al-Muntazar (Muhammad the Awaited One), "disappeared" in 874 C.E. as a child with no sons, creating a major dilemma for the line of not only political and military but also religious succession. Shii theology resolved this dilemma with the doctrine of the Hidden Imam, according to which the twelfth Imam had not died but rather "disappeared" or gone into hiding for an unspecified period of time. He is a messianic figure who is expected to return as the divinely guided Mahdi at the end of time to vindicate his followers, restore his faithful community, and usher in a perfect Islamic society of justice and truth.

In the interim, there is no imam in the physical realm to lead the community. Instead, the role of guiding the community is to be filled by religio-legal experts, or *mujtahids* (those capable of independently interpreting Islamic law). The role assigned to the religio-legal experts led, over time, to the development of a clerical hierarchy, at the top of which were religious leaders who were acknowledged by their followers as *ayatollahs* (signs of God) because of their reputations for knowledge and piety.

The Message of Islam's Politics

The main political message of Islam is that Muslims are required to establish a just society on earth that recognizes God as the source of all authority, law, and order. How this society is to be established and under what format and institutions has been open to interpretation by various groups across time and space. Historically, Islam's role in the state reinforced a sense of common identity for Muslims, as well as a sense of continuity in Muslim rule, success, and power from the time of Muhammad to the dawn of the European colonial era. The existence of an Islamic ideology and system, however imperfectly implemented, both validated and reinforced a sense of a divinely mandated and guided community with a unifying purpose and mission, giving the Islamic state a divine raison d'être. It was this belief in the divine mandate of the Muslim community that gave Muslims the impetus to spread their rule and empire over the entire Middle East and major portions of Africa, South Asia, and Southeast and Central Asia, as well as into Spain and southern Italy on the European continent.

Since Islam was revealed, Muslims have been involved in an ongoing process of understanding, interpreting, defining, redefining, and applying Islam to all aspects of their lives. It is a process in which the Word of God as revealed in the Quran has been interpreted and applied through the teachings and preachings of human beings. Because not all texts have a single clear meaning, it has been necessary in every time and place to reflect upon and interpret texts in accordance with political and social contexts, typically reflecting the power structures and privileges of the time and place. The result has been the development of Islamic law, theology, and mysticism in response to the political and social questions particular to the societies in which they were developed. Although there is only one Islam, revealed in the Quran and Sunnah, many interpretations of Islam have existed over time and space.

Islamic Law

The detailing of Islamic law over the centuries has been one major way in which Islam has been given a prominent public role in the life of the Muslim community. The elaboration of Islamic law and the implementation of a system of Islamic courts and judges were among the most important activities of the Muslim community in the first centuries following Muhammad's death. The delineation of Islamic law provided the believer with specific duties and responsibilities, reflecting Islam's emphasis on orthopraxy (correctness of behavior), rather than simply on orthodoxy (correctness of belief), so that obedience to God's law and religious observance are key duties in Islam. Thus, Islamic law, rather than theology, has occupied the primary stage in the development of the Muslim community historically.

Islam's worldview is a vision of individual and communal moral responsibility and accountability in which Muslims are to strive or struggle (*jihad*) in the path (*shariah*) of God in order to implement God's will on earth, expand and defend the Muslim community, and establish a just society. The purpose of Islamic law in such a vision is to provide the guidelines and requirements for two types of interactions: those between human beings and God, or matters of worship (*ibadat*); and those between human beings, or social transactions (*muamalat*). Both types have private and public dimensions. Islamic law is comprehensive in its coverage, ranging from regulations for carrying out religious rituals, marriage, divorce, and inheritance to setting standards for penal and international law.

Historically, the major elaboration of Islamic law occurred between the seventh and tenth centuries C.E., largely during the rule of the Umayyad Dynasty. Rather than being a purely intellectual exercise, the elaboration of Islamic law was motivated by the real religious and political concerns and issues of Muslims of that time. Many Muslims felt that the Umayyads were illegitimate usurpers of power, particularly as dissatisfaction arose over time due to increasing social and economic stratification within the empire, the rise in corruption and the abuse of power, and the incorporation of "foreign" ways into Islamic civilization and religious practice. Islamic law was developed largely in response to these conditions as a means of placing limitations on the power and autonomy of the ruler and placing it instead in the hands of religious scholars.

The development of Islamic law continued to flourish during the tenth century under the patronage of the Abbasid Dynasty. The Abbasid caliphs had led a rebellion that ultimately overthrew the Umayyads, placing them in a position of needing religious legitimation and justification for their rule. By officially sponsoring the study of Islamic sources and the elaboration of the law, the Abbasids gained religious legitimacy in the eyes of their subjects. It is important to note, however, that the elaboration of the law was the work of scholars (*ulama*), rather than judges, the practice of the courts, or government decrees.

Theology

Because of the primacy of orthopraxy over orthodoxy, theology does not play as central a role in Islam as Islamic law. Theology is understood to be the domain of the *ulama* (religious scholars) because there is no ordained clergy in Islam. Historically, although they did not necessarily serve in official posts, the *ulama* (religious scholars) were considered the guardians and interpreters of Islam. As such, they often served in an advisory capacity to Muslim rulers. The *ulama* who advised the rulers were not part of a clerical hierarchy; nor were they necessarily associated with any organized house of worship. Rather, they constituted an unofficial intellectual and social class in society, serving in a variety of capacities. Their authority was due to popular acclaim and their role as the collective voice of society's conscience, rather than to official licensing.

The *ulama* as a class played a primary role in the state's religious, legal, educational, and social service institutions. They worked as theologians, legal scholars (*fuqaha*), and legal advisers (*muftis*) who were responsible for the administration and application of the law and the Shariah courts. They ran the schools and universities, educating those who aspired to both religious and public offices. They oversaw and administered funds from religious endowments (*waqf*) and royal grants, which were used for a variety of social benefits, such as the construction and maintenance of hospitals, roads, bridges, mosques, schools, and student hostels. Over time, the *ulama* became a religious establishment that operated alongside and was often dependent upon the political establishment. In many empires, the ruler appointed a senior religious leader to serve as Shaykh al-Islam (head of religious affairs), a position that still exists in many Muslim countries.

Islamic theology did not grow out of any theological or dogmatic necessity. Rather, it developed due to particular sociopolitical contexts that led to a need for a religious resolution to specific problems. Examples of theological problems addressed are the Kharijite split from Ali, early Muslim–Christian polemics, and the penetration of Greek thought into the Islamic world during the early Abbasid period (750–1258 c.e.).

The first major theological issue faced by Muslims was the Kharijite withdrawal from the Muslim community over their declaration that Ali had abandoned his right to the caliphate by failing to subdue Muawiyyah's rebellion and find and punish Uthman's assassin. The theological issues that arose from this incident were the question of the religious implications of grave sin, its effect on membership in the Islamic community, and the religious legitimacy of a political ruler. The Kharijites believed that only two categories existed in the world: believers and nonbelievers, or Muslims and non-Muslims. In their opinion, anyone who failed to adhere to their extreme interpretation of Islam was to be considered outside of the Muslim community because they would thereby hold the status of non-Muslims. They believed that they had the right to determine the status of others and thereby expel them from the Muslim community if they were classified as non-Muslims.

The majority of the Muslim community rejected the Kharijite position, believing that only God on Judgment Day is capable of determining who is to be excluded from the Muslim community and, therefore, Paradise. The majority of Muslims did not believe it was appropriate for human beings to declare others as apostates and expel them from the Muslim community, except in cases of obvious acts of apostasy, such as denial of the existence of God. The majority maintained that an individual's faith, rather than specific actions, should determine his or her membership in the Islamic community. They further believed that the primary work of Muslims should be calling others (*dawah*) to the worship and service of God, rather than judging and condemning them, because only God is capable of judging. Historically, one of the most important groups carrying out missionary work was the Sufis.

Sufism

Sufism, or Islamic mysticism, like the development of Islamic law, began as a seventh-century reform movement. The expansion of the Islamic Empire, its growing contact with other civilizations whether through diplomacy or conquest, and the tendency of the Umayyad caliphs to establish elaborate courts and court rituals, as well as imperial lifestyles and material luxuries, led some pious Muslims to be concerned that dynastic rulers and their royal courts were more interested in power and wealth than they were in submitting to the will of God. Although some turned to Islamic law as the solution to the excesses of the Umayyad court, believing that stricter adherence to the Quran and Sunnah was in order, Sufis felt that simply knowing God's will and following God on the external path through Islamic law was insufficient. They desired a deeper, internal spiritual experience of the presence and reality of God. The path to this internal experience became known as Sufism.

Sufism began as an ascetic movement that renounced dependency on the things of this world and encouraged detachment from them. Sufis believed that dependency on worldly things was a seduction and distraction away from the central reality of God. They desired instead to return to the purity and simplicity of the early Muslim community. Disdaining the materialism of imperial Islam, the early Sufis emphasized the need to devote themselves completely and selflessly to the fulfillment of God's will, study the Quran and Sunnah, perform their religious duties, focus on the centrality of God and the Last Judgment, deny their own material desires, repent from sin, and carry out good works. Although this approach would appear to be apolitical by its nature, the historical reality is that Sufi orders have played an important role in the political life of Muslims, particularly during the period of European colonialism.

The Sufi orders played an important role in the spread of Islam through missionary work. The Sufi tendency toward eclecticism, signified by their adoption and adaptation of local non-Islamic customs and practices, and the strong devotional and emotional content of their practices enabled it to become a popular mass movement. Although this opened the Sufi orders up to charges by the more orthodox *ulama* that they were unfaithful to the tenets of Islam, as well as a threat to the established religious order, this spirit of openness and willingness to incorporate local traditions into their practices allowed the Sufis to expand rapidly and to wield great power over their adherents. Sufism became integral to popular religious practices and spirituality.

Over time, Sufism's strengths which allowed it to become a popular mass movement also became its weaknesses. Premodern reformers and modernists, both secular and Islamic, targeted Sufism as the culprit in the decline and corruption of Muslim faith and societies. They believed that Sufism's flexibility and openness to local practices and beliefs, however superstitious, over time had led to the corruption of Islamic practices and beliefs. Furthermore, critics charged that the tendency of Sufis to focus on purely spiritual experiences and the afterlife had resulted in the passive withdrawal of Sufi adherents from engagement in the affairs and problems of this world. Thus, many reformers believed that the reform of Sufism was a necessary prerequisite for the revival of Islam and for Muslim societies to successfully recover the power and prestige of past Islamic empires.

However, the reform of Sufism was not restricted to impositions from without. Many Sufi orders chose to reform themselves from within. In fact, the vast majority of African *jihad* movements in the nineteenth century were led by heads of reformist, politically oriented Sufi orders who sought to reform Sufism from within by realigning the orders in accordance with the Shariah. These leaders redefined Sufism, reinterpreting the orders to stress a this-worldly, activist Islam, as opposed to the earlier otherworldly, passive Islam.

Consequently, Sufi orders have played an important role in politics, particularly in the struggle against European colonialism and, most important, in South Asia and the African continent. For example, in Algeria, the Emir Abd al-Qadir, head of the Algerian Qadiriyah Sufi order, as well as a member of the Naqshbandiyah and Akhbariyah orders, led the resistance against the French for more than thirty years. As the head of the order and a recognized Sufi leader, Abd al-Qadir was officially recognized as "commander of the faithful" (amir al-muminin), extending his religious and political legitimacy across Algeria. The popularity of Sufism as a mass movement greatly aided Abd al-Qadir's quest for uniting Algerians in resistance to the French occupation. Although he ultimately surrendered to the French in 1847 after seventeen years of military opposition to French rule, Abd al-Qadir remained a powerful symbol of resistance to Western colonialism.

Islam and Nonbelievers: Politics and People
outside the Tradition

Historically, in many countries throughout the world, the implementation of a state religion has encouraged intolerance, oppression of, and/or second class status for other faiths because the dominant faith has been able to make use of the coercive power of the state to achieve its own interests and influence, much as the state has been able to use religion to legitimate its policies in the eyes of the people.[3] Intolerance is not necessarily limited to other religions, for oppression also often extends to members of the same confession who do not share or support the state's interpretation of religion.

Of further concern is the reality that a small fringe of extremists may take the law into their own hands when they feel that another individual or group is not adhering to religion according to their own understanding of it. Examination of the texts of Islam and the historical experience of Muslims ruling over non-Muslims provide some useful guidelines for consideration of the issue of religious minorities under Muslim rule today.

The Quran teaches that God deliberately created a world of diversity (Q 49:13): "O humankind, We have created you male and female and made you nations and tribes, so that you might come to know one another." Muslims, like Christians and Jews before them, believe that they have been called to a special covenant relationship with God, constituting a community of believers intended to serve as an example to other nations (Q 2:143) in establishing a moral social order (Q 3:110). The special status of both Jews and Christians within Islam is due to Muslim recognition that God revealed His will through His prophets, including Abraham, Moses, and Jesus. Indeed, Quran 2:62 states: "Those who believe— the Jews, the Christians, and the Sabaeans—whosoever believe in God and the Last Day and do good works, they shall have their reward from their Lord and shall have nothing to fear, nor shall they come to grief."

There are two categories of non-Muslims in Islam: *dhimmis* and *kuffar*. *Dhimmis* are those who are not Muslims but who are entitled to a special contractual relationship with Muslims on the basis of their own religious beliefs. Historically, this special status was most frequently granted to the Ahl al-Kitab, or People of the Book, defined as those possessing a sacred scripture but who did not accept Muhammad's prophethood. In practice, this meant Jews, Christians, Magis, Sabaeans, Samaritans, and Zoroastrians. Under the protective *dhimmi* relationships, adult male *dhimmis* of sound mind paid a poll tax (*jizyah*) on their incomes in exchange for protection by Muslims.

Dhimmis did not enjoy a legal or social status equal to that of Muslims, however. In many instances, *dhimmis* were required to wear special clothing, barred from certain occupations, and restricted as to where they were allowed to live. In public, they were required to conduct themselves quietly and inoffensively and were forbidden from proselytizing or publicizing their religion or religious activities. In exchange for this, *dhimmis* were provided with protection of their lives and property; defense against enemies; freedom of religious practice, including the right to live under the authority of their own religious leaders and laws; and the right to govern themselves. These rights and regulations were applied in different ways and to varying degrees over time and space. Generally speaking, under the Islamic Empires, *dhimmis* enjoyed far greater tolerance than their minority counterparts in Europe.[4] However, over time and space, the right to privately practice one's religion came to mean that *dhimmis* could not build or repair structures for worship without permission from the government, testify against a Muslim in court, or marry a Muslim woman.

In his early years, Muhammad had expected Jews and Christians, as People of the Book, to be his natural allies. The Quran itself confirms the sending of prophets and revelation to Jews and Christians and recognizes them as part of Muslim history (Q 5:44-46, 32:23, 40:53). Muhammad initially presented himself as a prophetic reformer reestablishing the religion of Abraham. For example, like the Jews, the Muslims initially faced Jerusalem during prayer and fasted on the tenth day of the lunar month. Muhammad made a special point of reaching out to the Jewish tribes of Medina. The Jews of Medina, however, had political ties to the Quraysh tribe of Mecca, so they resisted Muhammad's overtures. Shortly afterward, Muhammad received a revelation changing the direction of prayer from Jerusalem to Mecca, marking Islam as a distinct alternative to Judaism.

When Muhammad consolidated his political and military control over Medina, he recognized the reality of religious pluralism in the Constitution of Medina (c. 622–24 C.E.). The Constitution states that believers, including Jews, constitute a single community, or *ummah*, which is responsible for collectively enforcing social order and security and for confronting enemies in times of war and peace. Tribes remained responsible for the conduct of their individual members, but a clear precedent was set for the inclusion of other religions as part of the broader community led by Muslims. The Jewish population was granted the right to internal religious and cultural autonomy, including the right to observe Jewish religious law, in exchange for their political loyalty and allegiance to the Muslims.

Muslims point to the Constitution of Medina as evidence of Islam's inherent message of peaceful coexistence, the permissibility of religious pluralism in areas under Muslim rule, and the right of non-Muslims to be members of and participants in the broader Muslim community. This state of affairs could have continued to exist had not the Jews of Medina maintained their ties with the Meccans, despite their relationship with Muhammad and the Muslims. These ties became a source of conflict over time. Furthermore, after each major battle between the Muslims and the Meccans, one of the Jewish tribes was accused of breaking their treaty with Muhammad, establishing a relationship of distrust between Muslims and Jews. As a result, some Jews were exiled and the Muslims ultimately engaged in a war to crush the remaining Jews of Medina, who were regarded as a political threat to Muslim rule in and consolidation of Arabia. The primary issue here was one of politics, rather than religion.

The foundation and expansion of the Islamic Empire brought the issue of religious minorities under Muslim rule to the forefront of Muslim politics. The inhabitants of conquered territories were offered three choices: (1) convert to Islam, which enabled them to enter into the community of believers, granting them full citizenship or membership in the new empire; (2) pay a special poll tax (*jizyah*), which enabled them to enter into the *dhimmi* relationship in which they were allowed to practice their own faith and be ruled in their private lives by their own religious laws and leaders, although this meant accepting a more limited form of citizenship; and (3) fight or be killed for resisting or rejecting Muslim rule. The fact that conquered peoples were given the right to maintain their own religious affiliation and autonomy was unusual for the time, reflecting a spirit of openness and pluralism which was not apparent in other empires. This spirit was further reflected in the tendency of the Islamic Empires to incorporate the most advanced elements from surrounding civilizations, including Byzantine and Sassanid imperial and administrative practices and Hellenic science, architecture, art, medicine, and philosophy.

Christendom, particularly the Eastern Orthodox Byzantine Empire, experienced the early conquests and expansion of Islam as a political, cultural, and theological threat to its own hegemony. However, the reality was that Byzantium and Persia shared cultural and ethnic ties to the Muslim conquerors. In fact, for the non-Muslim populations of Byzantium and Persia, Islamic rule meant simply a change in rulers rather than a loss of independence. Christian and Jewish subjects, as *dhimmis*, assisted their Muslim rulers with the collection and translation of the great books of science, medicine, and philosophy from both East and West. Despite initial fears, the Muslim conquerors thus proved to be far more tolerant than imperial Christianity had been, granting religious freedom to indigenous Christian churches and Jews, most of which had been persecuted as schismatics and heretics by the Orthodox Church. As Francis Peters has observed:

> By an exquisite irony, Islam reduced the status of Christians to that which the Christians had earlier thrust upon the Jews, with one difference. The reduction in Christian status was merely judicial; it was unaccompanied by either systematic persecution or blood lust, and generally, though not everywhere and at all times, unmarred by vexatious behavior.[5]

Other positive historical examples of religious tolerance under Muslim rule include Sultan al-Nasir of Bejaya's request to Pope Gregory VII in 1076 C.E. for the ordination of a local priest to care for the Christian population and the arrangements made by the Christian emperor Charlemagne and the Abbasid Caliph Harun al-Rashid for Christian travel to the Holy Land through the establishment of a hostel in Jerusalem for Christian pilgrims and hostels constructed and run by the Christian Cluniac order along the way.

The most frequently cited example of interreligious tolerance in history, though, is that of Muslim rule in Spain (al-Andalus) from 756 to about 1000, which is usually idealized as a period of interfaith harmony or *convivencia*, living together. Muslim rule of Spain offered the Christian and Jewish populations seeking refuge from the old ruling class system of Europe the opportunity to become prosperous small landholders.[6] Christians and Jews further occupied prominent positions in the court of the caliph in the tenth century, serving as translators, engineers, physicians, and architects. Bishops were even sent by the Umayyads on important diplomatic missions.[7] The archbishop of Seville had the Bible translated and annotated into Arabic for the Arabic-speaking Christian community.

Islamic history also contains positive examples of interfaith debate and dialogue, beginning in the time of Muhammad. Muhammad himself had engaged in dialogue with the Christians of Najran, resulting in a mutually agreeable relationship whereby the Najranis were permitted to pray in the Prophet's mosque. The fifth Sunni caliph, Muawiyyah (661–69 C.E.), regularly sent invitations to the contending Jacobite and Maronite Christians to come to the royal court to work out their debates with each other. The Syrian Christian John of Damascus was also invited to appear in the court of the caliph to debate the divinity of Jesus and the concept of free will.

Debates involving both Muslims and Jews occurred in Spanish Muslim courts, and a sixteenth-century interreligious theological discussion between Catholic priests and Muslim clerics was presided over by the Mughal emperor Akbar. Although these debates were not always conducted between "equals" (indeed, many were held to "prove" that the other religion was "wrong," as was also the case for dialogues initiated by Christians), the fact that the debate was permitted and encouraged indicates some degree of open exchange between faiths, one of the highest stages of educational and cultural achievement in the Muslim world.[8]

Furthermore, Muslims maintained an open-door policy to Jews escaping from persecution in Christian Europe during the Inquisition. Even during the Crusades, Muslims practiced a tolerance of the practice of Christianity—an example that was not followed by the other side. For example, some treaties concluded in the thirteenth century between Christians and Muslims granted Christians free access to sacred places then reoccupied by Islam. The great Christian saint Francis of Assisi met Muslim leader Salah al-Din's nephew Sultan al-Malik al-Kamil in 1219, leading the Sultan to grant freedom of worship to his more than 30,000 Christian prisoners when hostilities were suspended, as well as the choice of returning to their own countries or fighting in his armies.[9]

The Ottoman Empire has long served as one of the prime examples of positive treatment of religious minorities in a Muslim majority empire. The Ottomans officially recognized four religiously based communities, known as millets: Greek Orthodox, Armenian Gregorian, Muslim, and Jewish. Under the millet system, Islam assumed the prime position, but each other millet was placed under the authority of its religious leaders and permitted to follow its own religious laws. The millet system enabled the empire to accommodate religious diversity, placing non-Muslims in a subordinate position to Muslims and offering them protected status. Minority religions further had the right to hold government positions in some cases. Thus, religious pluralism and tolerance were important components of Ottoman statecraft.

Conclusion

Islam has a strong history of faith as a guiding force in both the private and public spheres. This history has provided a series of symbols, slogans, and precedents, which have been called upon in the modern era to provide legitimacy to rulers, governments, and political systems, as well as to respond to many of the challenges of the modern era. The next chapter addresses the modern interpretations and adaptations of Islam in politics.

Notes

1. Cited in Mark Juergensmeyer, *Terror in the Mind of God: The Global Rise of Religious Violence* (Berkeley: University of California Press, 2000), 79.

2. For a more detailed discussion of Ibn Taymiyyah, see Rudolph Peters, *Jihad in Classical and Modern Islam* (Princeton, N.J.: Markus Wiener Publishers, 1996), 43–54.

3. Hugh Goddard, *Christians and Muslims: From Double Standards to Mutual Understanding* (Surrey, England: Curzon Press, 1995), 133.

4. Bernard Lewis, *The Arabs in History*, rev. ed. (New York: Harper & Row, 1966), 93–94.

5. F. E. Peters, "The Early Muslim Empires: Umayyads, Abbasids, Fatimids," in *Islam: The Religious and Political Life of a World Community*, ed. Marjorie Kelly (New York: Praeger, 1984), 79.

6. Lewis, *Arabs in History*, 121.

7. Ibid., 124.

8. Tamara Sonn, "The Dialogue between Islam and the Judeo-Christian Tradition," in *Religious Issues and Interreligious Dialogues: An Analysis and Sourcebook of Developments Since 1945*, ed. Charles Wei-hsun Fu and Gerhard E. Spiegler (New York: Greenwood Press, 1989), 437.

9. *Recognize the Spiritual Bonds Which Unite Us: 16 Years of Christian–Muslim Dialogue*, Pontifical Council for Interreligious Dialogue, *Nostra Aetate* (Vatican City: Pontifical Council for Interreligious Dialogue, 1994), 4.

Suggested Readings

Esposito, John L. *Islam and Politics*. 4th ed. Syracuse, N.Y.: Syracuse University Press, 1998.

———. *Islam: The Straight Path*. 3d ed. New York: Oxford University Press, 1998.

———, ed. *The Oxford Encyclopedia of the Modern Islamic World*. New York: Oxford University Press, 1995.

———, ed. *The Oxford History of Islam*. New York: Oxford University Press, 1999.

———. *What Everyone Needs to Know about Islam*. New York: Oxford University Press, 2002.

Goddard, Hugh. *Christians and Muslims: From Double Standards to Mutual Understanding*. Richmond, England: Curzon Press, 1995.

Haddad, Yvonne Y., and John L. Esposito, eds. *Islam, Gender and Social Change*. New York: Oxford University Press, 1997.

Peters, Rudolph. *Jihad in Classical and Modern Islam*. Princeton, N.J.: Markus Wiener Publishers, 1996.

Seven | **Modern Islam** |

John L. Esposito with *Natana J. De Long-Bas*

IN CHAPTER 6, WE ADDRESSED THE FIVE QUESTIONS BEING ASKED IN THIS VOLUME OF
every religious tradition with respect to the formative period of Islam. Because
the answers to the first two of those questions (dealing with the classical sources
and theory of politics) are the same for modern Islam as they were for classical
Islam, we do not reiterate our findings here, but rather refer the reader to the first
two sections of chapter six.

Across the globe, from North Africa to Southeast Asia, from New York City
to London and Paris, Muslims, like many believers of other faiths in the modern
age, struggle with the question of how to live out and apply their faith in a global world. Though some believe that religion should be restricted to private life,
others, believing that Islam is a comprehensive way of life that should serve as
the guiding ethical force for all actions, struggle to implement Islam in public life.
Many twenty-first-century Muslims, like their ancestors, point to the Quran, the
lives and times of Muhammad and the Companions, and Islamic law as embodied in the Shariah (Islamic law) as a blueprint for an Islamically guided and socially just and moral state and society. But with the demands of the modern era,
these same people question how to interpret and reinterpret their history to allow
Islam to speak to their life situations.

In Muslim-majority countries, Muslim activists disillusioned with Western secular ideologies have pressed for the implementation of Islam in the public sphere
of politics with slogans like "Islam is the solution" and "The Quran is our constitution." Muslims living in non-Muslim-majority countries struggle with the
question of their appropriate assimilation into and participation in these societies,
whether economically, socially, or politically, while maintaining their Muslim
identity.

One of the greatest challenges for Muslims today is understanding why a religion that enjoyed great prestige and prosperity in the past has failed to maintain
such glories in the present. Sunni Muslims, in particular, look to the vast conquests and great empires of the past as evidence of God's favor upon Muslims
when they fulfilled their divine mandate to spread God's Word, guidance, and
governance. Viewed in this light, the increasing decline and powerlessness of the
Muslim world from the eighteenth century through the present can only be
understood as a reflection of their failure to adhere to God's will. It is this worldview that has, in part, given rise to the Islamic revival that began in the eighteenth
century and experienced a major resurgence and reformulation in the twentieth

century. This revival has in turn sparked debates and theories about the relationship between Islam and politics resulting in a multiplicity of interpretations over space and time.

Modern Islam's Theory of Politics

As has been explained above, Islam's theory of politics applies equally in the modern era as it did in the classical period. Because we have already discussed this aspect of Islam's politics in chapter six, we refer the reader there for further insight into the issue of Islam's theory of politics.

The eighteenth through the twentieth centuries were a period of remarkable upheaval and renewal in the Muslim world. The internal failures and declines of the previously powerful and wealthy Islamic empires gave way to European colonial power, resulting in an increasing sense of powerlessness and frustration. However, rather than passively accepting their colonial overlords and their accompanying Christian faith and secular political ideology, many Muslims turned to their own faith in search of answers not only as to why their own societies had failed in the face of Western power, but also as to how they could recover their past power and prestige. The common response was a revival of interest in Islam as a faith and religio-political ideology. Although the forms of the religious, social, and political revivalist movements varied, as did the political and socioeconomic circumstances of the countries in which they occurred, all of them shared a common concern about the deterioration of the religious, social, and political practice of Islam and a conviction that the revival and renewal of Islam as the center of life both individually and communally was therefore the cure.

The Medium of Expressing Politics in Modern Islam

Although the movements of the eighteenth through the twentieth centuries shared a belief in the need for the revival and rejuvenation of Islam as the solution to the socioeconomic and political circumstances in which they arose, the forms of expressing this goal politically varied across time and space. What follows is an analysis of some of the most common political expressions of Islam according to time period, beginning with the eighteenth century.

Eighteenth-Century Islamic Revival and Reform

Eighteenth-century reformers generally sought to reenact the paradigmatic drama of early Islam by either restoring or recreating the ideal, early community-state as it existed in Muhammad's time. They believed that they were thereby reestablishing God's rule on earth in the same way as Muhammad had done. Revivalist movements combined religious practice with political action and established Islamic states based upon Islamic law (the Shariah). Their *jihad* was not so much about holy war against outside oppressors as it was about purifying, defending, and restoring the internal integrity and orthodoxy of their community from the inside first with the further goal being to build up its earthly strength and eventually expand.

To achieve these goals, the reformers first established sociomoral reform movements designed to create a religious community-state that would spearhead an attempt to return society to a more pristine practice of Islam. They taught a direct return to the Quran and Sunnah and reinstated the practice of *ijtihad* (independent reasoning). Their purpose in doing so was not so much to find new solutions or to resolve new problems as it was to rediscover the meaning of the original message in its original time and place. They believed that implementing this vision would resolve the problems of corruption and powerlessness facing Muslim societies of their own time and place. Those who disagreed with or resisted this reform-minded interpretation of Islam were to become subject to *jihad* as holy war. Consequently, although reformism initially appeared to be simply a matter of reforming and reviving religious practice, it clearly took on political dimensions, particularly as the movements gained increasing numbers of adherents. Indeed, one of the integral components of the revivalist worldview was the assertion that the righteous community established by Muhammad at Medina should serve as the timeless and eternal model that all Muslim communities should emulate.

Revivalist movements looked to the rich history and tradition of revival (*tajdid*) and reform (*islah*) to address the internal failures and external threats to their societies. The concepts of *tajdid* and *islah* are contained within the fundamental scriptural sources of Islam, the Quran and Sunnah. Both call for a direct return to the Quran and Sunnah as the basis for the revival and renewal of Muslim faith and society. Both also call for a reassertion of *ijtihad* to reinterpret and revitalize Islam through these sources.

The Quran uses the term *islah* to refer to the work carried out by the prophets (Q 7:170, 11:117, 28:19). Also called "messengers" and "warners," the prophets in the Quran, who include the biblical prophets, were essentially reformers who called sinful individuals and communities back to God's path. Muslim reformers throughout history have followed this same pattern, calling individuals and communities to realign themselves with the norms and ethics of the Shariah by doing and enforcing what is good and avoiding and prohibiting what is evil. This work takes on political dimensions when carried out at the community level because it provides a common bond and rationale for community life and direction.

One of the most important and influential movements dedicated to *islah* historically was the eighteenth century "Wahhabi" movement, which began in Arabia. This movement was the result of an alliance between a reform-minded jurist and theologian, Muhammad Ibn Abd al-Wahhab (1702–92 C.E.), and a tribal chief, Muhammad Ibn Saud (d. 1765 C.E.), in 1744 C.E. The movement had important political implications because it sought to politically unite the tribes of Arabia under the religious banner of Islam. Religious purification was combined with military action to enforce religious precepts and principles from the top down, rather than relegating religion to the purely private, individual sphere.

One of the major purposes of this movement was to purify the practice of Islam from superstitions and popular practices that were not based upon the teachings of the Quran and Sunnah. In particular, the movement's ideologue, Muhammad Ibn Abd al-Wahhab, sought to eradicate the popular practices of veneration of saints and the use of amulets, activities which constituted *shirk* (idolatry) because they asserted that people or objects other than God possessed the power to grant requests. Ibn Abd al-Wahhab asserted the absolute equality of all believers in the eyes of God, so that no one enjoyed special status or a favored position except through piety.

One of the most controversial ways in which Ibn Abd al-Wahhab tried to eradicate these practices was through the destruction of shrines and tombs that were popularly venerated, including those of holy men and even Muhammad himself and his Companions. In the process, Shii, as well as Sunni, shrines were destroyed, setting the stage for Wahhabi-Shii tensions which continue to this day, as evidenced by ongoing tensions between Saudi Arabia and Iran.

Muhammad Ibn Abd al-Wahhab also taught the radical rejection of *taqlid*, or adherence to past tradition, in favor of *ijtihad*, or the use of independent reasoning in direct interpretation of the Quran and Sunnah. Ibn Abd al-Wahhab did not support a literal interpretation of scripture. Rather, he emphasized the need to contextualize the Quran and Sunnah so as to know the exact situation facing the Muslim community at the time. This enabled him to distinguish, for example, which Quranic prescriptions were intended to apply to every time and place versus those which were situation specific. Likewise, this approach allowed him to determine the same for Muhammad's Sunnah so that attributes or responsibilities specific to Muhammad could be separated from those applicable to a political or religious leader of another time and place. This became particularly important as Ibn Abd al-Wahhab outlined the responsibilities of an imam (religious leader) versus those of an amir (political leader), particularly with respect to *jihad*.[1]

Preaching a message of absolute monotheism (*tawhid*), Ibn Abd al-Wahhab sought to reassert the absolute uniqueness and sovereignty of God in every aspect of life at both the individual and communal levels. He emphasized the importance of "conviction of the heart" and the need to gain converts. Although the Wahhabi movement has often been accused of "conversion by the sword," that is, a militant form of *jihad*, Ibn Abd al-Wahhab himself denounced this method as being incapable of producing "conviction of the heart." Instead, what he proposed was a policy of missionary work (*dawah*), in which adherents would carry on dialogues and study with non-Wahhabis to encourage them to return to the straight path of Islam.

Historically, this missionary work was carried out through letter writing and traveling for direct dialogue and debate, the purpose being expansion of the Wahhabi community through conversion to Wahhabi religious beliefs. The historical record also includes instances in which communities targeted for debate and dialogue disagreed with and resisted the Wahhabi interpretation of Islam. In these cases, the inhabitants were declared to be unbelievers and thus became subject to military activity to place the territory under Wahhabi control. This policy was in keeping with the classical historical practice of providing the inhabitants of areas under conquest with the choice of conversion, entering into an alliance relationship, or becoming subject to the sword. Thus, rather than remaining a strictly religious movement, the Wahhabi movement was one in which religious ideology informed and guided political activity. This alliance of religion and politics remains intact today in the Kingdom of Saudi Arabia.

The concept of *tajdid* has its origins in a saying of Muhammad: "God will send to this *ummah* (Muslim community) at the head of each century those who will renew its faith for it."[2] Muslims believe that a renewer (*mujaddid*) will be sent at the beginning of each century to purify and restore Islamic practice to the straight path (*shariah*), thereby regenerating and revitalizing the Muslim community. Over time, the belief in the *mujaddid* took on popular religious forms, the most important of which was belief in the Mahdi ("divinely guided one"). The Mahdi claimed to be God's appointed and inspired representative on earth, although he did not hold prophetic status.

One of the most prominent revivalist movements with a proclaimed Mahdi was that which arose in the Sudan in the eighteenth century. In this case, a charismatic Sufi leader, Muhammad Ahmad, proclaimed himself the awaited Mahdi who had come to reform his degraded society. Like Muhammad Ibn Abd al-Wahhab, the Sudanese Mahdi perceived his society to be corrupt and in decline. He blamed the existence of popular, foreign, and un-Islamic practices—such as the veneration of saints, prostitution, gambling, widespread immorality and corruption at all levels of society, including political and religious, and the use of alcohol—for the state of his society. He particularly singled out the fact of Egyptian-Ottoman rule as having led to the current state of degradation in the Sudan. He accused the Egyptians of disobedience to God and Muhammad, alteration of and deviation from the Shariah, and blasphemy, thereby justifying a *jihad* against these unbelievers.

The Mahdi's proposed solution was to be the eradication of these practices in favor of a return to the "pure" interpretation of Islam that was practiced by the early Muslim community during the time of Muhammad and the Rightly Guided Caliphs. Unlike the egalitarianism of the Wahhabi movement, the Mahdi claimed special status for both himself and his followers, whom he called Ansar, after the Companions of Muhammad. The Mahdi set as a primary goal of the movement independence from foreign rule so that an Islamic state could be established with himself as supreme ruler and the Shariah as the law of the land.

This return to past examples was taken so literally that the Mahdi actually reinstituted the caliphate, believing that even the political structure of the early Muslims must be replicated in order to return to the "straight path" of Islam. Although the Mahdist state ultimately was overthrown, its influence lives on in the collective memory of Sudanese Muslims and through the Mahdi's descendants, who remain active in Sudanese politics today. For example, the Mahdi's great, great-grandson, Sadiq al-Mahdi, remains the head of the Mahdiyah Sufi order and served as prime minister from 1986 until 1989.

Nineteenth-Century Islamic Modernism

By the nineteenth century, most Muslim countries were in a sufficient state of internal decline that they became vulnerable to European imperialism. Muslims experienced the defeats of their societies at the hands of Christian Europe as a religious, as well as political and cultural, crisis. This was particularly the case because European armies were typically accompanied by Christian missionaries, who attributed their conquests not only to superior military technology and economic power but also to the superiority of Western Christian civilization and religion. Because religion took on such political overtones on the part of the West, it is not surprising that some Muslims looked to the combination of religion and politics to provide a solution. Muslim responses to European colonialism ranged from resistance or struggle, justified as *jihad* in the defense of Islam in the face of the Christian onslaught, to accommodation and/or assimilation with the West.

Those Muslims who advocated resistance to the West turned to the example of Muhammad, who, having faced rejection and persecution by the Meccans, chose to emigrate (*hijra*) from Mecca to Medina, from where he built his power base. Ultimately, he engaged the Meccans in battle and won. Some Muslims chose to follow this example, but such efforts were generally ineffective in the face of modern weaponry and technology and numerically superior European forces. In the end, not only did military engagement prove to be fruitless but emigration to a "safe" Muslim territory independent of European colonial control proved logistically and physically impossible for most.

Other Muslims, discouraged by the failure of Muslim societies to successfully oppose European colonial armies, believed that simple imitation of past Muslim practices or the reimplementation of the early Muslim community's practices was insufficient, given modern technology and methods. Instead, they believed that Western technology was compatible with Islam so that what was really needed was a modern reinterpretation or reformulation of Islam.

These Islamic modernists taught that religious doctrines and practices needed to be reinterpreted (*ijtihad*) in light of modern needs so as to provide religious, educational, and social reform. For example, they reinterpreted Quran verses to introduce reforms enhancing the status of women by restricting polygamy and the husband's unilateral right to divorce, enhancing the woman's right to divorce, and providing greater regulation of maintenance payments and child custody. Others believed that the best long-term plan was to harness religion to political and social activism, a tendency often referred to as "Islamic fundamentalism." These approaches remain in existence in the contemporary Muslim world, although their relative power and influence have varied over time.

Islamic modernists provided an Islamic rationale for the reinterpretation of Islamic law and doctrine and the adoption and/or adaptation of modern ideas, technology, science, and institutions by asserting the compatibility of Islam and reason. They looked to the glories of past Islamic empires and their significant contributions in mathematics and science to argue that Islam was a religion of science, progress, and reason. They called upon Muslims to reclaim the beliefs, values, and attitudes that had made the Islamic community successful and had contributed to the creation of Islamic empires and civilization in the past. They claimed that the decline of the Muslim community was not due to any flaw in Islam per se, but rather lay in Muslims' departure from the dynamic of Islam as practiced by Muhammad and the early Muslims. To remedy this, Islamic modernists like Muhammad Abduh (1849–1905 C.E.) in Egypt and Sayyid Ahmad Khan (1817–98 C.E.) and Muhammad Iqbal (1876–1938 C.E.) in India called for a process of purification and reconstruction, or renewal and reform, to replace the prevailing static medieval religious worldview with a more dynamic interpretation of Islam that was capable of adapting to and incorporating modernity.

Islamic modernism took on political form to the extent that it was concerned with the overall reform of society. The raison d'etre for Islamic modernism was the confrontation between the Muslim world and the West in the form of European colonialism and the global debate about the relationship between religion and science. In the process, Islamic modernists and conservative traditionalists came into conflict, because conservative traditionalists (represented by the *ulama*) accused Islamic modernists of selling out to the West. Islamic modernists defended their position by asserting the need to break with strict adherence (*taqlid*) to the past in order to reinterpret Islam (*ijtihad*) so as to move into the future. Modernists insisted upon the need to understand the past historical and social contexts in which Islamic law had originally been interpreted in order to determine its applicability to modern society. They also emphasized the need to place the Quran and *hadith* in context to understand their meaning in their own time. A distinction was made between the unchanging laws of God (*Shariah*) and human interpretations (*fiqh*), which were subject to reformulation and change.

Modernists implemented their reforms in a variety of forms—political action and legal, educational, and social reforms. For example, Muhammad Abduh introduced changes in Egypt's Shariah courts when he was appointed mufti (head of the religious court system) of Egypt. He used his position as a judge to reinterpret and apply Islam to modern conditions, combining a return to the fundamental sources of Islam (the Quran and Sunnah) with modern rational thought. He further called for training new religious leaders capable of implementing this new methodology to achieve social reforms, such as improving and protecting the status of women. Likewise, Sir Ahmad Khan and Muhammad Iqbal rejected the classical formulations of Islam in favor of returning to the Quran and Sunnah. They also promoted educational reforms to combine the best of Western education with a modernist interpretation of Islam so as to prepare a new generation of Muslim leaders capable of leading the Indian subcontinent into the modern era.

Muhammad Iqbal in Pakistan provides a prominent example of the Islamic modernist critique of the West. Although he admired the dynamic spirit, intellectual tradition, and technology of the West, he nevertheless criticized their use in supporting European colonialism, the moral bankruptcy of secularism, the materialism and exploitation of capitalism, and the atheism of Marxism, themes that remain a part of contemporary Islamist discourse. Iqbal posited the vitality and dynamism of early Islamic thought and practice as a remedy and called for the reinterpretation of Islam and Islamic law in order to develop Islamic models that could serve as alternatives to societies built upon Western ideologies.

Most important from a political point of view, Iqbal identified precedents in Islamic belief and traditions that could be reinterpreted to yield Islamic equivalents of Western democracy and parliamentary government. He claimed that the most important political ideal in Islam was its assertion of the brotherhood and equality of believers, beliefs that he believed represented democracy. In fact, he asserted that, rather than his borrowing the concept of democracy from the West, the reverse was true. Democracy was actually an Islamic ideology: "Democracy has been the great mission of England in modern times . . . it is one aspect of our political ideal that is being worked out in it. It . . . makes it the greatest Muhammadan Empire in the world."[3]

Iqbal also used his belief in the unity and brotherhood of all believers to reject the secular Western ideology of territorial nationalism because he believed that this threatened the overarching unity of the Muslim community. That is, in Islam, territorial borders should not be considered the most relevant criterion for determining loyalty relationships. However, despite this theoretical objection, Iqbal, like many other Islamic modernists, tempered his religious idealism with a political realism that led him to recognize the need for Muslims to achieve national independence from their European colonial overlords. It was this political realism that permitted him to become the "father" and ideologue of modern Pakistan because he was increasingly convinced that communal harmony would not be possible for a Muslim minority living in a Hindu-dominated state. His call for a separate homeland for Muslims was geared toward allowing Muslims to preserve their distinctive Islamic identity, way of life, and solidarity.

Despite its important contributions to the revitalization and reinterpretation of Islam, Islamic modernism attracted only a small intellectual elite of followers. It never developed into a popular or mass phenomenon. Islamic modernism served as the theoretical springboard for legitimating and Islamizing modern ideas and institutions, such as the nation-state, democracy, parliamentary government, and the notion that legal experts were qualified to interpret Islam. However, the systematic reinterpretation of Islam and the development of effective and popular organizations to preserve, propagate, and implement its message did not occur until the emergence of twentieth-century organizations like the Muslim Brotherhood in Egypt and the Jamaat-i Islami in South Asia.

Twentieth-Century Islamic Political Activism

The Muslim Brotherhood and the Jamaat-i Islami serve as models for many of the contemporary Islamic movements and organizations active in the Muslim world today. The springboard for the development of these movements was the continued presence and power of Europe in the Muslim world and the apparent failure of Islamic reformers to block the spread of Western political and cultural penetration of the Muslim world. Like the revivalist and modernist movements that preceded them, the Muslim Brotherhood and the Jamaat-i Islami sought to recapture the strength and vitality of the early Islamic period and to harness religion to political and social activism. But their methods, agendas, and popularity have differed. The most important and influential thinkers of the contemporary movements are the founder of the Muslim Brotherhood in Egypt, Hasan al-Banna (1906–49 C.E.), the founder of the Jamaat-i Islami in Pakistan, Mawlana Abul Ala Mawdudi (1903–79 C.E.), and the Egyptian Muslim Brother who radicalized Islamic revivalism, Sayyid Qutb (1906–66 C.E.).

Hasan al-Banna and Mawlana Mawdudi both were influenced by and built upon the eighteenth-century models for revival and reform, particularly the Wahhabi and Mahdi movements. Like the Wahhabis and the Mahdi, al-Banna and Mawdudi insisted upon returning directly to the Quran and Sunnah for reinterpretation. However, unlike the Wahhabis and the Mahdi, both al-Banna and Mawdudi were modern, although not necessarily Western oriented, in their activities, organization, and ideological agendas. They sought to engage and control the modern world, rather than to escape from or avoid it. Both emerged at a time when the Muslim world was weak, in decline, and mostly occupied and ruled by foreign powers.

Both the Muslim Brotherhood and the Jamaat declared Islam to be a self-sufficient, all-encompassing way of life and an ideological alternative to Marxism and Western capitalism. As such, they claimed that Islam was the ideological and organizational solution to the major issues facing the twentieth-century Muslim world, namely, European colonialism and the revitalization and development of Muslim societies and their fortunes. Because the religio-cultural penetration of the West through education, customs, laws, and values was blamed for the downfall and subservience of Muslim societies to the West, they believed that the solution was necessarily a religio-cultural reassertion of Islam in these fields, rather than a simple adoption of Western institutions and ideas.

Turning back to the fundamental sources of Islam, the Quran and Sunnah, the Brotherhood and the Jamaat looked for Islamic equivalents of Western ideas and institutions, thus reinterpreting and Islamizing matters such as legal and educational reforms, government accountability, and popular participation in the political process. Religious ideology thus informed, motivated, and inspired both political and social activism and became a means of protecting Muslim identity and culture. In contrast to Islamic modernists who sought to render Islam compatible with Western culture, the Brotherhood and the Jamaat sought to create a more indigenously rooted Islamic state and society through a process of renewal and Islamization.

Although the Brotherhood and Jamaat rejected Westernization, they did not reject modernization. In fact, they incorporated modern methods and means into their institution building, provision of services, and even proselytizing, making use of the mass media, modern technology, and organizational skills. Although their message was based upon the Quran and Sunnah, it was clearly written for a twentieth-century audience because it addressed the challenges of modernity and analyzed the relationship of Islam to modern issues, such as democracy; nationalism; Zionism; Marxism; capitalism; modern banking; law and education; the status, education, and right to work of women; and international relations.

While they differed on some issues, the Brotherhood and the Jamaat shared an ideological worldview based upon the Islamic historical tradition. This worldview, which has guided many contemporary reform movements, includes the following common beliefs:

1. In Islam as a comprehensive way of life in both state and society, private and public spheres;
2. In the Quran and Sunnah as the fundamental scriptural sources of Islam;

3. In Shariah (Islamic law), as derived from the Quran and Sunnah, as the sacred blueprint for all aspects of Muslim life, both personal and communal;
4. That Muslims have a divine vocation to reestablish God's sovereignty and rule over the earth through the implementation of the Shariah and that fulfillment of this vocation will result in success, wealth, and power for the Islamic community in this life as well as the next;
5. That the current state of decline and subservience of Muslim societies is due to the fact that they have not fulfilled their divine vocation and have not adhered to the Shariah;
6. That the restoration of Muslim identity, pride, power, and rule can occur only through a return to Islam, reimplementation of the Shariah, and following of God's guidance for both state and society;
7. That modern science and technology must be harnessed and used within an Islamically guided and oriented context to prevent the Westernization and secularization of Muslim society; and
8. That a social revolution must be undertaken to set the stage for the establishment of an Islamic state and society.

The Brotherhood and the Jamaat looked to the example of Muhammad and the early Muslim community in Mecca for their organizational example. They found a paradigm in the early Muslim community for righteous living within a broader society. That righteous community was to serve as a dynamic nucleus from which a true Islamic reformation or revolution was to be launched. The Brotherhood and the Jamaat determined that the most effective means of building such a dynamic nucleus in the contemporary era was to produce a new generation of Islamically oriented but modern educated leaders to lead a dynamic social, rather than violent political revolution with the ultimate goal of establishing an Islamic state and society.

Consequently, both movements recruited followers from different educational institutions, including schools, universities, and mosques, and from a variety of professions, ranging from professionals to students and laborers, largely from the lower-middle and middle classes. The major difference between the two organizations was its power base—the Muslim Brotherhood worked to develop a broadly based mass populist movement, whereas the Jamaat was more elitist and hierarchical in membership. The Jamaat's primary goal was to train leaders who were intended to come to power, whereas the Brotherhood sought to achieve change through popular demand across society.

As was mentioned above, both the Brotherhood and the Jamaat sought to establish an Islamic state through the gradual Islamization of society through a process of social change, rather than through violent political revolution. Rather than rapidly overthrowing the current order, both organizations taught that Muslims needed first to reclaim and reappropriate their Islamic identity and practice, beginning at the grassroots level and gradually working their way up through society and institutions to achieve Islamization. Therefore, both organizations disseminated their interpretation of Islam, which combined personal religious commitment with modern learning, technology, and social and political activism, through the provision of social services, as well as publications and preaching.

In addition, to encourage Muslims to seek to revive and strengthen Muslim societies through Islam as the divinely revealed foundation for state and society alone, they discouraged adherence to self-generated Western ideologies like capitalism and communism, which they accused of promoting values anathema to Islam, namely authoritarianism, corruption, social injustice, and economic exploitation. They preached that Western secularism, with its separation of church and state, was morally bankrupt and inherently fallible and would ultimately lead to the moral decline and downfall of Europe and North America. The revitalization and reformation of Islam therefore, in their view, should be in a return to revelation, rather than dependence upon human reason.

A group within the Muslim Brotherhood of Egypt became radicalized during the late 1950s and 1960s when it was engaged in confrontation with and suppressed by the Egyptian state, under the presidency of Gamal Abd al-Nasser. As the group was targeted for state persecution and, ultimately, eradication, its chief architect, Sayyid Qutb, transformed the ideological beliefs of Hasan al-Banna and Mawlana Mawdudi from a social into a violent political revolution with the ultimate goal of physically overthrowing the Egyptian state. That is, whereas al-Banna and Mawdudi had focused more on a vision of social change, Qutb's program was blatantly political and radical in focus. Although he represents an extremist minority within Islamic activists, Qutb is important for study because of his influence on contemporary militant extremist movements. His approach has become synonymous with Western understandings of *jihad* as holy war.

Qutb's rejection of the West was based upon his own personal encounters with it. Although born and raised in Egypt, like many other young intellectuals of the time, he studied Western literature and admired the West as a young man. In 1948, he published a major work, *Social Justice in Islam*, in which he argued that, unlike Christianity and Communism, Islam possessed its own distinctive social teachings. In his view, only Islamic socialism, as rooted in Islam's comprehensive vision of life, avoided the corruption and failures of atheism and secularism. In 1949, he traveled to the United States to study educational organization. Although he set out on his journey in admiration of the United States, he quickly experienced a strong dose of culture shock that drove him to become more religiously observant and severely critical of the West, which he experienced as sexually permissive, morally decadent, and anti-Arab (due to U.S. government and media support for Israel).

Qutb returned to Egypt in 1951. Shortly thereafter, he joined the Muslim Brotherhood and quickly emerged as the organization's most influential ideologue, particularly among the younger, more militant members. He directly experienced the Egyptian government's harassment of the Brotherhood during his imprisonment and torture in 1954 for alleged involvement in an assassination attempt against then-president Nasser. Qutb was imprisoned for ten years, during which time he wrote prolifically. His most important and influential Islamic ideological tract, *Signposts* or *Milestones*, was written during this time. In it, he took the ideas of al-Banna and Mawdudi to their literalist, radical, and revolutionary conclusions. Qutb's prison experience radicalized him, pushing him into an increasingly confrontational worldview in which the world was absolutely divided into two strict categories: the party of God and the party of Satan, or those committed to the rule of God and those opposed to it. In this worldview, which was reminiscent of the seventh-century Kharijite movement, there was no middle ground between the forces of good and evil.

Qutb's vision of a bipolar world included both the confrontation between Islam and the secular West and the confrontation between Islamic activists and repressive, anti-Islamic governments and societies. Qutb included Nasser's regime in this latter category. Qutb advocated the formation of a group (*jamaa*) of true Muslims within the broader faithless and corrupt society in order to oppose it. Like Muhammad and the early Muslims, Qutb viewed his Islamic movement as a righteous minority surrounded by unbelief (*kufr*) and ignorance (*jahiliyyah*). Here Qutb reinterpreted the concept of *jahiliyyah* as ignorance from its classical meaning of pre-Islamic to a more modern meaning of "anti-Islamic."

In Qutb's worldview, *jahiliyyah* was the result of the displacement of Islam's God-centered universe, where the responsibilities of the community are the primary concern, by the Western-minded and -oriented, human-centered universe, where the rights of the individual have taken priority. The driving purpose of Qutb's worldview was political—the immediate, revolutionary creation of an Islamic system of government. He understood this to be a divine imperative, rather than simply an alternative ideology to capitalism and communism. He encouraged armed, rather than passive, struggle as the only way to implement the new Islamic order because of the violence his movement experienced at the hands of the authoritarian, un-Islamic Egyptian government. Qutb was executed by the Egyptian government in 1966.

Qutb's radical declarations against governments in both East and West, defining them as "enemies of God" against whom true believers were obligated to wage holy war, represented a significant departure from the teachings of al-Banna and Mawdudi, as well as most classical scholarship. Classical scholars tended to emphasize the importance of maintaining social order even in the case where the ruler was unjust, and al-Banna and Mawdudi focused on evolution from the grassroots level upward. Qutb, however, preached the revolutionary overthrow of any government deemed to be "un-Islamic" or "anti-Islamic" according to his interpretation, so as to implement an Islamic state and society from the top down. His formulation has inspired many other radical, extremist movements since then.

One of the ways in which Qutb's influence is most apparent is the interpretation of *jihad* ("to strive" or "to struggle") as a call for the violent overthrow of an unjust order, as exemplified by twentieth- and twenty-first-century militant extremist movements. These movements have reinterpreted Quranic prescriptions about just wars versus unjust wars in ways differing greatly from classical interpretations. At issue are definitions of concepts, such as aggression and defense, as well as the questions of when the command to sacrifice life and property to defend Islam is appropriate, and how to define the "enemies" of Islam. For example, the Quran speaks again and again of the "enemies of God" and the "enemies of Islam," often defining them as "unbelievers." Although other Quranic verses appear to make it clear that such people should be physically fought against only if they behave aggressively toward Muslims, some Muslims have interpreted the call to "struggle" or "strive" against such enemies to be a permanent engagement required of all Muslims of every time and place until the entire world is converted to Islam.

A major example of this kind of thinking is found among those responsible for the attacks on the World Trade Center and Pentagon on September 11, 2001. Such extremists claim that they have a divine mandate to kill and maim "the enemies of God" (Muslims and non-Muslims alike). Osama bin Laden justified his declaration of war against the United States because of his perception of U.S. crimes against Muslims—specifically the presence of non-Muslim U.S. troops in Saudi Arabia, the homeland of Islam; U.S. economic sanctions imposed against Iraq, which have resulted in the deaths of thousands of civilians; and unconditional U.S. support for the state of Israel, which is held responsible for the suffering of the Palestinian people—which placed the United States in the position of the aggressor. Thus, in bin Laden's mind, there is a call for "self-defense" in the face of U.S. military and economic aggression.

Definitions of "attacks" or "offensive" actions against Muslims have changed in the twentieth and twenty-first centuries, reflecting current social thought. Rather than restricting "attacks" and "offensive" actions to purely military activities, current definitions of aggression include economic, cultural, and environmental aggressions, such as disparities between wealthy and poor nations and the globalization of Western culture. For example, when Ayatollah Ruhollah Khomeini called the United States the "Great Satan," he was referring to the perceived cultural aggression against Iran by the United States through the media and advertising, as well as through U.S. support for the shah. It was in response to this perceived aggression that Khomeini declared that the most binding command in

Islam is that which instructs the Muslim to sacrifice life and property to defend and bolster Islam.[4]

Other twentieth- and twenty-first-century interpretations of *jihad* are focused on the Muslim vision of order and social harmony. Recognizing that Muslims have a responsibility to strive for a just society, Muslims in the twentieth and twenty-first centuries have considered the struggles for educational and social reform, the fight against drug use and addiction, the fight to clean up neighborhoods and slums, and the efforts to establish good schools and to provide education for all children to be ways in which communities engage in *jihad*. Personal endeavors in *jihad* include the individual discipline required to keep the fast of Ramadan, to do what is good and avoid what is evil, and to fulfill family responsibilities. Clearly, contemporary Islamic movements and societies, though all in agreement about the ultimate goal of establishing an Islamic state and society, continue to debate about whether evolution or revolution is the appropriate method for its accomplishment and the nature of the state, from caliphate to modern parliamentary governments.

The Message of Islam's Politics

Classical definitions of the role of Islam and the state have undergone revision in modern times. Up until the nineteenth century, Muslims generally thought of politics in terms of the Muslim *ummah* (understood as the universal Islamic community) and either a universal caliphate (in which its religious character was emphasized) or diverse sultanates (in which its political character was emphasized). The dominant vision was that of the unity of the universal Muslim community, or *ummah*, which recognizes no geographic, linguistic, ethnic, or national boundaries, and the responsibility of the *ummah* to obey the just ruler. The modern nation-state, in the European sense, did not exist before the nineteenth century. Politics was more a matter of dynasties and rulers (referred to as *dawlah*) than a matter of communal participation in a system.

The first mention of the territorial state was made in the nineteenth century by the Egyptian scholar Rifaah Rafi al-Tahtawi (1801–73 C.E.), who emphasized the concept of *watan* (fatherland), as opposed to *dawlah*. The use of *dawlah* to refer to a territorial state dates to the nineteenth-century Ottoman Empire, when the "state" became distinct from "dynasty" or "government." Nineteenth-century Islamic scholars also distinguished between the politics and administration of religion (*al-din*) versus the politics and administration of the "kingdom" (*al-mulk*), positing that the two had been united only during the eras of the Four Rightly Guided Caliphs (632–61 C.E.) and Caliph Umar ibn Abd al-Aziz (r. 717–20 C.E.).

The proclamation of Islam as being both a religion and a state (*din wa-dawlah*) dates to the early twentieth century, when Muslims were confronted with both the abolition of the Turkish caliphate and the territorial division of Muslim communities under the impact of European colonialism. Under such circumstances, the vision of the caliphate that should be reinstated provided an alternative to fragmentation by insisting upon the unity of the Muslim *ummah*. It also provided an alternative vision to the territorial nationalism of Europe. Those who supported the continued existence of the caliphate defined it as a combination of spiritual and political authority in its ideal form, so that an Arab caliphate, for example, should serve as a state for both Arab Muslims and Arab non-Muslims.

Although the caliphate had come to a forcible end with the fall of the Abbasid dynasty to the Mongols in 1258 C.E., it remained a powerful religious symbol of political legitimacy. The Ottoman sultans adopted the title of caliph to lend religious legitimacy to their rule. The Ottoman claim to the caliphate was abolished in 1924. Since then, there have been occasional calls among Islamic revivalists for a revival of the caliphate as a means of maintaining unity of the broader Muslim community, but such calls have not garnered popular support. Instead, other organizations, such as the Organization of the Islamic Conference, have been formed to try to unify policies between Muslim countries.

Twentieth-century visions of the ideal state have varied. Whereas some have spoken of the necessity of a Muslim state, defined as a state founded as a homeland for Muslims (i.e., the creation of the state of Pakistan), others, like Mawlana Abu al-Ala Mawdudi (1903–79), the founder of the Jamaat-i Islami, called for the foundation of a specifically Islamic state, a God-centered one run only by true believers with the Quran and Sunnah as guides. Mawdudi was, as a result, vehemently opposed to both nationalism and democracy because he perceived both to be secular ideologies in which sovereignty belonged to the territory or the people rather than to God. Stated belief in Islam as a faith was insufficient in Mawdudi's political vision. According to Mawdudi, that faith must be placed into action in all spheres of the state—political, economic, and legislative, as well as moral. Likewise, Egypt's Muslim Brotherhood proclaimed Islam as a religion and a state, a spirituality as well as an action. Both the Muslim Brotherhood and the Jamaat-i Islami sought the Islamization of both society and state, but this was to be done from the grassroots level on up, rather than by a revolutionary overthrow of the current political system.

An alternative, and more radical, vision of the relationship between Islam and politics was presented by Sayyid Qutb (1906–66), whose work was discussed above. In Qutb's vision, the foundation of an Islamic state is incumbent upon all Muslims and is to be achieved by force, if necessary. Establishment of the Islamic state is to precede Islamization of society, because Qutb posits that the Islamic state is necessarily in a position to impose Islamization from above. In his vision, human rulership in all of its forms is to be rejected so that the kingdom of God can be established on earth. All non-Islamic influences, such as patriotism and nationalism, are to be rejected so that Islamic culture cannot be polluted. According to Qutb, God's kingdom on earth is to be established via physical *jihad* (struggle), not just through teaching or preaching. Only when the new Islamic order has been established should followers turn to the detailing of laws and systems of government. Many militant Islamic groups today have pursued Qutb's ideology, seeking to confront and overthrow secular states.

The Islamic revival that began in the late 1960s was accompanied by a revived interest in the subject of the appropriate relationship between Islam and politics. The mainstream position recognizes that Islam, although in part a devotional religion, also has a public dimension. Mainstream Muslims believe that Islam should serve as a moral guide in developing new forms and systems of both state and government in accordance with modern circumstances. Political Islamists, in particular, believe that a distinct Islamic model of the state and government are clear, making their immediate establishment mandatory. However, to date, Islamists have failed to present a blueprint for such a state or government, focusing instead on the need to first create an Islamic order.

The most conclusive evidence that the Quran and *hadith* do not specify a form for Islamic government or an Islamic state is the fact that contemporary Islamic movements do not all seek the same type of polity. Nor do the states that consider themselves "Islamic" necessarily share the same form of government. Countries may share certain principles, such as the application of the Quranically prescribed *hudud* punishments or the prohibition of usury, but the actual forms of government vary widely. Some Islamic states, like Saudi Arabia, are hereditary monarchies, whereas others are military dictatorships (Sudan) or are republics with elected parliaments (Iran and Pakistan). Many of them do not even mutually recognize each other as Islamic states. Clearly, a variety of political forms of Islamic government are possible, although common social and moral features may exist.

The theory of the Islamic state that has had the most direct impact upon actual government due to its implementation is that of Ayatollah Ruhollah Khomeini (1902–89) in Iran. Khomeini taught that Shiis did not necessarily have to wait for the return of the Hidden Imam to have a pious government, but that such a government could exist currently, provided that it had an appropriate leader. The hallmark of Khomeini's vision of the Islamic state was his declaration of the doctrine of *vilayat-i faqih*, or the rule of the jurist. This doctrine was based upon a reinterpretation of the Shii doctrine of the Hidden Imam, in which the *ulama* (religious scholars) serve as the Hidden Imam's representatives during his absence.

According to this system, the *ulama* are responsible for the interpretation of Islamic law and the most learned in Islamic law is to serve as the leader of the country. This doctrine was implemented in the Islamic Republic of Iran in

1979, with Khomeini as the Faqih, or supreme jurist. Within a short time after the revolution, both Iran's government institutions and parliament were dominated by the *ulama*. Although an elected parliament is responsible for enacting legislation, the *ulama* retain control over legislation through the Council of Guardians, a group of appointed *ulama* who must verify that any and all legislation passed by the parliament is in accord with Islamic law. By granting the government primacy in Islam, the Islamic government therefore held the right to break any contract or stop any activity deemed contrary to the Shariah or to the interest of the country.

The role of the *ulama* in politics is an increasingly contested issue in Iran today as Iranians grapple with the realities of the contemporary global and increasingly technical and scientific world of today, the argument being that the *ulama*, as more traditional scholars, simply do not possess the scientific and technical expertise to deal effectively with contemporary realities. Instead, it is believed that religious experts need input from experts of other professions. This is particularly true with respect to the need to reinterpret, expand, and reform Islamic law.

Islamic Law

With respect to Islamic law, the contemporary Muslim community faces two major interrelated issues. The first is the necessity of distinguishing between the eternal principles and values of the Quran, which are to be applied consistently and without change to all sociopolitical contexts, and those that were revealed as specific responses to specific historical situations. The other major challenge is the need to separate out divine prescriptions from human interpretations. Many of the *ulama*, representing the traditional and conservative strains in Islam, continue to equate the Shariah, God's divinely revealed law, with its interpretation as found in the legal manuals developed by the early law schools. Other more reformist trends, like those represented by Muhammad Abduh and Muhammad Iqbal, have insisted on the distinction between the divinely revealed law (Shariah) contained in the Quran and Sunnah and human interpretation (*fiqh*) and application of those laws which is the product of social custom and reason. Those that are considered to be unchanging relate to the Muslim's duties and obligations to God (*ibadat*, or worship), whereas those that are subject to change relate more to interpersonal relations (*muamalat*, or social obligations), because these are contingent upon social and historical circumstances. Consequently, contemporary leaders of Islamic activist movements have reclaimed the right to *ijtihad* for the express purpose of reinterpreting Islam to address today's issues and needs.

Legal reforms remain a contested issue in many contemporary Muslim countries. Most Muslim states have Western-inspired legal codes addressing everything but family law. As the heart of the Shariah and the basis for a strong, Islamically oriented family structure and society, Islamic family law has remained intact in most Muslim countries. However, significant reforms in Islamic law occurred during the twentieth century, most notably with respect to the protection and expansion of women's rights.[5]

However, these legal reforms have been the subject of considerable conflict and debate. Since the 1980s, the Islamic resurgence has often been accompanied by attempts to reimplement classical family law and to reverse modern reforms. Furthermore, since the 1960s, there has been increasing pressure for the reimplementation of Islamic law in the public sphere, as well, in countries as diverse as Afghanistan, Iran, Pakistan, and Sudan. Islamization of the law has occurred most notoriously through the reimplementation of the *hudud* punishments for alcohol consumption, adultery, theft, fornication, and false witnessing. Other, less controversial Islamization measures guided by Islamic law include the prohibition of interest and the development of an Islamic banking and financial sector. Although in some cases, such as Afghanistan under the Taliban, reimplementation of Islamic law has meant restrictions on the rights of women, this has not necessarily been the case in other countries, like Egypt, Iran, and Pakistan, where women vote, work, and hold political office.

Contemporary Islamic reforms tend to focus on political issues: the relationship between Islam and the state, the reform of Islamic law, the promotion of religious and political pluralism, the push for popular political participation or democratization, and the rights of women. The question of the compatibility of Islam and democracy has taken center stage during the past few decades.[6] Some Muslims, such as the ruling family of Saudi Arabia, reject any discussion of the issue at all, claiming that Islam has its own system of government. Others claim that Islam and democracy are incompatible because Islam is a divinely revealed system, whereas democracy is based upon un-Islamic, Western, human-made principles and values.

However, there are those who point to traditional Islamic concepts like consultation (*shura*) and consensus (*ijma*) as providing the basis for the reinterpretation of the Islamic understanding of politics in support for adopting modern forms of political participation and democratization, such as voting in parliamentary elections, which involves the consultation and consensus of the masses, and the appointment of a parliamentary body as a legislative branch, because passing bills into laws would require consultation and consensus on the part of the lawmakers. Muslims supporting these concepts point to the past example of Muhammad's senior Companions forming a consultative assembly (*majlis al-shura*) to advise Muhammad and to the selection and election of Muhammad's successor (the caliph) through a process of consultation and consensus. Muslims reinterpret and extend this notion to the creation of modern forms of political participation and government, such as the election of heads of state and members of parliament.

The close relationship among the state, religion, and society throughout Islamic history has made the relationship of Islam to the state and the place and role of the Shariah in the contemporary Muslim world one of the greatest questions and challenges facing contemporary Muslims. For most, the question is not whether change should occur, but rather how much change and what kinds of change are possible, permissible, and even necessary. The question of change is vital to both private and public life for Muslims. Tied to the question of change are the questions of who should determine those changes by reinterpreting Islam and according to what standards.

Although the *ulama* (religious scholars) have traditionally regarded themselves as the appropriate guardians of religion on the basis of their extensive knowledge of the Quran, *hadith*, and Islamic law, the reality is that many contemporary Muslims believe that the traditionally educated and oriented *ulama* do not have the necessary expertise to address contemporary issues, such as technology, medicine, and science. Furthermore, many of the *ulama* are seen to be too closely linked to the authoritarian regimes under which they serve, approving and religiously legitimating the unpopular policies of the state. Because governments in many countries control and distribute the funds used to build mosques, appoint and pay the salaries of religious leaders and judges, and approve the topics or outline the Friday mosque sermons, traditional religious leaders have become increasingly accused of preaching the government interpretation of Islam.

Consequently, it is not surprising that the majority of contemporary reformist leaders are not religious scholars but lay people who are Islamically oriented and politically and socially activist. These leaders argue that they have the appropriate expertise (technical, medical, economic, social, and legal) to address contemporary issues and therefore should be counted as qualified "experts" in the reinterpretation of Islam for the contemporary world.

These changes in religious leadership have led to more serious questioning of the nature of authority, the state, and society. How are their Islamic character to be determined and defined? And by whom? Should the traditionally trained *ulama* retain their prerogative in interpretation of Islam? Or should the new class of laypeople with a modern education take over? Or should there be some combination of the two, where the *ulama* remain the interpreters of Islam and Islamic law but with the advisory assistance of laypeople with more modern expertise?

Islam and Nonbelievers: Politics and People outside the Tradition

One other major issue facing Muslim and Islamic states today is the status of non-Muslim minorities. Concern has arisen in recent years about the status of religious minorities under Muslim rule, because Islam has been reasserted as the state religion in many countries. In the contemporary era, many of those seeking to establish Islamic states in the Muslim world look to history to determine the status of non-Muslims. Although many call for a strict reinstatement of the gradations of citizenship that accompanied *dhimmi* status in the past, others recognize that this approach is not compatible with the pluralistic realities of the contemporary world and international human rights standards.

Those who advocate gradation of citizenship according to religious affiliation believe that an Islamic state, defined as one in which Islamic law is the law of the land, must necessarily be run by Muslims because only Muslims are capable of interpreting Islamic law. This position has been advocated by Islamization programs in Afghanistan, Iran, Pakistan, and Sudan that have legislated that only Muslims have the right to hold senior government positions. However, this status is not satisfactory to non-Muslims who wish to enjoy full and equal rights of citizenship.

Islamists have been on the forefront of the debate over religious pluralism, affirming that pluralism is the essence of Islam as revealed in the Quran and practiced by Muhammad and the early caliphs, rather than a purely Western invention or ideology. They point to the Islamic empires that permitted freedom of religion and worship and protected the *dhimmis* as evidence of the permissibility and legality of pluralism. Though many militants and mainstream conservative or traditionalist Muslims advocate classical Islam's *dhimmi* or the millet system, reformers call for a reinterpretation of pluralism. By the mid-1980s, recognizing the need to open the one-party and authoritarian political systems ruling the Muslim world, many Islamists began using the word "pluralism" for the political process, as well, so that, by 1990, they were using the term to explore conflict and differences in Muslim society, as well as the legitimacy of a multiparty system.[7]

Particularly problematic for the Muslim world today is the lack of accountability of current regimes. Increasingly, many Muslims promote the use of *ijtihad* (interpretation) and *shura* (consultation) as the function of the whole people and the recognition of the equality of all men and women. The universal implementation of *ijtihad* in the Muslim world is intended to rejuvenate political and social systems within the parameters of Islamic history, fulfilling the needs of modern society. The system could also result in the answerability of Muslim governments to the people combined with each individual Muslim's responsibility to God for his or her actions, demonstrating the positive fusion of Islam and democracy.[8]

Mainstream moderate Muslims and Islamic activists today are working to reexamine their faith in the light of modern society and to develop a new body of literature on diversity and pluralism. Its premise is that pluralism is a foundational principle of nature revealed by the Quran, which promotes the equality of all humanity in stating that God created the world to be composed of different nations, ethnicities, tribes, and languages (Q 30:22, 48:13). Thus, pluralism in systems, civilizations, and laws was intended to be permanent (Q 5:48, 69). Islamists believe that the purpose of these differences was not the promotion of war and discord but rather to serve as a sign from God that all people should strive to better understand each other.[9] As a result, Islam should not seek the eradication or negation of the "other" but should favor mutual acceptance and appreciation, because differences are intended to encourage competition in virtue among nations and guarantee progress (Q 2:251). Islamists point to the Quranic phrase used for the Muslim community—*ummatan wasat* (middle community)—as one that avoids extremes.

This body of literature also addresses the so-called universal values of pluralism, democracy, human rights, and the rights of minorities and women, debating the following contemporary concerns:

1. Can an Islamic state maintain normal relations with non-Islamic governments?
2. Can the Islamic polity tolerate political differences within its ranks without disobeying God's commandments?
3. Can the Islamic majority (Sunnis) tolerate the differences in religious interpretation of Islamic sectarian groups?
4. Can a Muslim nation grant equal status and opportunities to religious minorities in a reconstituted Islamic state, allowing them to continue the role granted to them by nationalist governments?
5. Can women have a public role in an Islamic state?

Debates about religious pluralism occupy an important space in Islamic literature. For example, some suggest that the early Muslim community practiced pluralism, highlighting the Prophet's debates with and granting of freedom of religious thought and practice to Jews and Christians, in particular, setting a precedent for peaceful and cooperative interreligious relations. Furthermore, the fact that the *ulama* throughout history have exercised *ijtihad* (independent reasoning in interpreting Islamic law) indicates that the quest for truth may be considered to be de facto and valid pluralism. They negate the claims of various Islamic groups to have "the" one and only truth because Muhammad recognized the infallibility only of the community as a whole, not of the individual. ("My people will never agree in error.")[10]

The Tunisian scholar and leader of the Renaissance Party, Rashid al-Ghannoushi, advocates the parliamentary system as a legitimate means for universal participation in the political process and an opportunity for the rotation of authority through honest election as a means of avoiding dictatorship and fulfilling the role of the Islamic institution *majlis al-shura* (consultative council). He cites *shura*, *ijtihad*, and *ijma* as principles for managing state institutions, the economy, and social affairs, because "Divine law, therefore, manifests itself as the will of the people who, by expressing support or opposition, ratify the law and their approach to Islam and, consequently, their approach to modernity."[11] Democracy also provides the framework for dialogue and a remedy for the "ills of radicalism."[12] He discusses pluralism as part of the "Islamic heritage," as evidenced by peaceful existence of Jews in Muslim countries during the Middle Ages. Jews then were free to excel in their field of choice on the basis of skill, rather than religious affiliation. He cites the Quranic principle "There is no compulsion in religion" as the basis for religious, cultural, political, and ideological pluralism in Muslim society.[13] Clearly, the questions of religious and political pluralism have been interconnected in the contemporary Islamic debates on the topic of non-Muslim status in countries ranging from Egypt to Indonesia.

The question of the appropriateness of non-Muslims serving in official capacities in Muslim majority countries or in self-proclaimed Islamic states remains a problematic issue in many countries. These difficulties are reflected in debates such as the Egyptian dispute over whether Copts, members of an ancient Christian church, should be allowed to serve in the army and whether they should have to pay a special tax, so that the classical *dhimmi* relationship can exist. Similar debates have occurred and continue to exist in Indonesia, Malaysia, Lebanon, and Pakistan.

Furthermore, theoretical acceptance of nonbelievers has not always been observed in the contemporary Islamic world. One has only to consider the records of discrimination—against Bahais in Iran; Ahmadis in Pakistan; Christians in Egypt, Nigeria, and Sudan; and Arab Jews in Syria—to recognize the failures of many modern states to accommodate differences at an institutional level. One state that has successfully established interfaith cooperation and coexistence is Indonesia, although in recent years it also has experienced problems of religious intolerance and intercommunal violence.

Ironically, in recent years the debate about minority status has taken on new meaning for Muslims as many Muslims have emigrated to Europe and the United States where they themselves constitute the minority. Islamic jurisprudence has been challenged to address the issue of minority rights and duties within a majority community from a new perspective. Is it possible for Muslims who live in Muslim-minority communities to be full citizens and to participate politically and socially in non-Muslim-majority communities not governed by Islamic law? What should be the relationship between Islamic law and civil law? Which is to prevail? How is Islamic law to be practiced in a non-Muslim-majority country? And what should be the relationship between Muslims and the non-Muslim state?

These questions have been faced in the past, although in different circumstances. In classical exegesis, written during the days of the expansion of the Islamic empires, Muslims living in non-Muslim territories were encouraged to migrate from them so that they would not be contributing to the strength or prosperity of non-Muslims. Although it was preferable for Muslims to live in Muslim territories, nevertheless, the reality was that this was not always possible. Consequently, classical jurists did allow Muslims to live outside of Muslim territories (*dar al-Islam*) if they were free to practice their religion there. Muslim jurists today offer a variety of opinions.

In the contemporary era, there remain some jurists who continue to counsel emigration from non-Muslim territories. However, others have permitted and even encouraged Muslims to live permanently as loyal citizens in their new homelands while preserving their Muslim identity and faith. Rather than focusing on differences and legalistic interpretations, they recognize that Muslims share a common ethical and moral code with other religions, which could be used to build a more just society in which economic injustice, materialism, excessive individualism, consumerism, sexual promiscuity, and violence would be condemned. Such recognition of common goals offers unity in the midst of diversity and points toward the possibility of pluralism through mutual recognition of common values based upon authentic revelation.[14] In this order, anyone who works toward the establishment of a just society would be considered as submitting to God's will.[15]

Conclusion

Islamic history continues to provide symbols and slogans for contemporary political and religious movements. When Muhammad brought his reformist message to Arabia, he was rejected and persecuted by the Meccans, creating a paradigm for "Islam in danger." Just as the early caliphs and Islamic revivalists and reformers throughout history issued the call of "Islam in danger" as a means of rallying the Muslim community to defend their faith, so twentieth-century independence struggles in Afghanistan, Bosnia, Chechnya, Kashmir, and Palestine have used this paradigm to garner popular support for their causes.

This is not to say that Muslims are always united. Monotheistic does not mean monolithic. In fact, there continue to be a variety of interpretations of Islam. Although the one most talked about in the West tends to be the explosive, radical, extremist strain, the broader and more representative "revolution" in the Muslim world is a quiet one taking place through Islamic discourse and social and political activism. In all cases, the question is not whether Islam has a role to play in the political lives of Muslims but, rather, what role Islam should play.

Notes

1. These options are outlined in Muhammad Ibn Abd al-Wahhab, *Kitab al-jihad*. A detailed discussion of this treatise can be found in Natana J. De Long-Bas, "Muhammad Ibn Abd al-Wahhab: An Intellectual Biography," Ph.D. diss., Georgetown University, 2002.

2. John O. Voll, "Renewal and Reform in Islamic History: Tajdid and Islah," *Voices of Resurgent Islam*, ed. John L. Esposito (New York: Oxford University Press, 1983), 33.

3. Muhammad Iqbal, "Islam as a Political and Moral Ideal," in *Thoughts and Reflections of Iqbal*, ed. S. A. Vahid (Lahore: Muhammad Ashraf, 1964), 52.

4. Cited in Mark Juergensmeyer, *Terror in the Mind of God: The Global Rise of Religious Violence* (Berkeley: University of California Press, 2000), 79.

5. For a more detailed analysis of Muslim family law and contemporary reforms, see John L. Esposito with Natana J. De Long-Bas, *Women in Muslim Family Law*, 2d ed. (Syracuse: Syracuse University Press, 2001).

6. For a more detailed analysis of the relationship between Islam and democracy, see John L. Esposito and John O. Voll, *Islam and Democracy*, 2d ed. (New York: Oxford University Press, 2002).

7. Yvonne Yazbeck Haddad, "Islamists and the Challenge of Pluralism," Occasional Paper (Washington, D.C.: Center for Contemporary Arab Studies, Georgetown University, 1995), 3.

8. Brian Beedham, *Muslims and Westerners: The Reformation of Cultures* (London: Eleni Nakou Foundation, 1997) 13.

9. Haddad, "Islamists and the Challenge of Pluralism," 6.

10. Ibid., 7–8.

11. Rachid Gannouchi, "The Battle against Islam," *Middle East Affairs Journal* 1, no. 2 (1992): 5.

12. Gannouchi, "Battle against Islam," 8.

13. Gannouchi, "Battle against Islam," 7.

14. Terence L. Nichols, "Social and Religious Pluralism and the Catholicity of the Church," in *Religions of the Book: The Annual Publication of the College Theology Society, 1992*, vol. 38, ed. Gerard S. Sloyan (Lanham, Md.: College Theology Society, 1996), 76.

15. Tamara Sonn, "The Dialogue Between Islam and the Judeo-Christian Tradition," in *Religious Issues and Interreligious Dialogues: An Analysis and Sourcebook of Developments Since 1945*, ed. Charles Wei-hsun Fu and Gerhard E. Spiegler (New York: Greenwood Press, 1989), 446.

Suggested Readings

Abdo, Geneive. *No God But God: Egypt and the Triumph of Islam*. New York: Oxford University Press, 2000.

Esposito, John L. *The Islamic Threat: Myth or Reality?* 3d ed. New York: Oxford University Press, 1999.

———. *Unholy War: Terrorism in the Name of Islam*. New York: Oxford University Press, 2002.

Esposito, John L., with Natana J. De Long-Bas. *Women in Muslim Family Law.* 2d ed. Syracuse, N.Y.: Syracuse University Press, 2001.

Esposito, John L., and John O. Voll. *Makers of Contemporary Islam.* New York: Oxford University Press, 2001.

Nasr, Seyyed Vali Reza. *Mawdudi and the Making of Islamic Revivalism.* New York: Oxford University Press, 1996.

Sachedina, Abdulaziz. *The Islamic Roots of Democratic Pluralism.* New York: Oxford University Press, 2001.

Tamimi, Azzam S. *Rachid Ghannouchi: A Democrat within Islamism.* New York: Oxford University Press, 2001.

Eight | **Hinduism** |

Brian K. Smith

THE MANY AND VARIEGATED TRADITIONS THAT HAVE BEEN SYNTHESIZED UNDER THE umbrella term "Hinduism" are often characterized in the Western imagination as "otherworldly" or "world-negating." The stereotypical image most commonly associated with Hinduism is the ascetic, the world-renouncer, the homeless wanderer, the cave-dwelling meditator, the holy man or *sadhu* who has transcended the concerns of this world and pursues liberation from the bonds of karma and rebirth. Although most strands of Hinduism do indeed include such renunciatory ideals and practices, Hinduism has always been mostly oriented toward the this-worldly concerns of the laity or the "householder."

This-worldly Hinduism is the religion of caste identity and obligation, of knowing and doing one's proper and inborn religious "duty" or dharma, of properly fulfilling oneself in each of the stages of life (the four *ashramas* of religious student, householder, forest-dweller, and world-renouncer) before moving on to the next, of maintaining and preserving a cosmic order by integrating one's own life and society as a whole to its dictates. Visions of a well-ordered society have been an integral part of the canonical tradition of Hinduism, complementing and contextualizing the mysticism and renunciation of otherworldly Hinduism. Although the many sects and branches of Hinduism vary in their theology, metaphysics, doctrines, and beliefs, they have traditionally all tended to adhere to the system of *varnasharma dharma*, religious duty calibrated to one's class or caste and one's stage of life. Hinduism has usually been oriented around questions of religion in society; the renunciation of the social world, and the obligations it demands of individuals, is usually envisioned as the culmination of one's prior perfection of religiously ordained social duties.

This-worldly Hinduism is thus a religion of dharma wherein everything has a place and, ideally, everything is in its place. Dharma is the principle of cosmic order, the condition of possibility for ordered cosmos rather than anarchic chaos. It is the foundation of all things, the force that preserves order and ensures morality, and as such is the "highest good": "Dharma is the foundation of the whole universe. In this world people go unto a person who is best versed in dharma for guidance. By means of the dharma one drives away evil. Upon dharma everything is founded. Therefore, dharma is called the highest good" (Taittiriya Aranyaka 10.79).[1] Within this social and cosmic ordering of things, each individual has his or her special role to play. Every individual has their "own dharma" (*svadharma*), and fulfilling it to the best of one's ability contributes to the macro-cosmic order.

Two figures stand out in this-worldly Hinduism as counterbalances to the world-renouncer, figures who are pivotal for the maintenance of social, and therefore cosmic, order. There is first of all the married householder, who supports not only himself and his family through proper work and religious rites but also through the giving of alms and other gifts is the very source of sustenance of members of the other stages of life. This stage of life, deeply implicated in the social world of work and relationships and in the this-worldly religious sphere of preservation and maintenance of the cosmos, is said to be the best stage of life: "Just as all living creatures depend on air in order to live, so do members of the other stages of life subsist by depending on householders. Since people in the other three stages of life are supported every day by the knowledge and the food of the householder, therefore the householder stage of life is the best. It must be carried out with zeal by the man who wants to win an incorruptible heaven (after death) and endless happiness here on earth" (Manu Smriti 3.77–79).[2]

The second personage critical to the promotion and stability of the social order, and of dharma more generally, is the traditional Hindu king, the ultimate householder and patriarch ruling over his "household," society at large. Since the times of the ancient Vedas, Hinduism has had a theory of sacred kingship wherein the ruler is not merely a great man or primus inter pares but also the creation of the gods and himself the very embodiment of a deity, charged with the all-important task of overseeing the social and political order. The proper administration of the polity by the righteous and strong king results both in the stability necessary for individuals and groups to fulfill their proper duties and in the harmonization of social order with the cosmic order as a whole. Conversely, a weak, inept, or immoral king who does not align himself and his subjects with the dictates of dharma is doomed to failure and becomes the cause of chaos among his people—a chaos that is said to have disastrous cosmic ramifications.

Within this vision of kingship, the god-king can, according to the texts, wield virtually absolute power. We shall see that many scriptural passages describe the king's powers in stark, even cruel terms. For it is "punishment" in the symbolic form of the scepter (*danda*)—the "big stick" or rod of punishment and coercive power—that often is said to underlie and characterize the king's rule: "The scepter conduces to the acquisition of what is not acquired, the preservation of what has been acquired, the growth of what has been preserved, and the distribution among worthy people of what has grown. It is on it that the proper functioning of society depends. . . . There is no such means for subjugation of beings as the scepter, say the ancient teachers. . . . The king, severe with the scepter, becomes a source of terror to beings. The king, mild with the scepter, is despised" (Artha Shastra 1.4).[3]

Hinduism, in other words, condones and legitimates political power verging on the dictatorial (and this, perhaps, is one of the sources of another and opposite Western stereotype concerning Hinduism, that of the "Oriental despot"). But Hinduism also tempers these absolutist powers by insisting that the king himself be both self-disciplined and under the rule of another. The ideal ruler is one who, like the ideal world-renouncer, has attained mastery over his desires and his senses; the paragon of this-worldly activity mirrors the model of other-worldliness. The ruler, then, should be a kind of this-worldly *yogin* whose rule over others is predicated on his rule over himself.

Moreover, it is crucial, according to many texts of the tradition, that the king closely align himself with those most closely associated with religion: the Brahmins or priestly class. It is ultimately only in consort with, or rather in subordination to, the Brahmins and the principles of religion they represent and embody that the king can rule effectively and legitimately—at least according to the sacred texts composed and preserved by these very Brahmins. Such an ideal alliance between the principles of temporal power and spiritual authority carries with it a certain ambivalence, however, that highlights the sometimes unresolved tensions between the this-worldly and otherworldly aspects of Hinduism.

Kingship and the religious roots of political power have thus received great attention in the sacred literature of Hinduism. These texts raise and scrutinize the following questions, among others: Why is a king necessary, and what is his function? Who is a proper king? What are his rights and powers, but also what are his limitations and obligations? What is the king's particular duty or *svadharma* and how does it relate to the preservation of dharma more generally? And what kind of associations is he to forge with the Brahmins and the Hinduism they represent, preserve, and broker? In sum, what is the role of the king in establishing and maintaining a religiously legitimate and beneficial political and social order, and what should that order look like?

Classical Sources of Hinduism on Politics

The classical—one might even say "orthodox"—traditions of Hinduism all trace their lineage back to the canonical texts known as the Vedas. The Vedas, which were composed beginning in the middle centuries of the second millennium B.C.E., and supplemented for at least a millennium after that, are a heterogeneous collection of different types of treatises compiled by different ritually based schools of thought and practice. All of these texts, in one way or another, pertain to the central preoccupation of Vedic religion: the performance and philosophy of ritual sacrifice. The later traditions that were founded upon and drew their authority from them regarded the Vedas as "revealed," that is, as existing eternally and not composed by human beings but rather "seen" or "heard" by the ancient sages.

It is in the Vedas that we first encounter an ancient Indian political philosophy set in a religious context. The idea and religious roots of kingship are found in the earliest strata of these texts, often nestled within cosmogonic accounts or within discourses concerning the meaning and performance of sacrifice. In these works, the king is often identified with one or another of the Vedic gods, but especially with Indra, the apotheosis of the warrior-king. Here also we see formulated the extremely influential and enduring idea that different classes have various functions in the social order; whereas Kshatriyas or warriors are given the exclusive prerogative to rule, Brahmins or priests are said to hold a monopoly on spiritual authority. Kings are advised to place themselves under the guidance of Brahmins for their rule to be efficacious. Rituals designed to confer spiritual authority as well as temporal power on the king also date from this period. Of especial importance were the royal consecration rite (Rajasuya) and the "horse sacrifice" (Ashvamedha), both of which rituals continued to be performed in later Hindu states long after the Vedic period came to an end.

During the Vedic age, the rights and obligations of the various orders or classes of society were increasingly concretized and formalized. This process came to a head in the post-Vedic texts called the Dharma Sutras (a.k.a. "Shastras" or "Smritis"). Although, like most ancient Indian texts, the Dharma Sutras are very hard to date, a recent estimate puts them at around the middle of the third century B.C.E. at the earliest.[4] It is in these works that we get detailed instructions on the religiously grounded duties of each of the social classes, and, specifically, some of the first codifications of the duties of the righteous king. Indeed, some of these treatises go into great detail, instructing the king in his rights and obligations and how he is to conform all behavior to the dictates of dharma—"religious law" or "righteousness."

But at about this same time a different kind of text was also produced that was designed to guide the Hindu monarch. This was the Artha Shastra, supposedly composed by Kautiliya, an adviser to the emperor Chandragupta Maurya. This book was not about dharma or religion but rather concerned *artha*, the pursuit of economic and political self-interest. The Hindu tradition had by this time formulated the notion that, in addition to dharma, there were two other religiously valid "goals of human life"—pleasure (*kama*) and *artha*—and that a well-balanced life would consist in the regulated pursuit of all three.[5] While the king was himself ruled by religious law or dharma, he was also very much encouraged to look after and promote his own (and his subjects') self-interest.

The Artha Shastra, a classic of political science in world literature often compared with Machiavelli's *The Prince*, purports to instruct the Hindu king in how to safeguard and maximize that self-interest. Topics covered range from the proper subjects in which a king should be educated and the importance of intellectual and moral discipline to the nuts and bolts of statecraft: the organization of the polity, how to guard against treachery in the court, the most effective use of spies, policing the populace and administering justice, how to conduct foreign affairs and war to one's best advantage, and so forth. Although Kautiliya's Artha Shastra is the classic work of this genre, other and lesser known texts centering on political advantage, the rules of government, and the "science of the use of force" (*danda niti*) were also later produced.

It is also necessary in this context to mention the two great epics of the Hindu tradition, the Mahabharata and the Ramayana, both of which revolve around the topic of kingship and rule. The Mahabharata is a massive, sprawling work that centers on the tale of a war fought by two sides of the same family for rule over "Bharata" or India. Among the many topics covered in this epic is that of political theory and *rajadharma*, the duty of kings. The Ramayana, the legendary story of Rama, who represents the Hindu ideal of warrior nobility and righteous rule, often discusses the need for proper government and the chaos that results in its absence. In its portrait of Rama himself, the Ramayana offers Hindus an image of the perfect ruler. Finally, the encyclopedic texts known as the Puranas (written beginning in the first millennium c.e.) contain, inter alia, religiously based advice and guidance for the Hindu king.

Hinduism's Theory of Politics

As was mentioned above, the religious grounding for the Hindu vision of an ideal social and political order can be traced back to the earliest texts of the Hindu tradition, the Vedas. Already in the Rig Veda (ca. 1200 B.C.E. or earlier) the four principal social classes are depicted as issuing forth from the time of creation as parts of the dismembered primordial Cosmic Man: "When they divided the Cosmic Man, how many parts did they apportion him? What do they call his mouth, his two arms and thighs and feet? His mouth became the Brahmin (priest); his arms were made into the Kshatriya (warrior and ruler); his thighs the Vaishya (commoner); and from his feet the Shudras (servants) were born" (Rig Veda 10.90.11–12). Each class is associated with its distinctive quality: the Brahmin with the mouth, by which he recites the sacred texts in his liturgical functions; the Kshatriya with the arms representing physical and coercive power; the Vaishya with the thighs (or loins) symbolizing fecundity and productivity; and the Shudra with the lowly (and polluted) feet, indicating the "base" nature of the lowest class but also that the Shudra is the "basis" upon which society stands. This myth of origins is elaborated in a later text in which the duties or dharmas of each of these classes are enumerated:

> But to protect this whole creation, the lustrous one made separate innate activities for those born of his mouth, arms, thighs, and feet. For Brahmins, he ordained

teaching and learning (the Veda), sacrificing for themselves and sacrificing for others, giving and receiving. Protecting his subjects, giving (to the Brahmins), having sacrifices performed (by the Brahmins), studying (the Veda), and remaining unaddicted to the sensory objects are, in summary, for a Kshatriya. Protecting his livestock, giving, having sacrifices performed, studying, trading, lending money, and farming the land are for a Vaishya. The Lord assigned only one activity to a Shudra: serving these (other) classes without resentment. (Manu Smriti 1.87–91)

In this way, the particular duties of the four classes—here is, *in nuce*, the much more complicated system of caste—are grounded in religious ideology, with the Brahmin at the top followed by the warrior-ruler, together making up the ruling classes. Below these two are the masses or commoners, the Vaishyas and Shudras. These classes, their duties and their relative rank in the hierarchy, are portrayed as aboriginal and "natural," and thus indisputable and eternal.

Within this scheme, it is the Kshatriya alone who is given the right to rule and the duty to protect others. In the Vedas, the Kshatriyas are said to be infused with certain innate powers that explain their unique capabilities to wield power over others. They are consistently associated with "virility," "power," "force," "might," "physical strength," "vigor," "fame" and "glory," "distinction," and thus with "rule" (*raj*). The tools of physical and military power, the weapons of war and violence, are clustered in the hands of the Kshatriya. The ideal member of this class is described as "an archer, a hero, and a great charioteer" and as "one who kills his enemies and contests with rivals" (Shatapatha Brahmana 2.1.2.17). Strong in arms and legs and fitted with armor, he performs his manly and heroic deeds (Taittiriya Brahmana 3.8.23.3). The other three classes (including the Brahmins) are sometimes said to be "subordinate to him" (Taittiriya Samhita 2.5.10.1), or to "approach the Kshatriya respectfully" and be "subject to him" (Jaiminiya Brahmana 1.285).

In the ancient Vedas and subsequent sacred texts, the king's power over those he rules is described in absolute terms, although not without recognition that this power is also derived, at least in part, from his subjects. He is the "lord of all" or the "lord of the people" (Atharva Veda 3.4.1), and the notion that the king is "lord of the earth" and the "father" of his people (the "children") is frequently encountered in Hindu texts.[6] But it is also only "through the people that the power of rule becomes strong" and it is "by means of his people that the Kshatriya wins what he desires to win" (Shathapatha Brahmana 4.3.3.6; 5.4.3.8). The ruler should be "surrounded" and "guarded" on all sides by his subjects (Shatapatha Brahmana 3.6.1.24), for they are his "protection" (Atharva Veda 3.3.5).

Conversely, many Vedic texts depict the ruler's subjects as existing mainly for his own exploitation. The king is said to have a "share in the people" so "whatever there is among the people, in that the ruler also has a share" (Shatapatha Brahmana 9.1.1.18). The king's subjects are to be "restrained," "brought to order," and made "steady and faithful" by the ruler through the implementation of coercive force (Taittiriya Brahmana 3.3.6.10; Aitareya Brahmana 1.9; Shatapatha Brahmana 5.3.4.15), and in all events the hierarchical distinction between ruler and ruled must be established and maintained: "The ruler (is) higher than the people, and therefore the people here serve, from a lower position, the Kshatriya who is placed above them" (Shatapatha Brahmana 2.5.2.6). There should, in sum, never be what one text calls a "categorical confusion" between the inferior and the superior, and one must take care never to "make the people equal and resistant to the ruler" (Shatapatha Brahmana 10.4.3.22); one must, as is proper, make them "compliant and obedient" (Shatapatha Brahmana 2.5.2.34).[7]

The stark embrace of political exploitation in the Vedas is nowhere more explicit than in the discourse of "food" and "eaters": "The Kshatriya is the eater, and the people are food. Where there is abundant food for the eater, that kingdom is prosperous and grows" (Shatapatha Brahmana 6.1.2.25). In one text, the ruler is equated with a deer and his subjects with grain: "He thus makes the people to be food for the ruler, which is why the ruler feeds on the people" (Shatapatha Brahmana 13.2.9.8). The commoner is summarized as a "tributary to another, to be eaten by another, and one who may be dispossessed at will" (Aitareya Brahmana 7.29).

Such a portrait of the king's absolute powers in relation to his subjects continues in some later texts, most notoriously in the Artha Shastra (where, e.g., the king's dictates are said to overrule law and custom and dharma itself, 3.1.39), in the many texts that extol the necessity of the "rod of punishment" or *danda* as the king's proper tool (see below), and especially in the Narada Dharma Shastra, where the king is to be obeyed and even worshiped, no matter what:

> Whatever a king does is right, that is a settled rule; because the protection of the world is entrusted to him, and on account of his majesty and benignity towards living beings. As a husband though feeble must be constantly worshiped by his wives, in the same way a ruler though worthless must be constantly worshiped by his subjects. (18.21ff.)

The king, the very embodiment, protector, and instigator of one of the principal "ends of life" in Hinduism—"profit," "material advantage," or political and economic self-interest (*artha*)—is given wide latitude to pursue this end with whatever means are necessary:

> (The king) should try hard to get what he has not got and to guard what he has got; he should make what he guards grow, and he should deposit in worthy receptacles of charity what he has made to grow. He should realize that these are the four ways of accomplishing the human goals; never tiring, he should strive to employ them properly. By means of his army he should seek what he has not got; by careful attention he should guard what he has got; he should make what he guards grow

by means of the pursuit of self-interest (*artha*); and he should deposit in worthy
receptacles of charity what he has made to grow. (Manu Smriti 7.99–101)

At the same time, the king's power to rule is tempered and restrained by several factors, including simple practical considerations. As the Artha Shastra notes,
a king who is hated by his subjects cannot expect to easily succeed in his goals
(8.3.16) and a ruler who is overly severe in wielding the coercive "rod of punishment" "becomes a source of terror to beings," whereas the just use of such power
confers honor upon him (1.4.8, 10). "Use of the royal prerogative to advance the
ruler's own ends," notes Drekmeir, "was considered to be theft of the people's
wealth—and was as grave an offense as failure to provide security. . . . In meeting
the responsibilities of his office, he must guard against provoking the people
unnecessarily, and he must always take public opinion into account."[8] It is ultimately in the king's best interests to curb his own excesses and to attend to the
welfare of those he rules, for "in the happiness of the subjects lies the happiness
of the king and in what is beneficial to the subjects his own benefit" (Artha Shastra 1.19.34).

But aside from the restraints that derive from sheer self-interest or practicali-
ty are those of religion. Already in the ancient Vedas and continuing into the period of classical Hinduism, the king's rule is limited and constrained by the claim
of the Brahmin, the representative of religion, to a hierarchically superior place.
The Brahmins, it will be remembered, are created first and from the highest part
of the creator god's body; they are, therefore, "the most excellent; there is nothing more excellent than this. He who knows this, being himself the most excellent, becomes the highest among his own people. The Brahmin has nothing
before it and nothing after it" (Shatapatha Brahmana 10.3.5.10).

Although the Kshatriya has indeed been afforded an exclusive right to the exercise of physical and political power, it is the Brahmin who wields the supposedly
superior powers of religion, especially embodied in their monopoly over the sacrificial rituals, knowledge of the Vedas, and expertise in dharma. Even in the early
texts, the Brahmins did not hesitate to assert their superiority over the Kshatriyas
(see, e.g., Aitareya Brahmana 7.15). And in the later texts on religious law or dharma, the Brahmins promote their own status to the utmost, on the basis of the
superiority of their birth and their connection to religion. "The Brahmin is the
lord of the (other) classes because he is preeminent, because he is the best by
nature, because he maintains the (ascetic) restraints, and because of the preemi-
nence of his transformative rituals" (Manu Smriti 10.3). Or again:

The Brahmin is the Lord of this whole creation, according to the law, because he
was born of the highest part of the body, because he is the eldest, and because he

maintains the Veda. . . . The very birth of a priest is the eternal physical form of religion (dharma); for he is born for the sake of religion and is fit to become one with
ultimate reality. For when a priest is born he is born at the top of the earth, as the
lord of all living beings, to guard the treasure of religion. All of this belongs to the
priest, whatever there is in the universe; the priest deserves all of this because of
his excellence and his high birth." (Manu Smriti 1.94, 98–101)

Even a young Brahmin boy is to be thought of as superior to even the most wiz-
ened of Kshatriyas: "A ten-year-old Brahmin and a hundred-year-old Kshatriya
should be regarded as father and son, and of the two of them the Brahmin is the
father" (Manu Smriti 2.135).

Complementing and often superseding the notion that the king was a divine
figure was the Brahmins' claim to be themselves "human gods." The Brahmins,
it is said in the Veda, are the "divine class" (Taittiriya Brahmana 1.2.6.6), born out
of the "womb of the gods" (Aitareya Brahmana 3.19), and, like the "other gods,"
equally deserving of sacrifices:

There are two kinds of gods, for the gods are gods, and those Brahmins who have
studied and teach the Vedas are human gods. . . . Oblations into the fire are (sacrifices) to the gods, and sacrificial fees (paid to the Brahmin priests are sacrifices) to
the human gods, the Brahmins who have studied and teach the Veda. With oblations into the fire one pleases the gods, with sacrificial fees one pleases the
human gods, the Brahmins who have studied and teach the Veda. Both these
gods, when gratified, place him in a condition of well-being. (Shatapatha Brahmana 2.2.2.6)

As "human gods," the Brahmins from earliest times claimed exemption—
while nevertheless demanding protection—from the rule of the Kshatriyas.
Already in the Vedas, the Brahmins were insisting on both security against oppression and exclusion from capital punishment (Shatapatha Brahmana 11.5.7.1)—
exemptions they further codified in law by the time of the Dharma Sutras: "(The
king) should never kill a priest, even one who persists in every sort of evil. . . .
There is no greater (act of) irreligion on earth than priest-killing; therefore the
king should not even conceive in his mind of killing that (kind of) man" (Manu
Smriti 8.380–81). Another text on dharma declares that "The king should exempt
such a man (i.e., a Brahmin) from six things: He should not be subjected to cor-
poral punishment, imprisonment, fines, banishment, upbraiding, and abandon-
ment" (Gautama Dharma Sutra 8.12), and yet others prohibit the king from con-
fiscating property from the Brahmins (e.g., Baudhayana Dharma Sutra
1.11.15–16).

The Brahmins, at least in the sacred texts they composed and preserved, refuse
to admit that they are under the sovereignty of the king. The Vedic ritual for con-

secration of a king includes rites whereby the Brahmins are made "higher" and the king "lower" (e.g., Shatapatha Brahmana 5.1.1.12), for, as it is said frequently, the Brahmins are ruled by a different king—"King Soma," the divine ruler of the sacrifice (e.g., Aitareya Brahmana 7.29ff.). Even the king's power of punishment and enforcement of the law is, according to some texts, not to be applied to the Brahmins, who are represented as self-sufficient agents wielding their own legitimate power: "A Brahmin who knows the law need not report anything to the king. By means of his own power, he may chastise those men who have wronged him. Between his own power and the power of the king, his own power is stronger; therefore a Brahmin may suppress his enemies by means of his own power alone" (Manu Smriti 11.31–32). And should the warrior class be so rash as to be "overbearing" in any way to the Brahmins, the latter claim the right to "subdue" them since Kshatriyas owe their very existence to the Brahmins: "If the Kshatriyas become overbearing toward the Brahmins in any way, the priests themselves should subdue them, for the Kshatriyas were born from the Brahmins" (Manu Smriti 9.320). Thus, in sum, it is declared that "The king rules over all except the Brahmins" (Gautama Dharma Sutra 11.1).

But while the priestly authors of the sacred texts maintain that Brahmins can, if necessary, live in independence apart from the Kshatriyas, they also insist that the reverse is not true. A Brahmin will, under the proper circumstances, find it advantageous to "obtain a king," that is, to find himself in the employ and under the protection of a pliant ruler. But a king who wishes to rule successfully—let alone righteously—must ally himself with and place himself under the control of the priests. If he does so, his rule will prosper: "It is perfectly in order for a Brahmin to be without a Kshatriya, but were he to obtain a king that would be advantageous. It is, however, quite improper for a Kshatriya to be without a Brahmin. . . . Therefore a Brahmin is indeed to be approached by a Kshatriya who intends to take any action, for his success depends on the act having been impelled by a Brahmin" (Shatapatha Brahmana 4.1.4.6).

It is, then, by placing himself under the guidance and authority of the Brahmin that the king's inclination to tyranny is restrained and his connection to the spiritual principle of dharma is established and preserved. The legitimacy and success of the king's rule depend on forging a bond with a Brahmin priest, with a *purohita* (literally "one who is put ahead") who is said to become one half of the very self of the king he serves. It is in this relationship that the two ruling classes are conjoined into a mutually advantageous consortium, a complementary union between political and temporal power and spiritual authority. "Therefore a Brahmin who has a Kshatriya (patron) is superior to another Brahmin; and therefore a Kshatriya (king) who has a Brahmin (as his personal priest) is superior to another Kshatriya" (Taittiriya Samhita 5.1.10.3). The Manu Smriti explains it thus, "Kshatriyas do not prosper without Brahmins, and Brahmins do not prosper without Kshatriyas; Brahmins and Kshatriyas closely united thrive here on earth and in the world beyond" (Manu Smriti 9.322).

This, then, is one of the principal ways in which political power is made subservient to spiritual authority in the Hindu tradition. The king's rule, seemingly absolute and often apparently tyrannical, is (at least in the texts of Hinduism) severely constrained and morally channeled through his necessary connection to the Brahmin priest. "He should appoint as his personal priest a Brahmin who is learned, born in a good family, eloquent, handsome, mature, and virtuous; who lives according to the rules; and who is austere. He should undertake rites only with his support, 'for a Kshatriya, when he is supported by a Brahmin,' it is said, 'prospers and never falters'" (Gautama Dharma Sutra 11.12–14). When the monarch is in this way harnessed, disciplined, restrained and under the supervision of his priest, his kingdom prospers and "does not come to an early end, life does not leave him before his time, he lives to a ripe old age, he lives life to the fullest, and he does not die again" (Aitareya Brahmana 8.25).

Such an important and intimate relationship holds its own dangers, however, and one of the interesting tensions inherent in Hindu thinking about religion and politics turns on this very union between king and priest. Because the alliance requires the two to join together so closely, the texts warn against Brahmins and Kshatriyas entering into this kind of bond with just anybody: "A Brahmin should not desire to become the purohita of just any Kshatriya, for thereby that which is well made and that which is poorly made unite. Nor should a Kshatriya make just any Brahmin his *purohita*, for thereby that which is well made and that which is poorly made unite" (Shatapatha Brahmana 4.1.4.5). The problem is particularly acute for the Brahmin. For he is the principle of spiritual purity, and by the very establishment of such a personal relationship with the king (so necessary for the king's legitimacy), his purity is thereby compromised. The Brahmin *purohita* is said to take on the traits of the Kshatriya he serves (Aitareya Brahmana 8.24; Manu Smriti 12.46; Mahabharata 12.76); as "half of the self" of the king he serves, the priest also takes on the sins and bad karmic deeds of that king (see, e.g., Pancavimsha Brahmana 13.3.12). The food of a king ingested by a Brahmin takes away the latter's "brilliant energy" (*tejas*), as do his gifts (Manu Smriti 4.218; Mahabharata 13.35.23). Thus some texts even recommend that the Brahmin avoid "service to a king" (e.g., Manu Smriti 3.64) and others depict the royal priest as a contemptible figure (Mahabharta 13.93.130). All in all, the relationship is often regarded with ambivalence on the part of the Brahmin authors of various scriptures. As Heesterman writes, "The *purohita* cannot be a proper brahmin because he is stuck in the sphere of antithetical relations where he has to exchange his purity for the impurity of his patron."[9] Such a dilemma did not, however, prevent Hindu texts from insisting upon this relationship as a means of mitigating the king's power and legitimating his rule.

Another method for tempering the otherwise absolutist powers of the Hindu king was to subject them to the strictures of dharma or religious duty. This was, of course, the principal duty of the king's personal priest: to instruct and guide the king in his "particular duty" or *svadharma*. Because dharma has a superhuman origin, it was binding on all and could be avoided by none; "since law (or dharma) was theoretically beyond the reach of men, the king was confined on pain of supernatural reprisal to administrative decrees consonant with the religious and social code that governed the community."[10] Otherwise put, "Restraints on the king were not formal; they were the restrictions imposed by the obligation to uphold custom and sacred law and to fulfill the requirements of rajadharma [the "dharma of kings"]."[11]

Rajadharma, according to the various law books on the subject, can be encapsulated as protection of his subjects from internal and external threats to their stability and well-being, from chaos within and without. "To take care of creatures is the special duty of a king, and he attains success by fulfilling it," according to one text (Vasishtha Dharma Sutra 19.1); according to another, the king's particular duty is to "destroy enemies and protect his own people" (Artha Shastra 14.3.88).

Protection from external threats means primarily defending the kingdom from its enemies, and virtually all the law books and other treatises on kingship require martial strength of the Hindu king. "The king should not turn back in battle," says one such text, but then goes on to note that a righteous king will fight according to the rules: He should not "strike with barbed or poisoned weapons. He should not engage in battle people who are afraid, intoxicated, mad, or delirious, or who have lost their armor; as also women, children, old people and Brahmins, unless they are trying to kill him" (Baudhayana Dharma Sutra 1.17.9–12).

Conversely, texts based on political realism like the Artha Shastra are far less scrupulous in their advice to the king for carrying out foreign policy, both in times of peace and those of war. The king should unhesitatingly and ruthlessly pursue his advantage; he should "march when by marching he would be able to weaken or exterminate the enemy" (Artha Shastra 9.1.44). Protection from external threats also is said to include protection from natural and supernatural disasters, or as one list would have it, protection from the "eight great calamities" of fire, floods, disease, famine, rats, wild animals, serpents, and evil spirits (Artha Shastra 4.3.1–2).

Diplomacy and foreign relations were included in this aspect of *rajadharma*; they were methods for insuring the protection of the kingdom from external threats and sometimes were constituted as war by other means. The famous theory of the "circle of states" put forward by Kautilya in the Artha Shastra, whereby one's immediate neighbor was one's natural enemy, and the neighbor's neighbor one's natural ally, also called for an elaborate system of undercover agents and spies—all designed to further the king's own interests by secretly "striking again and again" at his enemies and undermining their strength and stability:

> In this way, the conqueror should establish in the rear and in the front a circle (of kings) in his own interest, with the excellences of the constituent, called the ally. And in the entire circle he should ever station envoys and secret agents, becoming a friend of the rivals, maintaining secrecy when striking again and again. The affairs of one who cannot maintain secrecy, even if achieved with particular success, undoubtedly perish, like a broken boat in the ocean. (Artha Shastra 7.13.42–44)

In sum, a king who fails to protect his subjects, in all the ways at his disposal, from external threats to their security is compared with a barren wife, a dried-up milk cow, or a bull that bears no burden.[12]

Protection from internal threats to stability entails the king's administration of law and order. The king is to be both the chief of police and the chief magistrate, and both functions are summarized and symbolized in the form of the "rod of punishment" or *danda*. The proper use by the king of coercive force allows for "the orderly maintenance of worldly life" (Atharva Veda 1.4.4), for without it internal chaos would surely follow. The Hindu view of human nature is, as we shall see below, rather pessimistic, and as such the king's duty to enforce morality or dharma becomes all the more important. "The only way that a man might be kept pure and righteous was by the fear of *danda*," writes Spellman. "In the absence of a king or when people do not fear *danda*, the inevitable result is anarchy and strife."[13]

The administration of justice was another element of the king's obligations to ensure internal order. The law books and the treatises on kingship go into great detail on this subject. The Manu Smriti, for example, dedicates a whole chapter to the topic, instructing the king to hold legal hearings every day and decide cases "in accordance with arguments taken from local practices and from authoritative teachings" (8.3), but also allowing him to rely upon his own powers of intuition to determine guilt or innocence:

> [The king] should take his place on the throne of justice, with his body covered and his mind concentrated, bow low to the Guardians of the World, and begin to hear the case. Recognizing both what is profitable and what is not profitable, and what is intrinsically just and unjust, he should hear all the cases of the parties in the order of their classes. He should discover the inner emotion of men from the outward signs, by their voice, color, involuntary movements, and facial expressions, by their gaze and their gestures. The inner mind-and-heart is grasped by facial expressions, involuntary movements, gait, gesture, speech, and changes in the eyes and mouth. (Manu Smriti 8.23–26)

It is especially the king's duty to uphold the religious law or dharma of the various classes and castes to ensure the proper order and functioning of society: "When all laws are perishing the king here is the promulgator of laws, by virtue of his guarding the right conduct of the world consisting of the four social classes and the four stages of life" (Artha Shastra 3.1.38). Keeping order in caste India meant making certain that everyone kept in their proper place. This required the king to oversee the performance of the individual duties of the constituents of his kingdom, but also to guard against miscegenation. The "intermixture of castes" was abhorred and feared as the ultimate sign of internal chaos. It was the king's duty to protect the lives of the "fourfold human race," to ensure and promote their "increase" and "protection" and, especially, their "nonintermixture and adherence to the dharma" (Gautama Dharma Sutra 8.2–3).

As part of the king's duty or *rajadharma*, and as yet another means for keeping the powers of the king in check and assuring that his activities conform to religious principles, it is often declared that the king must himself be a model of personal conduct and ascetic restraint. He should, as we have seen above, "remain unaddicted to the sensory objects" (Manu Smriti 1.89); elsewhere it said that the king should be "correct in his actions and speech and trained in the three Vedas and logic. Let him be upright, keep his senses under control, surround himself with men of quality, and adopt sound policies. He should be impartial toward his subjects and work for their welfare" (Gautama Dharma Sutra 11.2–6). The king who properly and legitimately wields the "rod of punishment" is one who "speaks the truth, acts after due consideration, is wise, and is conversant with religion. . . ." Conversely, one who is "lustful, partial and mean" is himself destroyed by that very rod. "For the rod of punishment has great brilliant energy, and for those who are undisciplined it is hard to maintain; if a king swerves from justice it strikes him down, together with his relatives, and then his fort, his territory, and the whole world, with all that moves and does not move" (Manu Smriti 7.26–29).

One reading of the most famous text on Hindu political science, the Artha Shastra, sees that work as promoting a legitimating rationale for kingship based not on the sacrality of the office but rather on the world-renouncing principle of the ascetic restraint of the senses. The king's authority, in other words, is to replicate the authority of the world-renouncer or the otherworldly Brahmin, whose purity derives from his detachment from the things and interests of worldly life:

> The ideal Kautalayan king has an authority and a legitimation not derived from the community but all his own. For here the king's basic qualification is not his sacrality or divinity, but the *indriyajaya*, the victory over the senses, which sets him free from being at the mercy of worldly interests. In this way he becomes the worthy counterpart of the ideal Brahmin, who is equally detached from worldly concerns.[14]

Thus it is that in the Artha Shastra itself the "whole of this science" of politics and statecraft is said to rest on the king's mastery over himself. The ideal king mirrors the ideal ascetic who has attained control over his senses, his desires, and his emotions:

> Control over the senses, which is motivated by training in the sciences, should be secured by giving up lust, anger, greed, pride, arrogance and fool-hardiness. Absence of improper indulgence in (the pleasures of) sound, touch, color, taste and smell by the senses of hearing, touch and sight, the tongue and the sense of smell, means control over the senses; or, the practice of (this) science (gives such control). For the whole of this science means control over the senses. A king, behaving in a manner contrary to that, (and hence) having no control over his senses, quickly perishes. (Artha Shastra 1.6.1–4)

It is, the text declares, especially important for a king to overcome lust and anger, for "lust means the favoring of evil persons" and anger entails "the suppression of good persons. Because of the multitude of evils (resulting from them), both are held to be a calamity without end" (Artha Shastra 8.3.65). Controlling these two vices has very practical ramifications for the king's rule. Kings "under the influence of anger are known to have been killed by uprisings among the subjects"; anger can lead the king to oppression of his people which, in turn, can result in rebellion (Artha Shastra 8.3.5–7, 14–22). Elsewhere also, the king is advised to "make a great effort to avoid the ten vices that arise from desire and the eight that are born of anger, which (all) end badly":

> For a king who is addicted to the vices born of desire and pleasure loses his religion and profit, but (if he is addicted to the vices) born of anger (he loses) his very self. Hunting, gambling, sleeping by day, malicious gossip, women, drunkenness, music, singing, dancing, and aimless wandering are the group of ten (vices) born of desire. Slander, physical violence, malice, envy, resentment, destruction of property, verbal abuse, and assault are the group of eight (vices) born of anger. (Manu Smriti 7.45–48)

Most important, the king should be morally restrained because the king is the model for his subjects; his behavior influences them, and, according to Hindu political philosophy, in a very direct way. The king's adherence to the guidelines of dharma and the rules of ascetic self-discipline ineluctably molds the moral quality of his people: "What character (the king) has, that character the constituents come to have. . . . For the king is in the place of their head" (Artha Shastra 8.1.17–18); or, again, "A king endowed with personal qualities endows with excellences the constituent elements not so endowed. One not endowed with personal qualities destroys the constituent elements that are prosperous and devoted (to him)" (Artha Shastra 6.1.16).

So it is that the king's self-control or "self-rule" (*svaraj*) is the condition of possibility for his effective rule over others: "Day and night he should make a great effort to conquer his sensory powers, for the man who has conquered his sensory powers is able to keep his subjects under control" (Manu Smriti 7.44). The king's behavior is even said to have cosmic ramifications: "Welfare, good rains, sickness, calamities, and death among the people owe their origin to the king,"[15] and it is often said that the king's relative righteousness determines the kind of cosmic era (ranging from the Golden Age to the degeneracy of the "Kali Yuga" or Dark Age) his subjects inhabit: "Let not this doubt be thine, whether the era is the cause of the king or the king the cause of the era, for know it to be certain that the king is the cause of the era."[16]

This almost mystical notion of the interconnection between the individual's self-rule and the righteous rule of the political order, the postulation that one should be able to rule oneself before attempting to rule others, is thus a fundamental principle of Indian political philosophy. It perseveres in the Hindu tradition all the way up to the twentieth century, when it was adopted by no less of a figure than Mohandas Gandhi, who made it the centerpiece of both his method on nonviolent resistance and his vision of an independent India. *Svaraj* in the sense of self-control was for Gandhi the proper means for attaining the correlative end of *svaraj* in the sense of political independence.

The Medium of Expressing Politics in Hinduism

We have seen how even in the earliest strata of Hindu literature texts extolling the divine right of kings to rule are encountered within accounts of the creation of the world as a whole. Other sacred works of the tradition provide myths of origins specific to kingship per se, and argue for his divinity.[17] The king, such myths of origin and legitimation insist, is not to be regarded as an ordinary being but as a god on earth, created to put an end to anarchy and fear. In the following text, the king is portrayed as comprising the various essences of the gods so as to establish order in a world that, without a king, was in utter chaos:

> For when this world was without a king and people ran about in all directions out of fear, the Lord emitted a king in order to guard this entire (realm), taking lasting elements from Indra (warrior king of the gods), the Wind (Vayu), Yama (god of death), the Sun (Surya), Fire (Agni), Varuna (god of the waters), the Moon (Candra), and (Kubera) the Lord of Wealth. Because a king is made from particles of the lords of the gods, therefore he surpasses all living beings in brilliant energy, and like the Sun, he burns eyes and hearts, and no one on earth is able even to look at him. Through his special power he becomes Fire and Wind; he is the Sun and the Moon, and he is (Yama) the King of Justice, he is Kubera and he is Varuna, and he

is Indra. Even a boy king should not be treated with disrespect, with the thought, "He is just a human being"; for this is a deity standing there in the form of a man. (Manu Smriti 7.3–8)

Another text explains how having the essences of eight great deities confers upon the king his distinctive powers and abilities:

Like Indra, the sovereign is able to protect the wealth and possessions. As Vayu or Air is the spreader (and diffuser) of scents, so the prince is the generator (and cause) of good and evil actions. As the sun is the dispeller of darkness (and the creator of light) so the king is the founder of religion and destroyer of irreligion. As Yama is the god who punishes (human beings after death) so also the monarch is the punisher of offenses (in this world). Like Agni (fire), the prince is the purifier and the enjoyer of all gifts. As Varuna, the god of water, sustains everything by supplying moisture, so also the king maintains everybody by his virtues and activities. As the god of wealth protects the jewels of the universe, so the king protects the treasure and possessions of the state.[18]

A similar set of correlations between the deities and the king's powers is formulated as part of the myth of origins found in the Vishnudharmottara Purana:

The king was emitted by the Self-generated One who had drawn together portions of the gods for the purpose of wielding the rod of coercive power in order to protect all living beings. Since no one is even able to gaze at him on account of his radiant energy, the king is, among the people, a lord like the Sun (Surya). When a person comes to participate in divine favor by looking on him, then because he is the source of delight for the eye, he becomes the Moon (Candra). When he spontaneously pervades the entire world by means of his mobile agents, the king becomes the Wind (Vayu) among the people. Whenever the king makes wrong-doers shrivel up, the king turns into Death (Yama), born of the sun, among men. Whenever the king, on account of his majesty burns angered and aroused men even though he might not desire to, he turns into Fire (Agni) among men. Whenever the king makes gifts of wealth on all sides for the sake of giving itself then he becomes Kubera (god of riches). Whenever he floods the world by showering down streams of wealth, the king is said to become Varuna (god of waters) by men learned in right conduct. Sustaining all of the people without distinctions by means of a heart strong in compassion, the king becomes lord of the earth. When he fully protects the entire populace with overlordship then he turns into Indra (warrior king of the gods), compassionate toward all living beings.[19]

The king is even given powers of metamorphosis due to his divine nature: "In order to make justice succeed, he takes all forms again and again, taking into consideration realistically what is to be done, (his) power, and the time and place. The lotus goddess of Good Fortune resides in his favor, victory in his aggression, and death in his anger; for he is made of the brilliant energy of all (the gods)" (Manu Smriti 7.10–11).

Some stories legitimate the king's sacred nature and right to rule by imagining a primordial state of nature without law, stability, and security. Other such myths start by positing a golden age in which there was no need for a king. Society was self-regulating as all people naturally conformed their behavior to dharma or righteous conduct. But then comes a "fall." Morality degenerates, and the typical Hindu vices of delusion, ignorance, desire, attachment to sense objects, and greed arise. Dharma is no longer observed, immorality is given free reign, and the proper distinctions between things breaks down. It is as a corrective to such chaos that kingship is established by the gods:

> Neither kingship nor king was there in the beginning, neither scepter (or rod of punishment, *danda*) nor the bearer of the scepter. All people protected one another by means of righteous conduct. Thus, while protecting one another by means of righteous conduct . . . men eventually fell into a state of spiritual lassitude. Then delusion overcame them. Men were thus overpowered by infatuation . . . on account of the delusion of understanding; their sense of righteous conduct was lost. When understanding was lost, all men . . . overpowered by infatuation, became victims of greed. Then they sought to acquire what should not be acquired. Thereby, indeed . . . another vice, namely desire, overcame them. Attachment then attacked them, who had become victims of desire. Attached to objects of sense, they did not discriminate between right and wrong action. . . . They did not avoid . . . pursuing what was not worth pursuing, nor, similarly, did they discriminate between what should be said and what should not be said, between the edible and inedible, and between right and wrong. . . . Then the gods approached Vishnu, the lord of creatures, and said, "Indicate to us that one person among mortals who alone is worthy of the highest eminence." Then the blessed lord god Narayana reflected, and brought forth an illustrious mind-born son, called Virajas (who became the first king).[20]

Kingship here and in many other texts is represented as coming into existence in the mythical time of beginnings to counteract the effects of a natural state of affairs (or the reversion to it) of chaos, anarchy, and immorality. This state of nature, devoid of the coercive rule of a king, is often depicted as one governed by the "law of the fishes" (an ancient Indian concept not dissimilar to the "law of the jungle"). "If there were no king on earth for holding the rod of punishment, the strong would then have oppressed the weak after the manner of fishes in the water. We have heard that men, in days of yore, in consequence of anarchy, were ruined, devouring one another like stronger fishes devouring the weaker ones in the water."[21] As Spellman notes, "In ancient India, the fear of anarchy was almost pathological. Underlying every concept of kingship was the doctrine of *matsyanyaya*—the analogy of the big fish eating up the little fish. . . . Without understanding this idea, there can be no understanding of kingship in ancient India."[22]

It is, indeed, out of fear of the unruly alternative of a world without law in which the unrestrained "survival of the fittest" prevails that the gods fashioned the first king and ordained him the restorer of order, the legitimate ruler, and the enforcer of righteousness—and, as such, the human "worthy of the highest eminence." "The coronation of king is the first duty of kingdom," according to the great Hindu epic, the Mahabharata, for without a king anarchy prevails:

A kingdom in which anarchy prevails becomes weak and is soon afflicted by robbers. In kingdoms torn by anarchy, righteousness cannot dwell. The inhabitants devour one another. An anarchy is the worst possible of states. The sacred texts declare that in crowning a king, it is Indra (the king of the gods) that is crowned (in the person of the king). A person who is desirous of prosperity should worship the king as he should worship Indra himself. No one should dwell in kingdoms torn by anarchy. Agni (the god of fire) does not convey (to the gods) the libations that are poured upon him in kingdoms where anarchy prevails.[23]

The consequences of a king who is too weak or overly scrupulous when it comes to enforcing order are similar to a world in which there is no king at all. Lawlessness and disorder overwhelm stability, and society falls into the ultimate sign of corruption and chaos—the intermixture of castes:

If the king did not tirelessly inflict punishment on those who should be punished, the stronger would roast the weaker like fish on a spit. The crow would eat the sacrificial cake and the dog would lick the oblations; there would be no ownership in anyone, and (everything) would be upside down. The whole world is mastered by punishment, for an unpolluted man is hard to find. Through fear of punishment everything that moves allows itself to be used. The gods, the titans, the centaurs, the ogres, the birds and the snakes, even they allow themselves to be used, but only under pressure from punishment. All the classes would be corrupted, and all barriers broken, all people would erupt in fury as a result of a serious error in punishment. (Manu Smriti 7.20–24)

The king's right to enforce the law, dispense justice, and administer punishment is summarized in the concept of *danda*, the scepter or "rod of punishment." The *danda*—and all it represents—is itself given its own myth of origins in which the Creator "emits" it as his own son and as the "protector of all living beings." This rod of punishment is also identified with the king ("the rod is the king"), who wields it in order to uphold dharma:

For (the king's sake) the Lord in ancient times emitted the rod of punishment, his own son, (the incarnation of) Justice, to be the protector of all living beings, made of the brilliant energy of ultimate reality. Through fear of him all living beings, stationary and moving, allow themselves to be used and do not swerve from their own duty. . . . The rod is the king and the man, he is the inflicter and he is the chastiser, traditionally regarded as the guarantor for the duty of the four stages of life. The rod alone chastises all the subjects, the rod protects them, the rod stays awake while they sleep; wise men know that justice is the rod. Properly wielded, with due consideration, it makes all the subjects happy; but inflicted without due consideration, it destroys everything. (Manu Smriti 7.14–15, 17–19)

The Message of Hinduism's Politics

In the face of the always threatening dangers of anarchy, and especially the fear of the socially disastrous "mixing of castes," the figure of the king played a crucial role in Hindu social and political thought. The wide latitude the king is given to exercise coercive power seems to have developed in direct correlation to the degree of anxiety regarding life without such restraints.

But the king himself must also be restrained, lest the powers he has been given are misused. He is always to be guided by *rajadharma*, the religious duty assigned specifically to the monarch, that includes the duty of maintaining a kind of yogic self-control one usually expects to find as an attribute of the king's social and religious opposite: the world-renouncer. And as we have seen above, the king's religious legitimacy, as well as his temporal success, also depends on his proper alliance with a Brahmin priest or *purohita*. The bond formed between the these two figures ensured not only that the king, the embodiment of the principle of power, would be restrained by the Brahmin, the embodiment of the principle of religion; it also acted as a potent symbol of religiously legitimated political leadership.

Such a union between king and personal priest is given a divine pedigree and transcendental origin in stories revolving around the relationship between the divine priest Mitra and the royal god Varuna. The two are represented as the apotheoses of two complementary principles. The Brahmin deity is "intelligence" or "inspiration," whereas the Kshatriya god embodies "capacity for action" or "skillfulness." The Brahmin priest thus "at once inspirits and inspires the King," as one scholar puts it.[24] One paradigmatic text on the divine couple portrays the two as originally separate. But whereas "Mitra, the Brahmin, could stand without Varuna, the Kshatriya," things were otherwise for Varuna: "Whatever action Varuna did uninspired by Mitra, the Brahmin, did not succeed." Only when the deities—and the powers they represent—were united, and the Brahmin was made "foremost" in the relationship, could the divine king rule effectively: "Whatever action, inspired by Mitra, the Brahmin, Varuna subsequently did succeeded" (Shatapatha Brahmana 4.1.4.1ff.).

The Hindu epics, the Mahabharata and Ramayana, are (among many other things) also legitimating narratives of ideal Hindu kingship. The rule of Yudhishthira in the Mahabharata is represented as one in which the virtue of the king fans out beneficially to all the elements of the polity:

> The kingdom became free from disputes and fear of every kind. And all the people became attentive to their respective occupations. The rain became so abundant as to leave no room for desire and the kingdom grew in prosperity. Indeed, during the realm of Yudhishthira, who was ever devoted to truth, there was no extortion, no stringent realization of rent debts, no fear of disease, of fire, or of death by poisoning and incantations, in the kingdom. . . . and accordingly, during the reign of Yudhishthira, who was ever devoted to virtue, his dominions grew in prosperity.[25]

In like manner, Rama, the hero-king of the Ramayana, is depicted in ideal terms as "majestic," "illustrious," "lord of the three worlds," the "greatest ruler in the three worlds," and so forth. He is the great exemplar and protector of dharma: "Rama's own personal dharma and his dharma as potential king are linked together. The ideal of kingship seen in Rama is based upon the relationship between Rama's own dharma and that of the kingdom. . . . The promotion of dharma is secured not just by statecraft but also by example."[26]

Also in the Ramayana, we are given a depiction of the ideal Hindu kingdom, a state ruled by the righteous god-king Rama and thus termed "Ramrajya." In this millenarian time, "the world would be happy, satisfied and delighted, and free from sickness, affliction, famine and fear. Men would not see the death of their sons, women would not become widows and would remain devoted to their husbands. There would be no danger of tempest, nor would people perish through drowning, nor would there be danger from fire, just as in the Golden Age" (Ramayana 1.1.71–73).

Hinduism and Nonbelievers: Politics and People outside the Tradition

This Hindu political and religious ideal of a "kingdom of heaven on earth" ruled by a righteous god-king (or the equivalent) has persisted throughout history. There have, however, been somewhat different visions of what such an ideal kingdom would look like, especially with regard to its social and religious composition. For while Hindu theory has always not only accounted for but assumed the diverse nature of the religious and social components of the polity, it has only been relatively recently that the modern idea (and problem) of religious diversity has come to the fore.

In the classical texts of the tradition, social—and also to some extent religious—pluralism is embraced as not only a fact of political life but as necessary to the proper order of things. "Unity in diversity" describes the Hindu system of *varnashrama dharma*, whereby religious and social duty is calibrated to one's inborn class and particular stage of life. The notion that there are, and should be, differences in the body politic is therefore no problem for traditional Hinduism; indeed, it is a *feature* of traditional Hindu political and religious thought. The king's job is to stand apart from the sometimes competing interests of the various classes and castes, to negotiate and mediate them, but in every case to do so according to the religiously fixed guidelines of dharma. As we have seen, one of the principal duties of the king is to ensure internal order by enforcing the dictates of the particular dharma assigned to the particular individuals and groups that constitute his kingdom.

This assumes, however, that all within the kingdom accept and understand these dictates, that all, in other words, are in some sense or another "Hindu." The extreme elasticity of the term has helped (many apparently unorthodox traditions like Buddhism, Jainism, and later Sikhism could be and have been incorporated under the concept at various times), as has the notion that social duty overrides sectarian affiliation (a Buddhist or Sikh merchant is still, after all, a merchant with all of the attendant social duties). Furthermore, the hierarchical nature of Hindu thought and organization has allowed certain Hindu texts a great freedom to encompass all sorts of beliefs and practices under one or another sectarian heading.

Take, for example, the classic syncretistic text of the Bhagavad Gita, which reorients Hinduism up until its time around a new center, the devotion to and worship of the deity Krishna. It is Krishna, the text declares, who is recipient of worship regardless of who the worshippers think they are worshipping: "When devoted men sacrifice to other deities with faith, they sacrifice to me, Arjuna, however aberrant the rites" (Bhagavad Gita 9.23). In this way, religious diversity can be easily tolerated, albeit within a hierarchical scheme of things.

But Hinduism also has acknowledged the possibility of heresy, of the existence of those who cannot be included even within the rather wide embrace of the religion. "Atheists" (usually referring to Buddhists and/or materialists) have sometimes been so designated, but especially those who deny the authority of the Vedas and the Brahmins (and thus the authority of the Hindu conceptualization of dharma) are cast beyond the pale. Although in practice Hindu kings since the rise of the heterodox religions of Buddhism and Jainism in the fifth century B.C.E. have not only tolerated but often enough patronized them, Hindu law books are not without passages that advise the king to banish those the Brahmins regard as dangerous competitors: "(The king) should quickly expel from the town gamblers, traveling bards, playboys, men who persist in heresy or bad actions, and bootleggers" (Manu Smriti 9.225). Such advice (assuming the heretics in question were Buddhists and Jains) was a practical impossibility from early times and was ignored by Hindu kings in all periods.

The institution of Muslim rule over much of north India in the second millennium C.E. put much of Hindu political thinking and policy into eclipse. Hindus could and did, however, accommodate themselves to Islamic rule, perhaps in large part because, as one scholar has noted, "The ideal activities of the king, in the Hindu and Muslim traditions, appear to have certain common characteristics":

> The king presides over a social order to be maintained rather than over an enterprise to be managed: he must mete out punishment in order to uphold justice; he should not interfere with the property of his subjects except to levy lawful taxes; he should take care to restore good customs, namely those in consonance with sacred law; he should protect and help widows and orphans. In order to perform his proper functions effectively, he must cultivate traits of character which, in the two traditions, prove to be very similar. He must develop and exercise self control; he must avoid intoxicating drink; even though his sexual impulses need not be kept under severe restraint, he must remain suspicious of the influence of women.[27]

The Muslims were succeeded by the British, who colonized and ruled India in the nineteenth and twentieth centuries. Resistance to their rule and movements organized to achieve independence often involved the resuscitation of ancient Hindu religio-political ideas and images. The vision of an independent India based on and guided by the "rule of God" or Ramrajya was particularly embraced by two very different and competing factions of the independence movement. On the one hand, Mohandas Gandhi envisioned an inclusivistic and ecumenical ideal of Ramraj, which was nevertheless self-consciously conceived as a spiritual alternative to Western secular notions of nationalism and statecraft.

On the other hand, a very different conceptualization of the concept of Ramrajya was formulated and propagated by the rather more exclusive and intolerant members of the Hindu nationalist or "Hindutva" movement. This latter understanding was one of a Hindu theocracy in which non-Hindus (primarily Muslims and Christians) would be relegated to the status of "guests." Both versions of Ramrajya were in direct opposition to the constitutionally secular nationalism that won the day in 1947. But the Hindutva movement has received large support over recent decades in India and, at least in some of its more radical factions, has not given up its ideal of a Hindu theocracy—the reconciliation of political power and spiritual authority.

Conclusion

Gandhi once famously remarked that those who believe religion is separable from politics understand neither one. The Hindu tradition, stretching over the course of more than three millennia, has, in this regard, tried to have its cake and eat it too. On the one hand, religion and politics are separable and separated in classical Hindu thinking. The functions of political power and spiritual authority are, from this point of view, distinct and held apart. Each is monopolized by a different class: the warrior-king's temporal power belongs to him and him alone, whereas only the Brahmin embodies spiritual authority. As such, the king represents (and is often said to wield) absolute power over the secular realm, whereas the Brahmin holds himself aloof from the compromises and impurity of the world and thus safeguards his own spiritual purity. This-worldly and otherworldly Hinduism, condensed and symbolized in the figures of the king and the world-renouncing Brahmin, are in this way juxtaposed while isolated one from the other.

But this Hindu version of the "separation of church and state" cannot and did not stand unmitigated. The state's legitimacy depended on its connection to religion, just as "the church" depended on the state for protection and support. This-worldly Hinduism could only be religiously validated with recourse to the transcendent values and prestigious practices of otherworldly Hinduism. Conversely, otherworldly Hinduism was only possible through the support, order, and stability provided by those pursuing this-worldly activities. The king needed the Brahmin (or what the Brahmin stood for), and the Brahmin needed the king (or what the king stood for).

This tension played itself out in various ways, as we have seen. The king is represented as an autocrat whose pursuit of his political self-interest is his highest duty, but also as a divinity, the earthly embodiment of transcendent deities. The king's duty involves him deeply in the affairs of politics, protection, warfare, policing, and law—and mostly "by any means necessary"—while at the same time requiring him to subordinate himself to the Brahmin priest and the restraints of religion. The king mucks about in the world of realpolitik—of the pursuit of one's own goals and desires—while simultaneously restraining himself through ascetic practices designed to turn him into a kind of disinterested *yogin*.

There is, argues Heesterman, an "insoluble dilemma" inherent in the Hindu view of political rule. This conundrum finds its focused expression in the problematic alliance between the king and his Brahmin priest. The king needs the transcendent legitimation that only such a relationship with the Brahmin can give him. "But once the king has succeed in establishing this relationship the Brahmin by the same token has lost the transcendent status that formed his literally priceless value."[28] By virtue of the very fact that the Brahmin has formed such a relation with the king, his power to legitimate the king's rule is thereby compromised. Otherwise put, the conundrum of the power and authority consists in the fact that the king "who has successfully enticed the Brahmin to serve him only obtains an empty husk, for the Brahmin then loses his special quality that was the reason to engage him."[29]

Nor is this dilemma really solved by insisting that the king combine in himself this-worldly and otherworldly features in the form of the active, politically powerful king who is also epitome of the yogic ideal of self-restraint. For while "the king has to win his independence of action at the price of renouncing worldly interests," it is not clear what then could "motivate the king, whose hard-won conquest of the senses has placed him above worldly interests, still to acquire and increase his worldly power."[30]

In Hindu religious texts, "Kingship remains, even theoretically, suspended between sacrality and secularity, divinity and mortal humanity, legitimate authority and arbitrary power, dharma and adharma."[31] And perhaps such a conundrum is not really unique to Hinduism, but a feature of all religions. The harmonization of such opposing principles is never easy, and is perhaps ultimately impossible. It is not easy to connect the transcendent and imminent, the religious and the political, without compromising both.

Notes

1. Unless otherwise noted, translations from the Sanskrit texts are my own.

2. All translations from the Manu Smriti come from *The Laws of Manu*, trans. by Wendy Doniger with Brian K. Smith (London: Penguin Books, 1991).

3. Translations from the Artha Shastra are taken from *The Kautiliya Arthasastra, Pt. II: An English Translation with Critical and Explanatory Notes*, 2d ed., trans. by R. P. Kangle (Delhi: Motilal Banarsidass, 1972).

4. See the introduction of *Dharmasutras: The Law Codes of Ancient India*, trans. by Patrick Olivelle (Oxford: Oxford University Press, 1999). I have drawn on this work for translations of the Dharma Sutras found below.

5. Another "goal" or "end" of life is also sometimes included: *moksha* or "liberation" from suffering and rebirth.

6. For references, see Jan Gonda's *Ancient Indian Kingship from the Religious Point of View* (Leiden: E. J. Brill, 1966).

7. For further citations and a discussion, see Brian K. Smith, *Classifying the Universe: The Ancient Indian Varna System and the Origins of Caste* (Oxford: Oxford University Press, 1994), 42–46.

8. Charles Drekmeir, *Kingship and Community in Early India* (Stanford, Calif.: Stanford University Press, 1962), 255–56.

9. J. C. Heesterman, "Brahmin, Ritual, and Renouncer," *Wiener Zeitschrift fur die Kunde Sud- und Ostasiens* 8 (1964), 21.

10. Drekmeir, *Kingship and Community*, 21–22.

11. Drekmeir, *Kingship and Community*, 256.

12. Mahabharata (Shantiparva 15; 78.14), cited in Drekmeir, *Kingship and Community*, 138.

13. John W. Spellman, *Political Theory of Ancient India* (Oxford: Oxford University Press, 1964), 108.

14. J. C. Heesterman, "Kautalya and the Ancient Indian State," *Wiener Zeitschrift fur die Kunde Sudasiens* 15 (1971): 9.

15. Mahabharata (Shantiparva 139.9), cited in Spellman, *Political Theory of Ancient India*, 211.

16. Mahabharata (Udyogaparva), cited in Spellman, *Political Theory of Ancient India*, 212.

17. Drekmeir contends throughout his important work on ancient Indian kingship that the "divinity" of the king lies primarily not in his person but in the office. See, e.g., *Kingship and Community*, 252: "In summary we may say that usually the concept of divinity was used metaphorically in ancient India to describe the functions of the royal office. . . . In India (as in the European Middle Ages) divine right, at least in the period before the decline of Mauryan rule, must be located in the institution of kingship and not in the king himself."

18. Shukranitisara 1.141–52. Cited in Drekmeir, *Kingship and Community*, 223.

19. Vishnudharmottara Purana 2.71; adapted from the translation in Ronald Inden's "Ritual, Authority, and Cyclical Time in Hindu Kingship," in J. F. Richards, ed., *Kingship and Authority in South Asia* (Delhi: Oxford University Press, 1998), 48–49.

20. Mahabharata 12.59.5ff. Cited in Ainslie T. Embree, ed., *Sources of Indian Tradition*, Vol. 1, 2d ed. (New York: Columbia University Press, 1988), 238–39.

21. Mahabharata (Shantiparvan 67.16ff.), cited in Drekmeir, *Kingship and Community*, 138.

22. Spellman, *Political Theory of Ancient India*, 4–5.

23. Mahabharata 12.67, cited in Ainslie T. Embree, ed., *The Hindu Tradition: Readings in Oriental Thought* (New York: Vintage Books, 1966), 107.

24. Ananda K. Coomaraswamy, *Spiritual Authority and Temporal Power in the Indian Theory of Government* (New Haven, Conn.: American Oriental Society, 1942), 12.

25. Mahabharata (Sabhaparva), cited in Spellman, *Political Theory of Ancient India*, 213.

26. Frank Whaling, *The Rise of the Religious Significance of Rama* (Delhi: Motilal Banarsidass, 1980), 64–65.

27. Peter Hardy, "Growth of Authority over a Conquered Political Elite: Early Delhi Sultanate as a Possible Case Study," in Richards, *Kingship and Authority in South Asia*, 223.

28. J. C. Heesterman, "Priesthood and the Brahmin," *Contributions to Indian Sociology* (new series) 5 (1971): 46.

29. J. C. Heesterman, *The Inner Conflict of Tradition: Essays in Indian Ritual, Kingship, and Society* (Chicago: University of Chicago Press, 1985), 155.

30. Heesterman, "Kautalya and the Ancient Indian State," 9–10.

31. Heesterman, *Inner Conflict of Tradition*, 111.

Suggested Readings

Biardeau, Madeleine. *Hinduism, The Anthropology of a Civilization.* Trans. Richard Nice. New York : Oxford University Press, 1989.

Coomaraswamy, Ananda K. *Spiritual Authority and Temporal Power in the Indian Theory of Government.* New Haven, Conn.: American Oriental Society, 1942.

Drekmeir, Charles. *Kingship and Community in Early India.* Stanford, Calif.: Stanford University Press, 1962.

Flood, Gavin D. *An Introduction to Hinduism*. New York: Cambridge University Press, 1996.

Gonda, Jan. *Ancient Indian Kingship from the Religious Point of View*. Leiden: E. J. Brill, 1966.

Herman, A. L. *A Brief Introduction to Hinduism: Religion, Philosophy, and Ways of Liberation*. Boulder, Colo.: Westview Press, 1991.

Hopkins, Thomas J. *The Hindu Religious Tradition*. Encino, Calif.: Dickenson Publishing. Co., 1971.

Klostermaier, Klaus K. *A Short Introduction to Hinduism*. Oxford: Oneworld, 1998.

———. *A Survey of Hinduism*. 2d ed. Albany: State University of New York Press, 1994.

Knipe, David M. *Hinduism: Experiments in the Sacred*. San Francisco: Harper San Francisco, 1991.

Larson, Gerald James. *India's Agony over Religion*. Albany: State University of New York Press, 1995.

Richards, J. F., ed. *Kingship and Authority in South Asia*. Delhi: Oxford University Press, 1998.

Spellman, John W. *Political Theory of Ancient India*. Oxford: Oxford University Press, 1964.

Veer, Peter van der. *Religious Nationalism : Hindus and Muslims in India*. Berkeley: University of California Press, 1994.

Nine | **Confucianism** |

Mark Csikszentmihalyi

WHEN JESUIT MISSIONARIES FIRST SENT ACCOUNTS OF CHINESE RELIGION BACK TO Europe in the sixteenth and seventeenth centuries, some attempted to draw a distinction between "idolatrous" religions, such as Buddhism and Taoism, and the more enlightened tradition of the sage Confucius that preserved some traces of natural theology. In the intervening centuries, elements of this essential distinction have been recast in several ways: the prevailing academic tendency to classify Confucianism as a "philosophy" and other traditions as "religions," Max Weber's idea that Confucianism served as the official ideology of an imperial bureaucracy that retarded the development of capitalism, and even contemporary attempts to adopt elements of Confucianism as a secular value system by some Asian governments. Whether as a remnant of an inspired theology, a humanistic ethical system, or a bureaucratic ideology perceived as unthreatening to modern states, each of these portrayals of Confucianism paints it as a unitary and coherent tradition. Yet the very diversity of these portrayals demonstrates that the term actually has a number of distinct referents, and suggests that the notion that Confucianism is a single discrete tradition is an oversimplification.

Historically, Confucianism refers to a number of separate but related traditions that in some way invoke the authority of Kong Qiu, the fifth-century B.C.E. figure on whom the Jesuits bestowed the latinized sobriquet "Confucius." Most important for the purposes of this essay is the transmission of the Confucian canon, at different times in Chinese history comprising the "Five Classics" (*wujing*), the "Four Books" (*sishu*), and the "Thirteen Classics" (*shisanjing*) and their accumulated commentaries. Owing to Confucius's putative authorship, editorship, and teaching of many of the canonical texts, the transmission and valorization of these texts by scholars is called Confucianism. By extension, the emphasis on these texts in the traditional educational system has often been labeled as Confucian. Another Confucianism is the bureaucratic structure that depended on the canon for the curriculum of its examination system, and on relevant aspects of Confucius's teachings as a code of professional ethics for its members.

On a personal level, family life in East Asia has been structured by a set of normative behaviors, such as the familial piety (*xiao*) advocated by Confucius, that are indexed to roles defined by the "five relationships" (*wulun*). Also, the veneration of Confucius by his family and disciples spawned a cult that became institutionalized through the establishment of an official network of Confucian temples in the Tang Dynasty (618–907 C.E.). Both proper family behavior and animal sacrifice at Confucian temples also are routinely labeled Confucian. Each of these strands of Confucianism has had its own distinct influence on Chinese politics, and the political significance of both Confucian family roles and Confucian liturgy each merit attention in its own right. Here, however, the focus will be on the politics reflected in the core texts of the Confucian tradition. Because the Confucian canon played a central role in the educational system and defined the ethos of the government official, its interpretation has historically been at the center of disputes over politics in the public sphere.

Classical Sources of Confucianism on Politics

Of the classical sources that became part of the Confucian canon, two are particularly influential in the formation of the religious justification of political authority. The earlier of the two is the record of the sage kings of antiquity, collected in the *Shangshu*, or the *Classic of Documents* (*Shujing*, hereafter *Documents*). The other is the teachings of Confucius, primarily as transmitted in the *Analects* (*Lunyu*), but also as expressed in the cryptic chronicle of the *Spring and Autumn Annals* (*Chunqiu*) and various other works such as those incorporated by the Qing Dynasty scholar Sun Xingyan (1753–1818 C.E.) into the *Collected Sayings of Confucius* (*Kongzi jiyu*). These two sources treat politics through a dual focus on the methods and character of exemplary rulers of the past, and on the description of a process of the cultivation of a set of virtues capable of imparting moral authority. Both sources distinguish between the ruler's virtue as the justification for their authority, and the sanction conferred by *tian* (usually translated as "Heaven") as the actual source of the authority. These canonical texts argue that political success or failure is a function of the virtue of the ruler, and in this way combine a religious view of moral perfection with a political system that imagined no alternative to imperial sovereignty.

Yet the emperor's sovereignty was always predicated on the proper performance of a set of religious duties that were especially stringent. In keeping with its limited institutional existence outside the social and political structures of the state, the objects of writing on spiritual perfection in Confucianism were often the very rulers and officials that constituted the government. The political and the religious spheres overlapped to the extent that the emperor himself, as "Son of Heaven" (*tianzi*), conducted the imperial rituals that provided partial proof of his moral fitness and so legitimized his authority. Lacking an autonomous base, the guardians of the *Documents* and the *Analects*, collectively known as the *Ru*, could lobby the emperor through memorials to the throne or indirectly criticize him by commenting on history, but had little purchase to call into question the structural features of the political system.

It is in this context that the contrast between the *Documents*, as case studies of the practices of past sage rulers, and the *Analects*, as a guide to behavior for princes and ritual experts, may best be understood. The *Documents* is a collection of orations attributed to the sage rulers of the past and their ministers. The dominant tone of its fifty-eight chapters is persuasive, and the dominant argument is the justification of the political authority of the speakers. As such, its first-person testimony is seen to contain both a guide for behavior for the sage ruler and methods that have been empirically proven successful by those rulers. By contrast, the *Analects* is a collection of dialogues highlighting the teachings of the "uncrowned king" (*suwang*) Confucius, and is less concerned with the regulation of the state as it is with self-regulation as a means to becoming a sage. Its application to politics is for the most part implicit, but is no less influential than the *Documents* because of the perceived connection between the governance of the self and of the state. The Chinese term for this connection is "inside a sage and outside a king" (*neisheng waiwang*), which illustrates how the orations of the sage kings and the dialogues of Confucius have traditionally been perceived to promote the same political message.

The *Documents* is widely regarded as a combination of authentic Zhou period texts and forgeries created centuries later. The core chapters thought to be genuine include: "Great Announcement" (*Dagao*), "Announcement of Kang" (*Kanggao*), "Announcement of Shao" (*Shaogao*), "Many Officials" (*Duoshi*), and "Lord Shi" (*Junshi*). These texts have traditionally been dated to the reign of King Cheng of Zhou (d. 1006 B.C.E.). By contrast, the thirty or so "new text" chapters, traditionally said to have been found in the wall of Confucius's home in the first century B.C.E., are generally believed actually to have been forged around the fourth century C.E. Nevertheless, for much of Chinese history the text as a whole was regarded as the record of the sage rulers of the Zhou, and the weight of its examples has exerted a strong pull on both policies and political organization, as well as on the expectations for the personal behavior of the ruler.

The chapter "Announcement of Kang" in the *Documents* exemplifies the larger work's mixture of information on the proper conduct of the ruler and models for the successful administration of the state. Addressed to Feng, one of the sons of King Wen, on the occasion when he was put in charge of his own domain or fiefdom, the text is variously attributed to King Cheng or to Cheng's uncle the Duke of Zhou, speaking on the king's behalf while he served as regent. The "Announcement of Kang" is itself internally divided into ten parts:

1. A description of the virtues of King Wen. Wen is described in the following terms: "He made bright his virtue and was attentive in punishments, he did not mistreat those who had lost their spouses." His achievements were so extraordinary that Heaven (*tian*, see below) provided him with the man-

date (*ming*, see below) to overthrow the Yin (i.e., Shang, the previous dynasty).

2. A charge to Feng to pacify and integrate the worthy men of the former dynasty into the current government. Part of this charge is to "seek to learn the wisdom of the former kings as a means to protect the people."
3. A charge to attend to the circumstances of his subjects. Although it is not always possible to understand the favor of Heaven (*tian*), the "feelings of the people are visible."
4. A plea to judge crimes not by their gravity, but by the intent of the perpetrator.
5. An argument that judicial fairness on the part of the ruler will lead to similar circumspection on the part of his subjects.
6. The maxim that once an attitude of justice is created in the people, virtuous behavior will become universally appreciated. Particular goals are the attitudes of familial piety and the bonds of friendship (*you*), "revealed by Heaven (*tian*)," so as to develop in a fair and just environment.
7. The imperative that a ruler needs to guide the people to good fortune and success.
8. The assurance that the ruler's judgments are really an expression of the judgment of Heaven (*tian*).
9. The statement that in order to render just judgments, the ruler must perfect his mind.
10. The observation that the mandate (*ming*) given him by Heaven (*tian*) is not unchanging, and so the ruler must always keep it in mind.

The "Announcement of Kang" ends with the statement that if Feng regularly heeds the announcement, his fiefdom will be passed down to his heirs across the generations.

Characteristic of the *Documents*, the proper effect of the "Announcement of Kang" on the intended audience was to inculcate an attitude of reverence (*jing*) in the ruler. Although it is possible to be corrupted by rulership and its privileges, the attitude of uncertainty in light of the possibility of the withdrawal of the Mandate of Heaven (*tianming*) outlined in the piece motivates the ruler to remain attentive to his own moral development and maintain judicial fairness. Attention to such motivations is also characteristic of the *Analects*, where moral self-cultivation is abstracted from the context of rulership and translated into contexts such as the conduct of lesser officials and the navigation of everyday life.

The development of an ethical system that could be applied to contexts besides rulership is one of the primary aims of the *Analects*. Because the sayings and dialogues that conveyed Confucius's teachings were composed and edited in the period beginning from the lifetime of Confucius (trad. 551–479 B.C.E.) and ending with its collation in the late second and early first centuries B.C.E., the *Analects* is properly attributed to both Confucius and his disciple tradition over the centuries following his death.

Judging by the offices held by those who used and commented on the *Analects* in the first century B.C.E., the collection was used by Grand Tutors to the Heir-Apparent and other officials in charge of ritual and the education of the crown prince.[1] In its twenty chapters, the *Analects* depicts Confucius interacting with others, either the rulers he meets in his travels or the disciples of his later career as teacher. A concern with attaining the ideal of the gentleman (*junzi*) is the unifying element in the *Analects*, and this ideal was certainly taken as normative by those who later read the text as a guide to proper ritual behavior for princes and officials charged with maintaining court etiquette. The *Analects* outlines the development of the character traits of benevolence (*ren*, a sensitivity to others), righteousness (*yi*, an obligation to act fairly), wisdom (*zhi*, an ability to assess circumstances), and trustworthiness (*xin*, being true to one's word). One must also locate oneself correctly with respect to one's family through familial piety (*xiao*, caring for other family members as befits one's role) and with respect to one's community through ritual propriety (*li*, regulating speech and demeanor as befits one's status). The cultivation of these virtues is the proper goal of the gentleman, and it is these characteristics of the gentleman that qualify him for public service. As Hsu Cho-yun has observed, in the Warring States period, the term gentleman changed from denoting members of the ruling clan, to "an admirable person whose virtue entitles him to a high moral position no matter what his social status was."[2] In the *Analects*, attaining the moral ideal of the gentleman is the ideal qualification for public service.

In the context of the view that moral perfection was the primary qualification for rulership, both the *Analects* and the *Documents* may be read as political texts. That view is explicit at times in the texts themselves, especially with respect to the social virtues of familial piety and ritual propriety. The importance of the cultivation of virtues like familial piety in early life and its connection with fitness for governing is made clear in *Analects* 1.2: "It is rare for a person who is pious to his parents and older brothers to be inclined to rebel against his superior. . . . Piety to parents and elder brothers may be considered the root of a person." Possession of this quality led the sage king Shun (trad. r. 2256–2205 B.C.E.), despite his humble origins, to be recognized as a suitable successor to the sage king Yao (trad. r. 2357–2256 B.C.E.), according to a narrative found in the *Documents*. Yet while the sage was at times recognized and promoted in this way, the counterexample of Confucius implied that there were also times when the sage was not promoted.

By the second century, the legend that Confucius had developed a perfect plan for governing, but had not been given the opportunity by *tian*, had become part of the standard lore of Confucius. In chapter 80 of his *Balanced Discussions*, the Han critic Wang Chong (ca. 27–97 C.E.) explains the idea: "Confucius did not rule as king, but his work as uncrowned king may be seen in the *Spring and Autumn Annals*." The myth that through his writings Confucius could prepare China for the government of a future sage king became part of the cult of Confucius and has colored the reception of his writings ever since. The story of Confucius reinforced the cosmological assumption that merit did not always guarantee authority, but that authority always had to be granted through *tianming*.

Confucianism's Theory of Politics

The notion that traditional China's social structure was inert and its political order unchanging is at once the product of official imperial narratives of historical continuity developed to provide the ruling dynasty with a useful version of the past and a relic of the enthusiastic European reception of the "timeless" aspects of Chinese civilization. It is true that myriad religious and cultural continuities lasted up to and even beyond the Cultural Revolution of the 1960s and 1970s, but their deployment to mask the developments and dislocations of Chinese history is a project that is being increasingly discredited. That China's history is full of revolutions is not simply a figment of Maoist historiography; it reflects a useful antithesis to the common vision of a static Chinese past. Yet within the dynamic processes of Chinese history, ethical norms and political structures preserved in the Confucian canon and in sanctioned approaches to its interpretation are among the more conservative elements of traditional culture.

One of the core mistakes of many revisionist accounts, however, is the inference that the conventional aspects of Confucian traditions were allied exclusively with the interests of the state or of the ruling class. There is no mistaking the ability of Confucian traditions to transmit core texts and concepts relatively intact across generations, but that does not imply that their influence has been uniformly conservative on the political level. Though one of the primary concerns of the texts of the Confucian canon is the theoretical task of defining legitimate authority, contesting that definition was a preoccupation of entrenched political powers, as well as reformers and peasant revolutionaries. Far from being solely reactionary or progressive, Confucian texts were read as providing a vision of a normative social order, one that was invoked both in defense of and as a challenge to the status quo.

Although no single concept fully encompasses this complex social vision, few are as central to Confucian political discourse as the doctrine of *tianming* (often translated as "Heaven's Mandate"). Briefly, *tianming* is the political authorization that the virtuous ruler receives from the nonhuman realm, and the bad omens the corrupt ruler receives from the same source. The two words that make up this concept, *tian* (often translated as "Heaven") and *ming* ("command," "decree," "fate" or most often "mandate"), are key to understanding the formulation of claims to legitimate authority by emperors and revolutionaries alike throughout Chinese history. The fact that the word used in both 1949 and in the 1960s to translate "revolution" is *geming* (literally, "changing the mandate") demonstrates the degree to which Confucian theories of legitimation are still implicit in contemporary political discourse.

At the core of the doctrine of *tianming* is the agency of *tian*, one of the cardinal elements of Chinese cosmology. *Tian* literally means "sky," and is at the same time the mechanism—at times intentional and at other times naturalistic—behind the movement of the cosmos, conveyed to human beings through supernatural omens or seasonal cycles. Combining aspects of the notions of "God," "Heaven," and "Nature," *tian* shares at least one fundamental similarity with all of these concepts: it often is used as the category that complements that of the "human." An example of the contrast between *tian* and the human is in chapter six of the Taoist classic *Zhuangzi* (also know as *Chuang Tzu*), which compares knowledge of "what humans have created" with that of "what *tian* has created." In this context, the eminent sinologist Herbert A. Giles (1845–1935) identified *tian* as an allusion to God, albeit "of course as seen through Taoist glasses."[3] Giles is correct to the extent that in the earliest texts, *tian* has some of the anthropomorphic characteristics of a "spirit" (*shen*) or deity.

Yet the glasses are somewhat askew—the perfect Taoist ruler is not acting at the behest of an intentional *tian*; instead, such a ruler is simply best able to understand and internalize the patterns of *tian* through dispassionate and reactive governance (*wuwei*). In early Confucian texts, a similar approach is sometimes advocated. The sage king Shun, as portrayed in *Analects* 15.5, is said to have governed in the same reactive way (*wuwei*) and simply "be reverent himself and face due south." A focus of the ruler's relationship to *tian* in the Confucian texts has to do with one particular aspect of *tian*'s influence on the world. *Analects* 16.8 says that one difference between the gentleman and the petty person is that the former is in awe of the *ming* (mandate) of *tian*, whereas the latter is ignorant of it.

Tian's direct influence on the ruler is most often associated with *ming*, literally "command" or "mandate" but more accurately a limited notion of "fate." *Ming* is what determines the avenues of opportunity available to a person, and so whereas some capacities and potential outcomes such as wealth and life span are a matter of *ming*, personal thoughts, associations, and actions are primarily a matter of individual choice—comparable to what some might call "free will." This view is seen most clearly in the words quoted by Confucius's disciple Zi Xia in *Analects* 12.5: "Life and death are a matter of *ming*, wealth and honor depend on *tian*." Similarly, in the "Announcement of Shao" from the *Documents*, "*Tian* bestows its *ming* in wisdom, in good and bad fortune, and in a set number of years."

When placed together, these terms connote the endorsement that the cosmos gives to a virtuous ruler in the form of bounty and favorable omens, and the condemnation it provides a despot in the form of blight and unfavorable omens. This mechanism underlies the traditional conception of the dynastic cycle, a Gibbonesque model wherein each dynasty begins with a virtuous founder claiming a change in *tianming* and finally ends with a debauched descendent forfeiting it amid waste and immorality. In this way, the continuity of the dynasty and maintenance of social order depend on the effect of the character of the ruler on *tianming*.

The concept of *tianming* has a long tradition in China, and its evolution begins with the key historical event of the twelfth century B.C.E.: the Zhou conquest. The earliest mentions of *tianming* occur in texts associated with the end of the Shang (or Yin) clan's rule of the central plain by the Zhou clan. These texts were primarily attributed to Kings Wen and Wu, and Dan the duke of Zhou. These Zhou founders talk about the original authorization of the Shang by *tian*, and also about how the Shang lost *tian*'s support, thereby justifying their own usurpation of the Shang.

The *Documents* has long been interpreted to imply that *tian* was a deity of the Shang that was adopted by the Zhou as an alternative to the Shang high deity, *Shangdi* ("Highest Ancestor"). As Creel pointed out in 1965, the idea that *tian* was a factor in the founding of the Shang was a projection back in time by the Zhou, and there is little evidence that *tian* was a significant element of Shang religion.[4] By contrast, *ming* appears more frequently in Shang materials, but as Liu Zehua has argued, the fundamental meaning of the term was transformed from Shang to Zhou:

> Just as in the Shang, the Duke of Zhou did not speak or act himself, but rather it was said that everything was the intent or command of *tian*. This concentration of power is seen in the "Announcements of Shao" in the *Documents*: "*Tian* bestows its *ming* in wisdom, in good and bad fortune, and in a set number of years." Here *ming* means to "give an order to an inferior." The basic sense of this phrase is that Heaven sends down its orders by endowments of sagely wisdom, dispatches good and bad fortune, and makes determinations of how long one's time will last. The Duke of Zhou continued the Shang belief in the Highest Ancestor, but also made changes. The most important was that, in the words of the Announcement of Kang in the *Documents*: "the mandate is not among those things that are constant." The meaning of this is that the great mandate bestowed by the Highest Ancestor is not unchanging.[5]

The concept of *ming* underwent a transformation from permanent in the Shang to conditional in the Zhou. This change is reflected in the different nature

of divination practices between the Shang and Zhou, something recent archae-
ological discoveries have demonstrated. The classical method of reading milfoil
stalks of the *Yijing* (Classic of Change) associated with the Zhou period is advisory in the sense that the cast hexagram determines a potential outcome at a particular moment but assumes that later actions might negate the predictive value
of the divination. The long-lost *Guizang* (Storehouse to Which Things Return),
classically described as the Shang method of reading milfoil stalks, was discovered at Wangjiatai in Hubei Province in 1993. This method associated an invari-
ant reading of either good or bad fortune with each hexagram, predicated on a
relatively fixed notion of contingency. Therefore, the hexagram deciphered in the
milfoil stalks was always based on a fairly rigid set of rules about how the symbols related to reality. In the same way, the eternal support of the Highest Ancestor of the ruling clan of the Shang was replaced by the concept that *tian* gave and
revoked its favor based on the qualities of the ruler.

The *Documents* in particular again and again narrates the intervention of *tian*
in human affairs through the change in *ming* that affects changes of dynasty. In
the "Many Officers" chapter of the *Documents*, for example, the duke of Zhou
addresses the officers of the declining Shang Dynasty and invokes the example of
their own ancestor's receipt of the *ming* from *tian*. He tells them of their founder,
the sage king Cheng Tang, who defeated Jie, the last ruler of the previous Xia
Dynasty (trad. 1750 B.C.E.). The duke of Zhou's narrative is almost exclusively
driven by the agency of *tian*: "[Jie] was immoral and dissolute and others accused
him of this, but *tian* did not care or listen to him. It relieved him of his original
ming, and sent down extreme punishment. Thereupon it commanded (*ming*) your
ancestor Cheng Tang to replace the Xia, and use the best people to regulate the
empire." This is one of many examples in which the rise of the Zhou is justified
by locating it in the theory of dynastic cycles tied to the notion of *tianming*. Just
as the virtuous founders of the Shang had replaced the debauched last ruler of
the Xia, so also the Zhou founders were replacing the last ruler of the Shang.

For the ruling clan of the Zhou, the notion of *tianming* authorized their own
conquest of the Shang, but at the same time raised the possibility of their eventual loss of legitimacy. Of course, what *tian* was looking for in a ruler was specifically indexed to the ethos of the ruling clan of the Zhou. As Poo Mu-chou has
written, "Yet if we examine the nature of the texts in which the term 'mandate
of Heaven' was employed, it can be seen mainly as encompassing political doctrines propagated by the Zhou court or its ruling apparatus."[6] The acceptance of
the doctrine of *tianming* for centuries after the waning of Zhou political authority meant that the Zhou polity became the model according to which the legitimacy of future governors or aspirants to governing was determined. In *Analects*
17.5, the recreation of the Zhou was the explicit political ideal of Confucius, who
seeks to "make a Zhou in the east," and in 3.14 avers "I follow the Zhou." In this

way, particulars of the Zhou image of the perfect ruler became fixed as requirements for securing the authorization of *tian*.

Among the central political doctrines of the Zhou was the notion that proper family behavior was a model for the operation of the state. This doctrine, that
there is a direct relationship between the familial piety of the ruler and the loyalty of his subjects, is one of the central reciprocal relationships that informed
the description of the ruler that the Zhou held would receive *tianming*. A celebrated passage in the "Daxue" (Great Learning)—a chapter of the *Record of Ritual* (*Liji*) that became part of the "Four Books" elevated to canonical status by
Zhu Xi (also known as Chu Hsi, 1130–1200 C.E.)—explains that "the gentleman
does not leave home, yet brings his teachings to the entire nation. His pious
behavior to his parents is the means to serve the state's ruler, his filial treatment
of his older brothers is the means to serve the state's elders, and his parental kindness is the means to employ the multitude."

This passage is based on an association between the natural feelings cultivated in the setting of the family and the behaviors required for good government.
The first section of the "Discourses of Jin" from the Warring States period *Discourses of the States* (*Guoyu*) adumbrates this idea: "Serve one's lord with reverence, serve one's father with piety." The relationship is more than metaphorical,
because there is an assumption that proper familial behavior leads directly to a
well-ordered state. This is shown in *Analects* 2.21, when Confucius justifies his
lack of participation in government by quoting from the *Documents*: "simply by
treating with piety those who one should, and by being friendly to one's elder and
younger brothers, one is putting governance into practice." The contemporary
Confucian scholar Tu Wei-ming paraphrases this statement as "taking care of
family affairs is itself active participation in politics."[7] Indeed, the essence of the
association between familial piety and good government is that a state of properly functioning families is in fact a well-ordered society, that politics is the set of
conventional relationships that may be projected from the natural connections
found in the family.

Familial piety is not the only parallel structure that connects the personal
behavior of the ruler with the mechanisms for good government. The individual's constellations of responsibilities outside the family are the subject of a set
of behaviors summarized as "ritual propriety" (*li*). Later writers portray Zhou
ritual as formally complex, and they stress both the adherence to rules and the
expression of the proper attitudes of reverence (in the case of sacrifice) or grief
(in the case of mourning). The later aspect is so important that on several occasions the *Analects* condemns formalism without the proper attitude. *Analects* 17.11
makes it clear that ritual propriety is not simply a matter of ritual: "Saying 'Rites,'
'Rites,'—does it refer only to jade and silk? Saying 'Music,' 'Music,'—does it refer
to bells and drums?"

Instead, for the ruler, the performance of the rites with the proper attitude is an important stage in the development of the proper virtues. For the society as a whole, participation in the rituals of Zhou assured the orderly interaction of its members. As Ivanhoe has written, the rites were intended by Confucius to remind people that "harmonious relationships between people is the ultimate aim of and justification for moral self cultivation. If one loses sight of this aspect of the rites, one can mistake the task of moral self cultivation as primarily or exclusively a private, perfectionist concern, and this can lead one to run rough-shod over the needs, interests, and feelings of others."[8] In the case of the ruler, consciousness of the intended end of ritual participation entailed attention to the good of others and of the society as a whole.

Excellence in the practice of the rites was then a means to ensuring social harmony. Yet harmony was not the sole end of ritual. In *Analects* 1.12, it is clear that ritual is more than just a means of establishing harmony in the society: "Harmony is the most valuable of the applications of ritual propriety. It is the most beautiful of the ways of the former kings, and both minor and great were done in this way. Yet some things did not work out. To understand harmony and so pursue it, without the ritual to regulate it, will leave some things that do not work out." This illustrates the degree to which ritual was theorized as the only means to harmony on the level of the society. Even pursuing the ostensible goal of social harmony will not reach that goal as successfully as pursuing it via the proper performance of ritual.

The proper familial and ritual behavior of the ruler was the key to the Confucian understanding of the Zhou model of good government. Arguments for the legitimacy or illegitimacy of later governments often focused more on whether the emperor was in accordance with the standards for personal behavior of the past than on specific elements of policy. Because of the perceived linkage between the ruler's familial piety and his subjects' loyalty to the state, and between the ruler's ritual deportment and social harmony, the focus on the characteristics of the ruler's personal behavior was not only a matter of morality but also implicitly one of politics. The connection between the two is best understood through the mediating concept of *tianming*, whereby personal behavior resulted in concrete political change. Judging concrete behaviors against abstract standards could, however, prove problematic. For this reason, much of the normative political discourse of Confucianism has been transmitted through stories of exemplary sage kings of the past.

The Medium of Expressing Politics in Confucianism

Early Confucianism has been described as a form of virtue ethics, and indeed the exemplars of the virtuous sage kings of antiquity were central to the development of the imperial state. At the same time, the emphasis on merit and virtue was always at least implicitly in tension with the actual criteria of kingship by which the imperial succession was usually determined. To rule, a contender to the throne needed to be viewed as the legitimate successor of the previous ruler. Generally speaking, legitimation is based on hereditary, religious, legal, political, military, or other criteria. In China, legitimation was often more concerned with the demonstration of merit by hereditary rulers through personal piety and through reliance on officials and advisers whose merit was a function of their immersion in the culture and canon associated with the former sage kings and with the "uncrowned king" Confucius.

Two central narratives spoke to these dual modes of political legitimation. The first, the cardinal political narrative of Confucianism, was the decision by the predynastic emperor Yao to pass on political authority to Shun, bypassing the norms of the hereditary transfer of power. Shun was deemed worthy to rule on the basis of his moral perfection, as exemplified by his pious behavior in relation to his family. This narrates the standard of legitimation during a period of good government: the peaceful transfer of power based on merit, accomplished without the intercession of outside authority. The other narrative was that of King Wen and his son King Wu, the former credited with overthrowing the last corrupt ruler of the Shang Dynasty in the twelfth century B.C.E., and the latter credited with founding the succeeding Zhou Dynasty with the help of his uncle the duke of Zhou. The founding of the Zhou Dynasty complements the story of Yao and Shun in that it narrates the intercession by *tian*, through the military actions of a virtuous person, to end a period of misrule.

The story of Yao and Shun is one of the central narratives of sagehood and politics in early China. In the "Canon of Yao" (*Yaodian*) chapter of the *Documents*, the basic story of Yao's anxiety at the incompetence of his sons is followed by the recommendation of Shun by Yao's minister Si Yue: "Although his father was stupid, his stepmother deceitful, and (his younger brother) Xiang was arrogant, he himself was able to have amicable relations with them through his familial piety, raising them up through his benign influence so they did not return to wickedness."

More detail about Shun's family's treatment of him are given in an extended dialogue about Shun in book five of the *Mencius* (*Mengzi*), the eponymous work associated with the second major Confucian theorist (trad. 385–304 B.C.E.) of early times. There, the story is recounted that Shun's parents sent him to repair a grain storehouse. Once Shun had climbed up the ladder to the top, his father removed the ladder and set fire to the storehouse. Failing to dispose of him, they had Shun dig a well, which, not realizing he had momentarily left it, they filled in. Other sources provide the story of Shun finding out that his family planned to poison liquor they were planning to serve him, and preparing himself by bathing in a bath of that time's anti-intoxicant, dog excrement. In such a context, his "amicable relations" with them are perhaps even more surprising.

Yet it is exactly this quality that distinguished Shun in the eyes of Yao and, by implication, in the eyes of *tian*. As recounted in *Analects* 20.1, Yao proclaims: "It is you, Shun. *Tian*'s succession has fallen on your person. . . If the area within the seas (i.e., China) sinks into difficulties, then *tian*'s benefits will be forever ended." Despite the usual association of *tianming* with the changing of dynasties, its application in the case of the succession of Yao by Shun indicates that it should properly be seen as a facet of all successions. For reasons outlined in the previous section, it was the pious behavior of Shun in the familial realm that identified him as the rightful successor to Yao.

The application of the theory of *tianming* to the case of Yao's ceding the throne to Shun illustrates the way in which Confucian ethics and its implicit theory of contingency challenge the principle of hereditary succession. It is Yao's realization that he should select a virtuous successor that leads him to select Shun. If he had not chosen such a successor, then his descendants might have faced the fate that was meted out to the corrupt rulers of the Shang by King Wen and King Wu.

Yet the corrective actions of *tian* are not automatic, as is illustrated by an early Confucian text that was discovered at Guodian in Hubei province in 1993 called *Frustration and Success Are a Function of the Age* (*Qiongda yi shi*). The text (dating to about 300 B.C.E.) argues that Shun would still be plowing his field if he had not met Yao. It argues that "meeting or not is a matter of *tian*." Indeed, the role of *tian* in the succession is central to the understanding of the Shun narrative in book five of the *Mencius*: "Shun served as Chancellor for Yao for twenty-eight years, something that was not a result of human agency, but a matter of *tian*. After the death of Yao, once the prescribed three years of mourning were completed, Shun retreated from Yao's son to the area south of the Nan River. When those among the feudal lords of the world went to court, they did not go to Yao's son, but to Shun. When they had cases to be adjudicated, they did not go to Yao's son, but to Shun. Singers did not sing of Yao's son, but of Shun. This is why I say that it was a matter of *tian*. Only after these things did Shun return to the central states and take the position of 'Son of *tian*.' Had he continued to live in Yao's palace and expelled Yao's son, it would have been a usurpation and not something given by *tian*."

As the early translator James Legge implies by his note "*vox populi, vox dei*" this notion of the action of the *tian* through the actions of the people is also an important political doctrine and will be examined at greater length below. Early Confucian interpretations of the narrative of Yao and Shun take pains to implicate *tian* in the transfer of authority from Yao to Shun, making explicit the idea that *tian* does not recognize heredity as a sufficient justification for granting political authority.

At the same time, these narratives demonstrate how *tianming* does not completely undermine the hereditary transfer of power. Despite his exceptional service as regent, there was little question that the duke of Zhou would cede his authority when King Cheng had attained majority. When King Wen took power, he distributed his fiefdoms to his close relatives. The Zuo commentary to the *Spring and Autumn Annals* for 514 B.C.E. reads: "In the past, when King Wu conquered the Shang and controlled a broad area of the world, he had fifteen principalities governed by his brothers, and forty governed by the clans of his concubines." Likewise, in chapter 1 of the *Historian's Records (Shiji)*, written around 100 B.C.E., it is asserted that Yao's family continued to participate in the administration of Shun: "Yao gave his two daughters in marriage to Shun so that he could observe how he dealt with people from his treatment of them." It also notes that Yao's nine sons attended to Shun's affairs. The third-century B.C.E. writer *Xunzi (Hsün Tzu)* explicitly attacks the notion that Yao "abdicated" the throne to Shun, arguing in chapter 18 of the *Xunzi* that the proper principle of succession is continuity of the policies of the previous ruler, "If a Yao succeeds a Yao, can we say a change has even occurred?"

The two narratives of nonhereditary succession play a central role in Confucian political writing because they reinforce the fundamental political principles of that writing. Specifically, the successful rebellion of the Zhou clan and the peaceful succession of Shun both illustrate the way in which *tian* can act to elevate a virtuous person to authority. Although the Confucian notion of contingency allows for the possibility that good people may not be recognized, at the same time it guarantees that dynasties at the end of their cycle will eventually be replaced.

The Message of Confucianism's Politics

An important debate in the interpretation of the Confucian canon was about the proper means of identifying the intercession of *tian*. By the fourth century B.C.E., references to omens interpreted as signs of Heaven's pleasure or displeasure with the character of the ruler or other parts of the government were becoming increasingly common. In the first century, the phenomenon became so important to the political discourse that records of these omens began to be integrated into the standard histories, as in Ban Gu's (32–92 C.E.) *Standard History of the Han (Hanshu)*. Though the esoteric interpretations of omens as signs that required special knowledge to decipher only grew stronger in the so-called apocryphal Confucian texts of the first centuries C.E., these methods developed alongside an exoteric tradition that read negative social conditions as signs of intercession of *tian*. This tradition, holding that *tianming* may be observed in the material wealth and satisfaction of the populace, has existed in China from the time of the *Documents*.

That the will of *tian* is evident in the material well-being of the people of a state is a lesson that Confucians have often read as a central message of the *Documents*. We have already seen how the "Announcement of Kang" specifies that whereas it is not always possible to understand *tian*, the feelings of the people are visible to the ruler. Other early Confucian texts also cite the *Documents* when they want to make similar arguments. For example, the "Black Robes" (*Ziyi*), another document discovered at Guodian in Hubei province in 1993 and dating to 300 B.C.E. at the latest, quotes the following passage from the "Lord Shi" chapter of the *Documents*: "In the past it was the Highest Ancestor in Geshen who looked down on the virtue of King Wen, and the great *ming* was concentrated in his person." It uses this quotation to complement a statement about the reception of the ruler's words by his people. Many scholars attribute this complementary statement to Confucius: "If one acts immediately following one's words, then the actions cannot be exaggerated. Therefore, if the gentleman first pays attention to his words and then acts, thereby bringing his trustworthiness full circle, then the people will be able to neither exaggerate his excellences nor diminish his faults." The implication is that the *tianming* being spoken of in the *Documents* is expressed through the approval or criticism of the people.

The Zuo commentary to the *Spring and Autumn Annals*, in an entry dated to 542 B.C.E., quotes similar ideas from the "Great Vow" (*Taishi*) chapter of the *Documents*: "Whatever the people desire, *tian* is sure to follow it." This is the same chapter quoted several times in chapter 5 of the *Mencius*. One quotation caps the explanation of how *tianming* was evidenced when Yao presented Shun to the people, and they approved of him. There the *Documents* is quoted as saying: "*Tian* does not speak, it simply indicates *ming* through actions and affairs." A second quotation of the *Documents* is even more explicit: "*Tian* sees through what my people see, *tian* listens through what my people hear."

In one sense, this understanding of *tianming* signals the naturalization of the concept of *tian*, because the cause-and-effect character of the relationship between bad rulership and negative social conditions is portrayed as self-evident. At the same time, the idea that *tian* still sees and hears, albeit through the eyes and ears of the people, is also consistent with an anthropomorphic divinity that is an embodiment of the society itself.

This interpretation of *tianming* allows for the retrospective legitimation of any succession, and it is the primary way the concept is applied in Chinese historiography. In chapter 12 of the *Xunzi*, the succession of Shun is explained in terms of the basic model that the people will follow an heir if he is worth but will turn to a sage if the heir is not. In *The Heir and the Sage: Dynastic Legends in Early China*, Allan examined the contrasting criteria of virtue and heredity for succession and explains this development in these terms: "This transformation removes the onus for breaking the rule of heredity from the ceding kings of the predynastic era and the rebel kings of the dynastic era by regarding all transfers of rule, both hereditary and non-hereditary, as equally valid manifestations of Heaven's will or as determined by the allegiance of the people."[9] Thus the notion of *tianming* was made congruent to the test of popular support.

This reading of the *Documents* was very influential in some later Confucian writing, and it is one of the central ways in which *tianming* was employed to criticize authority. In addition to the claims about the ruler's lack of familial piety or ritual propriety, concrete economic problems in the state could also be used as the grounds for claiming a change in *tianming*. The latter type of claim was not uncommon throughout Chinese history, and was amplified by later imperial writers such as Zhang Juzheng (1525–82) and Wang Fuzhi (1619–92). In response to China's encounters with the West, Liang Qichao (1873–1929) and other writers sought to replace Confucian political theory with the work of writers that he considered to be more realist political theorists such as Guanzi. Liang wrote that "The reason that Europeans and Americans are strong among the peoples of the world are a matter of methods of governing, and the reasons that Chinese are weak among the peoples of the world, are also only a matter of these methods."[10] As a result he advocated turning away from the Confucian classics to other writings he saw as more similar to the work of Machiavelli and Hobbes. Nevertheless, claims to moral virtuosity made for figures like Chiang Kai-shek and Mao Zedong in the twentieth century attest to the continuity of many of the ideas that find their roots in the *Documents* and the *Analects*.

Confucianism and Nonbelievers: Politics and People outside the Tradition

There are fundamentally two ways to address the issue of nonbelievers with respect to Confucian traditions: to examine historical systems of governance and self-cultivation that took issue with central Confucian claims, and to make problematic the rubric "belief" with respect to Confucian traditions. An examination of the major streams of thought that developed in counterpoint to the various Confucian traditions—such as Mohism, Legalism, Daoism, and Buddhism—will inevitably reveal some of the key differences in the way that religion operated in premodern China in comparison with the premodern West. These differences highlight the way in which "outside the tradition" carries a different meaning in China than it might in other parts of the world.

In early China, when the *Documents* and *Analects* were still forming, their approaches were criticized from perspectives rooted in the traditional governmental establishment, which found fault with the Confucian emphasis on allegiance to family and on individual self-cultivation. The earliest tradition that defined itself in opposition to the figure of Confucius was Mohism, which was founded by Mozi (a.k.a. Mo Tzu) in the fifth century B.C.E.. Mohist texts—centered on universalizing the altruistic impulse of "impartial caring" (*jian'ai*)—criticize the partiality inculcated by concepts such as familial piety. Instead, they promote a consequentialist scheme in which actions, especially those of the ruler, are deemed good if and only if they maximize the wealth, population, and social order of the state.

Although *tian* had a major role in Mozi's system, it was an automatic one in which "good actions" were rewarded and partial actions were punished. In this way, the theory of government resembled the one outlined above for early Confucians: it rewarded the ruler whose actions benefited the society; however, the definition of benefit was drastically different. In the third century B.C.E., Han Feizi (a.k.a. Han Fei Tzu) adopted from Mozi the notion that a well-ordered state was the goal of the ruler and designed a system of rulership based on the application of rewards and punishments in support of a universal legal code. Han Feizi's ideal ruler was intent on maintaining power at all costs and eschewed the niceties of Confucian moral self-cultivation. Both these texts are critical of the priorities of Confucian morality, and their alternative priorities to some extent influenced later Confucian writings.

These approaches, with vested interests in a strong centralized state, were explicitly critical of the early followers of Confucius but shared fundamental assumptions about the organization of the state. Both Mozi and Han Feizi accept the sovereign authority of a monarch and argue that the actions of the ruler are the primary determinant of the success or failure of the state. Neither of the systems accepts a strong version of the Confucian doctrine of *ming*, which introduces both a degree of uncertainty about the effectiveness of even the best potential ruler and a position from which to question the authority of the monarch. The systems of Mozi and Han Feizi offered an alternative to the theory of governance of the early Confucians. But because their audience was the ruler, they did not offer a comprehensive set of novel alternative values and beliefs outside that narrow focus.

This contrast underlines an important distinction between the early Confucian worldview and some of its counterparts further west during the same period. Though *tian* is often opposed to the human realm, faith or belief in *tian* was not contested across the different traditions. As such, issues of orthodoxy and heresy were focused on the area that the traditions contested: the conduct of the ruler. Consequently, early Confucian traditions lacked a confessional aspect. In this sense, the category of "nonbelievers" was fundamentally different in early China than elsewhere. This category was reserved for those opposed to the authority of the monarch and the state bureaucracy that supported him.

By the late sixth century c.e., however, Confucians had begun to define themselves in opposition to the followers of two other alternative systems, and they had begun to develop a rich vocabulary to engage issues of nonbelief. These two systems were Taoism and Buddhism, and combined with Confucianism are known as the "three teachings" (*sanjiao*) of China. Taoism is often misunderstood to refer primarily to a textual tradition in early China that includes the *Daodejing* (a.k.a. *Tao-te Ching*) and *Zhuangzi*.

Although these texts exerted an influence on later Taoism, they were just one of several important influences that included shamanism and medical and mantic practices. It was the arrival of Buddhism from South and Central Asia in the first century c.e. that sparked the formation of this hybrid religion and influenced its forms of organization. For the first few centuries after its arrival, Buddhism was received as fundamentally similar to Taoism and not essentially in conflict with indigenous systems. By the sixth century c.e., a recognition of some of the strong differences between Buddhism and China's indigenous religions led to officially sponsored debates between representatives of the "three teachings."

These court debates marked the beginning of Confucianism's move toward self-consciously defining itself as a tradition against—in competition with—Taoism and Buddhism. Particular areas of contention were the conflict between Confucian notions of familial piety and government participation and the Buddhist monastic ideals of renunciation and asceticism. Only rarely did this contention result in explicit conflict; mostly these differences were mediated through imperial proscriptions. More often, the result was accommodations through the integration of familial piety into notions of rebirth and integration of monastic with state and private institutions on one hand, and of spiritual exercises and institutions that existed independently of the social structure into Confucianism and Taoism on the other. A similar moment occurred in the sixteenth century c.e., when the arrival of Jesuit missionaries brought into focus differences between Christian views (which had actually been present in China for centuries) and the "three teachings." Because of the alliance between Christianity and European and American imperial interests, the attitude to these foreign religions erupted into open hostility in the nineteenth century.

For almost the first millennium of its existence, then, Confucianism did not identify itself as a "religion." Alternative political models did exist during that period. But because they were not rooted in a robust and distinctive religious worldview, proponents of the alternatives were not perceived of as being nonbelievers. As the arrival of Buddhism and then Christianity altered the identity of Confucian traditions, the resulting religious self-consciousness supported a distinction between insiders and outsiders, although again, confessed "belief" was not the determining criterion. Though the competing traditions did come into conflict, some form of mutual accommodation was the most common outcome.

Conclusion

Of the many Confucianisms that have existed throughout Chinese history, the narratives of the ancient sage kings as related in the classic texts—*Documents* and *Analects*—have exerted the cardinal influence on the construction of political authority in China. The notion of *tian* as the arbiter of moral claims through its bestowal of *ming* upon moral rulers and its rescinding it from corrupt rulers has meant that the justification of political authority was to some degree contingent on the moral self-cultivation of the ruler. The classical texts provided two narrative models of imperial succession, one in which human beings recognize the need to base political authority on moral authority and *tian* does not need to intercede, and one in which *tian* replaces an immoral ruler. The application of this conception of *tianming* is inherently ambiguous, and whereas the need to interpret changes in *ming* spawned a number of technical disciplines, it also led to an influential model that material wealth and satisfaction of the populace were a sign of the approval of *tian*. This model has been the source of religious claims to authority by emperors and revolutionaries alike throughout Chinese history, even to the present.

As the discussion of nonbelievers above made clear, the very definition of separate spheres of "religion" and "politics" is problematic in pre-modern China (whether this distinction is clear elsewhere in the premodern world is another question). Despite the reception of Confucianism as a unitary and primarily "philosophical" entity, the complementary strands of Confucianism represented by the *Documents* and *Analects* represent a comprehensive theory of religion and politics that has influenced every subsequent claim to authority in China. For this reason, the strands of Confucianism that they represent may best be seen as a binary entity that is inherently both political and religious.

Acknowledgment

The author thanks Zhang Zhenjun and Guo Jue for their comments on this chapter.

Notes

1. Mark Csikszentmihalyi, "Confucius and the Analects in the Han," in *Essays on Confucius and the Analects*, ed. Bryan W. Van Norden (New York: Oxford University Press, 2002), 134–62.

2. Hsu Cho-yun, *Ancient China in Transition; An Analysis of Social Mobility, 722–222 B.C.* (Stanford, Calif.: Stanford University Press, 1965), 159.

3. H. A. Giles, *Religions of Ancient China* (Chicago: Open Court Publishing, 1905), 44.

4. Herrlee G. Creel, *The Origins of Statecraft in China*, vol. 1 (Chicago: University of Chicago Press, 1970), 493.

5. Liu Zehua, *Zhongguo zhengzhi sixiangshi* [A history of Chinese political thought], vol. 1 (Hangzhou: Zhejiang Renmin, 1996), 18.

6. Poo Mu-chou, *In Search of Personal Welfare* (Albany: State University of New York Press, 1998), 30.

7. Tu Wei-ming, *Centrality and Commonality: An Essay on Confucian Religiousness* (Albany: State University of New York Press, 1989), 115.

8. P. J. Ivanhoe, *Confucian Moral Self Cultivation*. 2d ed. (Indianapolis: Hackett, 2000), 5.

9. Sarah Allan, *The Heir and the Sage: Dynastic Legend in Early China* (San Francisco: Chinese Materials Center, 1981), 31.

10. Liang Qichao et al., *Zhongguo liu da zhengzhi jia* [Six great Chinese political thinkers] (Taibei: Zhongzheng Shuju, 1964), 1.

Suggested Readings

Creel, Herrlee G. *The Origins of Statecraft in China.* Chicago: University of Chicago Press, 1970.

Csikszentmihalyi, Mark. "Confucius." In *The Rivers of Paradise*, ed. David Noel Freedman and Michael McClymond. Grand Rapids: William B. Eerdmans, 2001.

Ivanhoe, Philip J. *Confucian Moral Self Cultivation.* 2d ed. Indianapolis: Hackett, 2000.

Jensen, Lionel. *Manufacturing Confucianism: Chinese Traditions and Universal Civilization.* Durham, N.C.: Duke University Press, 1997.

Karlgren, Berhard. *The Book of Documents.* Stockholm: Museum of Far Eastern Antiquities, 1950.

Lau, D. C. *The Analects.* Harmondsworth, U.K.: Penguin, 1979.

Liu Zehua. *Zhongguo zhengzhi sixiangshi* [A history of Chinese political thought]. 2 vols. Zhejiang: Xinhua, 1996.

Xu Fuguan. *Rujia zhengzhi sixiang yu minzhu ziyou renquan* [Confucian political thought and democracy, freedom, and human rights]. Taibei: Baishi Niandai, 1991.

Ten | **Buddhism: The Politics of Compassionate Rule** |

Todd Lewis

"But what, Lord Buddha, is it that must rule the king?"
"It is the Dharma, monk!" replied the Buddha.
— *Anguttara Nikaya* III, cxxxii

THE SIXTH CENTURY B.C.E. IN NORTHERN INDIA WAS A TIME OF SPIRITUAL SEEKING unparalleled in the history of religions. Among the many individual teachers then regarded as having attained *nirvāna*, an exalted state of salvation, was one who called himself a "Buddha," one "awakened" by having seen reality clearly and fearlessly.[1] Feeling compassion for beings who suffered on the wheel of life and death, he founded the world's first missionary religion, created a community of monks and nuns (the *sangha*) who adopted his ascetic norms and meditative practices, and shared his teachings with all interested in hearing them, inspiring many and leading a few to enlightenment. The Buddha, born a prince, had renounced his own line to a royal throne; his early *sangha*, too, was taught to cultivate detachment from the householder's lifestyle, and so entanglements in worldly politics.

So for the student of world religions—and even for many scholars of Buddhism—a discussion of this religious tradition's relationship to politics might seem to be a strange, even barren, concern. Given the typical focus in the West on Buddhist texts dealing with philosophical beliefs and soteriological practices of the exemplary *sangha*, one might be tempted to view politics from the perspective of the spiritual elite and conclude that Buddhism counsels aloofness and that Buddhists should remain unconcerned with both worldly power and politics. Such an interpretation, however, would be lacking in the most rudimentary sociohistorical awareness and ignore a large corpus of canonical and popular texts. As it gained ever wider popularity beyond the ascetics and spread out of its region of origin, the Buddhist tradition developed in breadth and scope so that soon after the Buddha's death, most Buddhists were householders (more than 95 percent in most societies) and few—even among the monastic elite (as we will see)—were aloof from political concerns. In fact, we know that rulers across Asia were drawn to support Buddhism because of its positive contributions to political life: its emphasis on individual morality promoting social stability, its rituals designed to secure prosperity for the state as well as officials in power, and its authority through its respected monastics to bestow legitimization on rulers.

Buddhism has found acceptance in many kinds of societies, from nomadic communities to urbanized polities, from the tropics to the vast grasslands of northern Asia, from the Arabian Sea to the Pacific Ocean. One reason for this religion's successful trans-Asian pilgrimage has been not only an inspiring vision of the cosmos and salvation, but also its promise of householders securing worldly prosperity, participating in a moral civilization, and achieving a heavenly rebirth.

From its inception, Buddhism achieved broad support due to its flexibility, both doctrinal and institutional. This distinctive characteristic is based in part on the essential Buddhist belief that both individuals and societies are different as a result of possessing different karmic backgrounds—that is, persons have different past lives and so inherit unique and widely varying personalities, moral natures, and habits. Over time, even the same societies are subject to great changes as well. Buddhist acceptance of pluralism in social life is also due to the tradition's vast library of sacred literature but with no one text, canon, or institution ever gaining universal acceptance. Like all world religions, then, Buddhism is multivocalic; with few exceptions,[2] religious authority has been decentralized wherever the tradition has taken root. Before constructing a composite "Buddhist view of politics," then, it is important to note that in fact Buddhist political thought and practice were always region-specific and that this portrait necessarily entails broad generalizations.

The Classical Sources of Buddhism on Politics

The canons assembled by the major Indic schools that arose during the first 1,000 years after Shākyamuni Buddha (d. 480 or 380 B.C.E.) contain the most important sources for this study. These texts were redacted by monks, and most sections contain the Buddha's discourses on doctrine, monastic issues, and religious matters of prime interest to only monks and nuns. The religious concerns of householders, and any pronouncements regarding political philosophy, quite naturally found little place among long treatises discussing meditation methods, detailed philosophical analyses, or monastic discipline. It is instead in the canonical (and postcanonical) "popular texts" addressed to the householder community where political power and norms of rule find greater iteration.

Jātakas and *avadānas*, story narratives concerned with the previous lives of the Buddha, contain many sources of guidance in this domain (Brown 1955). Well over 800 of these story traditions exist, many in multiple recensions, and these were collected by all the canonical schools and woven into commentaries as well (e.g., Jones 1949–56; Khoroche 1990). Many relate teachings on the issue of political power. In these tales, the future Buddha Shākyamuni (properly termed a *bodhisattva*, "future Buddha") is often born in a ruling family; in many other narratives, he has dealings with political figures.

It is important to recognize that these "popular" stories were the most circulated sources for imparting Buddhist norms and doctrine across the broad sweep of Asian communities. Evidence for the centrality of these rebirth narratives comes from their early collection and the vast accumulation of story collections, indicating popular interest in these parables and the universal need for monk-scholars to redact them for use in teaching student-monks and householders. The ubiquitous place of these stories in Buddhist societies is made clear from the plethora of sculptures and paintings at *stūpas* and monasteries that illustrate key scenes from the most popular stories. This wealth of cultural evidence implies that from the earliest days onward it was the story narratives that shaped the spiritual imaginations and fixed the moral landmarks in the minds of most Buddhists, including the great majority of monks and nuns. That these "popular" stories were taken seriously and read carefully by the literati is confirmed by their translation into various vernacular languages and their use in the legal systems of Southeast Asia.

Another important source for our treatment of Buddhism and politics is a text that began as a letter from the famous philosopher Nāgārjuna that he addressed to a north Indian king, Gautamiputra Shatakarni (80–104 C.E.). This work devotes several chapters to the norms of just kingship and the practices of political rule, in certain areas down to specific policy recommendations; its circulation and importance went far beyond this ruler, because the text was eventually translated into Chinese and Tibetan (Hopkins 1998).

The life of Buddha constitutes another key source. Buddhists, like Muslims, have looked to the small and large details of their founder's life to inspire their own actions. Building on the scattered sources from the canons, and from oral sources now lost, monastic authors composed sacred biographies that recount the final life of the boy named Siddhārtha: a prince who is born in the modest Shākya kingdom located in the foothills of the Himalayas; who finds the householder life unsatisfying, leaves palace, wife, and child behind to pursue spiritual practices; and who achieves enlightenment, founding a community of celibate renunciants and householder supporters whom he leads for more than forty years until his death. These biographies draw upon the canonical sources that record pronouncements on a vast variety of subjects. For more than the past twenty-five centuries, Buddhists have carefully examined and interpreted these sources on almost every conceivable issue, both transcendental and pragmatic, including those pertaining to political power.

Buddhism's Theory of Politics

The very scattered passages in the monastic texts concerned with political thought and power relations might suggest that this area was only of tangential concern to the Buddha and his monastic followers, the monks and nuns of the *sangha*. The consistent concern in the canons for insuring good *sangha*–state relations, however, suggests that the Buddha and his early community took these matters very seriously (Thapar 1980).

In the *Mahāparinibbāna Sutta*, a popular text recounting the last months of his life, the Buddha lavishes praise on the Vajjian people, whose small ethnic state is ruled by a form of republican democracy and an ideology of social equality. He lauds their strength, justice, and social solidarity as a model to inspire the Buddhist *sangha*—his community of monks, nuns, and dedicated householders—after his own demise. (Modern Buddhist politicians have utilized this text to support their advocacy of republican democracy.)

But the world in which the Buddha lived, and in which early Buddhism flourished, was that in which kingship was the norm. (The Vajjian state was in fact eventually annexed by the kingdom of Magadha.) Political thought in the Buddhist sources very predominantly assumes the reality of kingship. In fact, one canonical passage explaining the origins of the world asserts that the evolution of the institution of kingship was a natural stage in the world's development, one in response to the world's degeneration from earlier eras when virtue was so strong that no rules or rulers were even needed. Kingship comes into existence and is needed to continue society's resistance against anarchy. Buddhaghosa's summary of the Pali Canon's creation account from the *Aggana Sutta* recounts the origin of kingship:

> Then they instituted boundary lines [on the land] and one steals another's share. After . . . the third time . . . they beat the offender with fists, earth clods, with sticks, etc. When thus stealing, reproof, lying, and violence had sprung up among them, they come together and said, "What if we elect some one of us, who shall get angry with him who merits anger, reproof, and banish him who merits banishment. . . . He was called the 'Great Elected One,' 'Lord of Fields,' . . . [and] 'King.'"[3]

And who becomes the world's first king? The commentary asserts that it was the future Buddha. This canonical text thus contains two original theories of political authority introduced by Buddhism into Indian political thought: a social compact theory that included a justification of social class and property rights; and a governmental contract theory for kingship (Gard 1962, 44).

The "natural law" of kingship in Buddhist thought is extended in the narratives imagining the animal and oceanic realms as well, with single species ruling ecological regions, and individuals within species assuming the role as king[4] (and, at times, queen). Because there is near-universal agreement among Buddhists that since the Buddha's demise the world has been on a downward spiritual and ethical course (Nattier 1991), subsequent writers when treating political rule assume that kingship is the norm.

Buddhist texts provide religious support for the place of kingship in society. Following the example of the Buddha in his last lifetime (and many births before this), which began when he was born as a crown prince, Buddhist doctrine sees an individual who becomes king doing so as the result of extremely good karma, a reward for almost immeasurable spiritual development in past lifetimes. Like the future Buddha in many incarnations, just kings can do great spiritual good; kingship's power can also be the cause of rapid descent into hells or lower births if the wealth and power over the multitudes is used selfishly or for evil.[5] Due to their potential for evildoing, Buddhist texts of all schools describe kings as a potential "danger" (along with bandits, snakes, poisons, fire, shipwreck) and commonly counsel great care in dealing with them.

What the tradition offers kings is to substitute a greater legitimacy based on *Dharma* (Pali, *Dhamma*; righteousness, justice, spiritual power) and the charisma of adhering to it for the legitimacy of rule based on power or mere inheritance (Gokhale 1969, 735). If this path is taken, a state can become a moral institution.

Even with his praise of the Vajjian republic, the Buddha's own rules in the *Vinaya* (the canonical books of monastic discipline) clearly advocate adapting to the laws and social practices of the region's monarchies. For example, no one could become a monk who was a deserter from a royal army or an escaped criminal; state law must also not be broken in other domains, because debtors could not join the order nor could slaves escape their masters; likewise, civil customs had to be respected, such as children having parental permission to become novice monks or nuns and spouses having to secure their partner's consent to receive ordination. Contrary to an oft-repeated stereotype about Buddhism in its early north Indian context, in no way can Buddhism be seen as a "social reform" movement. Throughout its first 1,700 years in India, there was no attempt to end the caste system or institute gender equality. Even within the *sangha*, the Buddha conformed to the patriarchal norms of his times and required all nuns to submit to the authority of monks.

Political power in Buddhist polities is founded on the Buddha's view that society should be organized with a spiritual exchange connecting householders with the monastic community in a symbiotic relationship. Buddhist institutions have always depended upon the laity making donations to them to earn merit and to garner worldly blessings for themselves, their families, and their communities. The *sangha*, in turn, was expected to maintain the rules of communal life and be spiritually virtuous, guaranteeing that the laity would earn good karma. Through their material support, monks and nuns could garner the resources for living simply, engage in spiritual practices, study, and preserve the tradition. As the faith developed and grew, the *sangha* also acquired lands and buildings that were donated, and it drew children from families to join the *sangha* wherever it took root. It also offered the Dharma to the householders through its monastics' public and private teaching. This central set of exchanges maintained Buddhism in ancient Indian society, and across Asia, and it was the political ruler who had to oversee its functioning (figure 10.1).

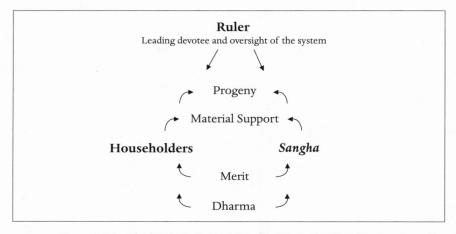

Figure 10.1. Ideal Religio-Political Exchanges in Buddhist Society

One distinctive weakness of Buddhism throughout its history was that it depended upon the state to protect this exchange and to maintain civil laws and civic order. Thus, Buddhist institutions relied on secular political to prosper.[6] Another dependency on outsiders concerned the maintenance of monastic discipline; although highly specific canonical guidelines set forth the rules by which monastic discipline was to be maintained, including the expulsion of those who broke the norms, the *sangha* still depended on the state to enforce such orders, because kings were invited to "purify the *sangha*" when conditions warranted (Rahula 1956, 67). Again, this essential juridical role indicates the importance of political relations in the maintenance of Buddhist institutions.

But this service was not a one-sided relationship. Leading monks in the *sangha* could offer those wielding political power the very highest terms of religious legitimation in the eyes of the Buddhist citizenry. The good king (governor, local official et al.) could be called a *dharmiko dharmarājā* ("just and righteous king"), *dharmarāja* ("just king"), *priyadarshī* ("one who sees the good [of others]"), or *mahāsattva* ("great being"). The terms *bodhisattvarāja* ("king who is a being [to be] enlightened") or *bodhisattvāvatāra* ("incarnation of a bodhisattva") were used across the Buddhist world,[7] usually implying that the ruler was considered the current incarnation of the future Buddha Maitreya (Sarkisyanz 1965).

The highest level of praise is reserved for the most extraordinary Buddhist king. He was the *cakravartin* ("wheel-turning just ruler and zealous devotee"), a spiritual ruler who sets the wheel of the Dharma in motion and establishes a just state, possesses miraculous possessions and assistance, and whose rule is marked by various supernatural signs. This figure, who is also recognized as a Hindu saint in Brahmanical political theory, in Buddhist reckoning is second in cosmic importance only to the Buddha.[8]

Despite the respect that the *sangha* may extend to those in political power, it is noteworthy that the Vinaya nonetheless contained a strict monastic rule that no monk or nun must ever bow to any secular authority, rulers included. This norm, to be observed regardless of a monk or nun's approval for a particular king, asserts symbolically that receiving ordination means moving into a form of existence that has transcended the householder's. The rule also seems intended to have the *sangha* act in unison, and not be divided by personal attachments of individual monks or nuns to political figures. It is also important to note that a bad king could be boycotted by the *sangha*, with monks and nuns uniting to "invert their bowls" and thereby refuse to accept meritorious alms and so proclaim that the individual is not worthy of his office.[9] Because individuals likewise hold power legitimately due to their righteousness, those who fail to maintain this standard can also be removed.

From antiquity to the present, there have been individual monks noted for their service to specific kings, none more significant than the monk who converted the ruler Ashoka, the monarch who first spread Buddhism throughout South Asia and beyond, and whose rule set the most important precedent for *sangha*–political relations thereafter. We now need to turn to this pivotal and paradigmatic political figure.

The Medium of Expressing Politics in Buddhism

When the world conquest campaign of Alexander the Great (355–323 B.C.E.) faltered in northwestern India, the small states on the Indus River weakened by his incursions were subdued and integrated into India's first great empire, that of the Chandragupta Maurya. When his grandson Ashoka (274–236 B.C.E.) assumed the throne, he followed Hindu norms of rulership, later set forth in the *Arthashastra*,[10] consolidated his frontier regions with brute force, directing an assault at Kalinga, a coastal region encompassing modern Orissa. The widespread destruction and bloodshed that his army caused in securing his victory, however, greatly dismayed Ashoka.

At just this time, the emperor encountered a charismatic Buddhist monk and became a staunch devotee. Now that he had extended the Mauryan empire across most of the Indian subcontinent, Ashoka sent ambassadors and scribes throughout his realm to explain "the Dharma" that the emperor embraced, and these reached the borders of his state, and beyond.

Ashoka's edicts—inscribed on rocks and tall pillars—were both general and specific in their explanation of Dharma, a principle he held as key to creating a good society. In Pillar Edict I, he writes, "Dharma is good. But what does Dharma consist of? It consists of few sins and many good deeds, of kindness, liberality, truthfulness, and purity."[11] Although several inscriptions allude to the value of meditation, Ashoka's chief concern was for Buddhism to be a moral force in society: "One should obey one's father and mother. One should respect the supreme value and sacredness of life. One should speak the truth. One should practice these virtues of Dharma."[12]

Having stated these principles and had them placed in prominent public places, Ashoka also sought to have his bureaucracy administer the empire with reference to them: "My officials of all ranks—high, low, and intermediate—act in accordance with the precepts of my instruction. . . . For these are the rules: to govern according to Dharma, to administer justice according to Dharma, to advance the people's happiness according to Dharma, and to protect them according to Dharma."[13] In the capital, Ashoka had trees and wells planted to aid travelers, declared certain days when animal slaughter was prohibited, and worked to limit religious conflict (Filliozat 1967).

His inscriptions also indicate that Ashoka went on a pilgrimage to the places where the Buddha had lived; texts recount that he unearthed the Buddha's relics in order to distribute them across his realm, building thousands of new sacred monuments called *stūpas* to enshrine them. Ashoka through his imperial edicts, official policies, and his patronage of notable monks and monasteries helped spread Buddhism from the Bay of Bengal to Afghanistan, from the Himalayan midhills to the island of Sri Lanka. Inscriptions indicate that he had sent emissaries to all the states of the known world, including the Greeks, the Chinese, and some (still unidentified) venues in Southeast Asia. The fate of the distant missions remains uncertain, but in South Asia the definite traces of the first Buddhist monuments (monasteries and *stūpa* shrines) can be dated to this era, as can the first systematic oral collections of the teachings.

Ashoka immeasurably abetted Buddhism's emergence as a broadly based religion that reached beyond the ascetics, one that did—given his strong political leadership—unify a civilization. Buddhist institutions soon dotted the major trade routes going north and south, east and west.

Although Buddhists in India eventually lost awareness of his inscriptions, they preserved memories of Ashoka's actions (with many embellishments) in post-canonical narratives such as the Sanskrit *Ashokāvadāna*,[14] the *Mahāvamsa*, and other chronicles of Sri Lanka (Geiger 1958), and the Thai text *Trai Phum Phra Ruang* (Reynolds and Reynolds 1982, 172–88). Strong summarizes the popularity of the Ashokan paradigm conveyed in the numerous narrative retellings:

Much of the appeal of the figure of Ashoka in the Ashokāvadāna lies precisely in the fact that he is both great king and simple layman. On a personal level, this involves him . . . with charismatic Buddhist saints who represent the Buddha and confirm for him his royal status; and, on the other, with abbots and ordinary members of the *sangha* with whom he enjoys a routinized relationship. At the same time, however, as a legendary model for Buddhists everywhere, this duality of roles represents a powerful combination; for as cakravartin and greatest donor of all time, Ashoka clearly was an ideal to inspire, while as a giver of ordinary gifts and routine supporter of the community, he was an example to actually be followed.[15]

Buddhist exponents in subsequent centuries invoked Ashoka as a model householder and ruler, one whose example challenged later Buddhist kings to see their vocation as a spiritual one. This idea of Buddhist kingship is expressed directly in this text's recounting of a dialogue between Ashoka and his teacher, the monk Upagupta:

[Upagupta:]
You have established your sovereignty, O Lord,
Keep on ruling conscientiously,
And always honor the precious Triple Gem.

The completely enlightened Buddha, that most excellent charioteer of beings, has entrusted us—you and me—with the safe keeping of his teachings which we are to maintain diligently amidst his flock.

[Ashoka:]
I distributed his reliquaries
And beautified the earth everywhere
With mountain-like *stūpas* of many colors,
With lofty banners and bejeweled parasols.
My son, myself, my house, my wives
The whole earth, even the royal treasure—
There is nothing whatsoever that I have not given up
For the Teaching of the Dharma King.[16]

The tradition's memory of Ashoka, then, established that charity, justice, concern with the common good, and generosity toward the *sangha* became the norms by which a "good Buddhist ruler" was measured. Since this time, too, Buddhists saw it as natural that communities had to depend on the assistance of upright rulers to realize their ideal of a moral and spiritual civilization. Only with political support can the *sangha*'s integrity be assured, the Buddha's monuments be maintained, and the teachings be passed down. In this pattern, Buddhist doctrines, monastic officials, and patrons entered into the secular and political history of the societies where it took root. At times, as with Ashoka, Buddhist monks and institutions were supportive of expansive states providing both political and moral legitimation for their integrating tribal peoples on their frontiers (Falk 1973), a process still ongoing in the mountainous regions of Southeast Asia (Lewis 1994; Tambiah 1984).

The Message of Buddhism's Politics

Just as compassion was the Buddha's central trait—witnessed through his choosing to teach tirelessly for forty years after his enlightenment—so did this ideal become central to Buddhist ethics. In many of the story narratives describing the dilemmas of rule, the recurring message is that political power should be wielded as a means of creating a society where compassion flourishes. Holding political power is not just an end, the coronation of one's past good karma, but the means to an end: shaping the world with justice and kindness. As Gokhale has observed, "The state was not merely a punitive instrument but primarily an agency for the moral transformation of man as a political animal. [The Buddhists] found in morality of a higher order the solution to the dilemma of power" (1966, 20).

In many *jātaka* narratives, a good king's duty is likened to a parent caring for children, or as a son caring for an aged parent.[17] Like the Buddha, a just ruler should understand that in a world marked by suffering, attention to collective welfare is needed; and that being in a position of wielding power, one must bear the burden of moral cultivation and detachment so as to dispatch one's political responsibilities fully. As the great Buddhist monk Buddhaghosa observes in his *Visuddhimagga* (IX, 124):

> For the Great Beings' minds retain their balance by giving preference to beings' welfare, by dislike of beings suffering, by the desire for the various successes achieved by beings to last, and by imparting impartiality toward all beings. And to all beings they give gifts, which are a source of pleasure, without discriminating. . . . And in order to avoid doing harm to beings they undertake the precepts of virtue. They practice renunciation for the purpose of perfecting their virtue. They cleanse their understanding for the purpose of non-confusion about what is good and bad for beings. They constantly arouse energy, having beings' welfare and happiness at heart. When they have acquired heroic fortitude through supreme energy, they become patient with beings' many kinds of fault.[18]

In the *Buddhacarita*, one of the influential biographies of the Buddha written by the Mahāyāna monk Ashvaghosa (active in the second century C.E.), the ideal

king and the norms of political rule are described in the case of King Suddho-
dana, the Buddha's father, and the Shākya state he governed. The king "ceased
from all evil, practiced all self-restraint, and rewarded the good;" "he surpassed
his kindred and citizens by his virtues;" he worshipped the gods and supported
brahmins; he commuted the sentences of criminals condemned to death, suppressed anger toward them, and sought to "reform their characters." All his country he viewed "like a father." The effect on the state was profound: "His servants
and citizens followed his example, like the senses of one absorbed in contemplation whose mind is abstracted in profound peace."[19] We encounter the idea of
virtue's contagiousness again below.

Many popular narratives focusing on kings and the principles that should
guide political rule convey a consistent set of virtues, although there are varia-
tions in emphasis. In Pali Jātaka #376, a sage advises, "O great king, a king should
rule his kingdom with righteousness, eschewing the four evil courses, being zealous and full of patience and kindness and compassion."[20] Here, an exhortation
to the king draws focus to an admonition against anger:

> In the village, in the forest, on the sea or on the shore,
> Ne'er be angry, prince of warriors 'tis my counsel evermore.[21]

Another Pali story (#387) summarizes the virtues that should be cultivated by
compassionate rulers, ending with a sage listing ten political virtues: "Great king,
it is good for a king to rule his kingdom by forsaking the ways of wrongdoing,
not offending against the ten kingly virtues and acting with just righteousness:

> Alms, morals, charity, justice and penitence,
> Peace, mildness, mercy, meekness, patience.[22]

A similar passage from another Pali story provides an overview of the virtues
that are consistently highlighted in individual narratives. It mentions King
Janasandha's exemplary practices, especially those that led to his kingdom enjoy-
ing prosperity and spirituality:

> The good King inspired all India with his almsgiving; the prison doors he opened
> for good and all the places of execution he destroyed, all the world he protected
> with the four sorts of beneficence [liberality, affability, impartiality, good rule], he
> kept the five precepts, observed the holy fasting days, and ruled in righteousness.
> From time to time, he would gather his subjects and declare the Dharma to
> them.[23]

We now turn to several of the principles of political power that are emphasized
again and again in popular Buddhist literature.

Forgiveness and Foregoing Revenge

In a story found in the Theravādin *Vinaya* (X, 2, 20), emphasis on forgiveness as a royal virtue is highlighted, as Prince Dighavu realizes a central ethical lesson: After King Brahmadatta murders his parents and destroys their kingdom, he patiently and diligently plots revenge. On the brink of accomplishing it, he recognizes the alternative causalities that would unfold if he undertook immoral or moral action, and sees his only course as forgiveness. With revenge merely a sword thrust away, he relents:

> If I should deprive you of life, O king, then your partisans would deprive me of life; my partisans again will deprive those of life. Thus by hatred that hatred would not be appeased.[24]

The futility of a king or government inflicting capital punishment in karmic terms comes up again and again in the royal narratives, with individual and collective retribution eventually boomeranging back in immediate and/or next lifetime effects. In Pali Jātaka #528, for example, when the king captures plotters of a coup against him, the future Buddha convinces him to forgo the ministers' suggestions of the guilty receiving execution or dismemberment, but instead be content with a more humane course: "depriving them of property and after having fettered them and sprinkled them with cow-dung, banishing them into exile." Similar in approach is the widely popular *Simhalasārthabāhu Avadāna*. It tells the story of a caravan trader who is shipwrecked and has his companions trapped and eaten by cannibalistic demonesses; when he later becomes king, he leads an army to attack these murderous spirits, but accepts their surrender in the following terms:

> "O Demonesses! After seeing all of your crimes, you deserve to be killed immediately." But after hearing their entreaties for mercy, he continued, "And in this land, you should live no more. You must never come back here so go and live in a dense forest in a far-off land. If you ever return to this town, I will certainly kill you all."[25]

In a few stories, we find the view expressed that kings should not even resist violent invaders who threaten their domains. In one instance, a king throws open the city gates and admits a marauding gang. After he himself is captured and thrown into a dungeon, the king's only defense is to extend thoughts of *maitrī* (Pali, *metta*; loving-kindness) to his chief tormenter. This causes his captor to feel "great torment in his body," burn as though "with a two-fold flame," and be smitten with great pain."[26] A similar story plot is found in Pali Jātaka #351, and the result is the same: Both kings regain their thrones without war or bloodshed.

This same spiritual method of nonviolent defense is evident in other Mahāyāna narratives as well. In one of the stories that is part of the *Pañcarakshā*, one of the most popular Buddhist texts translated across northern and eastern Asia, the king responds to invasion by telling the citizens not to fight, as he alone resorts to ritual:

> He proclaimed, "My dear subjects! It is my duty to safeguard the country and countrymen. You need not be afraid of anything. I will do all that is needed." After saying this, King Brahmadatta bathed and cleansed himself with many kinds of sweet-smelling waters. Purified in body, speech, and mind, the king appended the amulets of the *Pratisarā dhāraṇī* to his crown and armor, then went alone to meet the enemy. The men in the army of the enemy kings retreated and ran away in a panic.[27]

In another Mahāyāna story, we find the same threat again, but after the citizens express frank skepticism,[28] the king assures them that they can relax because he alone will repel the marauding army relying on his "meritorious actions": "King Brahmadatta went to the holy river and bathed. Then he went to the . . . temple that night, fasted, and worshiped Mahākāla.[29] He meditated on Mahākāla constantly. . . . As a result, the deity Mahākāla in his terrifying form appeared before the king."[30] The king praised Mahākāla and received the boon of the "eight supernormal powers," including being invisible, capability to be invulnerable to enemies, and gaining the power to vanquish enemies. The result? "Armed with such precious powers, when King Brahmadatta went like a lion to the battlefield with his hand raised high, his enemies were panic-stricken and ran to him for refuge."[31]

Thus, an observant Buddhist king need not perpetuate the endless cycle of revenge, even on those mindlessly assaulting civil order; instead, he can rely on the powers of tradition themselves: the force of loving-kindness, the causality of karmic retribution, and the power of rituals and chants bestowed by the Buddhas.[32]

Support of Buddhism and Spiritual Teachers

The good political ruler, as we have seen, can rely on the force of merit for benefiting his subjects. So it follows that performing meritorious deeds is a central attribute of Buddhist kingship. In the Buddhist reckoning of merit making, no action is more productive of generating good karma than making donations to spiritual seekers, with Buddhist saints the most productive "field of merit." We know from the testimony of the Chinese pilgrim Hsuan Tsang that some Indian kings followed the example of Ashoka and were generous to the ascetics in their realm (Beal 1983, 63), including their sponsoring the *pancavārsika* ("Five-Year Assembly") that Ashoka reputedly inaugurated, whereby every monk and nun in the *sangha* was fed and given robe cloth on a lavish scale (Strong 1983, 91–96). As many of the story narratives also reveal, royal donations to monasteries and sages were often repaid by their being sources of service to citizens[33] and purveyors of good advice. As one virtuous king notes:

> Because, O Prince, I never grudge great sages what is meet:
> Ready to pay them honor due, I fall before their feet.
>
> Me envying none, and apt to learn all conduct meet and right,
> Wise sages each good precept teach in which they take delight.
>
> I listen to the bidding of these sages great and wise:
> My heart is bent to good intent, no counsel I despise.[34]

If respected, the *sangha* can thus serve as a "repository of the conscience of the state" (Gokhale 1966, 22). Fostering political as well as social stability, members of the *sangha* often served in governmental administration in education, welfare, and in diplomatic relations (Gard 1962, 47).[35]

Some stories provide a negative lesson on this theme, showing the results of kings failing to heed the advice of wise monks and virtuous counselors. In the case of the *Sringabheri Avadāna*, it is the queen who offers her husband the king some good advice, to cease his daily hunting; ignoring her, he dies young and falls victim to great suffering in his subsequent lifetime.[36]

The Measure of Wielding Power: Seeking and Promoting Justice

A Buddhist in power must pursue justice in his realm and be just in his ruling practices. The popular texts counsel kings to choose their ministers wisely and monitor their agents carefully. Paying those in their employ regularly and fairly is important.[37] Rulers should also respect prisoners and appoint their punishments with compassion; invest in schools, resthouses, water systems, and medicines; exact taxes sensitive to the plight of farmers; and make certain that the police truly protect the citizens. The reckoning of Buddhist justice extends to nonhumans, including animals and suffering spirits.[38]

Kings in ancient India were often preoccupied with dispute resolution, deciding cases in their courts that arose between individuals. Being fair, not accepting bribes, and implementing a just solution are often cited as moral markers in the *jātaka* narratives.[39] In a frame story to one, for example, the Buddha addresses a king from the early state of Kosala: "'My lord king,' replied the Master, 'To judge a cause with justice and impartiality is the right thing; that is the way to heaven.'" He then notes that a king closely following the Buddha's precepts and acting rightly is not surprising.[40]

Justice must be sought in every part of the kingdom and extended to every kind of individual, regardless of class, caste, or occupation. As the poetic verses in Pali Jātaka #501 eloquently convey:

To friends and courtiers, warrior king, do righteously; and so
By following a righteous life to heaven the king shall go.
In war and travel, warrior king, do righteously; and so . . .
In town and village, warrior king, do righteously; . . .
In every land and realm, warrior king, do righteously; . . .
To brahmins and ascetics, warrior king, do righteously; . . .
To friends and courtiers, warrior king, do righteously; . . .
To birds and beasts, warrior king, do righteously; . . .
Do righteously, warrior king, from this all blessings flow
By following a righteous life to heaven the king shall go.[41]

The Politics of Collective Karma: Buddhist Polity as Commonwealth

It is commonly thought that the karma doctrine of Buddhism (and Hinduism) embraces a strict nexus of individualistic retribution: that is, what one person sows by intended action, one reaps oneself, whether in the present lifetime or in a future rebirth. But in fact this is not the full reality of human connection and karmic causality. *Jātaka* stories told by the Buddha about his previous lives clearly portray how a person's worldly and spiritual destiny can also be profoundly affected by simple proximity to significant others, especially spouses, shipmates, monks, and kings.[42]

But the potential for those wielding political power to affect their subjects is a relationship of the greatest magnitude. This truth is memorably and dramatically conveyed in Pali Jātaka #276 (a plot line also found in #483 and #494), when the deity Indra seeks to find out why heaven[43] is suddenly becoming so crowded. He investigates and discovers that the spiritual rule of a virtuous king is the reason; not only does the king's virtue lead citizens to reach the heavens, it also leads to the land's prosperity:[44]

> Then their king practiced the Kuru precepts and the Five Virtues. And then in the realm . . . the rain fell; the three fears were allayed; the land became prosperous and fertile . . . and then with his subjects went to fill the heavens.[45]

Many stories about rulers make this point, utilizing the same simile:

> Beneath the mild sway of a righteous king,
> Like shade from sun-stroke sheltering,
> His subjects may all dwell in peace,
> Rejoicing in their wealth's increase.
>
> . . . If the bull a course direct shall steer,
> The herd of cows straight follow in his rear.

> So should their chief to righteous ways be true,
> The common folk injustice will eschew,
> And through the realm shall holy peace ensue.[46]

A good king's virtue is highly influential through his example as leader. As another *jātaka* concludes:

> Should their chief to righteous ways be true,
> The common folk injustice will eschew,
> And through the realm shall holy peace ensue.[47]

Another idea found in these stories is that the natural world itself responds to a king's moral actions, [48] affecting all the citizens as a result.[49] Pali Jātaka #334 provides a good example of this view of connectivity: "In the time of unjust kings, oil, honey, molasses and the like, as well as wild roots and fruits, lose their sweetness and flavor; not only these but the whole realm becomes bad and flavorless; but when the rulers are just, these things become sweet and full of flavor, and the whole realm recovers its tone and flavor."[50]

A king's actions also affect the supernatural beings that share our world, a causal nexus that also can affect an entire nation. This is made clear in Pali Jātaka #213, where the result is not collective blessing but collective disaster:

> All the spirits that dwelt in the realm of Bharu with one mind were angry with the king, and they brought up the sea, and for the space of three hundred leagues they made the kingdom of Bharu as though it were not. And so for the sake of the king of Bharu alone, all the inhabitants of the kingdom perished thus.[51]

One final aspect of the king's collective influence is in his role as ritual leader. Ritual acts, in traditional Buddhist assessment, are choreographed moral actions garnering merit, drawing on the canonically sanctioned power inherent in repeating the Buddha's words and venerating his relics or images. Ritual texts for this purpose were translated into all Asian languages and utilized extensively, although few have been translated into Western languages (Lewis 2002). Many of the stories appended to them state that kings are especially enjoined to perform rituals to aid their countries. The most important ritual a king can do for his realm is enshrine or worship the Buddha's relics, or venerate a special Buddha image.

Another example of the linkage between political power and ritual power is the previously cited *Pancarakshā*, a text that contains special chants (*parittas, mantras, dhāranīs*) that were revealed by the Buddha to help kings protect their cities, farm animals, elicit supernatural assistance, and free the realm of diseases, including epidemics.[52] The king as promoter of rituals directed to solicit the compassionate intervention of the celestial bodhisattvas was pivotal in the Mahāyāna

Buddhist polities of highland and east Asia, and is featured in many texts, such as in the aforementioned *Simhalasārthabāhu Avadāna*.

Going further is the *Manjusrīmūlakalpa*, an early and widely disseminated Mahāyāna text, that attests that a just king must be on the Buddhist path and one who has produced the thought of enlightenment. In the text's description of the royal consecration, the ritual encodes many of the ideas already mentioned; the king also is asked to identify with Manjushrī, the celestial bodhisattva who symbolically wields a sword that cuts through delusion; and he must strive to be a *cakravartin* ruler who will serve all beings, human and nonhuman (Snellgrove 1959, 205–7).

Buddhism and Nonbelievers: Politics and People outside the Tradition

Whether or not people convert to Buddhist tradition—taking refuge in the Buddha, his teachings, and in the *sangha* of monks and nuns—believers aver that the destiny of all beings in this world is shaped by karma. So whether individuals follow the Four Noble Truths and the Eightfold Path, Buddhists believe that its general moral framework is universal, because all humans must proceed on the same progressive religious path: Starting with morality, one advances through many births to be capable of meditation; and as this is slowly mastered, there is the arising of salvific insight (*prajñā*); when this is complete, there is enlightenment and escape from future rebirth, that is, *nirvāna*.

This cosmic law operates regardless of whether individuals adhere to views of the world at variance with the Buddha's. So from the Buddhist perspective, those who adhere to monotheistic or polytheistic theologies, or who propitiate spirits, or those who are atheists or irreligious . . . are simply immature in their spiritual development, but eventually—in this or future lifetimes—will find the Buddhist path. Therefore, non-Buddhists must certainly be shown compassion because they are simply underdeveloped, like children, in their spiritual capacity. Toleration of non-Buddhists in Buddhist polities follows from this outlook.

What is also striking in the stories we have examined is that kings are urged to support all true spiritual seekers and teachers in their realms, including Brahmins; in many instances, and somewhat surprisingly to non-Buddhists, many texts lack any special call for favoring Buddhist monks or nuns to the neglect of others. So all beings and all spiritual seekers in a polity must be protected by the Buddhist ruler, even foreigners. As one story's praised king reflects on the success of his rule:

Thus merchants prosper, and from many a realm they come and go,
And I protect them. Now the truth, Uposatha, you know.[53]

So the general Buddhist view of political rule regarding nonbelievers is to accept pluralism, to protect and support all beings regardless of their religious affiliation, and to use power to support morality and mold a compassionate world. The measure of a political regime's success is its citizens' worldly prosperity, justice implemented in the state's workings, the presence of a vital *sangha*, and merit-making practices by citizens that would hold the promise of their heavenly rebirth.

Conclusion

The Buddhist approach to political power and rule builds upon the faith's core philosophy that sees as a universal truth the fact that all beings suffer and that compassion is the ethos to guide human action in the world. Beyond the basic principles articulated in the early texts surveyed, it is important to note that later Buddhist theorists did not develop many finely nuanced policies for wielding political power. In ancient India, however, the detailed articulation of statecraft methods received great attention by Hindu writers. We do know that statecraft in South Asian polities did follow the principles of the *Dharmashastras* and the *Arthashastra*, and not many of those in the Ashokan Buddhist model.

In fact, across the Himalayan, Sri Lankan, and Southeast Asian frontiers of India, where Buddhism spread and established its network of institutions, it was accompanied by Hindu and Brahmanical traditions at the ruling courts. Thus, Hindu theories of divine kingship, rule by force, and royal court ritualism at times influenced these otherwise predominantly Buddhist polities. The history of these frontier countries—up to the present—therefore cannot be viewed as being influenced solely by the Buddhist theories of political rule but by the confluence of these two Indic traditions (Reynolds 1972; Tambiah 1976, 102–31; Pathak 1974; Lewis 1994).

Having surveyed the features of Buddhist political philosophy, its acceptance of religious pluralism, and the universal exhortation not to resist evil or capital retribution, one might finally wonder how the tradition has even survived to the modern era or up to the present. The past 500 years have brought a multilayered and interlinked series of crises to Buddhist Asia: the decline and fall of kingship throughout the Buddhist world (in all countries but Thailand and Bhutan), the forceful imposition of colonial law by foreigners, the imperial quest for wealth, and confrontation with world religions that more readily sanction violence to defend or extend themselves.

Because most of the discourses and prescriptions for political action in Buddhist societies are based upon the presence and necessary intervention of a king, Buddhist societies have faced the unprecedented challenges of colonialism—and now independence—lacking the guidance of primary resources from their canonical tradition. Across Asia, there has been an urgently felt need to redefine the political foundations of Buddhism in a kingless world.[54] The rise of lay organizations across Asia and the general decline of monastics and monastic influences have dramatically changed the classical balances imagined in the early texts.

Is the history of Buddhism's decline and near disappearance from medieval South Asia (the Gangetic plain; ancient Gandhara and Sind, which correspond to modern Pakistan and Afghanistan), from Central Asia, and from Indonesia a product of its distinctively passive approach to political power and rule? Or did the tradition decline in these places centuries ago because there were no longer Buddhist kings to protect the faith? Does the exile of the Dalai Lama–led Gelugpa State in Tibet after 1959, the failure of Buddhists in Burma to resist military authoritarianism since 1960, or the inability of Buddhists to muster effective resistance to communist regimes in Southeast Asia (Vietnam, Laos, and Cambodia) reflect the inapplicability of the traditional political views to the postcolonial and posttraditional era (Gard 1962; Sarisyanz 1965; Lewis 1997)?

We conclude this essay with the sort of question commonly posed today in Buddhist societies: How can a Buddhist society following its classical political ideals hope to survive in the modern world where nations' "civil religions" require universal loyalty, violent retribution is often regarded as virtuous, and where showing compassion is regarded as political weakness? Modern Buddhist reformers now face many questions from citizens and rulers concerning the relevance and applicability of the traditional Buddhist norms of political rule.

Notes

1. Buddhist terms in this chapter will be rendered in the more familiar Sanskrit form, with the Pali term indicated in parenthesis at first usage. For citations of Pali texts, the original will be preserved, with the Sanskrit term indicated in brackets.

2. In this chapter, due to space limitations, I cannot include more than passing references to the unique and complex case of Tibet. In this vast high-mountain region, schools formed that allowed monastic officials to assume political power in a manner unseen elsewhere in the Buddhist world. See Dargyay 1988; Goldstein 1989, 1997; Richardson 1962; Stein 1972; Shakabpa 1967.

3. Translated in Warren 1995, 326.

4. E.g., see Pali Jātakas #407 and #270 (Cowell 1957, vol. 2, 242–43) where all land animals have the lion and among fish there is the "Ananda" (of uncertain identity, perhaps a dolphin); the story details birds seeking a king, as they reject the owl and decide on the golden goose. In more than half of the jātakas, the future Buddha is born as king of his group or species.

5. In one jātaka, the bodhisattva remembers his previous life as a king and how he had to be born in purgatory to "work off" the bad karma of royal acts. Accordingly, he feigns mental illness and physical disabilities to avoid becoming king.

6. Pali texts recommend that Buddhist kings establish officers to advise the king on policies relating to justice and religious support (Gokhale 1966, 18).

7. The Dalai Lamas of Tibet were identified as incarnations of the most popular Mahāyāna celestial bodhisattva, Avalokiteshvara.

8. Textual prescriptions indicate this king's extraordinary standing and state that the *cakravartin's* relics must be enshrined in a *stūpa*, and whose worship is considered meritorious.

9. The Ceylon Chronicles mention that this punishment was once set in place by the *sangha* for the seventh-century king Dathopatissa II (Wijayaratna 1990, 136).

10. This work details the Hindu theory of royal rule.

11. Nikam and McKeon 1978, 41.

12. Nikam and McKeon 1978, 43.

13. Nikam and McKeon 1978, 42.

14. The *Ashokāvadāna* is a Hinayānist work, but one that foreshadows Mahāyāna developments. It is translated in Strong 1983.

15. Strong 1983, 100.

16. Strong 1983, 242.

17. "Just as an aged father . . . ought to be cared for by an able-bodied son, so too ought all the people be protected by the king." Pali Jātaka #432; Cowell 1957, vol. 9, 305.

18. Nyanamoli 1976, vol. 1, 353.

19. Cowell 1969, 24.

20. Pali Jātaka #276 highlights the influence of a just king who upholds the "Kuru Precepts" of kingship: slay not the living; take not what is not given; walk not evilly in lust; speak no lies; drink no strong drink." Cowell 1957, vol. 3, 276. These are none other than five precepts for all Buddhist householders.

21. Cowell 1957, vol. 6, 151–52.

22. Cowell 1957, vol. 6, 173–74.

23. Jātaka #468, in Cowell 1957, vol. 4, 110.

24. Rhys-Davids and Oldenberg 1982, vol. 2, 305. This passage quotes the famous section at the beginning of the Pali *Dhammapada*.

25. Translated in Lewis 2000, 79.

26. Jātaka #282, in Cowell 1957, vol. 3, 274.

27. Translated in Lewis 2000, 135.

28. That this nonviolent and spiritual policy toward murderous lawbreakers was met with skepticism in ancient times finds expression where a spokesman is quoted replying in panic to the king's bold but seemingly foolhardy assurances, "We have no knowledge of what powers you have by virtue of your meritorious actions. We want you to demonstrate this power by resisting and destroying the present enemy. It will be pointless to repent after our country has fallen into the hands of its enemies!" Lewis 2000, 111–12.

29. Mahākāla is an Indic deity shared by both Hindu and Buddhist traditions. Related to Shiva, and associated with kings in later South Asian history, Mahākāla is thought to be a guardian of Buddhist monasteries, and utilized in Vajrayāna meditation traditions. See Lewis 2000, chap. 5.

30. Lewis 2000, 112.

31. Lewis 2000, 113.

32. That some Buddhist kings ignored these nonviolent precepts, and did not follow the Ashokan example entirely, should not be surprising. One famous example comes from Sri Lanka, where the fanatical early king Duttagamani (101–77 B.C.E.) does make an armed crusade to repel invaders. In the national chronicle, the *Mahāvamsa*, he is said to have attached a Buddha relic to his spear and marched into battle with 500 monks in attendance. This is clearly perceived as a deviation from the Buddhist norm in the text, which describes the efforts of 8 enlightened monks (Arhats) who were called upon to assuage his guilt at the killing he had caused. Their words of comfort are also in striking contrast to the norms of the early canon and popular narratives: "From this deed arises no hindrance in thy way to heaven. Only one and a half human beings have been slain here by thee, O Lord of men . . . unbelievers and men of evil life were the rest, not more to be esteemed than beasts . . . therefore cast away care from thy heart." Quoted in Smith (1972, 43), who notes that this passage may reveal that the *sangha* preserved it to underline the need for vigilance against such compromises in the future.

33. According to the Chinese *Tripitaka* [Taisho 16, #683], Buddhists should missionize by engaging in the follow services for local communities: "1. Build monastic halls and temples; 2. Plant Fruit trees, shade trees and then excavate bathing pools; 3. Freely supplying medicines to heal the sick; 4. Construction of sturdy boats; 5. Safe placement of bridges suitable for the weak or ill; 6. Digging wells near roads for the thirsty and weary; 7. Enclosing sanitary toilets." The value of these activities to local and state rulers was doubtless, in places, considerable.

34. Pali Jātaka #462 from Cowell 1957, vol. 4, 85.

35. The exceptions to this practice were classical India (300–1200 C.E.) where brahmanical texts argue against any ascetics serving the state, and in China where a Confucian civil service often disdained the social benefits of the Buddhist *sangha*.

36. Translated in Lewis 2000, chap. 2.

37. One king in Pali Jātaka #462 proudly proclaims: "Elephant troops and charioteers, guard royal, infantry— / I took no daily toll of daily dole, but paid them all their fee." Cowell 1957, vol. 4, 85.

38. Mentioned in Nāgārjuna's *Precious Garland* (Hopkins 1998, 74–83).

39. Pali Jātaka #527 has the future Buddha offering the following advice: "A king delighting in the law is blest, / And of all men a learned one is best, / Ne'er to betray a friend is good, / But evil to eschew is perfect bliss." Cowell 1957, vol. 5, 114.

40. Pali Jātaka # 151. Cowell 1957, vol. 2, p. 1. See also Pali Jātaka #247.

41. In Cowell 1957, vol. 4, 263.

42. I discuss stories in these areas in Lewis 2000.

43. According to Buddhist doctrine, heaven is a highly desirable rebirth venue, and praised as a goal of householder Buddhists; but it is impermanent and one must eventually be reborn in other spheres. Significantly, one cannot escape the world of rebirth (*samsāra*) from heaven.

44. Despite the universally declared individual hope for *nirvāna* in a distant time, worldly prosperity and heavenly rebirth were the two primary goals that have motivated Buddhist householders from antiquity to the present. The royal stories underline that these were the central concerns in the imagination of typical Buddhists in Asian societies.

45. #276 in Cowell 1957, vol. 3, 260.

46. Cowell 1957, vol. 4, 114–15.

47. Cowell 1957, vol. 4, 74.

48. This idea that the earth or nature will respond to the actions of a notable spiritual person—who declares his or her truthfulness and goodness—is actually found often in the canonical literature. There are numerous examples: the earth quakes after the enlightenment of a Buddha, and to affirm his imminent attainment of *nirvāna*. Trees blossom in response to a Buddha's deeds. The recitation of the Buddha's words can alter a region's environment, pacify serpents, and cause rain to fall. Early Buddhists also believed in a ritual practice called "An Act of Truth" that calls upon the unseen forces of the world to change worldly reality when a morally advanced person speaks the truth about his spiritual practice.

49. Many ritual traditions practiced in Buddhist polities—the king plowing the first furrow in planting, welcoming the rains, etc.—were based upon this belief (Gard 1962, 45).

50. Cowell 1957, vol. 4, 72.

51. Cowell 1957, vol. 2, 120.

52. The *Karunikarâja-prajnâparimitâ Sūtra* is another Mahāyāna ritual text designed for "protecting the country" (Gard 1962, 56).

53. Pali Jātaka #462, in Cowell 1957, vol. 4, 85.

54. The title of the recent book by H. L. Seneviratne (1999), *The Work of Kings: The New Buddhism in Sri Lanka*, captures just this reality: Buddhist reformers having to reinvent their Buddhist polity in the one country that has in many respects led the revival of Theravada tradition during the colonial and postcolonial eras. The initial results of these efforts—the rise of intolerant Buddhist nationalism, ethnic fratricide, civil war—have exposed the failure to invent modern Buddhist politics there and have led to the tragic failure to achieve the canonical ideals of tolerant and compassionate rule. The same pattern of Buddhist institutions and Buddhists succumbing to nationalism can be discerned in early modern Japan, where the Buddhist establishment likewise fueled nationalism and fomented imperialistic wars (Victoria 1997; Ketelar 1990).

References

Beal, Samuel, tr. 1983. *Si-Yu-Ki: Buddhist Records of the Western World*. 2 vols. New Delhi: Munshiram Manoharlal.

Brown, D. Mackenzie. 1955. "Didactic Themes of Buddhist Political Thought in the Jatakas." *Journal of Oriental Literature* 1(2): 3–7.

Cowell, E. B., trans. 1957. *The Jātaka*, 6 vols. London: Routledge & Kegan Paul.

———. 1969. *Buddhist Mahayana Texts*. New York: Dover.

Dargyay, Eva K. 1988. "Srong-Btsan Sgampo of Tibet: Bodhisattva and King." In *Monks and Magicians*, ed. Phyllis Granoff and Koichi Shinohara. Oakville, Canada: Mosaic Press.

Falk, Nancy Auer. 1973. "Wilderness and Kingship in Ancient South Asia." *History of Religions* 13(1): 1–15.

Filliozat, J. 1967. *Studies in the Asokan Inscriptions*. Calcutta: R.D. Press.

Gard, Richard A. 1962. "Buddhism and Political Authority." In *The Ethic of Power: The Inter-*

play of Religion, Philosophy and Politics, ed. Harold W. Lasswell and Harlan F. Cleveland. New York: Harper & Row.

Geiger, Wilhelm, ed. 1958. *The Mahavamsa*. London: Luzak and Company,.

Gokhale, B. G. 1966. "Early Buddhist Kingship." *Journal of Asian Studies* 26: 15–22.

———. 1969. "The Early Buddhist Theory of the State." *Journal of the American Oriental Society* 84(4): 731–38.

Goldstein, Melvyn C. 1989. *A History of Modern Tibet, 1913–1951*. Berkeley: University of California Press.

———. 1997. *The Snow Lion and the Dragon: China, Tibet, and the Dalai Lama*. Berkeley: University of California Press.

Hopkins, Jeffrey. 1998. *Buddhist Advice for Living and Liberation: Nagarjuna's Precious Garland*. Ithaca, N.Y.: Snow Lion,.

Jones, J. J. 1949–56. *The Mahāvastu*, 3 vols. London: Luzac and Co.

Ketelar, James Edward. 1990. *Of Heretics and Martyrs in Meiji Japan: Buddhism and Its Persecution*. Princeton, N.J.: Princeton University Press.

Khoroche, Peter. 1990. *Once the Buddha Was a Monkey: Arya Sura's Jātakamālā*. Chicago: University of Chicago Press.

Lewis, Todd T. 1989. "Mahāyāna *Vratas* in Newar Buddhism." *Journal of the International Association of Buddhist Studies* 12 (1): 109–38.

———. 1994. "The Himalayan Frontier in Comparative Perspective: Considerations Regarding Buddhism and Hinduism in Diaspora." *Himalayan Research Bulletin* 14(1–2): 25–46.

———.1997. "The Anthropological Study of Buddhist Communities: Historical Precedents and Ethnographic Paradigms." In *Shamanism, Altered States, Healing: Essays in the Anthropology of Religion*, ed. Steven Glazier. Westport, Conn.: Greenwood Press.

———. 2000. *Popular Buddhist Texts from Nepal: Narratives and Rituals of Newar Buddhism*. Albany: State University of New York Press.

———. 2002. "Representations of Buddhism in Undergraduate Teaching: The Centrality of Ritual and Story Narratives." In *Teaching Buddhism in the West: From the Wheel to the Web*, ed. Victor Hori and Richard P. Hayes. Surrey, U.K.: Curzon.

Nattier, Jan. 1991. *Once Upon a Future Time: Studies in a Buddhist Philosophy of Decline*. Berkeley, Calif.: Asian Humanities Press.

Nikam, N. A. and Richard McKeon, eds. and trans. 1959. *The Edicts of Ashoka*. Chicago: University of Chicago Press.

Nyanamoli, Bhikkhu, trans. 1976. *The Path of Purification (Visuddhimagga) by Bhadantacariya Buddhaghosa*. Berkeley, Calif.: Shambhala.

Pathak, Suniti Kumar. 1974. *The Indian Nitishastras in Tibet*. Delhi: Motilal Barnarsidass.

Rahula, Walpola. 1956. *History of Buddhism in Ceylon*. Colombo: Gunasena.

Reynolds, Frank. 1972. "The Two Wheels of Dhamma: A Study of Early Buddhism." In *The Two Wheels of Dhamma*, ed. Bardwell Smith. Chambersburg, Pa.: American Academy of Religion.

Reynolds, Frank E., and Mani B. Reynolds. 1982. *Three Worlds According to King Ruang*. Berkeley, Calif.: Asian Humanities Press.

Rhys-Davids, T. W., and Hermann, Oldenberg, trans. 1982. *Vinaya Texts*. 3 vols. Delhi: Motilal Banarsidass.

Richardson, Hugh E. 1962. *Tibet and Its History*. Oxford: Oxford University Press.

Sarkisyanz, E. 1965. *Buddhist Backgrounds of the Burmese Revolution*. The Hague: M. Nijhoff.

Seneviratne, H. L. 1999. *The Work of Kings: The New Buddhism in Sri Lanka*. Chicago: Chicago University Press.

Shakabpa, Tsepon W. D. 1967. *Tibet: A Political History*. New Haven, Conn.: Yale University Press.

Smith, Bardwell L. 1972. "The Ideal Social Order as Portrayed in the Chronicles of Ceylon." In *The Two Wheels of Dhamma*, ed. Bardwell Smith. Chambersburg, Pa.: American Academy of Religion.

Snellgrove, David L. 1959. "The Notion of Divine Kingship in Tantric Buddhism." *Studies in the History of Religions* 4: 204–18.

Stein, R. A. 1972. *Tibetan Civilization*. Stanford, Calif.: Stanford University Press.

Strong, John S. 1983. *The Legend of King Asoka*. Princeton, N.J.: Princeton University Press.

Tambiah, Stanley J. 1976. *World Conqueror and World Renouncer: A Study of Buddhism and Polity in Thailand against a Historical Background*. Cambridge: Cambridge University Press.

———. 1984. *Buddhist Saints of the Forest and the Cult of Amulets*. Cambridge: Cambridge University Press.

Thapar, Romila. 1980. "State Formation in Early India." *International Social Science Journal* 32(4): 1–28.

Victoria, Brian. 1997. *Zen at War*. New York: Weatherhill.

Warren, Henry Clarke. 1995. *Buddhism in Translations*. Delhi: Motilal Banarsidass.

Wijayaratna, Mohan. 1990. *Buddhist Monastic Life*. Cambridge: Cambridge University Press.

Retrospective on Religion and Politics |

Jacob Neusner

DESPITE THE DIVERSITY OF THE WORLD'S MAJOR RELIGIONS, AS WE HAVE OBSERVED throughout this volume, politics permeates each religious tradition. A politics theorizes an ongoing exercise of power, of coercion that includes legitimized violence. Here we have shown for world religions that politics addresses a religious issue and—more to the point—makes a religious statement, as much as, not uncommonly, religions take up political ones and engage in political action. People expect from religion not only private solace but also ultimate solutions to shared problems; that means they anticipate from religion acts of power, not only affirmations of conscience. Though these acts of power may from the religious perspective originate in the sacred realm—in God—they very much affect the human, and social, domain. Therefore, religion integrates the private and the public.

In the public sphere, religion produces political consequences, shaping attitudes and ideas that make an impact on issues of public policy. Why so? Religion comprises what people do together, not just what they believe in the privacy of their hearts. In other words, religion functions socially. And because it operates within society, religion may function politically, sometimes through legitimate violence and coercion. Before the seventeenth century in the West, and throughout much of the world even today, religion integrated politics, economics, and philosophy, imparting its character and purpose to them all, expressing its statement of self-evident truth through them all.

Of course, all religions speak of power, and thus to some extent of legitimate violence. In their view, power is exercised by or in behalf of God and his divine agencies. But religions also talk politics in another manner. A religion's intellectuals claim to explain the workings of power. That is, they try to explain why things are the way they are. And in accounting for why legitimate power works, why things are as they are, they commonly propound a causative theory of how things began. Further, the assertion of how things began serves as justification for the religion's legitimate violence, for when we say how things originated, we implicitly claim that that is how things were when they were right, and therefore how they should be even now. The chapters in this volume are drawn together around the politics of religions. In our treatment of this critical subject, however, we have not limited our analysis to data that directly concern coercion and violence, legitimate or otherwise. Quite to the contrary, we have extended our interest to the consideration of all aspects of the social order that the religion under study means to describe. It would have been impossible to treat politics as dis-embedded from myth and philosophy and from economics and theology.

In the end, the comparative study of religion offered here supplies insight not simply into politics but also into the nature of religious systems of the social order. Each account here reveals how that system that is under study delivers its message through the topics it selects for detailed analysis, what its message is, and why it chooses (in this case) politics as the appropriate medium for stating its message. Politics is well captured for religions in the laconic, searing judgment of the social order of Babel: "Brick served them as stone, and mud served them as mortar" (Gen. 11:3); religions have nothing better with which to work than the human materials at hand.

At stake in the issues raised here is understanding the world we face at the advent of the twenty-first century, a world in which in many parts of the world religion and politics form a tight alliance. As William Green suggests in the introduction, the United States is the exception to the rule of the union of religious belief and political behavior. As a matter of fact, we in the West have long ago formulated a theory of the social order that distinguishes religion from politics, church or synagogue or mosque or temple from institutions of state. We in the United States define politics in an acutely secular way as the theory of the legitimate exercise of violence, and reserve for the state the power of physical force, assigning to religion the moral force of persuasion. This is expressed clearly by Mitchell's penetrating observation that:

> In the West, the rightful employment of coercion is generally reserved for political powers, the civil and military authorities at their various levels. Persuasion, on the other hand, is generally left to the social powers, consisting of the many voluntary associations that influence individual behavior (church, family, community, etc.). Primitive tribes . . . recognize no distinction between the social and the political. The tribe functions as an extended family, organized in a strictly hierarchical fashion. . . . Everyone has his place in the pyramid, and every social subgroup is a subordinate part of the whole. Some societies have maintained a unified, hierarchical, and essentially tribal structure. . . . Most Western nations are still political societies, with a political system easily distinguishable from the rest of society, and a political hierarchy representing just one way in which the society is organized.[1]

Here Mitchell rightly underscores that in the West, political power is limited, and the social powers stand on their own: "Christianity . . . confirmed the distinction between political rule and social life, providing Western civilization with both a cosmological basis for the distinction and a powerful new social order to counterbalance the political order."[2] One may speculate that the first three centuries of Christian history, with the Church confronting a hostile state, introduced the distinction between the Church as an autonomous social entity and the empire: "It claimed for itself the right to function free of government interference and made itself responsible for many matters of public welfare and moral, at the same time leaving the use of coercion to civil authorities alone."[3] The systemic message of earliest Christianity appropriated a politics of division, perhaps turning necessity into the occasion for a restatement of the systemic perspective on the coming of God's Kingdom under Christ.

So it is easy for us to miss the extreme and radical character of that theory of distinction between church and state, religion and politics, for that distinction is not only familiar in the politics of our own country but also a given of the Christian civilization that defines Western civilization. As a result, we in this country find exceedingly difficult the task of understanding a different utilization of politics from the Christian and Western, secular one, with its critical distinctions, as Mitchell has expressed them in most current form. But that is exactly the task facing both individuals and religions from around the globe. We must all wrestle with the fundamental differences between two disparate worldviews. One is a religiously sanctioned political order wherein the spheres of politics and religion are, at least theoretically, neatly distinguished one from the other. The other is a religiously sanctioned political order incorporating the divine realm and its power, and whose purpose is to achieve the goals set forth and sanctioned by God.

The upshot of the character of Western Christian and secular politics, with its critical distinction between and among power in various modes—political from prophetic, for instance—is simple: We find exceedingly difficult the task of making sense of a politics that serves for systemic purposes in religious systems. We have no theory that encompasses a politics embedded in the religious theory of the social order, shaped by that theory, given legitimacy and purpose through that theory. Hence we cannot hear the religious messages that politics, when embedded in an encompassing, religious theory of the social order, wishes to set forth.

We are unable to make sense not only of those enormous portions of the world in which politics and religion cohere and deliver a single, uniform, and cogent statement. We also cannot formulate in our own context a theory that will explain to us the political aspirations of religious societies, with the result that important components of the political order in this country, on both right (viz., the former Christian Coalition) and left (viz., the National Council of Churches) come to the public square with pronouncements on public policy that invoke theological principles and express them. Consequently, religious groups appear to speak a kind of gibberish, intelligible only to themselves, when in fact they mean to make a statement not only to, but about, the social order that encompasses us all. They address the definition of what it means to be a human being, what God wants of us, how we are to relate to one another and assume public responsibilities—deeply religious categories of thought. But the rest of us hear, and fear, yet another pressure group, but an illegitimate one.

In the pages of this book, we have surveyed the other ways, besides the American one, in which God rules—or negotiates. Consequently, the book has both described how each major world religion formulates its politics and how they have laid the groundwork for potentially fruitful dialogue between many different groups. The trajectories of those dialogues will define the future of our religions and our politics.

Notes

1. Brian Mitchell, "The Distinction of Powers: How Church and State Divide Us," *Religion and Public Life* 2 (1995): 2.
2. Ibid.
3. Ibid.

Glossary |

Aggadah: The rules of correct conviction, exegesis, and interpretation.

Apostles', Nicene, and Athanasian Creeds: The creeds of the Early Church that spelled out Catholic Christian belief in such basic areas as the Trinitarian nature of God and the divine and human natures in Jesus.

arhat: Enlightened monk, or a perfected saint, who has reached *nirvāna* and will be released from *samsara* at death.

ashram: A stage of life in Hinduism; also refers to a hermitage or secluded place for meditation.

Bavli: Talmud of Babylonia (ca. 600 C.E.), a Rabbinic commentary on the Mishnah.

bodhisattva: "Future Buddha," or person who is to become fully enlightened; in Mahayana Buddhism, one who reaches enlightenment but vows to continue rebirths in *samsara* to assist others.

Brahmins: The priestly ("divine") class in Hindu society, the highest rank of society based on their ritual purity.

Buddha: "Enlightened One"; Siddhartha Shakyamuni Gautama (ca. 563–483 B.C.E.) became the Buddha, with whom the religion of Buddhism is associated.

Catholic: With a lowercase "c," the word means "universal or all-embracing"; capitalized, the word refers to the Roman Catholic tradition.

Christology: The study of the words and story of Christ, and more precisely his sacrifice on the cross.

danda: The scepter, "big stick," or rod of punishment and coercive power.

Dead Sea Library: The collection of written documents (e.g., scrolls) of the Jewish sectarian religious community living in caves located in the mountains overlooking the Dead Sea; see also *Qumran.*

dharma: A term central to Hinduism with multiple meanings, including (1) personal duty or responsibility, social obligation; (2) religious law or righteousness; (3) the principle of cosmic order, the condition of possibility for ordered cosmos.

ecclesiology: The study of the theological understanding of the church.

episcopacy: The system of church government by bishops (from the Greek *episcopoi*), for example, in the Anglican, Lutheran, Orthodox, and Roman Catholic traditions.

Epistles: Books of the New Testament that focus on the meaning of Jesus Christ's life and teachings for the life of the Early Church, as interpreted by Paul the Apostle, Peter, James, and John.

eschatology, eschatological: From the Greek *eschaton*, meaning "the end" or "end times."

Eucharist: The Christian sacrament of Holy Communion, the *theia koinonia*, or fellowship with God; called the "Divine Liturgy" by the Orthodox.

evangelical: The segment of Protestant Christianity that stresses certain core beliefs rooted in the Bible, such as personal conversion and salvation by faith in the atoning death and resurrection of Jesus Christ, and the Bible as the sole authority in matters of faith and life.

familial piety (xiao): One of the two core social virtues of early China, emphasizing the respect and care that should be exhibited by children toward their parents, which they then will receive from their own children. In the *Analects* (*Lunyu*), Confucius notes that familial piety (*xiao*) and brotherly devotion (*di*) are the roots of acting with benevolence.

Five Classics (wujing): Five classic works associated with Confucius, made canonical by the 651 compilation of the corrected meanings of the Five Classics (*Wujing zhengyi*). These works are the Classic of Changes (*Yijing*), the Classic of Poetry (*Shijing*), the Classic of Documents (*Shujing*), the *Spring and Autumn Annals* (*Chunqiu*), and the Records of Ritual (*Liji*).

five relationships (wulun): The five paradigmatic family relationships are ruler and subject, father and son, elder and younger brother, husband and wife, and friend and friend.

Four Books (sishu): The four core classic philosophical works made canonical during the Song Dynasty Confucian revival by Zhu Xi (1130–1200). These works are the *Analects* (*Lunyu*), *Mencius* (*Mengzi*), and the "Great Learning" (*Daxue*) and "Inward Harmony" (*Zhongyong*) chapters of the *Records of Ritual* (*Liji*).

Gospels: The first four books of the New Testament—Matthew, Mark, Luke, and John—which focus on the life and teachings of Jesus of Nazareth and are the central classical Christian source for information on the life of Jesus Christ.

hadith: The prophetic traditions of Islam, which are narrative reports that record the sayings and deeds of Muhammad.

Halakhah: The norms of correct conduct.

Hebrew Scriptures: Jewish canonical sacred texts, roughly corresponding to Christianity's "Old Testament," also known as the Written Torah, which is divided into three sections: Torah, Prophets, and Writings. Also known as the First Testament.

hijra: The emigration of Muhammad from Mecca to Medina, which eventually developed into a practice of making pilgrimage to Mecca at least once in the life of a Muslim.

immanence: The usual category used to refer to the divine as existing within the universe as people may perceive it; the opposite of transcendence.

Islam: An Arabic word meaning submission, related to the Arabic word for peace, *salaam*, but also the name of the religion mediated by the prophet Muhammad.

Israel: (1) The alternative personal name of the patriarch Jacob, son of Isaac. (2) The collective name of the Hebrew people who are descended from Jacob.

jihad: Often mistranslated as "holy war," the word actually means to "struggle" or "strive" and refers to the Quranic command to Muslims to exert themselves to realize God's will on earth, to live a virtuous life, to spread the Islamic community throughout the entire earth by preaching and teaching, and to fulfill the universal mission of Islam.

karma: Literally, "action," "deed," or "work"; in Hinduism, it means the law of consequences with regard to one's actions, which determines the future cycle of rebirth.

Kharijites: A Muslim group that interpreted the Quran and Sunnah literally and believed that the Quranic injunction to "command the good and prohibit evil" was a religious mandate that was to be implemented absolutely and without compromise at the political level.

Kshatriyas: The classical "noble," warrior, or ruling class in Hindu society, the second social stratum.

Liturgy: A rite or body of rites prescribed for public worship; it plays an especially prominent role in the theology of almost all Orthodox Christians in modern times; also a synonym for the Eucharist.

ming: Literally, "command" or "mandate," "fate."

Mishnah: A Rabbinic philosophical law code (ca. 200 C.E.).

New Testament: A collection of books (Gospels, Acts of the Apostles, Letters, and the Apocalypse) consituting the part of the Bible exclusive to Christianity; also known as the Christian or Second Testament.

nirvāna: "Blowing out" of the fires of life, liberation from suffering and rebirth, the spiritual goal of Buddhist practice; popularly conceived as perfect bliss or even paradise.

Old Testament: See *Hebrew Scriptures.*

Oral Torah: The corpus of Rabbinic writings from the Mishnah to the Yerushalmi through the Bavli, along with certain compilations of biblical interpretation known as Midrash books of the same period.

Pali Canon: Earliest collection of Buddhist sacred texts, including the Tripatika, or "Three Baskets" (Vinaya, Sutta, and Abhidhamma), written in ancient Sanskrit.

Pentateuch: The Greek term for the first five books of the Hebrew Scriptures— Genesis through Deuteronomy—also known as the Torah.

Qumran: A site adjacent to the Dead Sea where the Dead Sea library was found, and where a Jewish sectarian communal group lived.

Quran: In Islam, the eternal, literal, uncreated, and final Word of God, revealed to the prophet Muhammad one final time over a period of twenty-two years (610–32 C.E.) to serve as a guide for humankind (Q 2:185); claimed to be the corrective to the one eternal message of God initially revealed to but corrupted by Jews and Christians (Q 5:19).

raj: Rule.

rajadharma: The duty (dharma) of kings

Reformation: Reformation Christianity is the broad label applied to the diverse Christian movements that emerged in Europe and the West during the sixteenth century C.E.

Sadhu: Holy man, in Hinduism.

samsara: The cycle of rebirth.

sangha: One of Buddhism's three jewels: the community of monks, nuns, and householders (laity).

Second Vatican Council: Roman Catholic church council convened in 1962 by Pope John XXIII, which continued through 1965 under his successor Pope Paul VI, to deal with issues of modernity in the Catholic church; also called Vatican II.

Shii: The minority tradition of the Muslim community, which holds that succession of political and Muslim leadership and authority should be hereditary, passing through Muhammad's daughter, Fatima, and her husband, Ali, who, as Muhammad's first cousin, was Muhammad's closest living male relative.

Shirk: Idolatry.

Shudras: Classical servant class in Hindu society, the fourth- (lowest) level social stratum.

soteriology: The study of salvation as effected by Jesus Christ.

stūpa: Memorial Buddhist shrine or reliquary, often built in a mound.

Sufism: An Islamic mysticism that began as an ascetic movement, renouncing material things and encouraging a detachment from them and a return to the purity and simplicity of the early Muslim community; it played an important role in the political life of Muslims and in the spread of Islam through missionary work.

Sunnah: The example of Muhammad in both his words and deeds, recorded in the *hadith* literature, which enjoys authoritative scriptural status among Muslims.

Sunni: The majority tradition of the Muslim community, which holds that Muslim authority should pass to the most qualified person (the most pious and learned in matters of faith) rather than in hereditary succession, because it holds that all Muslims are equal in God's eyes, with no special status accorded to anyone on the basis of wealth or family.

svadharma: Personal, individual dharma.

Svaraj: Self-control or "self-rule."

Talmud: A Rabbinic commentary on the Mishnah.

tawhid: Muslim doctrine of absolute monotheism.

Thirteen Classics (shisanjing): The thirteen classics defined in the Song Dynasty. These works include the Five Classics (see "Five Classics") with the addition of the ritual texts *Ceremony and Ritual (Yili)* and *Rituals of Zhou (Zhouli)*; the three commentaries to the *Spring and Autumn Annals (Chunqiu)* named after Zuo, Gongyang, and Guliang (together taking the place of the *Chunqiu*); the *Classic of Filial Piety (Xiaojing)*; the dictionary *Approach to Refinement (Erya)*; the *Analects (Lunyu)*; and the *Mencius (Mengzi)*.

tian: Usually translated as "Heaven."

tianming: Literally, "Heaven's Mandate"; the political authorization that the virtuous ruler receives from the nonhuman realm, and the bad omens the corrupt ruler receives from the same source. The two words that make up this concept, *tian* (often translated as "Heaven") and *ming* ("command," "decree," "fate," or most often "mandate"), are key to understanding the formulation of claims to legitimate authority by emperors and revolutionaries alike throughout Chinese history.

tianzi: "Son of Heaven," a special name for the emperor.

Torah: Literally, "Instruction." When referred to as "the Torah," it can mean either (1) the first five books of Hebrew Scriptures, also called the Pentateuch, or (2) the collection of the entire "Written Scriptures."

Trinity: The Christian doctrine of three Divine Persons in one God: the Father, the Son, and the Holy Spirit.

ummah: The single, universal community of Islam.

Vaishyas: The merchant, business class in Hindu society, third social stratum.

varnasharma dharma: Religious duty calibrated to one's class or caste and one's stage of life.

Vedas: A varied collection of Hindu scriptures, all of which focus on the performance and philosophy of ritual sacrifice.

Vinaya: The canonical books containing rules and regulations for Buddhist monastic life and discipline; one of the three "baskets" *(tripitaka)* of the Buddhist canon.

Written Torah: Written Scriptures, the sacred texts of the Hebrew Bible.

wuwei: In Buddhism, literally, "nonaction," or action without attachment to the outcome, but also meaning dispassionate and reactive governance.

Yerushalmi: Talmud of the Land of Israel (ca. 400 C.E.), a Rabbinic commentary on the Mishnah.

yogin: An individual who practices yoga, techniques of spiritual discipline for overcoming bondage to *samsara* (the cycle of rebirth), often emphasizing breathing and meditation exercises. Three yogic paths are karma (action), jnana (meditation/insight), and bhakti (devotion).

zakat: An alms tax of 2.5 percent of the total wealth of each Muslim.

Contributors |

Bruce D. Chilton is the Bernard Iddings Bell Professor of Religion at Bard College. He is an Episcopal priest as well as a scholar of early Christianity and Judaism. He has written several academic studies that put Jesus in his Jewish context, including most recently *Rabbi Jesus: An Intimate Biography* (2000), together with comparative studies of Christianity and Judaism, such as *Redeeming Time: The Wisdom of Ancient Jewish and Christian Festal Calendars* (2002).

Mark Csikszentmihalyi is an assistant professor in the Department of East Asian Languages and Literature and the Religious Studies Program at the University of Wisconsin, Madison. He coedited (with Philip J. Ivanhoe) *Religious and Philosophical Aspects of the Laozi* (1999) and is completing a manuscript titled *Material Virtue: Ethics and the Body in Early China*.

Charles E. Curran, is Elizabeth Scurlock University Professor of Human Values at Southern Methodist University. His extensive work in the field of moral theology includes *Catholic Social Teaching, 1891–Present: A Historical, Theological, and Ethical Analysis* (2002) and *The Catholic Moral Tradition Today: A Synthesis* (1999), which was awarded first prize in its field of moral theology by the Catholic Press Association of America.

Natana J. De Long-Bas is a senior research assistant at the Center for Muslim–Christian Understanding at Georgetown University, where she completed her Ph.D. in history. She is an editor of and a contributor to the *Oxford Dictionary of Islam* (2002) and is coauthor of *Women in Muslim Family Law* (with John. L. Esposito, 2001).

John L. Esposito is university professor and professor of religion and international affairs at Georgetown University's Walsh School of Foreign Service. He was founding director of the Center for Muslim–Christian Understanding and is editor-in-chief of *The Oxford Encyclopedia of the Modern Islamic World* (1995) and *The Oxford History of Islam* (1999). His other publications include *Unholy War: Terror in the Name of Islam* (2002), *The Islamic Threat: Myth or Reality?* (3d ed., 1999), and *What Everyone Needs to Know about Islam* (2002).

William Scott Green is dean of the College, professor of religion, and Philip S. Bernstein Professor of Judaic Studies at the University of Rochester, where he founded the Department of Religion and Classics. He has written extensively on the history of Judaism and is associate editor of the *HarperCollins Dictionary of Religion* (1995) and coeditor of *The Encyclopedia of Judaism* (2000).

Todd Lewis is associate professor of world religions at the College of the Holy Cross. He was founding cochair of the Tibetan and Himalayan religious group in the American Academy of Religion, and he has written more than thirty journal articles and several books, including *Popular Buddhist Texts from Nepal: Narratives and Rituals of Newar Buddhism* (2000) and *World Religions Today* (with John Esposito and Darrell Fasching) (2002).

Martin E. Marty is the Fairfax M. Cone Distinguished Service Professor Emeritus at the University of Chicago. He has been president of the American Academy of Religion, the American Society of Church History, and the American Catholic Historical Association. He is the author of more than fifty books, including the three-volume *Modern American Religion* (1984, 1990, 1996) and *Righteous Empire* (1970), which won the National Book Award.

Jacob Neusner is a research professor of religion and theology and a senior fellow at the Institute of Advanced Theology at Bard College in New York. He has written or edited more than 900 books on Judaism and religious studies and is editor of the multivolume *Pilgrim Library of World Religions* (1996–98) and *World Religions in America* (2000).

Brian K. Smith is a professor of religious studies at the University of California, Riverside. He has written several books on the history of religion, including *Classifying the Universe: The Ancient Indian Varna System and the Origins of Caste* (1994).

Petros Vassiliadis is professor of New Testament in the Department of Theology at Aristotle University in Thessaloniki, Greece. He is currently president of the World Conference of Associations of Theological Institutes (WOCATI), vice president of the Society for Ecumenical Studies and Inter-Orthodox Relations, and he is the author of numerous journal articles and several books, including *Eucharist and Witness: Orthodox Perspectives on Unity and Mission of the Church* (1998) and *ΛΟΓΟΙ ΙΗΣΟΥ: Studies in Q* (1999).

Index

96–97; classical Islam and,
154–55; classical sources on politics, 87–92; defining, 85–87;
eschatological/nonhistorical
dimension of politics, 90–91,
94–95, 100; ethics as ecclesial
issue, 92; Eucharist and, 88–89,
91–92, 95; Jewish eschatology
and, 89–91; Kingdom of God and
Christ as *Logos*, 91; *koinonia* in
Eucharist, 91–92; the Liturgy
and, 88–89, 95–97; medium of
expressing politics, 95; message of
politics, 95, 96–100; and modern
sociopolitical concerns, 93–95,
101–2, 103nn5, 6, 7; monasticism
and, 100; nonbelievers and tolerance, 100–101; patriarch's role in,
104n22; Reformation Christianity
and, 85, 93, 110, 112, 118; teachings and life of Jesus Christ for,
89–91; theological presuppositions regarding truth/revelation,
87–88; theory of politics, 92–95;
Trinity doctrine and, 91–92
Ottoman empire, 138, 156, 174
*Oxford Dictionary of the Christian
Church*, 85

Pacem in terris (John XXIII), 74, 81
Pañcarakshā (Buddhist narrative),
244–45, 248–49
papal letters and encyclicals, 64–65,
73–74, 79, 80, 82, 87
Paul: early Christianity and, 38–41,
90–91, 98–99; Reformation Christianity and epistles of, 113,
115–17
Paul VI, Pope, 68, 74, 78
Pentateuch ("Written Torah"), 4–5,
12, 14–15, 21, 31–32

Peter, 41, 46–47
Peters, Francis, 154
Philo of Alexandria, 56–57
Photius, 99
Pius XI, Pope, 71, 73
Pius XII, Pope, 74
Plato, 14–15, 48, 53, 54
Platonism, 57
Pollitt, Katha, 1
Poo Mu-chou, 221
Porphyry, 54
primitive and early Christianity, 4,
5–6, 37–59; and adaptation to
political forms of this world, 5–6,
37, 38, 41–42, 49–52; Augustine
and, 52–55; "Byzantine synthesis"
and, 98–99; Christian epoch and
history as apocalypse, 38, 54, 55;
classical sources on politics,
38–41; distinction between
"primitive" and "early," 37; dual
loyalties to God and earthly masters, 37; eschatologies, kinds of,
38, 46, 58; eschatology and global
history, 52–56; eschatology and
medium of expressing politics,
45–49; eschatology and theory of
politics, 41–45, 90; God's will and
human will, 53; Gregory of
Nyssa and Christianized Empire,
49–51; Hebrew Scriptures and, 4,
6, 37, 39; history and philosophical reflection in, 55–56; and hope
of justice, 52–56; juridical eschatology, 42, 44–45, 46, 49; justice,
eschatological, 57–58; justice
and the imitation of Christ, 52;
message of politics, 49–56; New
Testament and, 37, 51; nonbelievers and apologistic literature,
56–57; nonresistance to evil and